WITHDRAWN
DUPLICATE

Theatres for Literature

A Practical Aesthetics for Group Interpretation

by

Marion L. Kleinau and Janet Larsen McHughes
Southern Illinois University at Carbondale

D1271420

Alfred Publishing Co., Inc.
Sherman Oaks, California 91403

PN
2081
R4
K57

*To those pioneers in interpretation theory and practice
who have preceded us, and whose work has made some
of these understandings possible.*

*To those students, graduate and undergraduate, who have given
unselfishly of their time and energies to help build The
Calipre Stage at Southern Illinois University at Carbondale.*

*And, finally, to our patient and supportive husbands, Marvin
and Bill.*

M.L.K.
J.L.M.

Copyright © 1980 by Alfred Publishing Co., Inc.

All rights reserved.

No part of this book may be reproduced or transmitted in any
form or by any means, electronic or mechanical, including
photocopying, recording, or by any information storage and
retrieval system, without permission in writing from the
Publisher:

Alfred Publishing Co., Inc.
15335 Morrison Street
Sherman Oaks, California 91403

Printed in the United States of America

Current printing last digit:
10 9 8 7 6 5 4 3 2 1

94300

Library of Congress Cataloging in Publication Data

Kleinau, Marion L   1926–
    Theatres for literature.

    Includes index.
    1. Readers' theater.   2. Oral interpretation.
3. Amateur theatricals.   I. McHughes, Janet Larsen,
1945–   joint author.   II. Title.
PN2081.R4K57   792'.023   79-24492
ISBN 0-88284-096-7

ERRATA: The following material was inadvertently left out of this printing. It will be corrected in future printings.

We wish to thank the following publishers, authors and translators for permission to reprint their copyrighted material:

"My Side of the Matter," by Truman Capote, *A Tree of Night* (Signet) Random House.

"Paul's Case" by Willa Cather from *Youth and the Bright Medusa,* Random House.

from *Breakfast of Champions,* Kurt Vonnegut, Jr., Delacorte Press/Seymour Lawrence.

"Glass Poem," by Karl Shapiro from *Poems 1940-1953.* Random House.

"The Jockey," by Carson McCullers, *The Ballad of the Sad Cafe,* Houghton Mifflin. Copyright 1955 Carson McCullers.

"Somnambule Ballad," by Federico Garcia Lorca, *Selected Poems,* Allen & Francisco Lorca, eds. Copyright 1955 New Directions Publ. Corp. Reprinted by permission of New Directions Publ. Corp.

"Antigone," by Jean Anouilh. *Five Plays,* Vol. I, Random House. Trans. Lewis Galantiere.

"Spring Hunt" and "Trophy" by Jerry Prater. Copyright Jerry Prater. Reprinted by permission of the author.

"November" by Paul H. Oehser from *Fifty Poems,* Washington:1954. Permission of the author.

"A Father to Be" by Saul Bellow from *Seize the Day.* Reprinted by permission of The Viking Press.

from *The Autobiography of Mother Jones,* Third Ed. Revised, 1977. Charles J. Kerr Publishing Co.

from *Voices from the Mountains,* by Guy and Candie Carawan. Reprinted by permission of Guy and Candie Carawan and Alfred A. Knopf, Inc.

"In the Zoo" by Jean Stafford, from *Bad Characters.* Copyright 1953, 1964, by Jean Stafford. Appeared originally in *The New Yorker.* Reprinted with the permission of Farrar, Straus & Giroux, Inc.

from *The Princess Bride* by Wm. Goldman, Harcourt Brace Jovanovich, Inc. By permission of the publishers.

"The Love Song of J. Alfred Prufrock" by T. S. Eliot from *Collected Poems 1909-1962.* Harcourt Brace Jovanovich, Inc. Permission of Publisher.

"Chicago" by Carl Sandburg from *Chicago Poems.* Harcourt Brace Jovanovich, Inc. Permission of Publisher.

"To Christ Our Lord" by Galway Kinnell. *What a Kingdom It Was,* Houghton Mifflin Co. Copyright 1960 Galway Kinnell.

"Forgive My Guilt" by Robert P. Tristram Coffin in *Apples By Ocean.* Macmillan Publishing Co. Copyright 1949 by Robert P. Tristram Coffin, renewed 1977 by Richard N. Coffin, Robert P. Tristram Coffin, Jr., and Mary Alice Westcott. Originally appeared in *Atlantic Monthly.*

from *Mythologies* by W. B. Yeats. Macmillan Publishing Company (pp. 43, 44, 70, 76, 86, 90, 106, 117, 118). Copyright Mrs. Wm. B. Yeats, 1959.

from "The Land of Heart's Desire" by W. B. Yeats, *Collected Plays.* Copyright 1934, 1952 by Macmillan Publishing Co. Reprinted with permission from Macmillan Publ. Co.

"The Hosting of the Sidhe" by W. B. Yeats, *Collected Poems.* Copyright 1906 by Macmillan Publishing Co., Inc., renewed 1934 by Wm. Butler Yeats.

"The Everlasting Voices" by W. B. Yeats, *Collected Poems.* Copyright 1906 by Macmillan Publishing Co., Inc., renewed 1934 by Wm. Butler Yeats.

"Heat" by H. D. *Selected Poems* of H. D. Reprinted by permission of New Directions Publishing Corporation. Copyright 1957 by Norman Holmes Pearson.

"Gacela of the Flight" by Federico Garcia Lorca. *Selected Poems.* Copyright 1955 New Directions Publ. Co. Reprinted by permission of New Directions Publ. Co.

"Lament for Ignacio Sanchez Mejias" by Federico Garcia Lorca. *Selected Poems.* Copyright 1955 New Directions Publ. Co. Reprinted by permission of New Directions Publ. Co.

"Scotia" and letter from Jacob Vowell. *United Mine Workers Journal.* By permission of UMW Journal.

"Deer Hunt" by Judson Jerome. Copyright by author, Downhill Farm, Hancock, Md. 21750. Reprinted by permission of the author.

"This Poem is for Deer" by Gary Snyder. *Myths and Texts.* Printed by permission of New Directions Publ. Corp.

"Death of Antonito el Camborio" by Federico Garcia Lorca. Copyright held by Angel Flores, 163 Malden Rd., Palenville, New York 12463. Trans. Robert O'Brien and Gordian Press, Staten Island.

"The Lifeguard" by James Dickey from *Drowning With Others,* James Dickey. By permission of Wesleyan U. Press. Copyright 1961 James Dickey. "The Lifeguard" first appeared in *The New Yorker.*

Misc. excerpts from *Mountain Life and Work*. Used by permission of The Council of the Southern Mountains, Drawer No., Clintwood, VA 24238.

"Haircut" by Ring Lardner in *The Lovenest and Other Stories* by Ring Lardner. By permission of Charles Schribner's Sons.

"Mother and Daughter" by D. H. Lawrence from *The Complete Short Stories of D. H. Lawrence,* Vol. III. Copyright 1933 estate of D. H. Lawrence. Copyright 1960 Angelo Ravagli and Montague C. Weekly. Reprinted by permission of The Viking Press, Inc.

"The New Dress" in *A Haunted House and Other Stories* by Virginia Woolf. Copyright 1944, 1972 Harcourt Brace Jovanovich, Inc. Reprinted by permission of publishers. *Caution:* All rights, including professional, amateur, motion picture, recitation, lecturing, public reading, radio broadcasting, and television are strictly reserved. Inquiries on all rights should be addressed to Harcourt Brace Jovanovich, Inc., 757 Third Avenue, New York, NY 10017.

"Pain" by Vladimir Nabokov in *The Portable Nabokov.* Copyright 1953, 1955, 1957, by Vladimir Nabokov. Reprinted by permission of Doubleday and Company, Inc.

from *A Portrait of the Artist as a Young Man,* by James Joyce. Copyright 1916 by B. W. Huebsch, 1944 by Nora Joyce; Copyright 1964 by the Estate of James Joyce. Reprinted by permission of the Viking Press.

"The Boarding House" from *Dubliners* by James Joyce. Orig. publ. by B. W. Huebsch, Inc. in 1916. Copyright 1967 Estate of James Joyce. All Rights Reserved. Reprinted by permission of The Viking Press.

"The Congo" by Vachel Lindsay. Copyright 1914, The Macmillan Publishing Company.

page 12—The figure should be as follows:

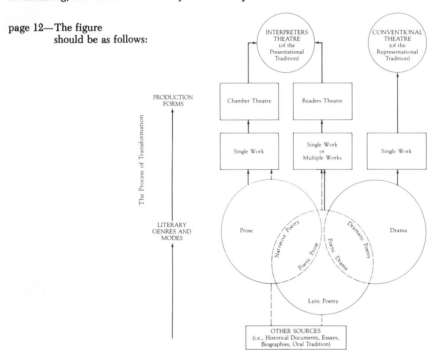

page 111—The example for technique 4 should be:

> **JOHN.** John said that he'd better be leaving. It was getting late.

> **BETTY.** Betty asked if he couldn't please stay just a little while longer. After all, he didn't have to go to work in the morning.

page 249—Figures 9.4d, e, and f are incorrectly labeled. They should be e, f, and d, respectively.

Contents

Preface—to the Instructor

For several years we've observed the arts of Readers Theatre and Chamber Theatre evolve into mature forms of theatre. We've known the special kind of excitement and fulfillment of directing and performing in these media. Yet many times we've been frustrated by our inability to explain to perceptive students our aesthetic identity in relation to other forms of theatre. The old definitions simply would not hold up in the light of our own experiments in group performance. *Theatres for Literature* is an attempt to respond to our needs and the needs of others for a more comprehensive theoretical framework for our art.

Working with these ideas has reaffirmed our belief in the value of group performance as a way of coming to know literature, and as a means of extending the student's literary learning experience beyond analysis. In small classroom exercises (finding the "voices" in a literary work, for example) and in larger preparation and rehearsal of scripts for public performance, we've seen students light up with new excitement about literature, as they see their analyses take on theatrical vitality. We believe, for these reasons, that *Theatres for Literature* may be useful for all teachers of literature, whether in the field of English, Oral Interpretation, or Theatre.

By defining the aesthetic position of Interpreters Theatre we've come to a fuller understanding of the essential presentational nature of our theatre form as it relates to other familiar theatre styles. We hope *Theatres for Literature* will be of value to all theatre directors who are interested in presentational staging.

We have tried to treat all aspects of Interpreters Theatre comprehensively, from analysis to scripting to production. Because many curricula offer separate courses in some of the activities covered in the book, we designed the book to be used either in sections or as a whole. Chapters 2 and 3 of Part Two: Image-inations are meant to be read as a unit on Readers Theatre; Chapters 4 and 5 are a similar unit on Chamber Theatre. Part Three: Realizations contains production information that applies to the entire book.

Our analysis of the orchestration of literature (Chapter 3) may be of interest to those who wish to experiment with the use of a chorus. Similarly, we have included a full treatment of compiling, from both literary and documentary sources (Chapter 6). Chapters 7, 8, and 9 explore the presentational nature of Interpreters Theatre, suggesting methods for using the performer's voice and body symbolically and for designing the technical aspects of an Interpreters Theatre performance. Chapter 10 examines some special audiences and objectives of Interpreters Theatre in a social context.

We are interested in showing students how to create and produce scripts, rather than in providing ready-to-stage scripts; we are therefore including examples of various scripting techniques in the test, with few "completed" scripts. The appendices offer practical suggestions for casting, blocking, and rehearsal for those students who may have had no course in directing. Finally, the "Suggestions for Further Reading" at the end of each chapter refer the student to other sources on literary analysis and production.

M.L.K.
J.L.M.

Carbondale, Illinois
January, 1980

Acknowledgments

We are grateful to the following contributing authors:
>   Robert B. Loxley for "Alternate Performance Environments" in Chapter 8
>   Ann S. Utterback for "Readers Theatre as Documentary" in Chapter 10
>   James W. Utterback for "Projections" in Chapter 8
>   Charlotte S. Waisman for "Practical Considerations for Selecting
>   Children's Literature" in Chapter 2

We extend our warm appreciation to Timothy Gura, Kathleen Miranda, Jill O'Brien, and Sheron Dailey Pattison for reading the entire manuscript and generously contributing suggestions; to Patricia Comeaux, Kristin Langellier, and Cynthia Miller for research assistance; and to the Department of Speech Communication at Southern Illinois University at Carbondale, for generous support and services.

M.L.K.
J.L.M.

PART ONE

Orientations: Getting Acquainted

This is a book about theatre—a special kind of theatre. This is also a book about literature, and how the art forms of theatre and literature can connect. When they do, they produce a special magic that has helped make theatre a vital part of human existence.

Our purpose is to help you share in the act of making theatre. Rather than providing you with ready-made scripts for staging, we're interested in making practical suggestions so that you can construct your own scripts and stage them yourself. To do this, we'll offer a theoretical basis as a guideline for your artistic decisions. We'll give many practical suggestions and examples to open doors, indicate possibilities, and extend horizons. You may not be familiar with all the examples or techniques we offer; we hope you'll be inspired to become familiar with new works and to risk trying different techniques in scripting and staging. The mark of a true artist is a willingness to experiment, to dream, to risk, and even to fail. The "great attempts" that don't quite make it are always better than the small safe attempts that fail to tap new creative resources. We hope this book will inspire you to "great attempts."

In *Theatres for Literature*, we're interested in breaking some of the bonds that may have limited creative vision in the past. We're also interested in reaffirming our traditions and conventions by placing them in a theoretical framework, but conventions are not rules. We are not attempting to set up rules. Instead, we're interested in freeing the way we regard literature and *Interpreters Theatre*. When we speak of Interpreters Theatre, it is helpful to distinguish it from what we call *Conventional Theatre*. These terms—Interpreters Theatre and Conventional Theatre—reflect two major traditions in the long history of theatre: presentationalism and representationalism. Both traditions are rich and varied. The presentational tradition includes such theatre forms as the Kabuki theatre of Japan, classical Greek staging, Elizabethan theatre, some modern explorations such as the Living Theatre, and Interpreters Theatre. The representational traditions includes the realistic settings of Italian Renaissance theatre, Restoration staging, nineteenth-century theatre including western realism, and most proscenium staging today. Both Interpreters Theatre and Conventional Theatre are interpretive, operate according to established conventions, and are *theatre*. We offer these two terms merely as a way of making important distinctions which we will discuss throughout the book.

Our ultimate interest is in the form of presentational theatre we call Interpreters Theatre. We wish to open doors long closed between the two art forms of Interpreters Theatre and Conventional Theatre. Interpreters Theatre *is* theatre, perhaps in its most fundamental form. What is theatre? Theatre is a living exchange of energies in space. All the techniques of stage production are open to all directors, whether they're working in Interpreters Theatre or in Conventional Theatre, to facilitate that fundamental exchange of energies. By the same token, any theatre director may choose to use only the human voice and body if such a choice serves the essential purpose of the script.

To clarify the concepts we're exploring, we've created new terms and used familiar terms in new ways. Words printed in bold type are some of the key terms in the Interpreters Theatre director's vocabulary.

Interpreters Theatre is an umbrella term that includes both **Readers Theatre** and **Chamber Theatre.** Artists who work in Interpreters Theatre are oral interpreters of literature. The activity is interpretive because literature is interpreted, or transformed, from the page to the stage.

The term *Readers Theatre* originally referred to the reading of plays, with participants seated or standing behind lecterns. Although Readers Theatre has grown into a much more active and experimental form, staging all kinds of literature, the original name is still used. When we refer to Readers Theatre, we mean not a static theatre *of* readers, but a theatre *for* readers, serving literary experience.

Chamber Theatre is dedicated to the staging of narrative literature. Originated by Robert S. Breen in the forties, Chamber Theatre explores the complicated relationship between a story and the person who tells the story. Breen suggests in his book, *Chamber Theatre*, that the delicate balance between story and storyteller is like the harmonics of chamber music (see "Suggestions for Further Reading," Chapter 1).

As you begin to work in these forms of Interpreters Theatre, you'll see that there are four stages to your creative interaction with a piece of literature. We're using the term *work* to refer to the literature as you discover it on the page. A work becomes a **text** when you have found your own interpretive vision of it; you can refer to "my text" and "your text" of the same work. A **script** is a text that is ready for performance, divided into parts with suggestions for staging. Finally, the **production** is the connection between the literary form and the theatre form. The challenge of transforming a literary selection from work to text to script to production is what draws us to Interpreters Theatre. We hope, as Robert Frost says, that "you come, too."

CHAPTER ONE

Perspectives on Our Art

A novel or poem or play remains merely inkspots on paper until a reader transforms them into a set of meaningful symbols.

Louise M. Rosenblatt, *Literature as Exploration*

We are about to enter the world of literature onstage. It's exciting. It's demanding. It's a creative world of many kinds of creators. The writer brings an imagined world to life through language. Silent readers explore that world and create meaning by taking the writer's literary world into their own realms of experience. In this sense, silent readers are creative artists in many of the same ways as original writers. But silent readers hear literature through their inner voices only; the literature seems to strain for audible speech and a visible body. The performers of literary works are the creative artists who lift literature out of its written form and lend it voice and body. At the same time, the adapter-director listens creatively to the voices of literature and finds ways (by constructing scripts and producing them) to release those voices into physical space and time, using the energies of the performers to bring the literary work to life for an audience. Finally, audience members in the theatre are the artists who, much like the silent reader, create meaning by taking the staged voices of literature into their own fields of experience.

Those of us who work in Interpreters Theatre are creative readers, performers, adapters, and directors. We face many of the same challenges the original writer of literature faces: we catch a vision (usually from a literary work) and seek ways to embody that vision. To bring our visions to life we need to be as creative in preparing and staging a script as the writer of the original work was in writing it.

We usually think of theatrical staging as the performance of plays. Interpreters Theatre has helped to change this emphasis: no longer is the action of a play the only action that can be realized onstage. The entire world of literature—nondramatic as well as dramatic—has an inner vitality that begs to be embodied in the theatre; Interpreters Theatre has become the vehicle for making that embodiment possible while retaining the literary structure of the work. No longer must we make a novel, a poem, or an essay into a play to stage it; through our work with Interpreters Theatre, we now recognize the inherent drama of all literary forms. As Broadway director Gerald Freedman remarked, "It's about time all of us in professional theatre recognize the wealth of staging possibilities in nondramatic literature. Broadway is no longer for plays alone."[1]

As we explore the staging possibilities in all literature, guided by the vitality of literary action, we find ourselves redefining or rediscovering theatre forms. We choose a theatrical form because the literary text calls for it; we don't attempt to cram every literary text into the same theatrical form. In effect, we seek theatres for literature rather than literature to fit in theatres. Some literature pushes adapter-artists toward experimentation, urging them to break existing conventions to stage certain formal features of the work. By this process new conventions are created. Other works may call for familiar traditions in production. When, for example, we sense the presence of a collective voice in a literary work, we may borrow the idea of a chorus from classical Greek theatre. When a literary speaker addresses the reader directly, we may stage that moment with the kind of face-to-face confrontation between actor and audience found in Elizabethan theatre. Sometimes formal elements in a work may suggest a near cliché in Interpreters Theatre: reading stands and stools. Such staging can be creative and exciting when the literary work *leads* to this theatre form.

The recognition of tradition and the willingness to experiment are both important in artistic practice. In all probability, every Interpreters Theatre production will use some traditional techniques, although they may be combined in new ways. Since we believe that experimentation in Interpreters Theatre staging is always in response to the demands of literary form, *Theatres for Literature* will proceed from an understanding of the literature toward an exploration of experimental possibilities in scripting and production.

How do we come to our understanding of literature? The building of a relationship with a literary selection is interpersonal; it begins with a series of discoveries about the distinguishing qualities, the strengths, and the conflicts within the world of the literature and within our own worlds. One of the excitements of transforming a literary work is the discovery of its living presence, which allows us to come to terms with another consciousness: that of the speaker in the literature. As we interact with the literary world, two very important things happen: we shape the literature through our interpretation of it, and the literature shapes us by stretching our experience. Such is the interpersonal dynamic of creating a text (our personal vision) of a work.

Any literary work that captures our imagination is a potential text. When we're attracted to a piece of literature, as when we're attracted to another human being, we want to learn as much about that "other" as we can. Fortunately, when we want to know a literary selection better we have many methods for doing so. These methods, called literary analysis techniques, help us understand how a poem, for example, thinks, feels, and moves. We even learn about its shape and rhythms. By coming to know many different kinds of poems, we grow in our understanding of the world outside us. But, because each of us is a unique person, each of us has a different text of the same poem, a text that is a blending of the world of the poem and our world. The various texts of the same poem have much in common—they share a structure and a nucleus of meaning —but their differences are what allow literature to grow and change through the centuries. As the readers of each new generation come to a literary work, they bring new perspectives to it and thereby create new texts. Some works cannot sustain these changes and they die a little; other works thrive on the continuous evolution of their meaning.

When we set out to stage a work of literature for Interpreters Theatre, we make a script from our text. Our text will resemble the work in many ways, but it will also contain our vision. On an interpersonal level, a text is like a strong friendship between two people. The relationship is sustained by a continual give-and-take, founded in respect. The script is a written record of the friendship; it reflects the worlds of both friends. A script, therefore, isn't designed to serve the work alone. It serves both the work and our vision of it, which is the text. This is what we mean by freeing the way we regard literature. Such freedom serves the creative artist best, and generates much of the excitement of Interpreters Theatre.

DEFINING INTERPRETERS THEATRE

"But I thought Interpreters Theatre used stools and reading stands. This one had costumes and a set!"

"If you carry your script, it's interpretation; if you don't, it's acting."

"Why are they moving around like that? I thought this was supposed to be Readers Theatre."

Interpreters Theatre has evolved in this century from the informal play readings of the twenties, through the formalization using stools, reading stands, and formal attire of the thirties and forties, through the awakening fifties, into the experimental sixties and seventies. Today in Interpreters Theatre, a general trend toward more fully staged and media-rich productions moves decidedly away from stools-and-stands readings toward an art form more closely resembling Conventional Theatre. Simultaneously, a countertrend advocated by theatrical innovators such as Peter Brook and Jerzy Grotowski moves toward an elemental theatre of empty space and ritual. This artistic crossover has made many of our former definitions obsolete.

More than ever, we need a definition of Interpreters Theatre that will allow for experimentation in production while retaining an aesthetic identification. Then Interpreters Theatre can acknowledge its kinship with the whole presentational tradition in theatre, while many of the experimental directors and writers in Professional Theatre today can recognize more clearly their alliance with Interpreters Theatre.

Whether traditional or experimental, Interpreters Theatre adapter-directors are distinguished by a unifying concern: they are interested in featuring **presentational form**. Our definition of Interpreters Theatre reflects this goal: *Interpreters Theatre is the actualizing of presentational form in literature.* The process of actualizing, or releasing into action, is twofold: it begins when you create your text and culminates with the staging of your production. If you're actualizing presentational form that you discover in literature, then your production will be presentational as well. Understanding presentational form in literature is easiest when you look at its effect—presentational form in the theatre—and at how it differs from representational form in theatrical staging.

Presentational Form in Production

The history of theatre can almost be written in terms of its alternating preoccupation with presentational and representational styles, although the distinctions are blurred in certain periods. To represent is to make a facsimile, to create a kind of believable verisimilitude. In stage terms, to represent is to materialize a fully created world onstage through the use of literal props and action. The audience is invited to look in on that world; part of the magic of representational theatre is being able to see into worlds that are normally inaccessible to us.

To present is to offer for acceptance and, implicitly, to request a responsive action on the part of the receiver. In stage terms, to present is to create symbolic images that evoke an active imaginative response on the part of the audience. The audience is invited to participate in the creation of the experience. Since Interpreters Theatre is part of the presentational tradition in theatrical art, it shares the dynamic of presentational staging: the performers and the audience mutually create an imaginative world. Presentational style is identified by any gesture or aspect of production that reaches out from the stage area toward the audience directly—no matter how fully that gesture may be enacted. The location of presentational action, therefore, isn't confined to the stage space, but moves out toward the audience. A character's nod of the head, for example, may be magnified into a complete bow, because the audience completes the gesture imaginatively. "Now I'm opening out like the largest telescope that ever was! Good-bye, feet!" exclaims Alice in Lewis Carroll's *Alice in Wonderland*.[2] Through her words, her gestures, and her downward focus, the performer of Alice invites the audience to see her grow taller and taller. Such participation in creating an image depends upon a kind of presentational confrontation between literary characters and audience as they combine their energies to create the literary experience onstage.

Presentational and **representational** styles differ in their use of space in the theatre. Representational theatre uses stage space as a container for action. The world of the play is localized onstage, as in a picture, and actors generally turn away from the audience toward the created environment. We call localized space in the theatre **pictorial space**. The essential aesthetic of Conventional Theatre (the representational tradition) is to use pictorial space primarily.

Presentational theatre, on the other hand, works against localizing action in a defined space because it is concerned with the audience's ability to help create the action imaginatively. Stage space is used, rather, as a point of departure into **acoustic space**. As Edmund Carpenter and Marshall McLuhan define it, acoustic space "has no point of favored focus. It's a sphere without fixed boundaries, space made by the thing itself, not space containing the thing. It is not pictorial space, boxed in, but dynamic, always in flux, creating its own dimension moment to moment."[3] For Interpreters Theatre, acoustic space refers to the whole environment of the theatre auditorium, as well as to the imaginative space of the minds of the audience.

Interpreters Theatre and other presentational theatre forms are identified by their existence in acoustic space. In fact, we can differentiate Readers Theatre and Chamber Theatre in part by the ways in which they use acoustic space.

Of the two Interpreters Theatre forms, Readers Theatre lives most fully in acoustic space. Readers Theatre is dedicated to featuring language, using the spoken word to stimulate imaginative sensory responses. Seeing, in Readers Theatre, comes primarily as a result of hearing, a phenomenon that has led some practitioners of Readers Theatre to refer to the form as "Theatre

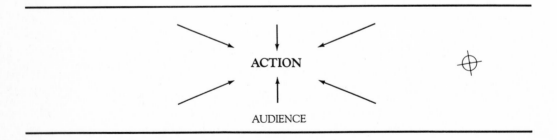

Figure 1.1: Pictorial space.

Figure 1.2: Acoustic space.

of the Mind."[4] (*Mind* in this context means imagination, which exists fully in acoustic space.) Traditionally, we've defined Readers Theatre by its ability to reach the imagination, or to suggest to the mind, through the ear.

Other stimuli, however, can evoke imaginative responses and are, therefore, part of a "sphere without fixed boundaries." Symbolic gestures, abstract movement, and offstage focus (see Chapter 7)—all of which appeal to the eye of the spectator and not to the ear—are just as evocative of imaginative response as words because of their **synecdochical** power—their ability to suggest a whole action by offering part of it.[5] Although these visual stimuli originate in literal space, their energies reach out to the audience.

As Carpenter and McLuhan originally defined acoustic space, it referred to the environmental presence of sound. We suggest the term be enlarged to include visual cues that operate in the same evocative manner as the spoken word. Acoustic space, then, is the location of action, both vocal and physical, in Readers Theatre.

The primary location of action in Chamber Theatre is also acoustic space, although Chamber Theatre interweaves the use of acoustic space with pictorial space more fully than does Readers Theatre. What makes Chamber Theatre so presentational is that the narrator, the central figure in any Chamber Theatre production, tells a story to the audience, directly recognizing their presence. Sometimes the narrator shows part of the action by materializing a scene in pictorial space; at other times the narrator tells the story in words alone, which "live" in acoustic space. The story, although it is staged with a fluid movement between acoustic space (telling) and pictorial space (showing), is dominated by the presentational action of the narrator, and ultimately exists in the imaginative space that surrounds storyteller and audience.

The diagram in figure 1.3 will help you visualize the spatial aesthetics of Readers Theatre, Chamber Theatre, and Conventional Theatre.

The production aesthetic of Interpreters Theatre is to start with an interest in acoustic space and presentational form. When the director of Interpreters Theatre chooses to add a representational detail or to use stage space pictorially, she does so consciously, in response to the demands of the literature being performed. The Interpreters Theatre practitioner is free to move scene onstage or to use space pictorially any time the script demands it, but each of those decisions represents a break from the general aesthetic informing Interpreters Theatre.

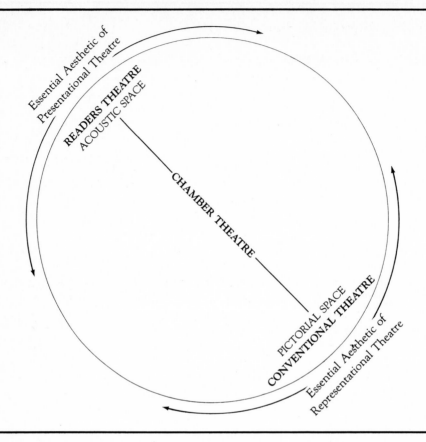

Figure 1.3: Spatial aesthetics.

Conventional Theatre practitioners operate from the general aesthetic of stage space as pictorial and action as representational. When a Conventional Theatre director instructs actors to turn outward from pictorial space toward acoustic space, as in asides, soliloquies, or placement of actors in the audience, she does so consciously and for a specific reason, recognizing that such decisions represent breaks from the general aesthetic informing Conventional Theatre. Theatre movements such as **Epic Theatre** tend to combine the aesthetics of both kinds of theatre. Chamber Theatre, owing great allegiance to the epic tradition, is likewise an aesthetic cross between the acoustic and pictorial uses of space.

In actual production, an Interpreters Theatre performance may have a free mixture of pictorial and acoustic space, just as a Conventional Theatre production can. Originating from different aesthetic positions, both directors have complete creative freedom to break their aesthetic ground or to remain within their original traditions. Rules and definitions don't determine production modes; the demands of scripts do. The demands of scripts for Interpreters Theatre are essentially presentational because of the evocative elements in the literature that have persisted through the transformation from work to text to script.

Presentational Form in Literature

All literature could be said to be presentational in that it suggests to the mind, but some aspects of literary works appeal to the imagination more obviously than others.

The use of *language* can be presentational. When the language of a literary work captures your attention because of some striking aspect of the words themselves or their arrangement, then language is functioning for its own sake rather than primarily for its referential value. Language that is more evocative than referential, relying on how words are used rather than on what they mean denotatively, has an essential presentational quality that can be featured in an Interpreters Theatre production.

Most literary works combine referential and evocative uses of language. In Shakespeare's *Macbeth*, for example, Macbeth's lines—"Before my body / I throw my warlike shield. Lay on, Macduff, / And damned be him that first cries 'Hold, enough!' " (act 5, scene 8)—are essentially referential because the language, although emotional, exists not so much for its own sake, but to refer to a physical action. In the same play, the witches' lines—"Double, double, toil and trouble, / Fire burn and cauldron bubble" (act 4, scene 1)—are more evocative because of the atmosphere they suggest through heightened sound value and rhythm. Such presentational lines can suggest physical action and often do, but their verbal texture is interesting for its own sake. The presentational aspects of the language in *Macbeth*—sound, imagery, rhythm—might become central features in an Interpreters Theatre approach to that play.

The communicative nature of language can also contribute to presentational form in literature. When there is a sense of directness between speaker and reader, as when the reader is confronted by a character, an image, or an idea, the stance or *action* is presentational. In lines such as, "Fruit cannot drop / through this thick air,"[6] the speaker thrusts the image of intense heat toward her reader with the choice of the word "this," as if presenting it for the reader to share.

When action is more *psychological* than physical, it suggests presentational form because such action tends to live in the interior world of ideas, emotions, and sensations rather than in the exterior world of literal action. Any literary work that probes consciousness—in pure lyrics, in stream of consciousness passages in prose fiction, in dramatic soliloquies—contains presentational action.

Literary action that exists in the realm of *fantasy* is presentational in nature. *The Lord of the Rings* by J. R. R. Tolkien—in which trees walk and talk—depends more on the reader's imaginative completion for its full effect than does realistic material. Tolkien himself has suggested the presentational aspects of fantasy. In *The Tolkien Reader*, he writes,

> Drama [that is, representationalism] is naturally hostile to fantasy. Fantasy, even of the simplest kind, hardly ever succeeds in Drama, when that is presented as it should be, visibly and audibly acted. Fantastic forms are not to be counterfeited. . . . For this precise reason—that the characters, and even the scenes, are in Drama not imagined but actually beheld—Drama is, even though it uses similar material (words, verse, plot), an art fundamentally different from narrative art.[7]

Presentational elements can also emerge through *ritual or mythic patterns* in a work. Our imaginations are captured by the ritualized quest of the hero in Maurice Sendak's children's story

A Checklist for Presentational Form

1. Is the language rich and evocative?
   Is the language interesting for its own sake (i.e., filled with rhythms, unusual word choice, sound values, etc.)?
   Does much of the action depend upon images that evoke the reader's imagination?
2. Is there a sense of confrontation between the literary speaker and the reader?
   Does the speaker recognize the reader directly ("dear reader" or "you") or indirectly ("We must never forget these horrors")?

Does the speaker seem to argue a position or explain motives ("The devil made me do it")?
3. Is the action more psychological or emotional than physical?
4. Is the work a fantasy?
5. Does a pattern of universal human experience —such as a quest or a ritual—structure the work so strongly that it calls attention to itself?
6. Is the action so extensive in scope that it defies representational staging and demands imagination for its realization?

Figure 1.4: Checklist for presentational form.

Where The Wild Things Are, for example, and by the underlying Egyptian fertility rite pattern of "The Vegetable King" by James Dickey because we're fascinated by the ways these works are structured.

You'll recognize other elements of presentational form in literature only as you attempt to place the literature on the stage. The action in some works seems too large in scope to be contained by the literal space of the stage. The windstorm in Shakespeare's *King Lear*, for example, is almost impossible to represent on stage because the storm is physically overwhelming. Furthermore, the storm has a psychological life as well as a physical one: the storm is in Lear's mind as well as in the outside environment. Any work containing huge actions—the epic marches of armies or the holocaust of an earthquake, for example—can best be realized presentationally rather than representationally.

In summary, the presentational aspects of a literary work are the elements that seem to reach out to the reader for a completion or realization of the experience. The accompanying checklist offers guidelines for discovering presentational forms in literary works.

FROM LITERARY FORM TO PRODUCTION FORM

A knowledge of the nature of presentational form in literary works helps you understand Interpreters Theatre in its various forms as "theatres for literature." We can characterize the major forms of Interpreters Theatre by their responses to and uses of presentational elements in literature. To probe the central presentational aspect of prose fiction—the relationship between the narrator, the story, and the reader—the conventions of Chamber Theatre were developed. A major focus in Readers Theatre is the featuring of presentational language structures. Because Interpreters Theatre today is devoted to literature of all kinds, it's useful to investigate the relationship between literary structures and forms of theatrical production.

Literary structure can be categorized by **genre** (referring to the type of literature—poem, play, or story) and **mode** (referring to the stance of the speaker—lyric, dramatic, or epic—within the genre). We're accustomed to thinking of literature by genre; many anthologies organize their contents according to these familiar distinctions. Modes, however, reveal aspects of the literature's communicative strategies and are particularly useful because they suggest presentational and representational tendencies within the work.

Aristotle was the first critic to define literature systematically according to the stances or positions the writer can take in relation to his or her literary work, and he suggested three major stances, or modes, in literature:

1. The mode in which the author seems to stand in the most open relationship to the reader or audience, as if she were sharing thoughts and feelings directly. This is the lyric mode, in Aristotle's sense.

2. The mode in which the author speaks sometimes directly to the audience and sometimes through characters who seem to speak for themselves. This is the epic or narrative mode according to Aristotle, which is constituted by a combination of the lyric and dramatic stances. In the epic mode, when the author speaks directly to us, he doesn't tend to share personal feelings; instead, he tells a story, which of course may be laced with private emotions.

3. That mode in which the author speaks only through characters who seem to have ideas and feelings entirely their own. This is Aristotle's dramatic mode.

Although classic literary modes often correspond to the familiar genres of literature (such as poems, novels, and plays), modes become most useful as critical tools when they aren't identical with the genre in which they're cast. Eugene O'Neill's play *Long Day's Journey into Night* is in the classic lyric mode because its autobiographical nature suggests that the author is directly revealing his personal thoughts and feelings about his family. Even though a poem generically, "John Brown's Body" is in the epic mode because it has the overwhelming presence of a story and a storyteller. Hemingway's "The Killers," a short story, tends toward the dramatic mode because the narrator's presence is minimized to allow the characters to speak for themselves.

As contemporary readers of literature, we sometimes have difficulty using the classical modes as analytical tools, despite the fact that we value modal structures as integral to literary form. The source of our difficulty seems to be that Aristotle's positions imply that the author can be a speaker in a work, whereas in contemporary criticism we tend to separate the author as a person in the real world from the literary speaker as a person in a fictive world.[8] In Aristotle's definition of the lyric mode, however, the implication is that the critic must know something of the life and ideas of the author (as with O'Neill's *Long Day's Journey into Night*) before he can determine whether a selection is lyric. Such knowledge isn't always available or desirable. Furthermore, our contemporary understanding of prose fiction includes the idea of an *implied author* and a *narrator* who, like the poetic persona, enjoy an existence separate from the author who created them.[9] Aristotle's classic definition of epic mode assumes identification of the storyteller with the author.

To clear up some potential confusions and to update the classic modal definitions, we suggest the following contemporary descriptions:

1. In the lyric mode, the *speaker* stands in the most open relationship to the readers or audience, as if sharing his or her own thoughts and feelings with them directly.

2. In the epic mode, a *narrator* tells a story by speaking sometimes directly to the audience, and sometimes through characters who speak for themselves. The epic mode is a combination of

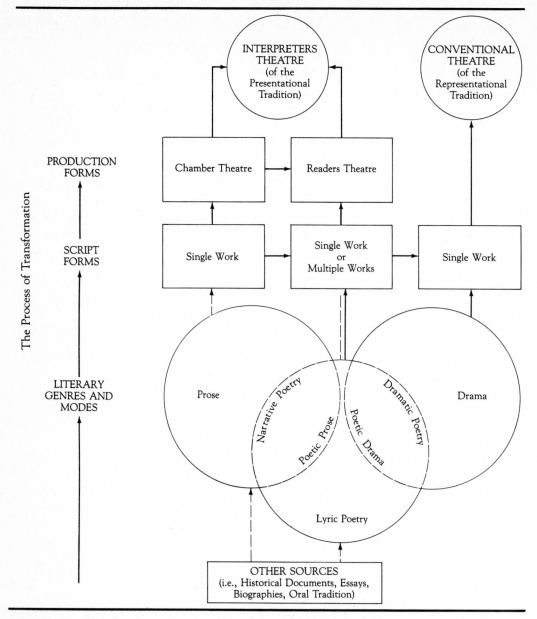

Figure 1.5: A generic-modal-production model. The interaction symbolized in the model is a dynamic process; for this reason, lines on the model suggest tendencies rather than demarcate strict boundaries.

the lyric mode (which features a speaker/narrator) and the dramatic mode (which features characters). A literary work is in the epic, or narrative, mode when the presence of a story and a storyteller is strong.

3. In the dramatic mode, *characters* speak to each other.

The major advantage of the new definitions is that they allow us to describe the shifts in attention and position of the literary persona rather than those of the author. *Long Day's Journey into Night* would therefore be dramatic, by our definition, although "John Brown's Body" would still be epic. In both the contemporary and classic senses, however, modes are powerful forces. A skillful transformer for Interpreters Theatre will use an understanding of literary modes to shape scripting and staging of the text.

The relationship among genres, modes, script forms, and production styles is symbolized by the diagram in figure 1.5.

Besides differentiating between **Interpreters Theatre** and Conventional Theatre in terms of their essential styles (presentational or representational) and uses of space (acoustic or pictorial), you can distinguish these theatre forms by variations in scripting and by genre and mode. Interpreters Theatre stages either a single work or multiple works brought together into a unified structure. The compiled script form, which may combine materials from many sources—poems, stories, newspaper articles, documents, drama, journals, and others—is actualized in Readers Theatre. The single work may be adapted for either Chamber Theatre or Readers Theatre. In the process of your transforming the single work for Interpreters Theatre, the literary structure leads you to script form and then to the choice of production style.

Although the model in figure 1.5 refers to literary works generically as either prose, poetry, or drama, we recognize the interrelation between genre and mode in literature. Modal tendencies may influence the choice of script and production style more than generic classifications.

We can make a modal distinction between Chamber Theatre and Readers Theatre. **Chamber Theatre** is the actualizing of presentational form in the epic mode. **Readers Theatre** is the actualizing of presentational form in the lyric and dramatic modes. Chamber Theatre is concerned primarily with the relationship between the narrator and the story she is telling. The narrator serves as a liaison between the audience and the characters in the story, overtly controlling the flow of the action. The narrator presents the story through a combination of dramatic showing (when characters sometimes contact the audience through presentational gestures and sometimes use representational action on stage) and lyric telling (when the narrator is always in a presentational confrontation with the audience).

Less defined as a production form than Chamber Theatre, Readers Theatre is highly presentational and may be characterized in these ways: (1) the major thrust of the action is outward, including the audience, (2) a chorus may be employed, and (3) the aesthetic qualities of language (such as sound, imagery, and rhythm) are emphasized. Since lyric and dramatic modes are featured in Readers Theatre, production focus is on individual characters in conflict (dramatic), speakers making personal statements (lyric), a chorus creating an atmosphere of sound and movement, or some combination of these elements.

When you seek an appropriate production form for a piece of literature, you'll be interested in the relationship between mode and genre in the literary world. In the genre of prose, for example, the relative balance between lyric and dramatic stances in the epic mode suggests script and production form. When the narrator in prose fiction dominates the action by expressing personal thoughts and feelings directly, as in much of Thomas Wolfe's fiction, the lyric mode predominates. Such poetic prose selections tend to find their production form in Readers Theatre. On the other hand, when a prose selection is mostly epic—lyric and dramatic stances are more evenly balanced—the best choice for production form is Chamber Theatre, because that medium is designed to probe the epic interaction of the narrator and the story.

The dramatic genre, which we usually think of as belonging in the Conventional Theatre form, may be realized successfully in Readers Theatre if the play has inherent presentational qualities within its structure. When a character opens up to the audience (as in a soliloquy), when characters seem to confront the reader by word or action with a way of life or an individual philosophical perspective (as in act 3 of "Don Juan in Hell," from George Bernard Shaw's *Man and Superman*), when the poetic language of the play rivals its interest in action (as in J. M. Synge's *Riders to the Sea*), or when the fantasy level cautions against representation (as in J. M. Barrie's *Peter Pan* and Shakespeare's *A Midsummer Night's Dream*), then Readers Theatre is a good production form to use. On the other hand, when the impact of the play seems to depend upon visually representing the action (such as in naturalistic drama or any comedy employing sight gags), the Conventional Theatre form is more appropriate. Much dramatic literature, however, may be realized in either Conventional Theatre or in a presentational form such as Readers Theatre; the choice of theatrical form is influenced by the nature of the play and your vision of it.

The genre of poetry seems to be best actualized in Readers Theatre, because the direct speaker-to-reader relationship in most poetry needs the essential face-to-face confrontation characteristic of the Readers Theatre medium. Such directness is most apparent in the lyric mode, where a speaker reveals intimate history (as in confessional poetry) or expounds upon nature (as in romantic lyrics), or wrestles with religious or philosophical concepts (as in metaphysical poetry). When the poetic persona assumes a storytelling stance, as in narrative poetry such as Robert Frost's "Death of the Hired Man," you may choose to emphasize the beauty of the poem's language through the Readers Theatre medium or the epic quality of the narration through Chamber Theatre. With narrative poetry and poetic prose, the distinction between Readers Theatre and Chamber Theatre becomes less important; in actual practice, you're apt to combine techniques from both production media when staging the selection.

Similarly, dramatic poetry and poetic drama may be at home in either Readers Theatre or Conventional Theatre, although dramatic poetry tends to be more comfortable in Readers Theatre. The dramatic nature of these literary forms may lead you to combine the more representational staging techniques of Conventional Theatre with the presentational emphasis of Readers Theatre.

STEPPING BACK

We've defined Interpreters Theatre in as many ways as we can—according to style, use of theatre space, and literary structure—to give you some formal guidelines. The definition of Interpreters Theatre has evolved throughout its history because people like you sought ways to allow literary works to speak. Interpreters Theatre forms evolve in response to changing literary form. From our contemporary vantage point, we can look back at the development of our art and suggest some of its defining characteristics now. But these definitions will be shaped and reshaped in the years to come because artists like you are willing to take risks or to defy conventions to serve their visions of a literary world. Definitions are transformed through time just as literary works are transformed through your interaction with them. In the chapters that follow, we shall turn our attention to the nature of both kinds of transformation.

NOTES

1. Gerald Freedman, Speech in honor of the retirement of Robert S. Breen from Northwestern University, Evanston, Ill., 13 May 1978.
2. Lewis Carroll, *Alice in Wonderland*, ed. Donald J. Gray (New York: W. W. Norton, 1971), p. 14.
3. Edmund Carpenter and Marshall McLuhan, "Acoustic Space," in *Explorations in Communication* (Boston: Beacon Press, 1960), p. 67.
4. See Leslie I. Coger and Melvin R. White, *Readers Theatre Handbook*, rev. ed. (Glenview, Ill.: Scott, Foresman, 1973), especially chap. 2, "Readers Theatre: Theatre of the Mind."
5. For an expanded discussion of synecdoche in Readers Theatre, see William R. Brown, Joseph Epolito, and Nancy Palmer Stump, "Genre Theory and the Practice of Readers Theatre," *The Speech Teacher* 23 (January 1974): 1–8.
6. H. D. [Hilda Doolittle], "Heat," in *Poetry in English*, ed. Warren Taylor and Donald Hall (New York: Macmillan, 1963), p. 570.
7. J. R. R. Tolkien, "On Fairy Stories," *The Tolkien Reader* (New York: Ballantine Books, 1966), pp. 49, 51.
8. See George T. Wright, *The Poet in the Poem* (Berkeley: University of California Press, 1962), especially chapter 1.
9. See Wayne Booth, *The Rhetoric of Fiction* (Chicago: The University of Chicago Press, 1961), especially chapter 3.

SUGGESTIONS FOR FURTHER READING

Bacon, Wallace A. *The Art of Interpretation.* 3rd ed. New York: Holt, Rinehart & Winston, 1979.

———. "Readers Theatre as a Humanizing Process." *Readers Theatre* (*News*), Fall 1975, pp. 3, 11.

Breen, Robert S. *Chamber Theatre.* Englewood Cliffs, N.J.: Prentice-Hall, 1978.

Carpenter, Edmund, and **McLuhan, Marshall.** "Acoustic Space." In *Explorations in Communication*, ed. Edmund Carpenter and Marshall McLuhan. Boston: Beacon Press, 1960.

Coger, Leslie Irene, and **White, Melvin R.** *Readers Theatre Handbook: A Dramatic Approach to Literature.* Rev. ed. Glenview, Ill.: Scott, Foresman, 1973.

Gilbert, Carolyn A. *Communicative Performance of Literature.* New York: Macmillan, 1977. chap. 6.

Gregory, Paul. "Paul Gregory Speaks." *Readers Theatre* (*News*), Winter 1974, pp. 3 and 5.

"Informal Conversations with the Leaders of Readers Theatre." *Readers Theatre* (*News*), Fall 1977, pp. 12–23.

Lee, Charlotte I., and **Galati, Frank.** *Oral Interpretation.* 5th ed. Boston: Houghton Mifflin, 1977. chap. 9.

Loesch, Katharine T. "Towards an Ontology of Literature in Performance." *Oral English* 1 (Fall 1972): 8–12.

Maclay, Joanna. *Readers Theatre: Toward a Grammar of Practice.* New York: Random House, 1971.

Pickering, Jerry V. *Readers Theatre.* Encino, Calif.: Dickenson, 1975.

———. "Readers Theatre as Theatre." *Readers Theatre* (*News*), Spring 1977, pp. 1–4, 18.

Tolkien, J. R. R. "On Fairy Stories." In *The Tolkien Reader.* New York: Ballantine Books, 1966.

Williams, David A. "Readers Theatre: The Heuristic Feast." *Readers Theatre* (*News*), Spring 1976, p. 5.

PART TWO

Image-inations: Listening To the Voices in Literature

"Let me out," cries the Dryad in Frank Stockton's romanticized version of the myth of the forest spirit, "Old Pipes and the Dryad." The main character, Old Pipes, has stumbled upon a Dryad tree in the forest.

> Old Pipes had never, to his knowledge, seen a Dryad tree, but he knew that there were such trees on the hillsides and the mountains, and that Dryads lived in them. He knew, too, that in the summertime, on those days when the moon rose, before the sun went down, a Dryad could come out of her tree if anyone could find the key which locked her in, and turn it. Old Pipes closely examined the trunk of the tree, which stood in the full moonlight. "If I see that key," he said, "I shall surely turn it." Before long he perceived a piece of bark standing out from the tree, which appeared to him very much like the handle of a key. He took hold of it, and found he could turn it quite around. As he did so a large part of the side of the tree was pushed open, and a beautiful Dryad stepped quickly out.[1]

Part 2 of *Theatres for Literature* is about beautiful Dryads and the keys that unlock them. Beautiful Dryads in literary worlds may be sensuous lovers, forces of evil, dilettante heroines, sophisticated jet-setters, or any of myriad clamoring voices that inhabit the pages of literature. We believe, with Walter J. Ong, that "literature exists in a context of one presence calling to another,"[2] and that literary language should be heard "as utterance, that is to say, as cries."[3] Characters and forces in their worlds call to us as we read, and we respond. Such is the joy of silent reading, which we've all experienced, that transforms the reader into a kind of creative artist. In this section, we're interested in developing another kind of creator—a "maker" who answers the cries of literary voices in a special way.

1. *The Best Short Stories of Frank R. Stockton* (New York: Charles Scribner's Sons, n.d.), p. 95.
2. Walter J. Ong, *The Barbarian Within* (New York: Macmillan, 1962), p. 59.
3. *Ibid.*, p. 28.

Guided by those voices calling from the pages of literature, you the maker will begin to capture fleeting images arising in your mind and shape them into a formal vision—an "image-ination," in which implicit presentational form is made explicit.[4] Image-inations are, therefore, transformed literary works. Each image-ination is unique, because it combines the particularized world of the literary work with the specialized vision of its adapter in a fully creative engagement. The process of transforming a literary work for Interpreters Theatre is thus a creative interaction between releasing and making. Voices in the literary work are released into acoustic space through the skill of the maker-transformer. You unlock the voices by creating a text; you give form to the voices by writing a script; you give body to the voices by staging a performance. In Part 2 we are interested primarily in the image-ination involved in the transformation of works to texts and then to scripts.

4. To the best of our knowledge, the term *image-ination* was coined by Leland H. Roloff, Northwestern University.

CHAPTER TWO

Transforming for Readers Theatre: Creating a Text

Great literature is simply language charged with meaning to the utmost possible degree.

Ezra Pound, *How to Read*

In a discussion of creative originality in literature, Sir Herbert Read says, "From time to time along comes a special kind of craftsman, special because he possesses a particular vision of the world, a peculiar way of seeing the world, and this leads to a modification of the traditional forms of expression, to a transformation."[1] We like to think of **transformation** in the sense in which physicists define it—to change one form of energy into another—because you, as an interpreter, can become that "special kind of craftsman" who changes the contained energy of printed literature into the dynamic energy of literature onstage. You make this transformation by discovering the lines of force within the text. This chapter is designed to show you how to discover and release power from a single work of literature and to shape—transform—its liberated energy into a script for Readers Theatre.

HOW TO BEGIN: SELECTING LITERATURE TO TRANSFORM

The transformation process grows from mutual love and respect between a literary work and a reader. To begin, ask yourself: Do I genuinely like this selection and does it like me? Look back to those stories, poems, and plays that have taken hold of your imagination. That tingle up the spine is real, and it's a trustworthy indication that you have connected with something. What literary works have forced you to put them down and think, have jabbed you, have caressed you, have enticed you to enter an unknown world? Turn first to those works or authors to find your materials for Readers Theatre.

You may prefer to engage the spirit of literary adventure. Seek works that aren't found in the usual anthologies. Look again at literature that once may have seemed forbidding or obscure to you. Don't hesitate to consider classical materials or to explore contemporary frontiers for experimental works. Let the excitement of adventure complement the satisfaction of the familiar. No horizon is off limits. Working in the medium of Readers Theatre, you're free to consider all literary forms—plays, novels, short stories, letters, diaries, essays, poems, songs—and even nonliterary forms such as journalistic pieces and documentary materials, but the works you'll choose to transform will meet one overriding requirement: they'll be rich in presentational form. If you can answer yes to many of the questions on the checklist for presentational form on page 10, then the literature you have in mind may indeed be good for transformation.

Practical Considerations

Once you have found a literary work that genuinely intrigues you, attracts your creative spirit, and is presentational in form, you're ready to consider the practical aspects of staging it.

First, consider the length of your production—whether, for example, you're interested in transforming a ten-minute selection as a class assignment, a thirty-minute piece, a reading hour, or a full-length two-hour production. If the selection you have tentatively chosen is longer than the performance time allotted, look at it for a scene or a segment that can be performed as a work in itself—a segment with a definite beginning, middle, and end. A well-planned director's note or an oral introduction should enable the audience to catch on to the action of a scene late in a play or novel. You may prefer a short poem for transformation if your assignment is to create a brief script.

Ideally, you should stage an entire work, but sometimes you'll need to cut for practical reasons, usually to arrive at a specified production length. (Cutting for aesthetic reasons will be discussed throughout this chapter.) Practical cutting of long works such as novels usually involves deleting whole scenes or excluding a character who is relatively unnecessary to the segment (or theme) you've chosen. At this point, it's important that your cutting be simple deletion or excerpting that won't substantially change the denotation of the original. Be careful and sensitive in your cutting of literature as you would be with any other kind of surgery on a living being. At this point, don't rearrange elements (lines of poetry or events of plot) so they seem to be the author's original arrangement. Transforming texts means recasting an author's work into a new form, but begin with as much of the author's text as you can to ensure that the newly transformed script will be truly a hybrid product of the author's original work and your creative imagination.

Another practical consideration in selecting literature is the audience. Who will comprise the audience? What are its collective tastes and interests likely to be? What are its general age and level of education? Would your selection raise the audience's understanding, widen its experience, and deepen its appreciation of literature?

Critics such as Wayne Booth suggest that every literary work has an **implied reader**—an ideal person to whom the work is addressed.[2] How does the implied silent audience of the literary work correspond to the theatre audience you anticipate? If there is a wide discrepancy between the implied and actual audiences, you may wish to reconsider your selection. Considerations of the audience are always sensitive and often difficult, but they are some of the most important factors in choosing material for transformation.

The demands of casting comprise the third practical aspect of literary selection. Will you have ready access to the kind and number of performers the work needs? Often a director chooses a work for transformation because of its special casting requirements—it calls for a large cast, an especially small cast, or an all-female cast, for example. Furthermore, a director may hesitate to select a play such as *Hamlet* unless she has a potential Hamlet. The flexibility of the Interpreters Theatre form allows a certain latitude in casting because Interpreters Theatre is engaged primarily in presentation, not representation.

Other preliminary considerations are performance rights and royalty fees. For any production other than a short classroom assignment (and even in those instances the copyright laws are tightening), you need permission of the author or publisher to stage a literary work. If you plan to adapt a play, you may have to pay the same royalty fees that Conventional Theatre directors would pay. Permissions for prose selections and poetry are often granted free of charge, but you must secure permission anyway. Royalties for children's works are generally quite reasonable, and many children's selections—such as fairy tales—are in public domain. Even for performances with no admission charge, publisher permission is required unless the literature is in public domain. Beware of neglecting to make an early inquiry for performance rights; a denial of permission can foil the best laid production plans.

Selecting Children's Literature

Transforming literature for children follows the same intuitive principles and takes the same careful analysis as does adapting adult literature for the stage. The one difference is that children comprise the audience; as an adapter sensitive to the interests of children, you need to choose literature that will captivate children's imaginations. Let the child in you help choose a poem, play, or story for performance. Don't hesitate to stage classics of children's literature that you loved when you were young; they're still great works, to each new generation.

What makes good children's literature? C. S. Lewis claimed that a book that could be enjoyed by children only was a poor children's book. Many of the best books ever written for children appeal to adult sensibilities as well. E. B. White's *Charlotte's Web*, *Peter and the Wolf*, Rudyard Kipling's *Jungle Book*, Mark Twain's *Adventures of Tom Sawyer*, *Grimm's Fairy Tales*, Saint Exupery's *Little Prince*, and myths and legends such as the Uncle Remus stories are just a few works with a wide audience appeal.

At the same time, there are significant differences between good children's literature and good adult literature. Children are not little adults. There are entire psychological, intellectual, and emotional areas of understanding that are beyond children's developing capabilities; good children's literature speaks clearly about what child readers can understand and subtly suggests larger understandings that children can perceive only when they're ready. As an adapter, you may wish to work with a selection with multilevel appeal that makes complexity available, yet retains clarity and simplicity on the surface level.

Often writers for children combine complexity and simplicity through the skillful use of comedy. Children of all ages love humor! The younger child is delighted by jokes and riddles. Repetition, slapstick, and chase sequences all add to the child's imaginative involvement, and suggest intriguing possibilities for staging. Comical characters and ridiculous situations often teach more effectively than serious reflective passages. Comedy can be used to point out the defects and flaws of our society, thereby providing guidelines for living. A trust in the powers of comedy to appeal to children, however, must not overshadow our essential interest in important values. Children can relate to serious concepts of death, war, and illness, among others, if the subjects are presented with dignity and sensitivity.

When choosing children's literature to stage for Interpreters Theatre, you're faced with a choice (and controversy) that doesn't have a counterpart when you work with adult literature: should you work with a realistic or a fantasy work? **Realistic literature** for children creates a convincing and recognizable world in which the events are not outside human experience. Realistic works often deal with sociological and personal problems a child faces every day (thereby suggesting that the child isn't alone in difficult situations). *The Dead Bird* by Margaret Wise Brown and *The Tenth Good Thing About Barney* by Judith Viorst sensitively explore the reality of death; *Where is Daddy? The Story of a Divorce* by Beth Goff helps children cope with troubled families; *Bang Bang You're Dead* by Louise Fitzhugh and Sandra Scoppettone explores the horror of war; Gladys Cretan's *All Except Sammy* tells about a young sports-minded boy who felt out of place in his family of musicians; Kriston Hunter's *Soul Brothers and Sister Lou*, Mildred Waler's *Lillie of Watts*, and Barbara Rinkoff's *Member of the Gang* all explore the problems of growing up black in the inner city.

Realistic literature for children also may explore past events. Scott O'Dell's *Island of the Blue Dolphins* is the story of the survival of an Indian girl alone on an island off the California coast from 1835 to 1853. The book suggests strong moral values as it teaches about a neglected period in our history. Irene Hunt's *No Promises in the Wind* is a gripping story of children who were starving during the Great Depression. Robert Louis Stevenson's *Treasure Island* combines nautical realism and exciting action.

Fantasy literature, on the other hand, often reveals worlds wholly outside a child's everyday experience, but those worlds tap deep resources of understanding within the child. Most of us grew up experiencing fantasy literature such as Mother Goose rhymes, fairy tales, and famous fantasy stories such as Lewis Carroll's *Alice in Wonderland* and J. R. R. Tolkien's *Hobbit*. Fantasies captivate our imagination because of their mystery; without overtly realizing it, we return to the world about us after reading fantasy with an increased understanding of the forces within each of us that make us behave as we do. Bruno Bettelheim, in his landmark study *The Uses of Enchantment: The Meaning and Importance of Fairy Tales*, argues (from a Freudian perspective) that fairy tales—in which good people "live happily ever after" and evil ones are always punished appropriately—help children construct healthy attitudes toward the world in which they live. Since fantasy worlds are separate from the child's own experience, they allow the child safely to explore the joys and difficulties of being human. In this way, fantasies enhance the child's understanding of reality.

Realism presents the world as it is; fantasy presents the world as it could be. Both are capable of presenting the world as it *should* be. Whether literature is realism or fantasy, the important question is whether it seems to reach out to you, whether it tantalizes you to adapt it for performance.

Practical Considerations for Selecting Children's Literature[3]

When selecting children's literature to stage, the age of the audience is of primary importance. You're very fortunate if you can control the exact age of your audience, so that you know you are playing to audience members with similar tastes and interests. Most likely, however, the ages in your audience will range widely. Fairy tales and animal tales are popular with younger children,[4] but the eleven-year-old and twelve-year-old prefer adventure, history, biography, and stories of real life. Although fantasies appeal to younger children primarily, there are some fantasy stories —such as those of J. R. R. Tolkien, Madeliene L'Engle, and Ursula le Guin—that hold the interest of older audiences. Similarly, realistic stories with historical interest tend to appeal to a wide variety of ages. The best advice for a widely diverse audience is to select literature that exists on several levels at once and can appeal to young children as well as to the parents (who often bring their children and stay for the performance).

When you adapt children's literature for either Readers Theatre or Chamber Theatre, be particularly conscious of the length of the whole work. The attention span of children ages four to seven is probably not greater than one hour; children ages eight to twelve can be attentive for two hours. Recognizing the demands of shorter attention spans, cut some of the longer speeches to be short and to the point. Long, talky dialogue is lost and inhibits the smooth flow of action. Children respond to overt physical action and to quickly moving plots, even at the expense of character complexity. The characters may even be served by these cuts: if action is sped up and extraneous business, subplots, and minor climaxes are diminished, the real conflicts in the text become more readily apparent for the audience. The performance features select perceptions of interesting characters in conflict. As with good adult literature, the very best children's literature will be difficult to cut. If you can avoid cutting and still maintain the child audience's attention, always do so.

You can also keep children's attention by designing the script to be full of action. Myles McDowell lists overt action as a key element distinguishing children's literature from adult fare.

> More important is the bias towards an active rather than a passive presentation of the material. By active I mean that the text concentrates on dialogue and incident rather than on the more passive mood which characterises description and reflection."[5]

One technique to make children's literature more active is to rewrite parts of the literary text, so that the children are drawn to make spontaneous audible or overt responses to the story. You may heighten the children's involvement by using redirected discourse: add to your text questions or repetition that encourage the audience to participate. For example, if your original text reads, "Oh, I can't find the princess. I wonder where she is," rewrite it by addition to read, "Oh, I can't find the princess. Do you know where she is? Can anyone tell me where she is?" (And any additional dialogue you need to elicit a response.) Consider the wide range of potential child responses and what your reaction would be in each instance. Be flexible!

When you've selected a literary work for its enticing literary qualities, its presentational form, and its practical suitability, you're ready to begin the actual process of transforming. The hard job of choosing material is behind you, and the creative task of transforming the work into a new script lies ahead. To begin, take a few moments to write down why you chose your selection. What is it about the work that attracts you? What images, visions, or feelings does it evoke in you? Do you have any notions, however vague, of how you might stage this work? This is important for two reasons: (1) your ideas at this point become part of your production concept, which will emerge more fully later, and (2) they'll form a guideline for the kinds of responses you wish to evoke from your audience.

How We Begin: Selecting a Sample Work to Transform

We've selected a sample literary work to show how a reader creates a text and transforms the text into a script for performance. We'll share two scripts with you because each literary work holds within it more than one text and many scripts. We hope you'll begin to see the creative possibilities in literature.

We've selected a short piece, the sonnet "Ozymandias" by Percy Bysshe Shelley. Using a brief work enables us to analyze the whole poem; the same principles are applicable to larger structures.

Ozymandias

I met a traveller from an antique land
Who said: "Two vast and trunkless legs of stone
Stand in the desert . . . Near them, on the sand,
Half sunk, a shattered visage lies, whose frown,
And wrinkled lip, and sneer of cold command,
Tell that its sculptor well those passions read
Which yet survive, stamped on these lifeless things,
The hand that mocked them, and the heart that fed;
And on the pedestal these words appear:
'My name is Ozymandias, king of kings:
Look on my works, ye Mighty, and despair!'
Nothing beside remains. Round the decay
Of that colossal wreck, boundless and bare
The lone and level sands stretch far away."[6]

We were initially attracted to the poem because it was one of those familiar works we had always liked but had never considered for Readers Theatre. We began to look at the world of "Ozymandias" with a new sensitivity to imaginative possibilities. The poem seemed to pack so many intriguing ideas into its brief form. Furthermore, its images were compelling enough to beckon us to investigate further.

Recognizing our attraction to "Ozymandias," we next investigated its potential for presentational form. We found that the richness of language ("vast and trunkless legs of stone," "shattered visage," "colossal wreck") created images that seemed to reach out to us, providing just enough information to suggest the ruins, yet withholding extensive descriptions. Furthermore, there are at least two perspectives in the poem: that of the "traveller from an antique land" and that of the mighty Ozymandias. The traveler and Ozymandias are separated not only by perspective, but also by mode. Ozymandias exists in the dramatic mode, whereas the traveler assumes the role of a narrator, telling a story in the epic mode. All the characters, whatever their modes, seem to address their audience directly, stating their positions, or perspectives, for all to hear. The work is well suited for any mature theatre audience, because the **implied audience** for Shelley's poem is all mankind.

Because "Ozymandias" is a sonnet, it has the characteristic emphasis on internal action, on ideas and emotions, rather than on physical behaviors. The poem finds much of its presentational form in the strong creation of setting—a setting that is simply presented to the audience members for their personal responses. In short, "Ozymandias" seems to be rich in presentational qualities that could be actualized onstage.

CREATING THE TEXT THROUGH ANALYSIS

Literary works, like people, contain powerful sources of energy. All individuals and all literary works have particular strengths that identify them. A human being may be a powerful athlete, muscular and rough in much the same way that a poem, such as "Chicago" by Carl Sandburg, is muscular and rough. Or a person may be quiet and tender, like a delicate Japanese haiku. Yet people and poems are rarely one-dimensional in their strengths. What makes living consciousnesses fascinating are their sources of power that either combine to give them complexity or that pull them in different directions to create conflicts of personality: the tough athlete, for example, who yearns for quiet times in which to write chamber music. You'll find the same kinds of complexity in literary worlds. In Robert Frost's "Stopping by Woods on a Snowy Evening," the speaker is pulled by two strong forces: the image of the "lovely, dark and deep" woods, which lures him to stay, and a sense of the many "promises to keep," which urges him on his way.

When the sources of power in literature reinforce each other or pull in opposite directions, they create **tensiveness**, in much the same way that two sources of live electricity can parallel each other to provide added strength or can create a spark when they intersect.[7] Defined by the Oxford English Dictionary as "the quality of stretching or straining," tensiveness is a condition of action and life-giving energy. The action of "Stopping by Woods on a Snowy Evening" is created by the tensive conflict between the image of the forest and the speaker's sense of responsibility. You feel the speaker struggle with the opposing forces of the poem's experience, and you know that this tensiveness is a sign of life. In general, life in literature comes from the patterns of interaction between sources of power.

We are interested in identifying the power sources in literature, because these forces will become the actual voices in the created script. The tensive quality of the literature is important because the way in which the forces collide and strain within the life-world of the literary work will create conflict and complexity in the created script. To create a living text from a literary work, and thus to create a vital script, you need to recognize the elements in literature that are sources of power and to understand the many ways in which these living forces connect.

Power Sources in Literature

The major source of power in a literary work is language; through language, literature lives on the page. Authors use language to create other kinds of structures within literary works; these elements become **power sources** for the text and voices in the script. Power in literature comes primarily from **ideas** or themes in the work, from **characters, imagery, sound structures, time systems,** and **plot structure**. It's obvious that characters can be given voices, but the possibility that other forces in a work may also have speaking roles is not so apparent. Any power source can become a voice in performance. By analyzing the power sources in your selection, you'll begin to understand which forces can become voices in your script.

Ideas

Ideas drive men and change civilizations. Notions of freedom, of honor, of deity, and of many other values have molded history. It is no wonder that, when a literary work contains dynamic themes, it surges with the power to move its readers. The dynamic quality of themes resides in their originality of treatment, in their posture in relation to their times, in their ability to embody enduring human needs and desires, in their capacity to contain conflicting perspectives, and in the potency of that which is withheld. William Faulkner concluded his acceptance of the Nobel Prize with an affirmation of the power of ideas in literature. "The poet's voice need not merely be the record of man, it can be one of the props, the pillars to help him endure and prevail."[8]

Ideas in literature are sometimes presented in such a way that they seem to be contradictory. When a direct conflict of ideas is captured in a single statement, it is usually called a **paradox.** In Mark 8:35 of the Bible, for example, "For whosoever will save his life, shall lose it; but whosoever shall lose his life for my sake . . . shall save it" is a paradox. By making such an obvious contrast in ideas, this paradox adds vitality to the notion of self-sacrifice. We often see paradoxes in other power sources: paradox in character traits (the lovable villain), for example, or paradoxical images (the silent scream). Some literary critics, such as Cleanth Brooks, argue that paradox—the tugs and pulls of opposite forces—is at the heart of poetry.[9] Brooks's expanded notion of paradox is very similar to our concept of tensiveness; we all sense the life-giving quality of this kind of conflict.

Another familiar kind of tensiveness is **irony. Verbal irony** is present when there is a contradiction between the meaning of an idea and the form of language in which it is cast. A familiar kind of verbal irony is sarcasm. **Dramatic irony** resides in the conflict between a character's understanding of events and the actual meaning of the events in which he is involved. If your literary work is ironic or paradoxical, you'll want to consider the possibilities for staging the contradictions, perhaps by using a chorus to embody the conflicting forces. In Sophocles' *Oedipus the King*, a classic example of dramatic irony, a chorus might be used to echo the earlier words spoken by Oedipus, "Upon the murderer I invoke this curse," at the very moment that Oedipus discovers that he himself is the murderer.[10]

Ideas are also given power by the force of implication rather than direct statement. Most literary works suggest more than they actually state, relying on the reader's imagination to recognize the power of the literary ideas. By so doing, literature works by indirection, creating imagined presences rather than direct statements. Imagined presences are always vivid. As Walter J. Ong notes, "Noises one hears, for example in a woods at night, register in the imagination as presences— personlike manifestations—far more than do movements which one merely sees."[11] If the writer can create enough noises in the night to set the reader's imagination afire, while at the same time withholding enough that is merely seen to allow that imagination to work freely, the force of an idea is increased.

Ideas in "Ozymandias"

Because we were first attracted to the ideas in "Ozymandias," it seems appropriate to look at the poem's philosophical level as a major source of its power. The idea informing this brief poem is very large indeed: that our pride is also our folly; that our egos will lead us to invest our energies in tangible memorials, whereas it is really only our mortality that endures. The idea is not unique, but the treatment of it in "Ozymandias" is: the idea is posed sparsely, mostly through visual images that are presented directly, without explanation. Since we have all felt self-pride, we can relate to some of the feelings Ozymandias had. This kind of connection between the world of the poem and our world is what helps us create our text of that poem.

Irony in "Ozymandias" is created by comparison of the self-confident words on the pedestal, "Look on my works, ye Mighty, and despair!" with the destruction surrounding the monument. The fact that only blowing sand remains, despite Ozymandias's intention to create a lasting memorial for himself, furthers the irony of the poem. In addition, it is ironic, on another level, that the passions of Ozymandias still seem to survive, despite the decay of the monument depicting them.

The ideas in "Ozymandias" are powerful also because they are presented through more than one perspective. Surely Ozymandias's display of self-pride is different from the judgments of the sculptor and the traveler; the contrast in perspective is one of the points of interest in the poem. Perspectives, however, are angles of vision taken by characters, another major source of power in literature.

Character

Often what draws us into a book is the vitality of another life. Instinctive voyeurs, people want to know about other people: how they live, how they think, how they feel. Characters in literature hold great fascination for us, and therefore are generators of literary power. There is no literature without some informing consciousness or character—a **persona** or speaker in a poem, a **narrator** and other characters in a story, or dramatic characters in a play.

Character refers to a consciousness created by the author, whether that consciousness belongs to a human being, an animal, or an otherwise inanimate object. Obviously, some characters are more fully realized than others. When a character is given a distinct voice and body, as in plays and novels, that character has been explicitly drawn by the author. Other kinds of characters, such as third person narrators and lyric personae, usually lack names, details of history, and defined physical appearance but, nevertheless, are distinctly felt presences as fully embodied in performance as explicitly drawn characters.

Characters are major sources of power in literature by virtue of their relationship to their world. Boldly drawn characters who seem to have lives of their own are powerful because they exhibit a distinctive force of personality through their interior thinking, their intense emotions, their authority, or their general vitality. To illustrate, think of literature as a moving film that allows you to stop the action at any time; the characters in that frozen moment who arrest your attention—because of their physical appearance, their actions, or their ideas—are powerful.

Children, in particular, are fascinated by boldly drawn characters, especially those who exhibit clear and predictable behavior. The younger the child, the more interesting the character must be externally. Many times children's works will feature flat or **stereotyped** characters as major sources of power. Although such flat characters are not normally desirable in adult literature, stereotyped figures are an important aspect of children's understanding of literary action. Young children need the clarity and reliability of predictable literary characters to help them sort out their complex world. Only when children grow older are they ready to appreciate multifaceted or round characters with traits of goodness and evil that strain at each other in a single body. In young children's literature, the tensiveness is between characters who represent strong recognizable positions; in older children's literature, tensiveness is clearly within characters who recognize the myriad choices they can make.

Many literary selections, for older children and adults, center around the powerful presence of more subtle characters. Subtly drawn characters such as narrators are powerful for reasons other than their personalities. Such characters achieve strength through their perspective and control on the world of the literary work. A narrator, for example, functions as the controlling force in any prose fiction and is always the central character in a Chamber Theatre production. Similarly, speakers in poems gain power as characters by their willingness to reveal personal attitudes and feelings. The richness of the lyric persona's character is directly related to the richness of the perspective, or vision, in the lyric poem; even though lyric personae are subtly drawn characters, especially in terms of their external appearance, they have powerful souls and minds. You come to know them as characters in the world, just as you know their more fully drawn dramatic counterparts.

Characters, whether they are subtly or boldly depicted, are carriers of all other power sources. It is through the speaking consciousness that the literature comes to you.

Characters in "Ozymandias"

There are four characters in "Ozymandias": the persona who opens the poem, the "traveller from an antique land," Ozymandias, and the sculptor who is merely referred to. The least defined of all the characters in the poem is the sculptor, who is identified only synecdochically by "hand." Yet the sculptor's attitude toward his subject is indicated by the word "mocked," and although he has no explicit voice in the poem, he speaks through the quality and character of his work, as do all artists.

Of the three remaining characters, the persona is least defined. He has no name. (Unless there is contrary evidence in the work, we assume that personae are the same gender as their authors.) In a sense, he relinquishes the poem to the traveler by letting the traveler tell the poem directly; yet the very act of stepping back is an act of strength on the part of the persona. He seems unselfishly to endorse the traveler's story by his silence.

Although the traveler, like the persona, is nameless, he is more fully defined because (1) he has so much voice (note the length and quality of his statement), and (2) he is given a role

Figure 2.1: Distance in perspective in "Ozymandias."

("traveller") and a locale ("from an antique land"). The traveler's attitude toward what he relates comes through clearly, although he seems to be objectively reporting what he has seen. Much of the traveler's power as a character, like the power of the poem itself, comes through what he doesn't say. He avoids philosophizing, relying instead on stark images that make his point: "wrinkled lip," "sneer of cold command."

Ozymandias, though given very little voice, is the fullest character in the poem. Despite our knowing his words are carved into the pedestal, we seem to hear them proclaimed by Ozymandias himself, a testimony to the living presence of the king. Other than the two lines on the pedestal, Ozymandias is defined by only five images: "two trunkless legs of stone," "shattered visage," "wrinkled lip," "sneer of cold command," and "heart that fed them"; yet his presence pervades the poem. Appropriately, the poem bears his name, always an indication of importance.

Much of the impact of the poem comes through the conflicting perspectives of its characters. Each character (with the possible exception of the persona, who appears to endorse the traveler's perspective) presents, or implies, a different answer to a single question of value: What should endure? Ozymandias seems to believe that the products of his power will endure. The sculptor seems to hold that the artist's vision of truth will prevail. Both the persona and the traveler see only the ruins enduring in the empty sands, although the persona has the additional perspective of seeing the enduring value of the traveler's story for the reader. We, as readers, interpret the natural decay of the statue as a metaphoric expression of the ravages of time and the insignificance of the human condition. It is as if the characters in "Ozymandias" and the reader of the poem were progressively distanced in perspective, as shown in figure 2.1. The diagram suggests possibilites for scripting and staging "Ozymandias" in Readers Theatre, particularly in terms of blocking. A director might want to arrange the sculptor, traveler, and persona onstage so that they are progressively more distant from Ozymandias.

Finally, we may look at the characters of this poem in terms of their relative degrees of authority. The persona has an authority of control; he initiates the poem and, we feel, could terminate it at any time. The persona gives the traveler a kind of importance by turning the poem over to him. The traveler also gains authority and credibility by his apparent reliance on factual proof; rather than sharing opinion alone, he points to physical objects that exist in nature and lets the objects speak for themselves. The traveler's authority grows in proportion to Ozymandias's loss of the tyrannical authority he enjoyed in his lifetime. Ozymandias has present vitality, but no authority. The sculptor, on the other hand, has an authority of vision that has gained momentum through time, because history has proven his mocking artistic version of the "king of kings" to be accurate. An understanding of the relative authority of characters in "Ozymandias" can help us in our later blocking, in costuming, and even in the choice of lines we give to the different characters.

Imagery

An image is an appeal to the senses through language, as if the words reach out to the reader for completion. Image power derives from the poet's ability to choose combinations of words that activate the reader's imaginative sensing and later cause the reader to sense in new ways—to hear and touch and see with intensification. Such vivid images as "the afternoon lies glazed upon the walls,"[12] "sawdust restaurants with oyster shells,"[13] and "a wild, glassy morning—all winds and glitter"[14] draw us imaginatively into the world of literature. When a literary selection is particularly rich in imagery, we say it has a high *sensory quotient*. Such works activate our senses because the images are alive and clear. They cause us to sense in new ways because the comparisons they make jar us out of our familiar ways of looking at afternoon sun, restaurants, and windy mornings. This kind of comparison is called a **metaphor**, a figure of speech that brings together two unlike elements, such as "my faith is a rock," "you're a dead duck," or "the long arm of the law." The value of a metaphor is that it focuses your attention on the **connotation**, rather than the **denotation**, of at least one of the elements and thereby intensifies our reaction to the comparison. Whenever authors evoke the connotations of words for literary effect, they depend on the reader's participation in creating the effects. Your image of a "glazed afternoon" will not be quite the same as another person's, because the word *glazed* is ambiguous enough to allow you to interpret it from your own experience. Metaphors therefore increase image-ination and are fundamental to presentational form.

Metaphors are only one way images occur in a piece of literature. Often images are presented directly to the reader, without bringing in a comparison, such as "the faint flush in her cheeks" or "the stiff twiggy stuff along the road." Their power derives from their simplicity and immediacy.

As you examine your selection for the nature and arrangement of its images, you gain a feeling for the fullness of its image life. Images central to your work may eventually become voices in the finished script. List images according to the sense channels to which they appeal: visual (to see); auditory (to hear); tactile, including thermal (to touch); gustatory (to taste); olfactory (to smell); kinetic (to move in space); and kinesthetic (to be aware of muscle contraction and release). Although such a classification doesn't take into consideration many of the complex sensations that pass through your body, it is useful because specific sense channel designations suggest possibilities for script formation. An auditory image, for example, might suggest a sound effect or an audible voice or it might lead to an action in response to sound.

Imagery in "Ozymandias"

There isn't a single line in "Ozymandias" without sensory appeals; "Ozymandias" has a high sensory quotient. All the other elements of power in the poem—its ideas, its sound patterns, its characters—relate to the stark image of the gigantic ruins in the empty desert.

The poem works with visual sensory appeals mostly, building a fascinating contrast between vertical visual images ("Two vast and trunkless legs of stone," "Half sunk," "pedestal," "colossal wreck") and horizontal images ("in the desert," "on the sand," "boundless and bare," "lone and level sands"). Although the setting is created primarily by visual images, thermal and tactile appeals are generated by the use of the words "stone," "desert," "decay," "wreck," and "sands." Auditory imagery contributes to setting through the subtle invocation of silence in the desert: the emptiness suggested by "nothing beside remains" and "lone and level sands" implies a silence as well. In contrast, the vitality of Ozymandias's words, even though they're etched in stone and literally appeal only to the eye, have a full auditory life, suggested in part by the use of direct quotation.

"Ozymandias" is an example of an unusual yet extremely functional use of kinesthetic imagery to create irony. The vitality of the ruler's "frown," "wrinkled lip," and "sneer of cold command" caught in a stone monument, half sunk and decayed at that, creates a strong appeal to the sense of kinesthesis. Ironic tensiveness resides in the use of an inanimate object—a monument—to capture the living essence of a passionate man. A Readers Theatre production of "Ozymandias" may feature that ironic conflict by letting Ozymandias's passion come through his voice only while his body remains immobile, or by giving Ozymandias a great deal of movement and then suddenly freezing his actions in the middle of a gesture.

Sound Structures

Sound structures in literature include both **tone color** and **rhythm**. Defined as the featuring of vowels and consonants for their sound values, tone color can be one of the strongest yet subtlest power sources in literature. Tone-colored works play with sound to help create meaning, so that the denotations of the words are enriched by the sounds used to produce them. A familiar kind of tone coloring is **onomatopoeia**, in which words are derived from the sounds of the actions or things they denote: *buzz, cuckoo, slap.*

Most tone coloring is not onomatopoeic, however. In the majority of literary works where sound is powerful, tonalities subtly suggest the mood and sensory life of the piece. In the first stanza of "God's Grandeur" by Gerard Manley Hopkins, the repeated sounds of vowels and consonants contribute to the fullness of praise in the poem.

> The world is charged with the grandeur of God.
>   It will flame out, like shining from shook foil;
>   It gathers to a greatness, like the ooze of oil
> Crushed. Why do men then now not reck his rod?[15]

When we read "God's Grandeur," we can almost "taste" the sounds of the words. In "the ooze of oil / Crushed," especially, sound helps to constitute tactile and visual images on an auditory level.

When the tones of syllables in a poem are identical, or nearly identical, we have **rhyme**, another very important aspect of tone color. Rhymes are most often at the ends of lines—as in "God," "rod," and "foil," "oil," in "God's Grandeur"—but they may be internal within the line itself—as in "men," "then." The rhyme scheme always contributes to the rhythm of a poem, returning the ear—and sometimes the eye, in eye rhyme—to the previous reference. Poets who are able to use rhyme as well as sounds, to link images or ideas, are using rhyme as a strong source of power.

An analysis of the sound structures in your literary selection reveals the patterns of sound in much the same way that a landscape designer's drawing of a garden shows the various patterns of foliage. An analysis of tone color and rhythm in a literary selection is a *soundscape* of that work. You can create a soundscape of any piece of literature. Although tone color and rhythm may be most prevalent in poetry, they are also strong sources of power in most prose and dramatic works.

Rhythm in literature may be defined as any regular recurrence of literary elements such as images, words, ideas, syntactical structures, sounds, pauses, vocal stresses, or shifts in attention of the informing consciousness. The rhythms of literary worlds become sources of power when they connect with the rhythms of human worlds—when the pulse or primal beat of a literary selection is felt in the muscles of its perceiver, whether that perceiver be a silent reader, an oral performer, or an audience member. Like rhythms of the human body, rhythms of the literary body are felt in terms of movement—the ebb and flow of strength—and are therefore of central interest to interpreters, who literally give moving bodies and voices to poetic worlds.

Rhythm in literature takes two essential forms: regular and irregular. In regular rhythm, the elements are repeated at evenly spaced intervals, so that power arises through the building of a regular pulse that fulfills our expectations. When skillfully employed, regular rhythm becomes a kind of pervading presence. In irregular rhythm, elements recur at uneven intervals, so that power arises from the element of surprise and the resultant forsaking of expectation. **Syncopation**, the temporary displacement of a regularly stressed element, is one of the most common examples of irregular rhythm. In Carl Sandburg's "Chicago," the irregular rhythm in the repetition of the word *laughing* is an important syncopated sound structure in this section of the poem.

> Under the smoke, dust all over his mouth, *laughing* with white teeth,
> Under the terrible burden of destiny *laughing* as a young man laughs,
> *Laughing* even as an ignorant fighter laughs who has never lost a battle,
> Bragging and *laughing* that under his wrist is the pulse, and under his
>   ribs the heart of the people,
>   *Laughing*!
> *Laughing* the stormy, husky, brawling laughter of Youth, half-naked,
>   sweating, proud to be Hog Butcher, Tool Maker, Stacker of Wheat,
>   Player with Railroads and Freight Handler to the Nation.[16] [Italics ours.]

Since all literature contains a speaker, one of the literary work's most basic rhythms is the pattern created by that voice as it speaks. There's the rhythm of the way the mind shifts from one event of consciousness to another. There's the rhythm of words put together into sentences. There's the rhythm of sound and silence, created spaces where intensity of thought or feeling seem to push sound away.

Often literary speakers—narrators and lyric personae, for example—set up pervasive rhythms, controlling the flow of the work through word choice and subtle language patterns, so that even when other characters speak, their rhythms become part of the larger movement of the work. On the other hand, sometimes the speech of a single character will contrast in rhythm with other characters in the same scene. In *Othello* (act 4, scene 2), notice how Desdemona and Othello each use poetic materials distinctively to create their own personal communication patterns. Desdemona's tendency to speak in a legato rhythm emphasizes her innocent reaction to Othello's stormy staccato accusations.

> DESDEMONA. Alas, what ignorant sin have I committed?
> OTHELLO. Was this fair paper, this most goodly book,
>   Made to write "whore" upon? What committed?
>   Committed! O thou public commoner!
>   I should make very forges of my cheeks,
>   That would to cinders burn up modesty,
>   Did I but speak thy deeds. What committed!
>   Heaven stops the nose at it and the moon winks,
>   The bawdy wind that kisses all it meets
>   Is hush'd within the hollow mine of earth,
>   And will not hear it. What committed!
>   Impudent strumpet!
> DESDEMONA.   By heaven, you do me wrong.
> OTHELLO. Are not you a strumpet?
> DESDEMONA.   No, as I am a Christian:
>   If to preserve this vessel for my lord
>   From any other foul unlawful touch
>   Be not to be a strumpet, I am none.[17]

Sound structures are so central to the interpreter of literature that we'll be discussing them many times in both the scripting process and the staging process. Tone color and rhythm are two of the most important aspects of presentational form, because they naturally inhabit acoustic space. When literary works are transformed for acoustic space, their sound structures, both vocal and physical, become concrete and recognizable.

Sound Structures in "Ozymandias"

By looking at the kinds of vowels that dominate "Ozymandias," you'll discover that much of the traveler's description comes through the use of open vowels—/æ/ (as in hat) and /e/ (as in bed) in particular. The effect of that tone coloring is that the openness of the vowels, in conjunction with the images, contributes to a sense of wide space, of a kind of emptiness. The /ou/ sound (as in so), though not as open a vowel, reinforces that sense. The cumulative effect of the many

/æ/, /e/, and /ou/ sounds is suggestive of a sigh, a background sound that pervades the poem, creating an additional level of meaning. The discovery of this sigh tone may lead to an idea for scripting. A chorus, for example, could create the sigh behind the traveler's words, adding to the despair of the poem.

When you examine the way consonants work together in the soundscape of the poem, you'll realize how intricately they're patterned. Four major consonantal patterns operate in the poem—a repetition of /s/ and /sh/ sounds, an /m/ and /n/ drone, a patterning of the dental sounds (/t/, /d/, /k/) and the incorporation of the soft /l/ sounds. The /s/ consonants pervade the work, providing a sibilant undertone that a creative transformer of literature may feature as the sound of wind and sand blowing on the desert. Through tone coloring, therefore, the poem achieves an auditory level that isn't indicated by the imagery analysis. The /m/ and /n/ sounds underlie the poem so fully that they create a constant hum, which works with the open vowels to help suggest the empty sigh.

In contrast to the sibilant /s/, the mesmerizing /m/ and /n/ and the liquid /l/, which are softeners of the poem's sound structure, the sharp intrusion of the abrupt dentals (/t/, /d/, and /k/ sounds) punctuates the placid scene with harsh tones. Images such as "colossal wreck" are set apart from the rest of the line because they are encased in sharp tones. A sense of the authority of the traveler comes from the way in which he punctuates his story by harsh, attention-demanding dental consonants.

The rhyme scheme of "Ozymandias" is not regular; we do not recognize it as a familiar sonnet rhyme. Yet rhyme in this poem is powerful because it's used to unite contrasting images through sound, contributing to an intricate soundscape. In this poem, images referring to life are united through rhyme with images referring to destruction and death; for example, the living word *frown* is slant-rhymed with the lifeless *stone*, *command* with *sand*, *kings* with *things*, and *despair* with *bare*. Since both vowel sounds and rhyme help to set up the two forces of life images and death images, we begin to see those clusters of images as strong sources of power. We sense that they create a major conflict, a tensiveness, which is at the heart of the poem.

Not all selections will be as rich as "Ozymandias" in tone color, although it's important in any work to analyze its sound patterns to determine what specific sounds to feature in the transformed script. Tone coloring is of major importance to a successful Readers Theatre script because presentational form often comes through the work's patterns in sound.

Now that we have a firmer idea of the way tone coloring operates in "Ozymandias," and especially of how it relates to imagery, we look at the poem's rhythms, to see whether they, too, connect with other power sources. If you are comfortable with prosodic scansion as part of your soundscape, you may wish to mark the poem with light and heavy stresses.[18] Such an analysis would reveal a specific contrast in rhythms that relates to character differences in the poem.

The persona seems to speak in exclusively rising rhythms (primarily iambic) although there is very little evidence (slightly more than one line) on which to base a description of the persona's characteristic rhythm. You will, however, sense a contrast when the traveler begins to speak. There's a sense of falling rhythm for the traveler; so many of his lines are syncopated, substituting stresses for unstresses in key positions, usually at the beginnings of lines and phrases, such as, "Two vast and trunkless legs of stone / Stand in the desert. . . . / Half sunk . . . / Tell that its sculptor . . . / Nothing beside remains." Finally, in contrast to the traveler's essentially falling rhythm, the words of Ozymandias stand out rhythmically (as well as emotionally and modally) from the traveler's story because Ozymandias speaks in a regular rising rhythm.

How does a transformer of literature use this information on rhythm? Recognizing that characters are distinguished rhythmically, as well as in other ways, the adapter may be led to insist on at least three separate voices—those of the persona, the traveler, and Ozymandias—in the script. Furthermore, in production, the director will want each character to maintain his characteristic rhythm.

Time

Like music, literature is a temporal art. Since literary worlds are alive, they live in time, and their speakers manipulate time—by remembering the past, living in the present, or dreaming of the future. These two aspects of literary time can become striking power sources: **literature in time** and **time in literature**.

We became aware of at least one way literature lives in time when we selected a work to transform. Literary works change in meaning and impact as time goes on because their language changes and their readers change. Our fascination with *Hamlet*, for example, has grown with the increase in our knowledge of psychology, particularly Freudian psychology. Conversely, the view of Jews as bloodthirsty moneylenders in *The Merchant of Venice* isn't a view we share today. A transformer of those texts, recognizing that their ideas have changed in time, would need to decide whether to feature or minimize those changes.

Another way in which literature lives in time is in its relation to clock time, or **public objective time**. Robert Beloof, in *The Performing Voice in Literature*, speaks of the poem's relation to clock time as its **structural time**—literally, the amount of time it takes to read (silently or orally) the poem.[19] Structural time becomes a power source in such poems as James Dickey's "Falling," which records on seven pages the thoughts and emotions of a stewardess as she falls to her death from an airplane. A similar plunge in the natural world would take less than one-twentieth of the time it takes to read the poem. The poem, therefore, seems too long; its expanded use of structural time builds unrelenting terror that can be featured in a performance of that poem. Filmmakers have long recognized the dramatic power of manipulating structural time; film techniques such as slow motion heighten emotional tension by emphasizing the difference between structural time and clock time.

Although transformers are interested in the practical considerations of the literature in time, the fascination of a work usually comes from the time in literature. Literary beings, like human beings, experience time according to its emotional value for them, rather than its physical length; consider the idiomatic expressions, "a big time," "a whale of a time," "a heavy time," "time flew," and "it seems like only yesterday." If the first truth about **subjective time** is that you (and your counterparts in literature) experience the passage of time emotionally, the second truth is that your mind often reorders the normal flow of time, despite the fact that time in the natural world is irreversible. The normal order of past to present to future pervades everyday existence, so that any disruption of that expected order becomes a source of interest and possible concern.

You have probably known persons who tend to prefer living in the past rather than in the present, or who exist in a wish-fulfilling future rather than in the harsh reality of the here and now.

Many literary works cultivate power by featuring the reordering of time. In Arthur Miller's *Death of a Salesman*, Willy Loman finds refuge from present-tense problems by living in the past. Some of Willy's past memories are fully staged, showing how immediate the past is for him. **Flashback**, which interrupts present-tense events to relive past experience, is a source of power in literature because it links past and present.

Some literary works play with time, obviously ignoring the normal rate of objective clock time to gain powerful effects. In "An Occurrence at Owl Creek Bridge," author Ambrose Bierce doesn't divulge the amount of clock time that passes in the story, but it is probably less than ten minutes. The action begins as a man who is about to be hanged is standing on the bridge with the rope around his neck, and ends with the man's death. The story progresses through clock time until the moment of the hanging; then clock time is suspended and subjective time takes over. As the man is dying, he hallucinates that he is escaping and swimming down the river. Although most of the pages of the story are devoted to the dying man's fantasy, his death takes only a few seconds of actual clock time. At the moment of the man's death, the reader is brought back to the exterior world of the bridge and the hanging corpse. The time systems—psychological time and clock time—which organize the events of this story have different rhythms and different imagery that could be used as contrasting features in production. Both time systems are brought together by a single climax—the death of the man.

Sometimes time shifts in literature are created by the author's use of different verb tenses. In "The Lifeguard" by James Dickey, past, present, and future tenses are interwoven in an intricate pattern. In the poem, a summer camp lifeguard returns, at night, to the spot on the lake where he failed to save a drowning boy earlier in the day. Overcome by guilt, the lifeguard admits his present-tense desire for future wish fulfillment as a way of undoing the past—("I *am* thinking of how I *may* be / The savior of one / Who *has already died* in my care" (italics ours)[20]—and proceeds to hallucinate that he does, indeed, save the boy. Much of the intrigue of Dickey's poem comes from the lifeguard's reordering of time according to his own psychological state.

When changes in the normal order of time flow seem to dominate the literary work's structure, or when subjective time of the character seems to contrast with the structural time of the work, then time is a strong power source.

Time in "Ozymandias"

Time is, of course, a major power in the poem because "Ozymandias" is ultimately about the effects of time on the life of all things, whether human or man-made. The ideas in Shelly's poem are timeless, containing as much significance today as they did two centuries ago, and that universality is one of the poem's strengths. Furthermore, two major tenses are used in the poem: past tense for the persona and present tense for both the traveler and Ozymandias. The contradictions between each character's grammatical tense and his actual temporal existence create much of the tensiveness within the power source of time. Although the persona employs past tense grammatically, he exists in the most immediate present tense for the reader, essentially because he speaks first. On the other hand, the traveler, who exists in past tense in relation to the persona, gains immediacy by using present-tense verbs. Finally, Ozymandias, who lived in antiquity, thrusts himself forward into the immediate present of the poem through the enduring present tense of his words on the pedestal. The brief structural time in "Ozymandias" and the broad historical time implied by the poem are pulling and straining the poem's dimension of time.

Plot Structure

The plot of a literary work, as we're defining it, is a patterned sequence of events—what happens when. The events that make up the plot may be objective (related to happenings or objects in the exterior world—"John went to the store") or subjective (related to happenings or objects of consciousness—"Images of his dead comrades floated through his mind"). Plot structure, or the organization of literary events, takes a variety of forms, one of the most familiar being a series of events that lead logically to a climax. Tension, caused by some sort of unstable situation (two men want to marry the same girl), increases until something in the situation shifts or gives way (the girl becomes engaged to one of the men). This results in a new situation (one man has seemingly won, but the other man will not give up). The tension builds again until another major shift in forces occurs (the engaged couple have a fight). This movement (rising action) continues throughout the literary work until the final climax occurs (the girl either marries her fiancé, or she gives back the ring and chooses the other man). This restores some stability and releases tension (the first man, defeated, leaves town). Climactic organization of this nature, sometimes called dramatic action, is highly defined in most plays. Plays usually have a central turning point, or **crisis**, after which the course of the action is more clearly shaped, leading to the highest point in the dramatic action, or **climax**. In classical tragedy, the crisis usually occurs when one character performs an act that changes the nature of the situation, and the climax is usually the death of the main character.

We don't usually think of lyric poems as having a plot structure, but most poems are built on an identifiable progression of events that are either objective or subjective. We believe, with John Ciardi, that most poems are structured around a balance point, or **fulcrum**.[21] The poem moves with a forward motion toward the fulcrum and then proceeds with what Ciardi terms a "counter-motion" after the fulcrum. **Counter-motion** simply means that what comes after the fulcrum balances everything that has gone before it, turning the reader's attention back toward the significance of what has already been said or experienced.

In Shakespearean sonnets, for example, the last two lines become the counter-motion of the poem. When the persona of Sonnet 29 concludes his poem with the lines, "For thy sweet love remember'd such wealth brings / That then I scorn to change my state with kings," his expression of love contrasts with all the feelings of depression he has shared in the first twelve lines of the poem. We learn how powerful his love is through its capability of overcoming his dejection.

Plot structure in most literary works is strongly related to the use of time because plot events happen in time; this relationship is especially important in the narrative mode. The narrator in a story may organize the plot around a simple progression through clock time (in the morning she drove the car to the park and stayed there until late afternoon), but time in literature is rarely so straightforward. Very often the plot of a literary work is organized by psychological shifts in time, so that time is suspended from its normal clock progression. As in "An

Occurrence at Owl Creek Bridge" and "The Lifeguard," psychological time shifts affect the order of events.

Space often works together with time to become an organizer of plot. A story may consist of a journey from one place to another, as in Homer's poem, *The Odyssey* (which traces the events of Ulysses' travels), or in William Faulkner's novel, *As I Lay Dying* (which follows the progress of a family as they move from one Southern town to another). Dramas such as Shakespeare's *Anthony and Cleopatra* (which shifts from scenes in Rome to Cleopatra's court in Egypt) and Thornton Wilder's *Happy Journey from Trenton to Camden* are also structured by their shifts in space.

Another aspect of plot organization has to do with whether the work moves in a single progression, or whether it moves by a series of more or less self-contained episodes. If the structure of your selection is **episodic**, you'll need to observe the organization of each episode as well as to discover the function of each episode in the larger sequence of the total work.

Some plots move through a kind of logical order that may be termed **cause and effect** (this happens because of that). Clues to this kind of logical patterning are found both in the language of the work ("but," "because," "therefore") and in the work's structure, when events are tightly interrelated and the author has been careful to include scenes that show reasons for the actions of characters.

If the causal principle doesn't appear strongly in the language or seem to be an active element in the organization of plot, the work probably operates in a coordinate manner (this happens, and that happens). This **contiguous** structure lets readers make their own connections because the author has juxtaposed events instead of explaining relationships between events.[22]

Because the basic structural organization of the literature becomes the basic structural organization of your script, it's important to have a clear idea of how the literary work has been put together. An understanding of the work's structure is absolutely necessary if you must cut your selection. In a longer work, such as a novel, you may have to cut out parts of the novel's structure or rearrange them slightly to achieve a manageable length in performance (beginning the script later in the book, perhaps, giving some of the important earlier information in a flashback). An episodic organization may allow you to cut whole sections of the work with ease, while structures with more continuity demand subtler aesthetic cutting. In drama or prose, multiple themes in the work are often carried in major and minor organizational structures—main plots and subplots. As you define how the ideas progress and how they interrelate, you'll see ways to eliminate one theme and to emphasize another, or you'll know which characters, if any, to delete. In a logically organized work, be sure to preserve the major causal links, because logical structuring implies a greater effort on the part of an author to carry the mind of the reader (and consequently your audience) along a specific pathway. A causal structure in a story, for example, means that the narrator will make a greater effort to help the audience follow the causal pattern.

Plot Structure in "Ozymandias"

"Ozymandias" is a sonnet and is therefore organized very tightly. The turning point, or fulcrum, in the poem comes at the twelfth line, with the words, "Nothing beside remains," or—some would argue—in the space between the eleventh and twelfth lines, as the traveler prepares to shift his attention from Ozymandias's words on the pedestal to the present scene of empty sand. In "Ozymandias," as in other poems, the crisis point is signaled by several devices: (1) a change in speakers, (2) a shift in time, (3) a movement from emotional subjectivity (the king's words) to cold objectivity (the traveler's observation), (4) a change in energy, from the fullness of Ozymandias's presence to the emptiness of the image of nothingness, (5) a shift from dramatic mode (Ozymandias) to epic mode (the traveler), and (6) a sudden reduction in sentence length. The poem turns on contrast—contrasts of images, energies, perspectives, and time frames. After building steadily to the high point of Ozymandias's energy-charged words, the poem seems to release its energy through the rather flat statements constituting the last three lines. The release is rhythmical because it suggests a repetition of the persona's flat opening in the first line and a half, thereby enveloping the passionate lines of the poem in a kind of recurring objective logic.

The Emerging Text

We've by no means exhausted the possibilities for power in literature, and not every selection will be powerful in all the ways we've discussed. Part of the enticement of literary analysis comes from the discovery that each work sets up its own field of forces.

Having analyzed our selection for major sources of power, we have a fuller understanding of what attracted us to "Ozymandias" and a greater respect for the skilled craftsmanship of the poem. The world of "Ozymandias" is more complex, existing on more levels simultaneously, than is apparent from a simple reading.

The literary work you've chosen to transform may demand an analysis more or less detailed than that of "Ozymandias," depending upon the complexity and length of the selection. The important thing is to come to know your selection in terms of its strengths and weaknesses, in much the same way you come to know a good friend. Transforming a work for Readers Theatre is an extremely creative act, in which you constitute meaning by engaging in a shared relationship between your world and the world of the literature.

That shared relationship is your text of a work. The text emerges for you when you can answer the question, "What is this work all about?" Although it appears simple, that question is deceptively complex: answering it requires you to bring together your understanding of all the power sources in your selection as they interact to create tensiveness.

Often, power sources work together to create universal patterns of tensiveness that pervade the whole work. When this happens, we sense the presence of underlying forms that involve all or many of the power sources. Underlying structures are important components of literary works' presentational forms because they create recognizable patterns through which literary experience is presented to you as reader.

When the forces of a literary work combine to form an underlying structure, you may sense the presence of a pervasive metaphor: this work is like something else. For example, perhaps you sense that the play *Endgame* by Samuel Beckett seems to be an elaborate chess game. The title is a strong clue to the pervasive metaphor of a chess game, and many of the individual power sources of the play—the apparent hierarchy of the character relationships and the contained environment, for example—suggest the chess game structure. You could feature that underlying structure in your Readers Theatre adaptation of *Endgame* by creating a set, costumes, and blocking that suggest the movement of chess pieces on a chess board.

In *Where the Wild Things Are*, a children's story by Maurice Sendak, the adventures of Max, the young hero, seem to follow the pattern of ancient journeys of the hero. The standard phases of mythic hero quests—departure or separation, initiation and confrontation, adventure or the coming of knowledge, and return—seem to be present in the story, creating an underlying metaphoric structure.[23] If you wished to feature that pattern in performance, you might create a script in which the journeying aspect of the story is featured.

Every observation you can make about a work will bring you closer to a full understanding of the richness of your text. Your answer to the question "What is this work all about?" will reflect all that your analysis revealed about the literary work, and it will also reflect you. Many of your ideas about the text will come directly from your analysis process, but others will be primarily intuitive or impressionistic. Accept your intuitive responses as well as your analytical notions. A truly creative transformation depends on a balance between intuition and critical thinking.

At this point in your interaction with your literary selection, it's time to step back awhile. You've immersed yourself in the work, creating your own special text of that work. Now, what about your interests as an adapter of scripts? You've mastered a lot of facts about the work, and you've even seen it flex its muscles, but what does that knowledge mean to you? Put the copy of your literary selection aside for a few days; as you go about your daily routine, think about the new literary world you've encountered. See it in your mind's eye; hear the voices speak; take it fully into your own world. Then, ask yourself: In light of all I understand about my text, what does it mean to me as I prepare to stage it? As you begin to formulate an answer to that question, you'll be creating your **production concept**—a specialized vision of your text onstage.

FINDING A PRODUCTION CONCEPT

The richer the literary world, and the more experienced a reader you are, the more voices you'll hear in your text and the more staging possibilities you'll imagine. The specific angle of vision you take toward your text at the time of creating the script is your production concept. The production concept will help you make every decision in the transformational process.

Most literary worlds are complex enough to support many production concepts; you go to see more than one production of the same work partly because you're interested in a new angle of vision. In a college Readers Theatre production of Ray Bradbury's *Something Wicked This Way Comes*, the adapter-director chose to feature the story's nonhuman, surrealistic dimension by concentrating on the horror and bizarre nature of the freaks in the story. At another college, a production of the same story followed a different concept: that *Something Wicked This Way Comes* is really about the very human, most realistic fears of aging, as seen particularly in the character of Charles Halloway. Both productions illuminated Bradbury's story, and both concepts were true to the personal interests of the directors.

Not only will different people have different production concepts of the same literature, but your personal production concepts of a single literary text will change as you change. Sometimes you'll return to a literary work you've known and discover that it holds a different meaning for you than it did when you read it earlier. Your production concept of that work will have changed in time. Director Robert Benedetti admits to a recurring fascination with certain texts, such as

The Trial by Franz Kafka, which he feels compelled to direct every three or four years. Each time he returns to *The Trial*, however, the story expresses something different for him—so different, in fact, that each production is a completely new experience.[24]

How Your Production Concept Develops

The production concept you adopt says much about you and much about the literary work you've encountered. As such, it's a living thing; it grows and changes in the process of your interaction with the work. You'll find four initial stages in the development of your production concept:

1. *Consider your first impressions of the literary work.* Return to the record of your initial responses to the literature you selected. What was it about this work that captured your imagination? It may have been something in the work—a vivid image, perhaps—that suggested possibilities for staging, or maybe it was the intensity of your emotional response that compelled you to select the work. When you wrote down those early impressions, you began creating a production concept.

2. *Create your text through analysis.* By analyzing your selection, you learn the kinds of power your work contains. Ideas for scripting and staging emerge throughout this process. Jot down these ideas. Once you see how the power sources interact in tensive patterns, you'll probably begin to imagine important moments of the text onstage. If you are like most adapter-directors, you'll visualize power sources in space: characters will speak in your head, images will suggest stage settings, or tone coloring will become sound effects. Even though these are often vague impressions, they may become very real components of your production concept.

When you find your text of a literary work, you'll have reached the first mature stage of your developing production concept.

3. *Allow for a soaking-in process.* All art takes time. You need to give the ideas you've gained from analysis and your vague impressions of scripting time to connect with your intuitive self. Ideas that are really important to you will continue to develop even when you aren't consciously aware of them. Those sudden inspirations, those flashes of insight that seem to be instantaneous, are really the result of a long soaking-in time. While you're playing volleyball or sleeping or doing the dishes, those creative ideas are working on you. When you hear of authors writing great poems overnight or composing plays in a matter of days, remember that most of these people are mature artists who've spent lifetimes in preparation for that moment of inspiration.

As you give yourself some breathing space from the intensity of your analysis, take another look at your first impressions of the work. Reread them in light of your analysis. Then, review all the ideas on production you recorded while you were looking at the work's power sources. Let these ideas float in your mind awhile. Don't be too eager to make definite decisions. Closing your mind too soon is the most uncreative thing you can do.

4. *Give form to your production concept.* How do you know when you're ready to formulate your production concept for the first time? Chances are, you won't wake up in the middle of the night with a sudden flash of inspiration. More likely, you'll merely begin to feel comfortable about certain ideas. Ideas have a way of prodding you to shape them into a workable form—to write down suggestions for voices, to design a set, or to describe a special casting requirement.

When it comes time to do this, you'll be ready. You'll have gathered together all of your impressions, sifted through them, and checked them against analysis; you'll probably also be facing several possibilities for scripting. To formulate a production concept is to choose among many possibilities.

This is another time you become strongly aware of the richness of the work you've selected to transform. How many possibilities does it offer you? The best works make formulating a production concept both easy and difficult: easy because those works are rich in possibilities; difficult because to choose one is to deny others. It may help to promise the text, as Benedetti did, that you'll return to it someday.

How do you write your production concept? Avoid the temptation to keep it in your head! Only by writing your ideas down are you able to gain perspective on them and thereby evaluate them more objectively. When you came to an understanding of your text, you undoubtedly had several answers to the question, "What is this work all about?" Now you must choose among your answers according to how many levels of meaning you feel you can realize in a single production. It's helpful to begin writing your production concept with these words: "[Title of the work] is about. . . ."

The body of your production concept should contain an organized statement of all your ideas on scripting and production that support the directions you've chosen. Every production concept is unique because literary works differ from each other and adapters differ from each other. Your written statement will reflect your creative vision of the forthcoming script at this point in your development. Your production concept will be continually reshaped as you find voices for your script and as you carry your script into casting and rehearsal.

Because the production concept is the major shaping force throughout the whole process of transformation, it should be clearly stated—to the best of your ability—before you begin to create your script. Clarifying your production concept will help you to release voices; to a large extent, the way you listen determines the voices you hear.

NOTES

1. Herbert Read, *The Origins of Form in Art* (New York: Horizon Press, 1965), p. 26.
2. Wayne C. Booth, *The Rhetoric of Fiction* (Chicago: University of Chicago Press, 1961), p. 138: "The author creates, in short, an image of himself and another image of his reader."
3. We are grateful to Charlotte S. Waisman for contributing the section, "Practical Considerations for Selecting Children's Literature."
4. When selecting literature for children, you may wish to note that many fairy tales are now considered sexist by some people. In *Cinderella*, for example, the central figure—a lone woman—waits and dreams for the handsome prince—an active, searching man—to change her plight. The fairy tale implies that life would be good for the ugly stepsisters, too, if they marry, especially if they raise their social position by marrying royalty. Accepting this notion, the sisters even cut off their toes (in some versions of the tale) to fit into the glass slipper. Bruno Bettelheim, however, refutes the notion that fairy tales—and

Cinderella, in particular—are sexist. He explains that "there are variations of the story in which Cinderella takes the initiative to be recognized, not waiting passively," and argues that "on the overt level, Cinderella's evading the prince tells that she wants to be chosen for the person she really is, and not for her splendid appearance." See Bruno Bettelheim, *The Uses of Enchantment: The Meaning and Importance of Fairy Tales* (New York: Alfred A. Knopf, 1976), pp. 236–277.

5. Myles McDowell, "Fiction for Children and Adults: Some Essential Differences," *Children's Literature in Education* 10 (March 1973): 55.

6. Rogers, Neville, ed. *The Complete Poetical Works of Percy Bysshe Shelly* 2 (Oxford: Clarendon Press, 1975), pp. 319–320. The editors of *The Norton Anthology of English Literature* note: "According to a passage in Diodorus Siculus, the Greek historian of the 1st century B.C., the largest statue in Egypt had the inscription: 'I am Ozymandias, king of kings; if anyone wishes to know what I am and where I lie, let him surpass me in some of my exploits.' Ozymandias was the Greek name for Ramses II of Egypt, 13th century B.C." See M. H. Abrams, ed., *The Norton Anthology of English Literature*, 3rd ed. (New York: W. W. Norton, 1974), p. 535.

7. See Wallace A. Bacon, *The Art of Interpretation*, 3rd ed. (New York: Holt, Rinehart & Winston, 1979), especially chap. 6, for a discussion of tensiveness in literature.

8. William Faulkner, "Acceptance of the Nobel Prize," 10 December 1950.

9. See Cleanth Brooks, *The Well Wrought Urn* (Harcourt, Brace, 1947), especially chap. 1, "The Language of Paradox."

10. Sophocles, *Oedipus the King*, trans. David Grene, in *Drama through Performance*, ed. Mark S. Auburn and Katherine H. Burkman (Boston: Houghton Mifflin, 1977), p. 16.

11. Walter J. Ong, *The Presence of the Word: Some Prolegomena for Cultural and Religious History* (New Haven, Conn.: Yale University Press, 1967), p. 164.

12. From Karl Shapiro, "Glass Poem," in *Poetry in English*, ed. Warren Taylor and Donald Hall (New York: Macmillan, 1963), p. 665.

13. From T. S. Eliot, "The Love Song of J. Alfred Prufrock," *T. S. Eliot: The Complete Poems and Plays, 1909-1950* (New York: Harcourt, Brace & World, 1952), p. 3.

14. From William Sansom, "Cat Up a Tree," *Three* (New York: William Morrow, 1947), p. 101.

15. Gerard Manley Hopkins, "God's Grandeur," in Taylor and Hall, *Poetry in English*, p. 466.

16. Carl Sandburg, "Chicago," in Taylor and Hall, *Poetry in English*, p. 535.

17. William Shakespeare, *Othello*, in *The Complete Signet Classic Shakespeare*, ed. Sylvan Barnet (New York: Harcourt Brace Jovanovich, 1972).

18. For aid in scansion and other matters of prosodic analysis, see George Saintsbury, *Historical Manual of English Prosody* (New York: Schocken Books, 1966); Harvey Gross, *Sound and Form in Modern Poetry* (Ann Arbor: University of Michigan, 1964); and Wallace A. Bacon, *The Art of Interpretation*, 3rd ed. (New York: Holt, Rinehart & Winston, 1979), especially chap. 9.

19. *The Performing Voice in Literature* (Boston: Little, Brown, 1966), pp. 207–210.

20. James Dickey, "The Lifeguard," *Poems 1957-1967* (Middletown, Conn.: Wesleyan University Press, 1967), p. 52.

21. John Ciardi, *How Does a Poem Mean?* (Boston: Houghton Mifflin, 1959), pp. 994–1007.

22. See Jonathan Raban, *The Technique of Modern Fiction* (South Bend, Ind.: University of Notre Dame Press, 1969).

23. For further reading on mythic hero quests, see Joseph Campbell, *The Hero with a Thousand Faces* (New York: Bollingen Foundation, 1949) and David Addams Leeming, *Mythology: The Voyage of the Hero* (Philadelphia: Lippincott, 1973).

24. Robert Benedetti, Speech in honor of the retirement of Robert S. Breen from Northwestern University, Evanston, Ill. 13 May 1978.

SUGGESTIONS FOR FURTHER READING

Bacon, Wallace A. *The Art of Interpretation*. 3rd ed. New York: Holt, Rinehart & Winston, 1979.

Bowen, Elbert R.; Aggertt, Otis J.; and Rickert, William E. *Communicative Reading*. 4th ed. New York: Macmillan, 1978.

Brooks, Keith; Bahn, Eugene; and Okey, L. LaMont. *The Communicative Act of Oral Interpretation*. 2nd ed. Boston: Allyn and Bacon, 1975.

Brown, Stephen J.M. *The World of Imagery*. New York: Russell and Russell, 1966.

Church, Margaret. *Time and Reality: Studies in Contemporary Fiction*. Chapel Hill, N.C.: The University of North Carolina Press, 1963.

Ciardi, John, and Williams, Miller. *How Does a Poem Mean?* 2nd ed. Boston: Houghton Mifflin, 1975.

Cohen, Edwin. *Oral Interpretation: The Communication of Literature*. Chicago: Science Research Associates, 1975.

Gross, Harvey. *Sound and Form in Modern Poetry*. Ann Arbor: University of Michigan Press, 1964.

Hemphill, George, ed. *Discussions of Poetry: Rhythm and Sound*. Boston: D. C. Heath and Company, 1961.

Langer, Susanne K. *Feeling and Form: A Theory of Art*. New York: Charles Scribner's Sons, 1953.

Lee, Charlotte I., and Galati, Frank. *Oral Interpretation*. 5th ed. Boston: Houghton Mifflin, 1977.

Lynen, John F. *The Design of the Present: Essays on Time and Form in American Literature*. New Haven, Conn.: Yale University Press, 1969.

Mendilow, A. A. *Time and the Novel*. New York: Humanities Press, 1965.

Meyerhoff, Hans. *Time in Literature*. Berkeley: University of California Press, 1960.

Roloff, Leland H. *The Perception and Evocation of Literature*. Glenview, Ill.: Scott, Foresman, 1973.

CHAPTER THREE

Transforming for Readers Theatre: from Text to Script

All poetry and all good prose invite me to utterance. I hope I do not sit muttering in public places; but if I cannot give voice, my ear harkens to unheard melodies.

Robert William Chapman, *Reading Aloud*

One of the most exciting aspects of transforming a literary work into a script for performance is seeking out *voices* in the text. You're familiar with the voices of dramatic characters, narrators, and lyric personae. When they share their feelings with you, they become real people for you, and you like or dislike them for many of the same reasons you respond to people in everyday life. Our concept of "voices" in literature includes characters, but it is much broader than that. There is, for example, the voice of the rhythm of the jungle drums that beat below the surface of Vachel Lindsay's poem, "The Congo":

> Fat black bucks in a wine-barrel room
> Barrel-house kings, with feet unstable,
> Sagged and reeled and pounded on the table,
> Pounded on the table.[1]

Consider also the voice of the /s/ and /sh/ sounds in "Ozymandias," which give to the poem the tonality of wind blowing across empty sand. Any power source in a literary work, if it is pervasive and strong enough, is a voice for the reader and can become an embodied voice in a script.

As you prepare to release voices in a literary text, you might turn to the work of the musical composer for some basic concepts; as a transformer for Interpreters Theatre, your interest in the sounds of voices in literature is very similar to the composer's interest in musical harmonies. As Arnold Tovey writes, "Music differs only in degree from literature."[2] Both music and literature derive form from the rhythms of bodily movement and from the rhythms of speech. Tovey also speaks of the rhetoric and of the drama of music, using terms which suggest that music speaks in many of the ways literature does.

As the composer selects instruments to carry melodies, deciding when and how each instrument is to be used, the literary adaptor discovers voices emerging from the lines of force within the text. As each instrument has its own characteristic quality, each literary voice has an identity, which may be specific, as a fully developed character, or generalized as a force or tonality.

45

The process of releasing the voices in the text is a process of opening up the literary world. It requires breaking apart the lines of force in a work to tap the harmonic interplay of its power for your script. Making a script of a text completes the second stage of its transformation.

Since transformers for Readers Theatre use both sound and movement in production, their creative task is to mediate between the impulse to compose musically (with voices alone) and the impulse to create meaning through movement (as in mime or dance). When you create your script, you see movement in space and you hear voices speak. This response to literature begins to lift it from the printed page into acoustic space or, as in the case of oral literature, to reshape it in acoustic space.

As adapter you seek clues to sound and movement in a literary work by identifying power sources. You then make covert action overt by releasing the voices of literature into a script that is performed. The covert movement of a text is suggested by such elements as a rhythmic beat or the physical gesture of a character. The covert sound of a text may be the tonality of a character, the pattern of tone color, the interplay of auditory images, or any other power sources that indicate how literature speaks to us. Wallace Bacon suggests that a central question for any interpreter who is considering both movement and sound is "How does a poem feel when it speaks?"[3]

How literature speaks is often the first concern in creating scripts. You find the voices of a text and discover the lines they speak before you lend them bodies and place them in space. This chapter will discuss scripting as a way of shaping the vocal life of literary texts. Techniques for shaping the movement of the script in space will be discussed in Part 3, "Realizations."

FINDING AND RELEASING VOICES IN THE TEXT

How do you begin to break a literary text into its voices? First, look for the characters in your selection—characters who are given a physical description and dialogue, narrators or poetic personae, and characters who are talked about but not given dialogue. These will be the major voices in your script.

Sometimes more than one character voice can be found in literature that seems to be spoken by a single voice. In the ballad, "Greensleeves," the italicized lines differentiate the persona's sung refrain from his spoken lament. The poem seems to interweave two states of being: one joyous and one depressed, one in the past tense and one in the present, one naive and one "sadder but wiser."

Greensleeves

Greensleeves was all my joy,
Greensleeves was my delight;
Greensleeves was my heart of gold,
And who but Lady Greensleeves.

Alas, my Love! ye do me wrong
   To cast me off discourteously:
And I have loved you so long,
   Delighting in your company.
     Greensleeves was all my joy . . .

I have been ready at your hand,
   To grant whatever you would crave.
I have both waged life and land,
   Your love and good will for to have.
     Greensleeves was all my joy . . .[4]

A single performer who is aware of the ambiguity of the persona's situation could speak and sing this poem. Yet there's a sense in which the singer of the lyrical refrain isn't the same person as the jilted lover who speaks the rest of the poem. An adapter might cast another performer as the singer to create an ironic tone in the poem. In this version, the singer's lines would constantly remind the lover of his earlier misconceptions about Lady Greensleeves, and subtly ask why he thinks it would be different the second time around. Another approach is to use a chorus to echo the refrain, and thereby reinforce the plaintive lyric quality of the song. These three interpretations of "Greensleeves"—that it is the ambiguous words of a single speaker, that it is ironic, or that it is melancholy—are only some of the possibilities suggested by the presence of what might be more than one consciousness or perspective. For the adapter, it's important to recognize that there seem to be two voices in this poem; the variations in scripting, from adapter to adapter, are what make transformation a creative process.

When you've determined the character voices in your selection, look back to your analysis of the other power sources. Are there forces other than character that seem to be voices? Tone coloring is an example, such as the pervasive sigh in "Ozymandias"—created by the /æ/, /e/, and /ou/ sounds—which could be considered a disembodied voice (see page 33). Other potential voices may be found in repeated images or words, such as the terrorizing image of the heart thumping below the floorboards in Edgar Allen Poe's story, "The Tell Tale Heart," or in the sentence, "There must be more money," in "The Rocking Horse Winner" by D. H. Lawrence. These kinds of sounds and images can be vocalized almost as a refrain running throughout a work to create atmosphere.

Another potential voice is a concept or presence that seems to pervade a work. Often forces of this kind are embodied in words a character speaks, but they seem to hold meaning of their own that gives them a separate life. In the following excerpt from scene 5 of *The Tragical History of Doctor Faustus* by Christopher Marlowe, the Good Angel and the Evil Angel are characters who enter briefly to influence Faustus as he contemplates selling his soul to the devil (Lucifer) in exchange for power and knowledge. Yet these angels are embodiments of larger forces, which are present even when the angels are offstage.

Scene V————Faustus *discovered in his study*

FAUSTUS. Now, Faustus, must
   Thou needs be damn'd and canst thou not be sav'd:
   What boots it, then, to think of God or heaven?

Away with such vain fancies, and despair;
Despair in God, and trust in Belzebub:
Now go not backward; no, Faustus, be resolute:
Why waver'st thou? O, something soundeth in mine ears,
"Abjure this magic, turn to God again!"
Ay, and Faustus will turn to God again.
To God? He loves thee not;
The god thou serv'st is thine own appetite,
Wherein is fix'd the love of Belzebub:
To him I'll build an altar and a church,
And offer lukewarm blood of new-born babes.
  [*Enter* Good Angel *and* Evil Angel]
GOOD ANGEL. Sweet Faustus, leave that execrable art.
FAUSTUS. Contrition, prayer, repentance—what of them?
GOOD ANGEL. O, they are means to bring thee unto heaven!
EVIL ANGEL. Rather illusions, fruits of lunacy,
  That make men foolish that do trust them most.
GOOD ANGEL. Sweet Faustus, think of heaven and heavenly things.
EVIL ANGEL. No, Faustus; think of honour and of wealth.
  [*Exeunt* Angels]
FAUSTUS. Of wealth!
  Why, the signiory of Embden shall be mine.
  When Mephistophilis shall stand by me,
  What good can hurt thee, Faustus? Thou art safe:
  Cast no more doubts.—Come, Mephistophilis,
  And bring glad tidings from great Lucifer;—[5]

Although the angels don't enter for several lines, you may recognize the presence of their influence in Faustus's opening speech. We seem to hear three voices in these lines: the temptation of the Evil Angel, the urging of the Good Angel, and the vacillation of Doctor Faustus as he feels these forces tugging at him. Since the clash between good and evil is at the heart of the play's conflict and central to its presentational form, a Readers Theatre production of *Doctor Faustus* might use these embedded voices to increase the physical presence of good and evil in the text. For example, an adapter could expand the roles of the Good Angel and the Evil Angel, keeping them onstage for longer periods than the original dramatic script indicates. In Faustus's opening speech of this scene, the Evil Angel and the Good Angel would become Voice 2 and Voice 3 respectively, with the vacillating Faustus taking Voice 1.

  VOICE 1. Now, Faustus, must
    Thou needs be damn'd and canst thou not be sav'd:
    What boots it, then, to think of God or heaven?
  VOICE 2. Away with such vain fancies, and despair;
    Despair in God, and trust in Belzebub:
    Now go not backward; no, Faustus, be resolute:
    Why waver'st thou?
  VOICE 1.   O, something soundeth in mine ears,
  VOICE 3. "Abjure this magic, turn to God again!"

VOICE 1. Ay, and Faustus will turn to God again.
VOICE 2. To God? He loves thee not;
    The god thou serv'st is thine own appetite,
    Wherein is fix'd the love of Belzebub:
VOICE 1. To him I'll build an altar and a church,
    And offer lukewarm blood of new-born babes.

Another approach would cast a chorus of voices that become Faustus's conscience, in much the same way that Greek choruses were used. A third idea suggested by the embedded presences in Faustus's speech is to cast three performers as Faustus, representing a kind of Freudian ego-id-superego relationship. As the three performers interacted onstage, the audience would be able to see which of the three forces dominated at any given moment. The flexibility of the Readers Theatre medium allows the adapter to experiment with splitting a character to make the inner tensions more vivid and to stage the split character in production.

A similar but more subtle presence is the apparent voice of authority that creeps into Antigone's speeches in act 1 of Jean Anouilh's version of this play. Much of Antigone's frustration comes from the conflict she feels within herself between what she wants to do and what she has been told, under threat of punishment, is her expected behavior. In this speech she recalls childhood orders given to her by others, translating them into her own words.

> ANTIGONE. Understand! The first word I ever heard out of any of you was that word "understand."
> Why didn't I "understand" that I must not play with water—cold, black, beautiful flowing water
> —because I'd *spill it on the palace tiles*. Or with earth, because *earth dirties a little girl's frock*. Why
> didn't I "understand" that *nice children don't eat out of every dish at once; or give everything in their
> pockets to beggars; or run in the wind so fast that they fall down; or ask for a drink when they're perspir-
> ing; or want to go swimming when it's either too early or too late, merely because they happen to feel like*
> swimming. Understand! I don't want to understand. There'll be time enough to understand when
> I'm old. . . . If I ever am old. But not now [italics ours].[6]

The voice of authority present in this speech is an earlier version of the larger voice of Creon's authority, which later condemns Antigone to death. The *italicized* phrases are those you can hear as another voice, a voice that has shaped Antigone's speech and action throughout her growing up and against which she rebels. By recognizing that voice of authority as a separate voice, the adapter follows the impulse to open up the literary world and expose its lines of tension.

Locating the voices, recognizing the particular forces in your selection that may be materialized to carry your production concept, is the first step in creating a script from your text. But how are the voices you hear in the text to be given bodies in the script? The following list of some of the conditions for the creation of roles will facilitate this process.

1. *A single character or other power source played by a single performer.* Individual performers speaking individual roles is by far the most familiar arrangement. Voices that correspond to explicit characters are usually fully embodied. When a character or presence is consistent throughout a whole text, or through a major part of it, the adapter will usually assign one voice (and body) to that entity.

2. *A single character or other power source played by more than one individualized performer.* If a single character seems to operate on more than one level (psychological, emotional, or philosophical), you may choose to break apart the lines of force within the individual character by

assigning more than one performer to a single character, as illustrated with "Greensleeves" and *Doctor Faustus*. In Paul Baker's experimentation with the play *Hamlet*, Baker saw several voices operating within the main character; according to his vision, Baker divided Hamlet's lines among three performers who interacted with each other to indicate the levels of Hamlet's personality.[7]

In the epic mode, certain proved sources in the text will suggest other kinds of voice divisions. First person narrators, for example, are sometimes divided into separate voices according to their positions in time. Third person narrators may be materialized by more than one voice and body whenever the text indicates several physical or psychological positions operating at once or in quick succession. The narration of *The Lord of the Rings* by J. R. R. Tolkien may be shared by several voices to emphasize the major geographical shifts in the story. For some selections, such as *Breakfast of Champions* by Kurt Vonnegut, Jr., in which the author intrudes into the narration, you may wish to cast both an author-figure and a narrator separately.

3. *More than one character or other power source played by a single performer.* Another way to assign voices to characters is to use one performer to play several roles, either for practical reasons, such as limiting the number of cast members by having one person play more than one incidental character, or for aesthetic reasons, such as using one voice and body for several characters to unite the characters as parts of a single force. In Jacques Offenbach's opera, *The Tales of Hoffman*, Hoffman falls in love with three different women; all three are played by the same actress to indicate that they're all versions of Hoffman's one idealized lover. By assigning a single voice to more than one character, you can unify related elements into a single powerful force, or you can simplify casting by allowing a single performer to play several differing characters.

4. *The use of a chorus.* A **chorus** can be one of the most versatile means of actualizing voices for the Readers Theatre script. Voices that seem to arise from power sources other than character are often vague and less easily distinguished; they usually appear, disappear, and reappear throughout the text. Most texts have a cluster of interwoven forces that can't be given individualized voices; they can be featured by using a chorus that picks up first one presence, then another. An individualized character who appears only once in the text may emerge from a chorus and then recede again into its ranks.

For some texts, you may want to use a chorus of performers to depict a single force. If the force is defined in the text as multiple but unified, such as the force of society, a chorus of voices can carry the thrust of many bodies acting with a single mind. You can also use a chorus of several performers acting as one body and voice to depict an explicit character, such as a character who has become an automaton, a mere pawn of a larger force.

You're apt to find a chorus most useful when the pervasive force being materialized is an elusive presence, such as the ghostly couple in Virginia Woolf's "A Haunted House" (see p. 60), is tonal or rhythmic, such as the /s/, /sh/ coloring in "Ozymandias" or the use of the word *laughing* in "Chicago," is imagistic, such as the images set in motion by the word *green* in "Somnambule Ballad" by Federico Garcia Lorca (see page 59), or is an idea or concept, such as the repeated phrase, "We must have more money," in "The Rocking Horse Winner" by D. H. Lawrence. With forces such as these, the use of a chorus allows greater range in the shaping of sound. We'll deal with the manipulation of voices for choral effects at greater length in our discussion of orchestration beginning on page 54. You may find the following Checklist for Finding Voices useful for determining the voices in your selection.

Checklist for Finding Voices

I. Make a list of characters in the text.
   A. Which characters should be given a single voice?
      1. Refer to your analysis of each character's perspective.
      2. Describe your impressions of the characters' physical and vocal manifestations.
   B. Should any characters be portrayed by more than one performer?
      1. Define the force that each voice will represent.
      2. Check to be sure the forces are strong and consistent enough to warrant individual voices.
      3. Are the voices performed by single performers or by a group of performers in a chorus?
      4. Describe your impressions of the voices' physical and vocal manifestations.
      5. Analyze the relationships between or among the voices; how will they work together?
   C. Are there two or more characters in the text who should be portrayed by a single performer? If so:
      1. Are there two or more characters who should be collapsed into a single voice (because their functions or styles are similar?)
      2. Are there two or more characters who, despite their distinctness, share traits in common that could be featured by a single performer playing them?
      3. Are there two or more distinct characters who should be played by the same performer, either for practical or aesthetic reasons?
   D. Are there characters that should be deleted?

II. Make a list of sources of power in the text other than character.
   A. Are any of them pervasive, functional, or independent enough to justify a voice?
   B. If so, should the voice be single or multiple?
      1. For single voices, describe your impressions of the physical and vocal manifestations of each voice.
      2. For multiple voices, answer the following questions:
         a. What does a multiplicity of voices (a chorus) accomplish for your script that a single voice does not?
         b. What functions will the chorus perform in the script?
         c. What are your impressions of the size and composition of the chorus?

Figure 3.1: Checklist for finding voices.

Releasing the Voices in "Ozymandias"

We can identify several possibilities for voices in "Ozymandias." Since we're planning to make more than one script, we'll be using the voices we hear in different combinations. Following our checklist, note that "Ozymandias" contains three major characters—the persona, the traveler, and Ozymandias—and one character inferred through synecdoche—the sculptor. Of the three major characters, none is multileveled enough to warrant division into more than one voice; since the characters appear in a brief sonnet form, this isn't surprising. We might conclude, then, that each of the three primary characters should have a single voice.

The inferred character of the sculptor presents an interesting problem in working with "Ozymandias." Depending upon the production concept, the sculptor could receive more focus than the printed version of "Ozymandias" suggests. The adapter might assign the sculptor's character to a separate voice, a chorus, or an individual voice coming out of a chorus. All options are creative possibilities.

Our analysis process shows that all basic power sources—ideas, characters, imagery, sound structure, time, and plot structure—are forces in "Ozymandias." The only strong forces we found operating independently of character, however, are imagery and tone color. We noted the pervasive sound value of the /s/, /sh/ repetition throughout the poem and the /ou/, /æ/, /e/ creating a sigh. A chorus of voices might be able to create a subtle background by using these sounds. A chorus might also be used to feature the contrast between life and death images by echoing words or phrases. Therefore, the idea of a small chorus (possibly five or six voices because "Ozymandias" is such a short selection) is an intriguing notion to us. We decided to list it as a voice possibility.

The most important vocal requirement at this point is the compatibility of the voices in "Ozymandias." For us, Ozymandias needs a deep, full-bodied baritone or bass voice, and the voices of the traveler, the persona, the chorus, and possibly the sculptor need to blend with his while using a higher register. Physical requirements for Ozymandias are simply that he be large, imposing, and capable of serious embodiment of the facial characteristics suggested in the poem. We also have a notion of the traveler as aged, possibly because we associate wisdom with longevity.

Now that we have identified some voice possibilities in "Ozymandias," we're ready to shape them in creative ways to actualize presentational form in the poem. There are as many ways to combine voices in literature as there are creative adapters. One choice is to break the existing text into voices without rearranging or adding lines. In "Ozymandias," this approach features the power sources of character and plot structure. Reorganizing the poem's elements—adding sound effects throughout the whole poem, for example—would emphasize the power sources of imagery and sound. The demands of the literature, your production concept, and audience analysis will all affect the making of your script.

"Ozymandias": Script Number One

Our production concept for the first script of "Ozymandias" suggests a creative treatment essentially following the order of voices in the printed poem, permitting us to feature the tensiveness between the brevity of the poem and the largeness of the idea.

"Ozymandias" is about the relationship between human endeavor and enduring time. Each character in the poem engages in a particular activity—speaking a poem, telling a story, making a statue, or building a monument—that reflects his personal vision of what endures. To Ozymandias, what endures are great monuments that attest to political might. The sculptor, on the other hand, relies on the power of the artistic vision. The traveler, who seems to move through time, offers the endurance of historical truth. Finally, the persona symbolizes the transcendence of poetic truth by uttering the poem.

This script also emphasizes the tensiveness among character perspectives. It relies on the power of each character's individual statement, or perspective, rather than on full orchestration. Some vocal overlay, echo, and sound effects will be employed and the visual power of the staging will reinforce the variations in character perspectives. (This script calls for special staging devices such as a lighted scrim behind which the sculptor and Ozymandias pose in a relief effect.) The script also features the power source of plot structure, emphasizing the economy with which the poem makes its statement. At the fulcrum, a long pause, a deliberate movement, and a change in focus shift the tonality of the script.

The voices we feature in this script are individualized, each played by a separate performer to help emphasize their distinctiveness. In addition to the three major characters—the persona, the traveler, and Ozymandias—the sculptor will be given a presence (through visual staging, sound effects, and dialogue) as a way of entering his character perspective into the world of the poem. For this script, we've chosen not to employ a chorus, whose collective presence may detract from the clarity of the four perspectives.

Ozymandias

CHARACTERS	SUGGESTED BACKGROUND MUSIC
PERSONA	Bartok's "Music for Strings, Percussion, and
TRAVELER	Celeste"
SCULPTOR	
OZYMANDIAS	

PERSONA. I met a traveller from an antique land
Who said—

PERSONA AND TRAVELER. [*In unison, with* Persona *fading out by "Stand"*]
Two vast and trunkless legs of stone

TRAVELER. [*As Traveler* speaks, the sculptor, behind a scrim, creates the sound effects of a hammer and anvil slowly, steadily, and loudly—about one to two beats per line.]
Stand in the desert. . . . Near them, on the sand,
Half sunk a shattered visage lies, whose frown,

SCULPTOR. Frown . . .

TRAVELER. And wrinkled lip,

SCULPTOR. Wrinkled lip . . .

TRAVELER. And sneer of cold command,
Tell that its sculptor well those passions read
Which yet survive,

SCULPTOR. Stamped on these lifeless things,

TRAVELER. The hand that mocked them and the heart that fed;
And on the pedestal these words appear:
"My name is Ozymandias, king of kings,"

OZYMANDIAS. [*Interrupting on the* Traveler's *word "kings"*]
My name is Ozymandias, king of kings,

Look on my works, ye Mighty, and despair!
[*Long pause, with* Traveler *and* Ozymandias *looking at each other.* Traveler *slowly turns toward audience.*]

TRAVELER.   Nothing beside remains. Round the decay
Of that colossal wreck, boundless and bare
The lone and level sands stretch far away.
PERSONA.   The lone and level sands stretch far away.

This script focuses on a particular condition of presentational form that is central in "Ozymandias": the sense of dialectic, or confrontation, between character perspectives. The characters (especially Ozymandias and the traveler, whose positions seem diametrically opposed) seem to speak for themselves directly to the audience, as if to present their points of view for consideration. It's right, we feel, for the sculptor to speak only in relation to his art, for indeed it is his work that communicates to the rest of the world. The persona and the traveler are united in perspective by two scripting techniques: speaking in unison and echoing the last line. The repetition of the last line has an additional presentational effect: it helps to set the image of "lone and level sands" firmly in the minds of the audience for their own imaginative completion.

By its relative faithfulness to the original printed form of "Ozymandias," this first script captures the poem's power of simple and direct expression. An orchestrated script of the sonnet, however, may sacrifice the power of an uncluttered plot structure to feature other levels of meaning in the poem. An orchestrated script of "Ozymandias" is as full as this script is spare. Each kind of script will have its own artistic virtue.

ORCHESTRATION OF THE TEXT

As a strongly lyric and presentational medium, Readers Theatre sometimes has a musical aspect. It is in the **orchestration** of the text that musical relationships are apparent. Orchestration means the manipulation of released voices and their melodies. Consider these voices as instruments; the portion of the script they speak is the melody they play. As a composer elaborates musical texture, intensifying his materials through techniques of **harmony** and **counterpoint**, so the adapter may work with voices, interweaving them to create a tapestry of sound, movement, and media.

Orchestration always implies the use of multiple voices, either moving simultaneously or in a contrapuntal arrangement. The presentational aspects of any literary material can be orchestrated to some extent according to the demands of your production concept, but selections with strong rhythmic and tonal patterns best lend themselves to this kind of manipulation.

Orchestration of vocal sound may range from a simple accentuation of selected moments in a script to an elaborate and total symphonic structure; powerful effects may be gained either through simple or elaborate approaches. Decisions affecting the manipulation of voices arise from your interaction with the text. How do you hear the script forming? To test your auditory imaginings, consider some of the values of orchestration and some of the problems that may occur.

The chief value to be gained through orchestration is the ability to reinforce elements of the text in varying ways. An idea, an emotion, a character presence, or an image structure may be augmented through the use of multiple voices, may be elaborated and thereby extended in time, or may be repeated in various places as an accompanying substructure of sound. Repetitions of important textual elements may be used, as in playwriting, for the purpose of foreshadowing future events, thereby helping to build a climax. Elaboration may be used to delay the occurrence of climax in such a way as to build suspense. Vocal sound effects may suggest auditory images in the work, such as the ticking of a clock or the pounding of a heartbeat. Such musical effects as echoing and vocal overlays provide not only elaboration and reinforcement of ideas and feelings, but also a general enrichment of the text.

Conversely, the careless use of orchestration can function against the text. You may unintentionally obscure plot line, idea, or some other important aspect of the text by an overelaboration of materials. It's possible to provide so much variation that the theme becomes too complex for an audience to grasp in a single hearing. Therefore, whether elaborate or simple, orchestrated elements need to be considered from the perspective of the viewing audience as well as from that of the creative artist.

Ultimately, decisions about orchestration will be determined by the way you want your script to flow. Orchestration retards the flow of time within the script, contributing to density rather than to straightforward progression. If you're working with a long work, and if the uninhibited movement of plot action is your major concern, you may wish to use no orchestration techniques or to use only touches of orchestration for accent. If you're working with a short work, and your major concern is the texture of the material, orchestration may be of major importance in your transformation of text into script. The decision about whether to orchestrate should always arise from your understanding of the text, and should not come from your desire to display your skill as an orchestrator.

Choral Structuring: Harmonics

The harmonic aspect of orchestration is the vertical sound structure, voice blended with voice in simultaneous layers of sound. Whenever multiple voices speak together, some kind of harmonic structure is created by the differing qualities of voices used. Script forms employing a total harmonic approach are sometimes termed *choral speaking, verse choir,* or *drama choir.*[8] Most orchestrated Readers Theatre scripts use a chorus in combination with more explicitly defined characters. The degree of harmonic structuring may vary from simple vocal unity in which all voices sound as one voice—a clear tone—to intricate structures in which voices use different pitches and qualities—a layered tone.

If your production concept includes the use of a chorus, you'll want to consider what your chorus will be composed of, particularly in terms of quantity: how many performers will you need? In considering the items on the checklist for finding voices (page 51), you estimated the approximate size of your chorus and listed the functions it will perform. Recheck your estimate to be sure it still meets the needs of your imagination. What does your chorus represent? Is it an overwhelming force, requiring a large number of voices, or a small intimate echo, best carried by a small group? If your use of the chorus will be extensive, and if you wish to create more elaborate tonal effects, choose a choral group large enough to include voices of varying qualities that can interact with each other. Some directors express a preference for a chorus of twelve or eighteen voices, because they can be divided in flexible ways. If your literary work is short or your use of choral effects limited, you may wish to use a chorus much smaller than twelve voices. Choral effects can be created by as few as two or three performers.

Most choruses contain a range of voice qualities. Voice qualities are classified as *dark*, very resonant and full-bodied voices; *medium*, average voices; and *light*, voices with high tonality and less chest resonance. Both male and female voices are found in all three quality types, with men tending to dominate the dark category and women the light category. A similar division of voices is used in singing choruses: soprano, alto, tenor, and bass. If you're familiar with these musical categories, you may prefer to use them.

Besides assigning voice qualities, you need to consider tempo, rhythmic patterns, and expressive quality, although these aspects of harmonics develop mostly as the script goes into rehearsal. Indicate on the pages of the script the nature of the choral effects you want, describing any sounds you wish your chorus to create in addition to the words of the text. Harmonics deals with a group of performers speaking in unison. If you're interested in the complexity of one vocal pattern playing against another, you'll want to work with counterpoint.

Choral Structuring: Counterpoint

Counterpoint is horizontal sound structure, the movement of voice against voice. By using counterpoint, you can enhance your script: you can create a musical background, you can reinforce any power source in the text by elaborating it, and you can add to the excitement of the text by heightening the conflict between one force and another. Contrapuntal techniques can create feelings of cacaphonous activity or harmonic serenity. The range of effects is as varied as there are scripts and orchestrators; your production concept will guide you to the degree of elaboration and the specific techniques to use.

Since techniques of counterpoint are best learned by example, we'll explore the ways some of the major contrapuntal forms can be realized in a script. Because a single text will rarely contain a variety of rhythms broad enough to support all the many methods of counterpointing, we've chosen several excerpts to illustrate the principles of orchestration. As you work with the examples, you'll become sensitive to the kinds of structures a particular work must have to permit the use of certain orchestration techniques. The methods of counterpoint are always suggested by forces in a literary work rather than those imposed by adapters on a literary work.

Voice and Accompaniment

A simple and familiar form of counterpoint is the single voice with a choral pattern played against it. Our first example is taken from the first paragraph of the short story, "The Fall of the House of Usher" by Edgar Allen Poe. The narrator has been requested to visit a boyhood friend whom he hasn't seen for many years. As he approaches the mansion in which his friend lives, the narrator is overcome by the sense of decay and gloom that envelops the house.

> What was it—I paused to think—what was it that so unnerved me in the contemplation of the House of Usher? It was a mystery all insoluble; nor could I grapple with the shadowy fancies that crowded upon me as I pondered. I was forced to fall back upon the unsatisfactory conclusion, that while, beyond doubt, there *are* combinations of very simple natural objects which have the power of thus affecting us, still the analysis of this power lies among considerations beyond our depth. It was possible, I reflected, that a mere different arrangement of the particulars of the scene, of the details of the picture, would be sufficient to modify, or perhaps to annihilate its capacity for sorrowful impression; and, acting upon this idea, I reined my horse to the precipitous brink of a black and lurid tarn that lay in unruffled lustre by the dwelling, and gazed down—but with a shudder even more thrilling than before—upon the remodelled and inverted images of the gray sedge, and the ghastly tree-stems, and the vacant and eye-like windows.[9]

The three images—"the gray sedge, and the ghastly tree-stems, and the vacant and eye-like windows"—seem to be **motifs** of the mysterious gloom surrounding the house. In fact, the same three images (in slightly different words) were used earlier in the same paragraph: "I looked upon the scene before me—upon the mere house, and the simple landscape features of the domain—upon the bleak walls—upon the vacant eye-like windows—upon a few rank sedges—and upon a few white trunks of decayed trees. . . ."[10] The power of these images emerges as a voice, which, sometimes lurking beneath the audible surface, can become an accompaniment to the narrator's lines. In our adaptation of some of these lines, two forces play against each other: the force of the man who tries to react rationally, and the force of the chorus who invokes the mysterious aura of the house, which cannot be explained logically.

CHORUS. [*Slowly*] Gray sedge . . . . ghastly tree-stems . . . .

NARRATOR.   What was it—I
CHORUS. vacant eye-like windows. . . . . [*low whisper*] Gray sedge . . . . .

NARRATOR. paused to think—what was it that so unnerved me in the contemplation
CHORUS. . . . . ghastly tree-stems . . . . vacant eye-like. . . . .

NARRATOR. of the House of Usher? It was a mystery all insoluble; [*pause*]
CHORUS. windows. . . . .

NARRATOR. nor could I grapple with the shadowy fancies [*pause*] that crowded
CHORUS. Gr———a—a—a—a—a———a———y Va—a—

NARRATOR. upon me as I pondered. . . . It was possible, I [*pause*] reflected [*pause*],
CHORUS. a——a—c—a—n—t   eye-like   windows

NARRATOR. that a mere different arrangement of the particulars of the scene,
CHORUS.

NARRATOR. [*pause*]   of the details of the picture, [*pause*]
CHORUS. Gray sedge, ghastly tree-stems

NARRATOR. would be sufficient to modify,
CHORUS. ghastly tree-stems [*rhythmically*] Gray .... sedge .... ghast ... ly

NARRATOR. or   perhaps   to   annihilate   its   capacity   for   sorrowful
CHORUS. .... tree .... stems ...... Va ...... cant .... eye .... like ....

NARRATOR. impression ...
CHORUS. win ..... dows ...

In a second form of voice and accompaniment, the choral pattern is composed of sounds carried by the tone color of the work. Two choruses, speaking sometimes together and sometimes separately, provide a pattern of human sound effects, which accompany the single voice. The example is from "Ozymandias."

TRAVELER. Round the decay   Of that colossal wreck
CHORUS 1 AND CHORUS 2.   S ——— Sh ——— S —— Shw ———

TRAVELER. boundless and bare   The   lone
CHORUS 1 AND CHORUS 2.   —— ou —— æ ——   [*as wind whistling*] Shw ———

TRAVELER. and   level   sands   stretch   far   away
CHORUS 1.   ———— Shw ——————— Shw ——————— Shw ———
CHORUS 2.   ou ——————— ɛ ——————— ou ——————— æ ———

The sibilant whistle suggests the blowing of sand, while the /æ/, /ɛ/, /ou/ sounds capture the sigh beneath the poem. By accompanying the traveler's words, the sound effect chorus adds to the vividness of the concluding setting and, thereby, helps to emphasize the contrast in the poem between the fullness of Ozymandias's living energy and the emptiness of the sands that outlast him.

Rounds and Echoes

The musical round and the echo rely on the rhythmic repetition of words or sounds. Simple yet fascinating, these techniques are based on all voice groups using the same words.

Familiar from camp songs, the **round** depends upon exact repetition of material that is rhythmically regular and has an even number of measures—two, four, six, or more. The round is composed of a sequence of voices, each entering at a different point in the phrase being repeated, but entering at regular intervals. Because of its absolute regularity, we will use a simple rhythmic sequence from Robert Southey's poem, "The Cataract at Lodore." The poem describes the development of a stream as it tumbles down through the rocks from the spring which is its source; the lines of the poem become longer as the stream becomes larger. The portion we have excerpted is in the middle of the poem. We also quote a few lines from earlier in the poem to help with context.

"How does the Water
Come down at Lodore?"
My little boy asked me
Thus, once on a time;

. . . .
From its source which well
   In the Tarn on the fell;
     From its fountains
   In the mountains,

. . . .
Collecting, projecting,
Receding and speeding,
And shocking and rocking,
And darting and parting. . . .[11]

Any number of voices may be used with these lines; we'll use a chorus of four parts, entering at three-beat intervals, for this example:

VOICE 1.	Col lect	ing, pro ject	ing, Re ced	ing and speed ing,						
VOICE 2.		Col lect	ing, pro ject	ing, Re ced	ing,					
VOICE 3.			Col lect	ing, pro ject	ing,					
VOICE 4.				Col lect	ing,					

VOICE 1.
VOICE 2. and speed ing,
VOICE 3. Re ced   ing and speed ing,
VOICE 4. pro ject   ing, Re ced   ing and speed ing,

Of course, a round can be carried on indefinitely. Our example shows how, by having voices enter every three beats, the triple rhythm is emphasized. This treatment elaborates the suggestion of the water dancing over rocks by adding some complexity to the simple movement of the lines.

    The same line can also be made into a round using two-beat intervals:

VOICE 1. Col lect ing, pro ject ing, Re ced ing and speed ing,
VOICE 2.   Col lect ing, pro ject ing, Re ced ing and
VOICE 3.   Col lect ing, pro ject ing, Re   ced
VOICE 4.   Col lect ing, pro ject ing

The restless urgency of the two-beat repetition adds an even greater complexity to the line, creating an interesting tension between the feeling of three, which is the norm of the poem, and a feeling of two. The two-beat rhythm moving against the three-beat rhythm makes the rather simple line more tensive.

    When using prose, or poetry that isn't composed in a regular rhythmic form, interesting patterns may be created by using imitation at irregular intervals. The following example is taken from "Somnambule Ballad" by Federico Garcia Lorca. The orchestration plays upon the word *green*, which appears consistently throughout the poem.

Green, how much I want you green.
Green wind. Green branches.
The ship upon the sea
and the horse in the mountain.[12]

The repetitions build in intensity so tone color and imagery are reinforced. Three voices are used because that number seems to gain a better rhythm and tonality in the repetition than do either two or four voices.

```
VOICE 1. Green, how much I want you, green
VOICE 2.                          Green, how much I want you,
VOICE 3.

VOICE 1. Green wind        Green branches        The ship upon  the sea
VOICE 2. green                         Green wind                Green branches
VOICE 3. Green, how much I want you,    green                        Green    wind

VOICE 1. and the horse in  the mountain.
VOICE 2.          The ship upon the sea and the horse in the mountain.
VOICE 3.                   Green branches        The ship upon the sea

VOICE 3. and the horse in the mountain.
```

Another use of simple repetition is exemplified by an excerpt from "A Haunted House" by Virginia Woolf. This short story is an impressionistic account of a ghostly couple who used to live in the house the narrator now inhabits. The storyteller feels the presence of the former owners, as they seem to move in shadows throughout the house. In the following brief section, the narrator describes a storm outside the house, while the inside, by contrast, is curiously still.

> The wind roars up the avenue. Trees stoop and bend this way and that. Moonbeams splash and spill wildly in the rain. But the beam of the lamp falls straight from the window. The candle burns stiff and still.[13]

In the orchestration of these sentences, parts of lines are repeated for an echo effect, while other lines are rearranged to create special rhythms and even rhyme. The last two lines of the script heighten the contrast between the stormy outside and the calm inside.

```
VOICE 1. The wind roars up the avenue. Trees stoop and bend this way and
VOICE 2.              The wind roa ——————————————— rs this

VOICE 1. that.          Moonbeams splash and spill       wildly in the rain.
VOICE 2. way   that way   this way      that way    splash and spill          wildly

VOICE 1. But the beam of the lamp falls straight from the window.
VOICE 2. [low]    The wind roars up the avenue              Moonbeams

VOICE 1. The candle burns stiff and still.
VOICE 2. splash            and        spill.
```

Augmentation and Diminution

To make shorter (to cut) is a common task for the adapter, especially when working with novels and long short stories. The manipulation of length is also an important technique for the orchestrator. **Augmentation** (to make larger) and **diminution** (to make smaller) are ways of working with the power source of structural time. A simple way to show how these techniques work is to manipulate duration and pause. In the line from "The Cataract of Lodore," Voice 2 is the norm against which we juxtapose the other two voices. Voice 1 is augmented so that its duration is twice as long as that of the diminished Voice 3. We've augmented Voice 1 by reducing the number of syllables per time unit, and diminished Voice 3 by increasing the number of syllables per unit.

VOICE 1. Col   lect   ing,
VOICE 2. Col lect   ing,   pro   ject   ing,
VOICE 3. Collecting, projecting, Re ced ing and speeding,

Augmentation can also take place through the manipulation of internal sections of the line (or of a larger segment of the work, such as a paragraph). In such cases the augmentation is accomplished by adding words. The example below, through its pattern of repetition, approximates the **madrigal** form.

VOICE 1. Collecting,   projecting,
VOICE 2.   Collecting,   projecting,
VOICE 3.   Collecting, projecting, Re

VOICE 1.   Receding, and speeding,
VOICE 2.   Receding   and speeding, and shocking,
VOICE 3. ceding   and speeding,

VOICE 1.   and shocking and rocking, and darting
VOICE 2. and   rocking, and darting
VOICE 3. and shocking and   rocking, and darting

VOICE 1. and part————ing
VOICE 2.   and part——ing
VOICE 3.   and part ing

The beauty of the madrigallike elaboration makes even stronger the image of the playfulness of the water as it swirls and flows. The shift from a repetition interval of three to an interval of one in the last line brings the chorus to an abrupt halt, as if suddenly interrupted.

In the following orchestrated example from "Ozymandias," augmentation is created by echoing and a slight rearrangement of the poem's word sequence. The effect is an elaboration of Ozymandias's words, almost as if they were reverberating through the stone passageways of a great monument. In the last line of this brief script, Chorus B begins to introduce the ironic notion that it is Ozymandias himself who should (or will) despair:

TRAVELER.   My name is Ozymandias
CHORUS A[1].   Name is Oz y man di as
CHORUS A[2].   Oz y man di as
CHORUS A[3].   Oz y man di as
CHORUS B.

TRAVELER.	King of kings					
CHORUS A¹.		King of kings				
CHORUS A².			King of kings			
CHORUS A³.				King of kings		
CHORUS B.	Ki————ng o————f ki————ngs					

TRAVELER.   Look   on my works   ye

CHORUS A.   King of kings   Look——Look

CHORUS B.   Lo————ok   on—— my —wor——ks

TRAVELER.   mighty   and despair

CHORUS A.   Look on my works   ye mighty   king of kings!

CHORUS B.   O————zy —— man—di—asss   desssssspa————ir

Finally, a selection may be augmented by the rearrangement of materials, by bringing lines, words, echoes of themes, from one part of the literary work and weaving them contrapuntally into the text of another part of the work. In our orchestrated version of Poe's "Fall of the House of Usher," we used images of decay from two sections of the story to accompany whole passages, creating not only an atmospheric accompaniment, but an augmented and counterpointed script as well.

Simple diminution is accomplished by deletion of content, cometimes with a powerful effect of sparseness and inevitability. To diminish the lines from "The Cataract at Lodore," we would remove one syllable in each foot, creating a marching rhythm of two beats: "Col lect, pro ject, / re cede, and speed." When this more driving rhythm is read simultaneously against the regular three-beat rhythm of the line, an interesting contrapuntal effect occurs.

VOICE 1. [*regular*]   Collecting, projecting,
VOICE 2. [*diminished*] Col   lect   pro   ject

VOICE 1.   Receding and speeding,
VOICE 2.   Re cede and   speed

Such effects are very useful to reinforce selected ideas or feelings and to keep the audience reminded of subtle threads running through the text.

When working with longer texts, this kind of orchestration may be spaced throughout the work. When manipulating sound, you'll demand more than one technique, and the text will often suggest other kinds of treatment than those we've described. Much of the excitement in transforming texts comes through your discovery of hidden voices and melodies.

"Ozymandias": Script Number Two

Our second script of "Ozymandias" features the forces of tone color and time imagery in the poem, rather than the power sources of character and plot. We orchestrated the sonnet to show how the sound structures in the poem powerfully suggest its setting in time and space.

In this production concept, "Ozymandias" is about a conflict between two major positions in time: the past and the present. Ironically, both positions are viewed from yet a third position:

the timeless, inevitable future. Just as Ozymandias and his power have decayed, the present intelligence (the traveler) will also pass, leaving only the poem, which *might* persist through time. The traveler, embodying the position of the present, is an unassuming common man, but he is also a man possessing a wide understanding of human power. Ozymandias, who embodies the position of the past, is a tyrannical king whose self-pride obscured his awareness of real human values. The chorus, which embodies the position of the future, communicates the ironic intelligence of endless time and space suggested by the poem as a whole. The chorus also helps to create the deserted scene of the present through its sounding of the /s/, /sh/ (wind) sounds and the /ou/, /ɛ/, /æ/ (sighing) sounds.

In this version of "Ozymandias," the chorus first sets the scene in sound. Then the two forces (past and present) confront the audience, each in turn making a low chanting statement that establishes his position—"My name is Ozymandias, king of kings" (past) and "A shattered visage," "Nothing beside remains" (present). The chorus, acting as the persona, then introduces the traveler. As the traveler describes the present scene, Ozymandias begins to emerge from the past, growing stronger until a major confrontation between traveler and king occurs, just before the fulcrum of the poem. At this point, immediately after Ozymandias has made his strongest statement, the chorus echoes the scene the traveler has described—"trunkless legs," "shattered visage." The evidence of the present prevails. After a pause, the traveler continues to describe the rest of the scene—"Nothing beside remains." As he does so, Ozymandias recedes back into the past. The traveler, however, does not achieve the ultimate victory. Even as he describes the leveling power of time, his own voice fades. The voice of the future (the chorus) is the only one left; it echoes the word *nothing* and then dwindles into sound alone, as if there were nothing left. Ultimately, time, the final victor, pronounces a verdict upon all human endeavor.

"Ozymandias": Script Two

CHARACTERS: CHORUS (*six voices; the chorus chants much of the time in an undulating tone alternating with whispers*)

OZYMANDIAS

TRAVELER

SOUND KEY
/æ/ as in "sand"
/ou/ as in "cold"
/u/ as in "who"
/ɛ/ as in "met"
/Shw/ as a wind sound

OZYMANDIAS.
TRAVELER.
CHORUS. Shw—————————————————/ ⌐u⌐ [changing pitch] ⌐ou—————

OZYMANDIAS. [*A soft slow chant: low pitched*] My name is Ozy   man
TRAVELER.
CHORUS. —ɛ——————— mm—————————————

OZYMANDIAS. dias   king   of   kings
TRAVELER.   ⌐u—————— Shw—————
CHORUS. —— æ————————/

OZYMANDIAS.
TRAVELER.   a   sha   tered   vis   age   Nothing   beside   re-
CHORUS.   Shw————————————————————————

OZYMANDIAS.
TRAVELER.   mai—————————ns
CHORUS.   Shw————————————ou————————————I met a

OZYMANDIAS.
TRAVELER.   Two vast
CHORUS.   traveller from an antique land [*three voices*] who said:
                          [*two voices*] who said:

OZYMANDIAS.   [*chant a little more insistently*]   My name is Ozymandias
TRAVELER.   and trunkless legs of stone stand in the desert
CHORUS.   æ————

OZYMANDIAS.
TRAVELER.   Near them, on the sand,
CHORUS.   ————ou—u————Shw————————
                                    æ————

OZYMANDIAS.   [*more insistent yet*] king of kings
TRAVELER.   half sunk,   a shattered visage lies
CHORUS.   æ————   [*low, soft*]   Shat tered visage

OZYMANDIAS.   [*stronger*]   king of
TRAVELER.   whose frown   and wrinkled lip   and sneer of cold command
CHORUS.   [*whisper*]   Shat————tered   shat————tered

OZYMANDIAS. kings
TRAVELER.   Tell that its sculptor well those passions read
CHORUS.   kin————gs   Mm————

OZYMANDIAS.   King of Kings
TRAVELER.   which yet survive stamped on these lifeless things
CHORUS.   ————————u————————Shw———— life—less

OZYMANDIAS.
TRAVELER.   Yet survive the hand that mocked them   and the heart
CHORUS.   [*soft, low*] Mocked themmmmm————

OZYMANDIAS. [*strong*] My name is Ozymandias.
TRAVELER.   that fed.
CHORUS.   Oz—y—man—di—assssssssss
                       [*one voice*] di—as
                       [*one voice*] dias

OZYMANDIAS.
TRAVELER.   And on the pedestal   these words appear: My name is
CHORUS.   [*low*]   trunkless legs

OZYMANDIAS.   [*very strong*]   My name is Ozymandias, King of Kings! Look on
TRAVELER.   Ozymandias, king of kings
CHORUS.   [*low*]   king——— of——kin———gs

OZYMANDIAS. my works, ye Mighty   and despair.
TRAVELER.   Look on my works, ye
CHORUS.   Migh——ty   des——pair

OZYMANDIAS.   Look on my works, ye Mighty, and despair!
TRAVELER. Mighty——
CHORUS.   [*stronger*]   dessssss——pa——ir

OZYMANDIAS.
TRAVELER.
CHORUS.   Ye Mighty———Look! [*pause*]   trunkless legs shat—

OZYMANDIAS.   [*weaker*]   d–e–s–s–s–sssssssss
TRAVELER.   Nothing beside remains
CHORUS. tered visage [*pause*]

OZYMANDIAS. pair   [*low*]   My name is O—zy—man—
TRAVELER.   Round the decay of that colossal wreck
CHORUS. æ——————— Shw——————m————

OZYMANDIAS. di—as   [*very low*]   desssssssssssspa——ir
TRAVELER.   boundless and bare   the lone
CHORUS. ———u———oʊ———   Shw——

OZYMANDIAS.
TRAVELER.   and   level   sands   stretch far away
CHORUS. [*three voices*]——Shw————Shw————boun——dlessssss
CHORUS. [*two voices*]————æ———ɛ——oʊ————Shw——

OZYMANDIAS.
TRAVELER.   [*chant*] stretch far a way.
CHORUS. a——————nnnnnnnnnd ba———re

OZYMANDIAS.
TRAVELER.   fa———r a——wa———y
CHORUS. Nothing beside rema———insssssss   No——thin——ng

OZYMANDIAS.
TRAVELER.
CHORUS. besi———de [*three voices*] No————thin————ng
         [*two voices*] Shw————

OZYMANDIAS.
TRAVELER.
CHORUS. Shw——wæ————oʊ————u———Shw————

This script features the poem's auditory level by employing a chorus to create the physical setting through tone color. The tensiveness between the desolate ruins today and the massive presence of the past, in the form of the king, also features the force of time in the poem. To realize our production concept, we've used a few more techniques of orchestration than in the first script: a choral line operating beneath a single voice, repetition (echo), rearrangement of lines, and augmentation and diminution.

STEPPING BACK

Creating a script from a text can be a thoroughly satisfying experience. When you build a script, whether orchestrated or not, its form reflects not only the work's structure but your patterns of thought. Our scripts of "Ozymandias" reveal two of the many patterns of voices we hear in the poem. As you read them, you may have heard other patterns. "Ozymandias" is rich; it suggests many readings and soundings. Even a subtle change in interpretation can produce a different production concept and a new script.

As you become attuned to hearing voices in literature, you won't be able to read a page without voices swirling in your head. Listen to the voices you hear, but learn to step back from them to check whether those voices are reflecting the power sources of the work. Are the voices you're hearing your voices only, or are you responding to lines of force in the work? As an adapter, you have a responsibility—not to recapture the original "author's intent"—but to achieve your best possible understanding of a work. When you listen to literary voices responsibly, you are able to choose among them sensitively, orchestrating only when the text can be served by it. The security of knowing that you have thoroughly explored the power sources in a literary work grants you freedom to use the techniques of script building creatively.

NOTES

1. Vachel Lindsay, "The Congo," in *Chief Modern Poets of England and America*, 4th ed., ed. Gerald DeWitt Sanders, John Herbert Nelson, and M. L. Rosenthal (New York: Macmillan, 1962), p. II-131.
2. Arnold Tovey, *The Forms of Music* (New York: Meridian Books, 1956), p. 101.
3. Wallace A. Bacon, *The Art of Interpretation*, 3rd ed. (New York: Holt, Rinehart & Winston, 1979), p. xv.
4. "Greensleeves," in *Poetry in English*, ed. Warren Taylor and Donald Hall (New York: Macmillan, 1963), p. 42.
5. Christopher Marlowe, *The Tragical History of Doctor Faustus*, in *A Treasury of the Theatre*, vol. 1, ed. John Gassner (New York: Simon & Schuster, 1951), p. 226.
6. Jean Anouilh, *Antigone*, in *Jean Anouilh (Five Plays)*, vol. 1 (New York: Hill and Wang, Mermaid Dramabook, 1958), pp. 11–12.
7. *Hamlet* by William Shakespeare, directed by Paul Baker, Baylor University, Waco, Texas, 1956.
8. We don't distinguish these as separate forms, but consider harmonic orchestration as an integral part of the total Readers Theatre spectrum and as an important tool to be used at the discretion of the adapter.
9. Edgar Allan Poe, "Fall of the House of Usher," *The Works of Edgar Allan Poe*, vol. 2 (New York: P. F. Collier & Son, 1903), p. 146.
10. Ibid., p. 145.
11. Robert Southey, "The Cataract of Lodore," *The Oxford Book of Children's Verse*, ed. Iona and Peter Opie (Oxford: Oxford University Press, 1973), pp. 94–97.

12. Federico Garcia Lorca, "Somnambule Ballad," *Selected Poems of Federico Garcia Lorca*, ed. Francisco Garcia Lorca and Donald M. Allen, trans. Stephen Spender and J. L. Gili (New York: New Directions, 1955), p. 65.
13. Virginia Woolf, "A Haunted House," *A Haunted House and Other Stories* (New York: Harcourt Brace Jovanovich, 1972), pp. 561–562.

SUGGESTIONS FOR FURTHER READING

Bacon, Wallace A. *The Art of Interpretation.* 3rd ed. New York: Holt, Rinehart & Winston, 1979. Chap. 13.

Brown-Agarowicz, Marjory Frances. *A Handbook of Creative Choral Speaking.* Minneapolis: Burgess, 1970.

Coger, Leslie Irene, and White, Melvin R. *Readers Theatre Handbook,* 2nd ed. Glenview, Ill.: Scott, Foresman, 1973.

DeWitt, Marguerite, ed. *Practical Methods in Choral Speaking,* Boston: Expression, 1936.

Gilbert, Carolyn A. *Communicative Performance of Literature.* New York: Macmillan, 1977. Chap. 6.

Gullan, Marjorie. *Choral Speaking.* Boston: Expression, 1931.

———. *The Speech Choir.* New York: Harper & Bros., 1937.

Haas, Richard, et al. *Theatres for Interpretation.* Ann Arbor, Mich.: Roberts Burton, 1976.

Long, Beverly Whitaker; Hudson, Lee; and Jeffrey, Phillis Rienstra. *Group Performance of Literature.* Englewood Cliffs, N.J.: Prentice-Hall, 1977. Chaps. 3, 6.

MacArthur, David E. "Readers Theatre: Variations on a Theme," *The Speech Teacher* 13 (January 1964): 47–51.

Provenmire, E. Kingsley. *Choral Speaking and the Verse Choir.* New York: A. S. Barnes, 1975.

Sandifer, Charles M. "From Print to Rehearsal: A Study of Principles for Adapting Literature to Readers Theatre." *The Speech Teacher* 20 (April 1971): 115–121.

Swann, Mona. *An Approach to Choral Speech.* New York: St. Martin's Press, 1964.

CHAPTER FOUR

Transforming for Chamber Theatre: Creating a Text

*I will try to point to a process that lies at the basis of fiction . . . that its
structure (as solid and stable a word as one can find) is in motion. It is
always and only in motion . . . a flow, a journey, a process.*

Alan Friedman, *The Turn of the Novel*

"Once upon a time, and a very good time it was," begins the narrator of *A Portrait of the Artist as
a Young Man* by James Joyce. Those words trigger memories of happy childhood moments when
the magic phrase, "once upon a time," signaled the exciting action to follow. When the child
pleads, "Tell me a story . . . *please*," the implied "you" is as important to the child as is the story
itself. Even if the facts of the plot remain the same, grandpa's version always differs from
mother's, and the child senses this difference. Who the storyteller is provides a central interest for
the story.

Throughout history, people have valued both the narrative tale and its teller, which is illustrated by the rich oral history of the epic mode, from the *Iliad* of Homer to the sung ballads of
Harry Chapin. Homer stands as a symbol of the **singer of tales** who has existed in many forms
from antiquity. With the advent of the printing press, the **writer of tales** took a position in literary history beside the singer of tales, bringing a new complexity to the epic mode. Today, in the
current movement toward postliteracy and a revival of an oral culture, a new figure in the history
of the epic mode, the **stager of tales**, has emerged. The stager of tales uses the art of transformation to combine the magic and power of the singer of tales with the complexity of the writer of
tales. The medium in which the stager of tales works is Chamber Theatre.[1]

Chamber Theatre stages the drama of storytelling. The singer of tales stands before an audience, peopling imaginative space with the characters of the story; the stager of tales places the
narrator before an audience, peopling physical space with those imaginative characters given
physical bodies. The drama of storytelling lies in the strategies by which the narrator brings the
story to life.

The two most important strategies that all narrators have at their disposal are **showing**
and **telling**, one of which she is doing at any given moment in a story. In literature, when narrators tell, they take a central position in the story by establishing a one-to-one personal relationship with the reader. In such moments, you as a reader are conscious of a single voice speaking to
you directly; that voice shapes your perceptions and conditions your attitudes toward events and

characters in the story. As narrators tell, they can also summarize events, introduce characters, shift time frames, and provide background information.

A narrator who shows steps back so you may see the story happen in your inner eye. Dialogue is the most obvious way a narrator shows; by stepping aside, the narrator allows the characters to speak for themselves. You see the scene because it unfolds before you. A more subtle kind of narrative showing occurs when the storyteller provides such detail that the reader can visualize the scene. In describing a room, for example, a narrator may tell that "the room was richly furnished," or she may show the reader that "the ornate patterns in the Oriental carpet were complemented by the gilded lions' heads on the Chinese Chippendale chairs." The telling narrator is simply providing information; she clearly doesn't wish you to dwell on the physical image of the room. The showing narrator emphasizes the room's physical presence by inviting you into the room through images. The degree of narrative showing or telling is the most important guideline for the physical movement of the narrator in a Chamber Theatre performance.

If you were to attend a Chamber Theatre production, what might you see? A narrator, or several narrators, sometimes speak directly to the audience and sometimes relate to characters. Characters may talk with each other or speak directly to the audience. Costume pieces, properties, and even a somewhat representational stage setting may be used. The narrator would sometimes tell the story directly to the audience and sometimes let the characters show the action of the story as in a traditionally staged play. In fact, the interaction between showing and telling—as when the narrator breaks into a scene and comments upon it or, in the middle of telling the audience about a character, signals the character to speak—becomes one of the most interesting features of Chamber Theatre.

In creating a script for this form, you'll learn something about how the epic mode functions, how to recognize and use the narrator's showing and telling, and how to divide lines among characters. You'll learn how to use the strategies of the narrator as a blueprint or pattern for your Chamber Theatre production.

SELECTING NARRATIVE LITERATURE TO TRANSFORM

When "Once upon a time" becomes "It was the best of times, it was the worst of times,"[2] or "Call me Ishmael,"[3] you begin to be aware of some of the ways in which narrators introduce themselves and their stories to readers. The narrator's voice, calling from the page, draws you into the world of literary experience. The more intriguing the voice, the more tempted you'll be to release it into action, to transform it into a script for performance. Although practical considerations are always important, the compelling reason for selecting a single work for Chamber Theatre is its quality of narrative action.

As an adapter of literature for Chamber Theatre, you'll be interested in literary works in which the lyric stance and the dramatic stance are in a balanced relationship. (Look back to Chapter 1 for an explanation of the lyric-dramatic tensions in epic literature.) Since Chamber Theatre is designed to feature the dynamic interrelationship between a storyteller's direct communication with a listener and his or her use of illustrative dramatic scenes to help unfold the story, the major focus is on the nature of the narrator who controls the epic balance.

The epic storyteller, the narrator, moves in a three-dimensional relationship. First, she is in an interpersonal communicative dimension, relating a tale to a silent reader or (as the narrator onstage in Chamber Theatre) to an audience. Some narrators are more aware of this audience than are others. Like the eighteenth-century storyteller who addresses a "Dear reader," Kurt Vonnegut's narrator in *Breakfast of Champions* recognizes the reader indirectly as he poses a rhetorical question: "I could go on and on with the intimate details about the various lives of people on the super-ambulance, but what good is more information?"[4]

Second, narrators live in an intrapersonal dimension—that is, they often relate to their own roles as storytellers. In "Wakefield" by Nathaniel Hawthorne, the narrator is very conscious of holding his story together: "But our business is with the husband. We must hurry after him along the street, ere he lose his individuality, and melt into the great mass of London life."[5] Although this narrator recognizes the reader through direct address, his major concern is with the process of telling a story.

Finally, narrators live in relation to the dimension of the story's action, functioning in various ways with the characters and events they bring into being. These ways of functioning form the major substance of the rest of this chapter. Here it is only necessary to note that the narrator's relation to the audience, to self, and to the story are major aspects of presentational form in the epic mode and become central in both the selection and the adaptation of literature for Chamber Theatre. The purpose of Chamber Theatre is to make this tridimensional relationship explicit onstage. In short, your interest as an adapter for Chamber Theatre will be in the narrator and in the act of narrating.

Works for Chamber Theatre should have not only an interesting narrator, but a narrative vitality that results from the storyteller's continual shifting of position in relation to the story being told and to the reader. Such movement in narrative attitude and position tends to evoke additional voices from the text—voices locked in past events, in interior worlds of characters' minds, or in the narrative consciousness itself. The adapter of literature for Chamber Theatre probes the story for those voices, transforming their implicit presence into explicit action onstage.

Once you've chosen a story to adapt for Chamber Theatre, refer to Chapter 2 for suggestions on how to record your initial impressions of the work. What is it about your selection that intrigues you, that makes you want to work with it? As you analyze your story, jot down any production ideas that occur to you. These notions on staging, along with your first impressions, will help form your production concept.

CREATING THE TEXT THROUGH ANALYSIS

A consideration of power sources in literature underlies the transformation process for Interpreters Theatre. Chamber Theatre, an Interpreters Theatre production form, explores the tensive relationship among power sources in the epic mode. The most important power source in the epic mode is **point of view.**

Point of View

Henry James was the first to crystallize the concept of point of view as a literary technique, although others had written about the phenomenon before he did. Percy Lubbock, in *The Craft of Fiction*, added the term to the common vocabulary of literary criticism and emphasized its importance: "The whole intricate question of method, in the craft of fiction, I take to be governed by the question of the point of view—the question of the relation in which the narrator stands to his story."[6] Brooks and Warren speak of "the mind through which the material of the story is presented" and call it "focus of narration."[7] Richard Eastman defines point of view or "angle of narration" as "the restriction of the reader's observation to a limited field of consciousness."[8]

The central mind in any story, the narrator, tells the story from a particular physical vantage point, with a definable attitude. This may be likened to an artist painting a picture, who views the scene from a definite location or angle of vision. If the artist were to move, the configuration of the scene would change. Artists also demonstrate their own feelings about the subject of a picture through coloring, design, and texture. Anyone viewing the final picture will see it from the same physical location as the artist and, if the observer is perceptive, will be able to determine something of the artist's feelings. In the epic mode, you see the fictive scene through the eyes of an observer who is located physically in relation to the action of the story. The difference between the picture and the literary work is that the narrator in literature, as in a film, may shift stance during the course of the narrative.

A narrator may be located at any distance from or at any angle to the action being performed. Distance from the action affords the narrator a wider angle of vision and possibly a greater objectivity, while a close position usually allows the narrator to observe subtle relationships. As a reader, you're located in the position of the narrator, you shift stance with the narrator, and you're able to discern, in the narrative style, the feelings of the narrator about the characters and events being described. The unity of the story and its ultimate effect will depend on the position and attitude of the narrator.

The physical and psychological positions the narrator takes toward the action combine to form the point of view of the story. Point of view, therefore, is a tensiveness among the narrator's position from which he views the characters and events, the narrative attitude toward them, and the characters and events themselves. In the epic mode, all other power sources serve to determine and to define the nature of point of view. As you begin to create your text from which a script will evolve, your first analytical step will be to consider the point of view in your literary work.

Point of view is traditionally identified on a basic level by person—that is, whether the story is told by a first person, second person, or third person narrator. (Second person narration is so rare that our discussion will be limited to first and third person. Narratives in the second person share many of the attributes of the first person narrative with the emphasis shifted from "I" to "you.") The choice of person by the author sets up specific conditions in the story and gives the reader an indication of the amount of information available to the narrator. Point of view is usually discussed under three major classifications: first person subjective, third person objective, and third person omniscient.

First Person Subjective

First person narrators are *characters in the stories* they narrate. Because they're characters, readers come to know them as people with names and personal histories.

Obviously, the first person narrator can know only that information that comes through outward observation and his or her own interior processes of thinking and feeling. Since first person narrators speak out of personal experience, they carry a high degree of believability; readers tend to believe those narrators because they've been witness to the events being related. The narrator's subjectivity, however, often results in a distortion of observable fact; readers may therefore question his or her **reliability**. A first person narrator may be either a major character who tells a personal story or a minor character who observes the action being related; each condition places the narrator in a different relationship with the other characters and events.

First Person—Major Character.
An "I" narrator who is the major character in the work tells his or her own story and is the center of the action. You often feel close to such storytellers, but you're also aware that they are subject to human error. Holden Caulfield in J. D. Salinger's *Catcher in the Rye* begins his story with a defensive attitude that continues throughout the novel. He feels the necessity to disparage most of the people he meets. Holden describes one of his fellow students, Robert Ackley, for example, as a boy who never brushed his teeth in all the time he knew him. Needless to say Holden's comments are characterized by a rather innocent exaggeration. As a reader, you instinctively like him and believe in his intensity of feeling and attitude, but you don't always believe in the accuracy of his observations.

First Person—Minor Character.
An "I" narrator who is telling someone else's story is usually near the periphery of the action and thus obtains a wider scope of vision than the narrator who is also the main character. Although first person observers can obtain more objectivity than protagonist narrators, they're still limited by inability to obtain privileged information—knowledge that wouldn't normally be available to an observer. They can tell only what they know to be true through experience and observation.

Sometimes a first person observer narrator convinces us of his or her reliability; the character of Nick in *The Great Gatsby* by F. Scott Fitzgerald convinces the reader of his ability to observe accurately and to judge Gatsby's actions in agreement with the judgment of the implied author. On the other hand, the barber who narrates Ring Lardner's "Haircut" quickly convinces us that he is no judge of character, as he tells of his admiration for Jim, the town's sadistic practical joker. The barber explains that one of Jim's funniest tricks was to pick out a name of a man in a strange town and then mail a postcard to him, saying, " 'Ask your Missus who kept her from gettin' lonesome the last time you was in Carterville.' And he'd sign the card, 'A Friend.' "[9] Throughout the story, the cruel nature of the tricks Jim played on others contrasts with the barber's praise of Jim. The barber is thus an unreliable narrator; we feel that the author holds different values than those expressed by the barber.

First person narrators, whether main characters or observers, reliable or unreliable, are as subjective as average human beings, and are believable because they have experienced in some way the story they are telling. We are often as interested in them as in their story, because most first person narrators constantly call attention to themselves, whether they intend to or not.

Third Person Objective

The most objective narrator, seeming to carry a high degree of reliability, is the one who isn't identified as a character in the story and who reports only what you as a reader could see if you were standing in the same location as the narrator. This point of view is often called *camera*, because it appears to be so objective; these narrators aren't able to go into the mind of any character, nor do they have omniscient powers of time and space. They usually limit themselves to changing scene, shifting your attention to different locations within the scene, and directing you to observe intricate details in the external environment.

Although language style always carries a suggestion of attitude and tone, and although a great deal of selection is taking place in terms of what the narrator observes, this narrator doesn't impose a sense of self on the reader, but lets details of character and environment speak for him or her. Notice the attention to detail in the following passage from "The Jockey" by Carson McCullers:

> Simmons cut into his beefsteak. He held his fork prongs downward on the plate and carefully piled on mushrooms with the blade of his knife. "He's crazy," he repeated. "He gives me the creeps."
>
> All the tables in the dining room were occupied. There was a party at the banquet table in the center, and green-white August moths had found their way in from the night and fluttered about the clear candle flames. Two girls wearing flannel slacks and blazers walked arm in arm across the room into the bar. From the main street outside came echoes of holiday hysteria.[10]

With a third person objective point of view, the reader tends to be more interested in the story and the manner in which it's related than in the narrator as a personality. This narrator constantly directs the reader's attention toward the objective aspects of the story, using details and events to evoke an emotional reaction from the reader. Part of the terror of stories such as "The Lottery" by Shirley Jackson comes through the objective matter-of-factness of the narration.

Third Person Omniscient

Omniscience usually refers to a narrator's ability to overcome the limits of personal subjectivity, of time and space, and of the inability to know the thoughts and feelings of another. For this reason an omniscient narrator always speaks in the third person and usually exists as an unidentified presence. The exception to this would be in those cases when the author seems to step into the story and address the reader directly ("I must interrupt this story here to tell you . . ."). Omniscience is a great convenience to a novelist because it allows greater flexibility in telling the story; the narrator may shift from an exterior view to an interior view at will, or may freely reveal knowledge of the past, present, and future. As a reader, you have the feeling that omniscient narrators know everything about their stories, although they choose to tell only selected information. The narrator may, in fact, relate much of the story as an objective observer, only occasionally exhibiting powers of omniscience. Such narrators are omniscient; why they avoid using omniscience becomes a major question for the adapter to answer. For narrators who do freely use their omniscient powers, it is the choosing to tell, show, or withhold interior information that defines certain general conditions of omniscience that may be termed (1) external omniscience, (2) multiple interior, or shifting omniscience, and (3) single interior omniscience.

Third Person—External Omniscience.

Externally omniscient narrators differ from third person objective narrators in that they aren't limited to a specific location, but may range through time and space. They comment upon the interior thoughts and feelings of one or more characters, indicating motivation and intention. Although these narrators know what characters are feeling and may tell about it, they don't show internal thinking and feeling processes in action. That privilege is reserved for internal omniscient narrators. External omniscience carries with it a strong weight of reliability; since these narrators know so much, they surely must be correct in their judgments.

Often an externally omniscient narrator is closely identified with the voice of the author in the work who might address the reader directly. In the following passage from "The Luck of Roaring Camp" by Bret Harte, the narrator not only seems to know all there is to know about the character being described—both external and internal conditions in present and past—but he indicates an awareness of the reader's presence in the first line.

> Perhaps the less said of her the better. She was a coarse, and, it is to be feared, a very sinful woman. But at that time she was the only woman in Roaring Camp, and was just then lying in sore extremity, when she most needed the ministration of her own sex. Dissolute, abandoned, and irreclaimable, she was yet suffering a martyrdom hard enough to bear even when veiled by sympathizing womanhood, but now terrible in her loneliness.[11]

Third Person—Multiple Interior, or Shifting Omniscience.

A narrator with shifting omniscience is identified by two major features: (1) the omniscience is interior, rather than exterior, permitting the characters' thoughts to be shown directly, and (2) the narrator enters the minds of more than one character, shifting between them with a narrative rhythm that suggests bouncing from one character to the next. Narrators with shifting omniscience are able to establish character relationships by skillfully juxtaposing the thoughts and motivations of one persona with those of another. In an excerpt from "The Boarding House" by James Joyce, the narrator's shifting omniscience helps set up one character's subtle manipulation of the others.

> Things went on so for a long time and Mrs. Mooney began to think of sending Polly back to typewriting when she noticed that something was going on between Polly and one of the young men. She watched the pair and kept her counsel.
>
> Polly knew that she was being watched, but still her mother's persistent silence could not be misunderstood. There had been no open complicity between mother and daughter, no open understanding but, though people in the house began to talk of the affair, still Mrs. Mooney did not inter-

vene. Polly began to grow a little strange in her manner and the young man was evidently perturbed. . . .

Mr. Doran was very anxious indeed this Sunday morning. . . . The recollection of his confession of the night before was a cause of acute pain to him; the priest had drawn out every ridiculous detail of the affair and in the end had so magnified his sin that he was almost thankful at being afforded a loophole of reparation. The harm was done. What could he do now but marry her or run away?[12]

By showing the thought processes of all three characters, and by interspersing interior views with his own commentary, the narrator features the *tensions* between Mrs. Mooney, Polly, and Mr. Doran. The question of reliability resides not with the narrator himself, but with the characters, since the narrator has sublimated his own voice to show the characters' thought processes directly. However, you can analyze the narrator's personality and value system by investigating whose thoughts are shown at any given moment. Does the storyteller take care to present all major sides of an issue, or does she emphasize one character's perspective?

Third Person—Single Interior Omniscience.
When a narrator is internally omniscient with only one character, the depth of the interior probing is usually greater than when the third person narrator shifts from character to character. The shared relationship between narrator and major character comes into primary focus, as though the major character were a kind of subjective narrator, telling the story from his or her own internal perspective. This kind of omniscient narrator engages in considerable self-effacement, so that the thought processes of the major character can receive the most emphasis.

In Saul Bellow's "A Father-to-Be," the central character, Rogin, observes a man on the subway who looks like the son Rogin imagines he might have if he were to marry his fiancée, Joan. The narrator perceives the stranger through Rogin's eyes and shows Rogin's subsequent mental associations to the reader.

His clear skin and blue eyes, his straight and purely Roman nose—even the way he sat—all strongly suggested one person to Rogin: Joan. He tried to escape the comparison, but it couldn't be helped. This man not only looked like Joan's father, whom Rogin detested; he looked like Joan herself. Forty years hence, a son of hers, provided she had one, might be like this. A son of hers? Of such a son, he himself, Rogin, would be the father. . . .

That was why he felt bound to him through all existence. What were forty years reckoned against eternity! Forty years were gone, and he was gazing at his own son. Here he was. Rogin was frightened and moved. "My son! My son!" he said to himself, and the pity of it almost made him burst into tears.[13]

One of the effects of limiting interior omniscience to one character only is that the reader gains a full knowledge of the major character, even to the extent (often) of seeing other characters only as they're reflected in the major character's eyes. Like other omniscient narrators, the third person storyteller with single omniscience enjoys a considerable measure of reliability as a narrator simply because she knows so much; that reliability at any given moment, however, is dependent on the accuracy of the judgments made by the character whose mind is being revealed.

If each type of narrator repeated the same story from his or her own point of view, the nature of the story would shift considerably with each change. Notice how the transitions from first person to third person and from subjectivity to objectivity to interiority affect the tone, style, and amount of information given in the following story.

First Person Subjective—Major Character

"I knew I was late for the office that morning, but I couldn't put it off any longer. I wanted to give her something, and the florist was close by. Why did I find it so hard to talk to her? I thought maybe the flowers would speak for me."

First Person Subjective—Minor Character

"I was wiping the counter and hoping we wouldn't have any early morning customers because I had so much work to do when Mr. Winston from the office complex down the street pushed open the door. He must be in the doghouse again, I thought. This will make the third time he's sent carnations to his wife this month."

Third Person Objective

"The man in the gray tweed coat pulled his car abruptly to the curb and hurriedly dashed across the sidewalk toward the florist shop. He darted a sideways glance as he pulled open the heavy glass door, as if to confirm that no one was watching him."

Third Person—External Omniscience

"Mr. Winston had been to the florist shop three times in the past month. His wife's love for plants made fresh flowers the perfect peace offering, and it had seemed to work . . . for a few days at least. He had tried everything to relieve her suspicions, but his late hours at the office had seemed to undo all the goodwill that the flowers had established. He was soon to discover that flowers wilt and suspicions grow."

Third Person—Multiple Interior, Shifting Omniscience

"Mr. Winston sighed nervously as he approached the florist shop. He was aware that he was becoming an all-too-familiar customer. It was just his luck, he thought, to have to deal with the same clerk each time.

"The clerk watched him approach. What color carnations would he send this time, she wondered. To her surprise, he stopped by the rose case. He must have *really* done it this time, she thought."

Third Person—Single Interior Omniscience

"Red roses. Long-stemmed, of course. Winston approached the counter. The same clerk. She's probably getting to know me pretty well, he thought. Too well. He made a mental note to change florist shops.

" 'Good morning, Mr. Winston. May we help you this morning?'

" 'Uh, yes. Red roses. A dozen. Send to Miss—uh, Ms.—Marcia Sutton, at my office address.' He smiled sheepishly. 'National Secretaries Week,' he blurted out, hoping that the bluff would work."

Like a piece of finely cut crystal, point of view is prismatic; it acts as a refractor of experience, determining what we see and how we see, by filtering events, characters, ideas, and images through the narrator's perspective. Once you've come to terms with the nature of point of view in your selection, you have a good understanding of the shape and faceting of your story's narrative prism.

Plot Structure

Intricately entwined with point of view in the epic mode, **plot** is the patterned sequence of fictional events that occur in the literary work. One of the narrator's primary tasks is to guide you on your journey through the events of the story, highlighting major action, filling in background information, calling attention to detail, and even suggesting camera angles. The tour is fascinating not only because of the personality of the guide, the narrator, but also because of the interesting twists and turns of the pathway it follows.

Although you may see some of the same sights on two different narrative trips, each story is a unique excursion by virtue of the interaction of plot and point of view. When a narrator tells you that "Frank loves Josie," for example, you're introduced to a situation you've encountered in literature many times before. How Frank loves Josie, what happens to Frank and Josie, and from what angle (where) you view their love constitute a plot of that story as it is told through the special world view of its narrator. This interaction between plot and point of view distinguishes the love story of Frank and Josie from all other romances. Plot is such a major structure in the epic mode that it brings together *all* the other power sources, creating life-giving tensiveness through the interaction of ideas, imagery (setting), character, time, and **style**[14] (including sound structures).

Ideas

One of the major reasons to choose a particular work of literature to adapt is a fascination with its themes and ideas. All literature derives power from the ideas that permeate it; in the epic mode, ideas generate a special interest because they come to the reader through a hierarchy of authority levels.

The statements of the narrator can be confirmed or contradicted by actions and ideas of the characters, or by the implied author who speaks through the work as a whole. In other words, the possibility that either the narrator or a character is unreliable makes it likely that some sort of ironic communication may be taking place in the epic mode. We're using *irony* to mean both verbal irony—a contrast between what a speaker says and what he means—and dramatic irony—a contrast between what a speaker says or thinks and the actual events. More than one set of values is often present in a literary work, and the search for levels of meanings is an important aspect of analysis. How do you view the opinions of Holden Caulfield in *Catcher in the Rye*, for example? Do you see the faults of the world through Holden's eyes or do you see an ironic juxtaposition between the faults of the world and the faults of Holden? Isn't Salinger sending the reader a double line of communication—a monologue from Holden and a subtle message from himself? Even more obvious is the ironic contradiction between the world view of the barber in "Haircut" and the world view the reader must judge to be that of Ring Lardner.

As adapter, you'll need to determine whether your literary work is ironic and, if it is, what kind of irony is present. When you believe the language used may have an intended meaning that isn't apparent on the surface, when there is an obvious contradiction (either stated or implied) between ideas, statements, or events, when language styles clash for no apparent reason, or when other kinds of incongruities appear, you'll recognize the presence of another level of communication. Does the narrator give the reader information that the characters don't have? Is the author making silent comments about the narrator? Are you, as the reader, and the narrator having fun at the expense of the character? Do you sense a tragic incongruity in the language and sequence of events in your selection? The ironic voice can convey humor, sarcasm, bitterness, pathos, tragedy, or any number of tonal nuances. A seemingly innocent comedy may hold a pathetic or bitter outcry against some aspect of life. A seemingly serious treatise may contain a jokester's wit. The doubleness of metaphor, paradox, and symbolism are all tools of the ironic writer.

When ironic tones are present, look for possible unreliability in the narrator or in a character in the story. Irony may become a major feature of a Chamber Theatre script and may be used as a principle for division of lines.

Imagery

While adapters of literature for Readers Theatre are interested in featuring the sensory life of their selection as part of the beauty of language itself, adapters of literature for Chamber Theatre are interested primarily in the way imagery contributes to setting and character. As the narrator unfolds the story, he describes actions and environments through the use of sensory appeals. The nature of the imagery used by a narrator is related to the point of view.

As with a camera lens, the narrator's relative distance from the scene being created determines the degree of panorama and detail in the imagery. A narrator who observes the actions from a distant perspective can see broadly, but not necessarily precisely. The narrator who is physically close to the action is limited in the amount he can see, but is nevertheless able to relate intricate detail. Objective narrators, like cameras, create images of characters in external environments. Subjective narrators focus on internal sensations of characters or on the external world as seen by characters.

Similarly, a narrator's attitude toward the scene being described will affect the color and shape of the images. Poe's narrators, for example, tend to see the world in dark colors and threatening shapes—images that contribute to the terror of the stories. The fragility of the images created by many of Katherine Mansfield's narrators, by contrast, gives her stories a characteristic delicacy. Imagery, particularly as it contributes to setting, is an important consideration in the transformation of the epic mode, because Chamber Theatre, more than Readers Theatre, uses pictorial space: the adapter will rely on an understanding of imagery for design of the stage setting.

Character

Character technically refers to any consciousness materialized by the author and, therefore, includes both the narrator and the participants in the action of the story. Throughout our discussion of Chamber Theatre, however, we make a distinction between the narrator and other characters in the story. Since the narrator is always given a voice and body in Chamber Theatre production, it becomes important to give as much attention to the analysis of the personality of the narrator as you give to any other major character of the story.

We look at characters in the epic mode in much the same way that we look at characters in other modes, but epic relationships suggest two additional aspects of character analysis: (1) the role of the narrator in shaping our understanding of other characters and (2) the nature of character thought processes.

The Role of the Narrator in Shaping Character

Since you see personae, objects, and events through the eyes of the storyteller, you can often learn a great deal about characters by studying the nature of the narrator who brings them to life. All narrators simultaneously reveal and withhold information; what a narrator tells or shows and how she or he tells and shows it not only shapes the story itself, but exposes the personality and value systems of that storyteller. When the objective narrator of "The Jockey" [see p. 73] observes, "He held his fork prongs downward on the plate and carefully piled on mushrooms with the blade of his knife," the reader gains a vivid impression of the character at the dinner table. But the adapter for Chamber Theatre also wants to know why the narrator chose those particular details and what the choice reveals about the nature of the narrator. Answers to these questions will come through analysis of similar details throughout the story, but it does seem clear at the outset that this narrator is a keen observer who values social graces. The storyteller's penchant for detail usually increases the reader's confidence in the accuracy of the observation and gives the narrator reliability.

In *A Portrait of the Artist as a Young Man* by James Joyce, the third person omniscient narrator is initially interested in building a close relationship between the reader and Stephen Dedalus; the narrator therefore chooses to show or tell only those actions which reveal the most about Stephen as he interacts with others in his world. The reader's **empathy** with Stephen is intensified by the narrator's vivid showing of such incidents as the pandying the young boy receives in his classroom:

> Stephen closed his eyes and held out in the air his trembling hand with the palm upwards. . . . A hot burning stinging tingling blow like the loud crack of a broken stick made his trembling hand crumple together like a leaf in the fire: and at the sound and the pain scalding tears were driven into his eyes.[15]

In this passage the narrator leads the reader into the sensory world of physical pain, deliberately excluding other emotions and social ramifications of the scene. Because the narrator is so close to the character, we perceive a rather selfless storyteller who seems to take a shared position in relation to Stephen—sharing the boy's childish language structures (as in the opening sentence of the book, ". . . this moocow . . . met a nicens little boy named baby tuckoo,"[16] and sharing attitudes and sensations throughout the story.

As the character of Stephen Dedalus matures, however, the narrator's partnership with him adjusts: Stephen gains independence from his narrator in much the same way that he gains personal independence from his family. While the narrator's empathy with Stephen isn't diminished, his sympathy for the character changes; he shows Stephen first as a fallible human being and, at the end of the book, as a character whose ego has distorted his view of the world. Stephen's later judgments of his friends are often colored by his own sense of superiority, as in his images of his fellow student Lynch:

> The long slender flattened skull beneath the long pointed cap brought before Stephen's mind the image of a hooded reptile. The eyes, too, were reptilelike in glint and gaze. Yet at that instant, humbled and alert in their look, they were lit by one tiny human point, the window of a shrivelled soul, poignant and self-embittered.[17]

As a reader, you may lose some confidence in Stephen's reliability, but you trust the perceptions of the narrator, whose decisions to reveal or withhold information seem always to be a function of his honest paternal concern for Stephen. In third person interior viewpoints, the narrator often serves as a guide, focusing upon the personalities and value systems of the characters in the story.

The personality and value systems of the storyteller are most obvious when the story is told by a first person narrator, especially when she is a major character in the story. There is a much greater sense of the personality of the narrator, with all the events and characters being filtered through a single limited point of view.

Some first person narrators tend to impose their value systems upon the story much more so than do others, and are therefore more visible throughout the story than are their less dominant counterparts. Holden Caulfield, for example, dominates *Catcher in the Rye* almost completely, rarely relinquishing his central position as teller of the story and peppering his narration with vivid word choices characteristic of his personality. Mrs. de Winter, the first person narrator of Daphne de Maurier's *Rebecca*, on the other hand, often steps aside to allow the action to be shown directly. Even in the long narrative passages of *Rebecca*, you can sense Mrs. de Winter's relative self-effacement.

Regardless of the degree of dominance, the *reliability* of the first person narrator is always in question. To what extent is the narrator reporting facts as we believe them to occur? Are there personal motives, conscious or unconscious, that would cause the narrator to distort the view of character we are shown? The narrator of Truman Capote's "My Side of the Matter," for example, needs to depict the other characters in the story as unjust persecutors to justify his own actions:

But it's what Eunice has done to Marge that really takes the cake. She has turned that girl against me in the most villainous fashion that words could not describe. Why, she even reached the point where she was sassing me back, but I provided her with a couple of good slaps and put a stop to that.[18]

This distortion of character seems fairly apparent to the reader, and is actually part of the charm of the story.

The narrator of "At the Zoo" by Jean Stafford, on the other hand, seems to be fair and reasonably reliable, questioning her own motives as she tells the story of herself and her sister:

Consequently, Daisy and I also became suspicious. But it was suspicion of ourselves that made us mope and weep and grimace with self-judgment. Why were we not happy when Gran had sacrificed herself to the bone for us? Why did we not cut dead the paper boy who had called her a filthy name?[19]

The narrator's self-evaluation leads the reader to accept her as objective and thus reliable. It is only at the end of the story that the reader realizes the larger implications of these questions and suspects the ability of the narrator to tell an accurate story. The narrator is in the club car of a train, writing a letter to her sister, to whom she has just said good-bye:

"There is a Roman Catholic priest (that is to say, he is *dressed* like one) sitting behind me although all the chairs on the opposite side of the car are empty. I can only conclude that he is looking over my shoulder, and while I do not want to cause you any alarm, I think you would be advised to be on the lookout for any appearance of miraculous medals, scapulars, papist booklets, etc., in the shops of your town. It really makes me laugh to see the way he is pretending that all he wants is for me to finish this letter so that he can have the table."[20]

The narrator's obvious paranoia causes you to reconsider your willing acceptance of her earlier account. Now you become painfully aware that all your understanding of the characters in the story is through the eyes of an obviously warped personality. Because your judgments of character have been shaped by the narrator throughout the story, you suddenly realize you must reevaluate what you've accepted as true.

The ways in which narrators shape characters are significant features of the epic mode and help determine the nature of a Chamber Theatre script. The other unique feature of the character power source in the epic mode is the ability of the narrative process to reveal the mental action of characters.

Character Thought Processes

Although lyric personae often engage in disclosure of personal thoughts, it is the epic mode that seems to feature most successfully the relationships between the interior worlds of characters' or narrators' minds and the exterior worlds of observable behavior. Much of the information known about characters in the epic mode comes through the narrator's ability to let readers become privy to the inner workings of the characters' consciousnesses. The reader's sense of sharing in a character's thought processes is strongest in stream of consciousness novels or in tales told in the first person by major characters.

As you examine characters (including narrators) in the epic mode, you discover a significant feature of the way in which the human mind works—a feature that can become a major focus of a Chamber Theatre script: mental action is inherently dramatic.

The Drama of the Human Mind

You carry in your consciousness a host of selves that can play imaginary roles for you at a moment's notice and that exist on at least three levels of consciousness. All of us have experienced a presence or tiny voice that speaks to us from time to time without our willing it to do so. Such dramatic voices are part of your **submerged self**—those imbedded forces that are the pricking of conscience, the gnawing hunch or instinct, or the feeling, simply, that "something told me this was the right choice" or "I had a feeling I shouldn't do it." Such voices are rarely separated from a person's sense of self; they make up a good deal of who you are, and as such are part of the core of your individual personality.

When you bring voices, or selves, to the conscious surface of thought, you begin to feel the presence of a **dramatic self**, a part of yourself that tends to be characterized somewhat separately, such as an alter ego, but still is part of your own consciousness. When you say, "I said to myself," or, "I keep telling myself," you invoke the presence of another voice within your mind—a listening self—which is more fully developed than the voice of your submerged self.

Your most dramatic staging of inner voices is your **projected self**—those parts you freely play within the confidentialities of your own thought processes. The action of your projected self allows you to take on the roles of external characters in a specific scene, often in an alternative time frame from the one in which you're currently living. Creative dramatists refer to the action of the projected self as evidence of human beings' inherent dramatic natures. Dorothy Heathcote suggests that there are two activities of the projected self: **preliving** (projecting selves into a future scene) and **reliving** (projecting selves into a past experience).

> Pre-living play takes place when we are looking forward to an event we fear or savour. . . . We "see" it in our minds happening in many different ways, trying to choose which is the most acceptable, which the most likely. We may indeed rehearse the words we shall use, and guess some of the replies that might come.[21]

Reliving inner dreams, according to Heathcote, "come[s] after such events, or after events that have gone strangely, inexplicably right or wrong. . . . How one plays with such events in one's mind!"[22]

The more complex you are as a person, the more various are your submerged selves, your dramatic selves, and your projected selves; collectively, they make up the inner workings and outer projections of your mind. Literary characters, like you, have hosts of selves that intrude on their thought processes from time to time. When you hear the direct words of a first person narrator or follow a third person omniscient narrator's probing of thought within characters, you're often aware of various voices or selves being revealed.

An example of the submerged self is found in "Horses—One Dash" by Stephen Crane: "Richardson longed to run. But in this threatening gloom, his terror [submerged self] convinced him that a move on his part would be a signal for the pounce of death."[23] The narrator of *A Por-*

trait of the Artist as a Young Man reveals Stephen's consciousness of the presence of a dramatic self
when he says: "Stephen had forgiven freely for he had found this rudeness also in himself towards himself [dramatic self]."[24]

In literature, projected selves engage more often in preliving than in reliving, as in the following example from "Paul's Case" by Willa Cather, when Paul imagines his father's reaction to
his late arrival: "He would not go in. He would tell his father that he had no car fare, and it was
raining so hard he had gone home with one of the boys and stayed all night."[25]

Often the submerged self, the dramatic self, and the projected self are interwoven in literature so that the *projected* scene is composed of two or more dramatic selves who reflect aspects of
submerged voices. An example of this phenomenon is found in "Pnin" by Vladimir Nabokov:
"Pnin debated with himself his next move [dramatic self] or, rather, mediated in a debate [pro-
jected scene] between weary-brained Pnin, [submerged self], who had not been sleeping well
lately, and an insatiable Pnin [submerged self] who wished to continue reading at home."[26]

As you become aware of the intricacies of narrator-character relationships in the epic
mode, you find that the power source of character is inherently tensive. The narrator's perceptions shape character, and character delineations reveal the narrator.

Time

Since Interpreters Theatre, like all theatre, is a temporal medium, adapters are always interested
in the way time functions in the literary selection they're about to stage. All literature exists in
time and time exists in all literature, especially the sense of time that is predominantly psychological in nature.

If time is a central power source in all literature, how can adaptors of the epic mode distinguish the specific characteristics of narrative time from the lyric mode's use of time or the temporal organization of the dramatic mode? Speaking generally, the pure lyric mode tends to be
more interested in subjective time, to step outside objective time while revealing inner thoughts
and feelings that have no real temporal connection to the external world, but that live in the persona's own psychological sense of time. In the dramatic mode, however, characters tend to live in
a kind of perpetual present tense, as time moves forward in each scene. Unlike the pure lyric's
form, dramatic action has a very real relationship to external clock time; character change occurs
in the objective time system of the world of the play or dramatic poem. Dramatic dialogue has
a presence that is of the here and now, largely because of the characters' use of present-tense
verbs in their conversation. Susanne Langer suggests that the dramatic mode is actually future-
oriented because characters in drama are always "becoming," always impelled toward the next
moment.[27]

The epic mode is most interested in the dimension of past time and how experiences in the
past intrude upon present time. The epic mode's use of time involves a temporal doubleness; the
mode is characteristically interested in the past as it relates to the present. The relationship between the temporal dimensions of past and present can take many forms. All narrators exist in
the present tense at the level of contact with the reader; their movement into the past, and out
again, constitutes the major double time frame of the epic mode: that the storyteller, who exists
in the present, tells a story that happened in the past. The third person narrator has no personal
identity in past time, but the first person narrator exists in both the present and the past.

A narrator uses several techniques to build the relationship between the past and the present. Flashback, one of the most common devices, is used by third person narrators to weave sections of past history into the story being told. The term *flashback* implies a kind of scenic presentation (flash), as if the narrator were able to recreate the past occurrence to show it to the reader directly. Identification of moments of flashback is important for the Chamber Theatre director, because variations in the time frames of action suggest specialized scripting and staging techniques to feature the contrasts in time.

First person narrators engage in four major relationships with past time: **reporting, reevaluating, recalling,** and **reliving**. To report is to refer to events in the past from a definite orientation to the present; the narrator's primary attention is on the present act of telling, as in the following example: "I went to a British school as a child—were they ever strict!" Reevaluating carries with it a blending of past and present. In a moment of reevaluation, the first person narrator reconsiders past experience in light of present tense awareness. The past, therefore, takes on a new significance or a new interpretation as a result of the present tense narrator's ability to see the past again: "I never realized it at the time, but those strict teachers really taught me how to think." As S. Alexander notes in *Space-Time and Deity*, "Memories are outgrowths of present perception."[28] In a curious way, reevaluated events are given a present tense time dimension while still retaining their pastness.

Recalling is more closely linked with the past than reporting or reevaluating. In moments of recall, images and thoughts become more vivid, stimulating some of the sensations and feelings of the past without reliving it: "Even in the fourth grade, I used to carry so many books home that my arms would ache. Sometimes the books were so heavy I thought I'd never make it home."

The past comes to life more fully when the narrator relives it, as if she were able to return, literally, to a past tense existence. Almost ironically, reliving the past gives it a presence that seems to remove it from its pastness and bring it into the present, such as when images and attitudes have such a degree of immediacy that the narrator, as character, seems to be feeling them again: "Once the teacher called on me when I wasn't prepared. I began to shake all over and got sick to my stomach. 'I-I'm sorry, Mr. Chaytor. I forgot to take my book home.'"

The differences between reporting and reevaluating in the present tense, recalling the past, and reliving the past are subtle, but they're very useful for Chamber Theatre adapter-directors for indications of line division and staging. To distinguish further these four states, consider your reactions to a common emotion, embarrassment. When you say you were embarrassed once, you're reporting; when you can laugh about it, you're reevaluating; when you remember how mortified you were, you're recalling; when your face begins to flush and your stomach knots, you're reliving. As first person narrators move from present tense reporting to recalling to reliving, they make the full transition from present to past and can, of course, return to the present as swiftly as they left it. Such movement in time is characteristic of the epic mode.

Narrators use many other techniques of temporal reorganization in the epic mode. Interior omniscient storytellers have the ability to relate simultaneous actions as a way of layering moments of experience. In Conrad Aiken's "Silent Snow, Secret Snow," for example, the reader is shown the stages in a young boy's progress toward schizophrenia. In one segment, the boy is sitting in his elementary school classroom, listening halfheartedly to the teacher explain a geography lesson. While the teacher is lecturing about the north and south poles, the boy's mind slips into an elaborate daydream about snow. To show that the boy's reverie and the teacher's lesson are occurring simultaneously, the narrator inserts half sentences of the teacher's lecture into the boy's thought processes, as if part of the boy is listening to the teacher while the other half dreams of snow. Exterior omniscient narrators can approximate the same effect by using the word *meanwhile*. A Chamber Theatre director can show simultaneity of events literally by staging them together, for example, and letting both scenes run at the same time.

The most significant contemporary technique of time-ordering is stream of consciousness narration, in which a storyteller reveals the thought processes of a character directly. Twentieth-century novelists such as James Joyce, Virginia Woolf, and William Faulkner have experimented most with stream of consciousness writing. When an omniscient narrator enters the psyche of a character, showing the character's thoughts directly, objective time is suspended and replaced by a new dimension of personal duration, or *dureé*, as Henri Bergson has named it.[29] Moments of *dureé* are always in present tense because they allow the reader to hear the character's thoughts as they occur. Such moments seem to be out of time in much the same way that the lyric expressions are out of time. Stream of consciousness sequences, then, tend to be lyric elements acting within the epic mode. Scripts of stream of consciousness novels are likely to use techniques described in Chapter 3, such as a chorus of voices, to highlight the essentially lyric quality of sustained consciousness shown directly.

Throughout analysis of the epic mode, the adapter for Chamber Theatre recognizes the essential power of time as an organizing principle of all narrative action. Narrators skillfully blend temporal states at every moment of storytelling; "once upon a time" is indeed an indicator that you are about to see and hear of people and events in time. Recognizing that time is a major power source, you can learn more about the specific ways time is manipulated by storytellers by examining the narrator's language.

Time Systems

Three major temporal systems are available to all narrators: **equivalent time, suspended time,** and **condensed time.** When narrators normalize the progression of time in a story to correspond to clock time, they are using equivalent time. In equivalent time, it takes the same amount of time to relate an action as the action itself takes (or took) to happen. All dialogue exists in an equivalent time system because it takes the reader the same amount of time to read (or perform) a line of dialogue as it does (or did) for the character to speak the line of dialogue. In addition to dialogue, blow-by-blow accounts of action (which could occur in the same amount of time it takes the narrator to relate them) exist in equivalent time: "He slammed his fist on the desk, and then slowly, steadily, reached for the letter."

A narrator will move into the suspended time system to halt the flow of the story temporarily to fill in details. In suspended time, it takes more time to relate an action than it takes (or took) to happen. An image, for example, flashes through a character's mind, but the storyteller needs considerable time to capture the image in words: "Suddenly, with an overwhelming feeling of *déjà vu*, the image of her father's face superimposed itself on the face of her husband, and the grizzled eyebrows, tightly set jaw, and piercing gray eyes seemed to live again for a brief moment."

When narrators speed up the progression of time in the story to cover information quickly, they're using condensed time. The familiar use of condensed time, "And they lived happily ever after," shows that the narrator in this time system takes less time to tell an action than it takes (or took) to happen.

All narrators tend to use all three time systems in an interwoven pattern. The movement, in fact, between the three systems sets up a kind of rhythm that is part of the story's style.

Verbal Actions Within Time Systems

Once the fundamental time systems have been identified, it becomes clear that characters and narrators often perform verbal actions in different time frames within time systems. To help describe those actions, we may use the familiar terms **scene, description**, and **summary**, which are verbal actions corresponding to the time systems of equivalent time, suspended time, and condensed time. Within an equivalent time system, for example, a character in dialogue may depict action in scene, may describe, or may summarize. Figure 4.1 shows the variety of actions possible within the three time systems and provides an example of each. As a narrator moves from an equivalent time system to a condensed time system, we sense a shift from showing to telling. Similarly, the verbal action of creating scene tends to be a kind of showing, whereas the verbal action of summarizing is an aspect of telling.

Time is one of the most significant power sources in the epic mode because all narration exists in time. Characters and events move through time; skillful narrators manipulate time in tight patterns, creating rhythms of showing and telling that can be overtly realized on the Chamber Theatre stage. An understanding of the way time shifts in an epic mode selection becomes one of several guides to the division of voices in a script. A temporal analysis also suggests special uses of stage space and clarifies questions of narrative focus in the staged Chamber Theatre production.

Style

It has been said that "a man's style is his mind's voice. Wooden minds, wooden voices." These words epitomize the close relationship between language style and character or personality. Our concern with style in the epic mode centers on the manner in which an individual character expresses in language his or her view of the world. From an examination of the style of a story, adapters gain two major insights into the work: (1) they learn something of the nature and attitude of the character using the language, and (2) they learn to distinguish which character (or which self) is doing the speaking or thinking. In other words, style gives you, as adapter, important clues to characterization and to action of the narrator in relation to the other characters in the story, thereby suggesting casting requirements and scripting techniques for Chamber Theatre.

Style and Character

Often one of the first aspects of style you notice in a work is the choice of words, or **diction**. Diction is an important indicator of the kind of mind being presented. Are the words predominantly short and simple ("The car began to move") or does the speaker use more complex

Narrator's Use of Time Systems	Narrator's or Character's Verbal Action Within Time Systems	
Equivalent Time	Direct and Indirect Dialogue (Characters)	Scene: Marge said, "As Clare's fingers touched the travel folder, she took a deep breath. Then she picked it up, and slowly handed it to him."
		Description: "Even in such a quick glance at the picture," continued Marge, "I noticed that her eyes began to dance, the corners of her mouth turned up, and her cheeks flushed with excitement."
		Summary: Marge said, "For years and years Clare has told me she wanted to go to Europe."
	Blow-by-blow Reporting of Action (Narrator)	Scene: Marge watched Clare as her fingers touched the travel folder. She took a deep breath, and then slowly handed it to her husband.
Suspended Time		Scene: In a flash Clare saw herself sitting at an outdoor cafe in Paris, sipping cognac and glancing covertly at the attractive man at the next table.
		Description: The folder she held in her hand was printed on slick paper with multicolored pictures of dancing girls and pyramids.
		Summary: Her gray eyes with their long lashes and carefully penciled brows spoke of the long years of her unfulfilled desire and rebellious dissatisfaction.
Condensed Time		Summary: Throughout all of her life she had wanted to travel but her father would never let her leave the farm.

Showing ←————————————————————————→ Telling

Figure 4.1: Epic time structures.

and unusual diction ("The Oldsmobile rocketed into motion")? Do the words seem charged with emotion ("I despise you!") or do they operate on a more precise, controlled level ("I don't approve of your actions")? Does the speaker choose concrete images ("rose") as opposed to speaking in more abstract terms ("beauty")? Does the persona tend to use evaluative adjectives and adverbs that connote a judgmental attitude ("She was a good little girl") or does she speak more descriptively ("She always helped her mother with the dishes")? What are the evidences of history or culture in the language? Use of idioms ("like rollin' off a log"), regionalisms ("Aw, shucks!") or old-fashioned words ("bundling") can evoke a whole world view in an instant. Even a character's profession may be signaled by his or her diction, as when a lawyer speaks of "judicial matters." In short, you may learn a great deal about the world of a character simply by studying the character's choice of words.

Syntax, or the way words are put together, is the second major aspect of style that helps to create character. The grammatical error in the sentence fragment "I got no," as opposed to "I haven't any" or "I have no," immediately connotes lack of education and cultural background. Also, poetic inclinations of a character may be revealed through the rearrangement of traditional sentence order—"Often have I thought of you" as opposed to "I have thought of you often." When a character or narrator builds cause and effect relationships (through the use of such words as "because of" and "therefore"), you see a careful reasoning process in operation. Other characters or narrators may deliberately structure their statements noncausally—"this happened, this happened, and then this happened"—which suggests a kind of existential interest in action. Kinds of sentences—long or short, simple or complex, interrogative or declarative, expressive or indicative, fragmentary or complete—shape the reader's impressions of the speaking character. Long or complex sentences often give an impression of formality, whereas short exclamations tend to suggest speed and informality and, perhaps, an impulsive nature. Questions can create a directness and intimacy between speaker and reader, and sentence fragments are typical of the casual conversationalist. How a character speaks is more indicative of personality than any aspect of external appearance.

Diction and syntax work together to create a rhythmic texture, which also characterizes the speaker. The nervous staccato of a series of short simple sentences or clauses contrasts with the stately undulations of rolling clauses, not only signaling variations in mood and attitude, but also suggesting fundamental personality differences. Notice the conversational casualness suggested by vocabulary and clause length in this passage from *The Pooh Perplex* by Frederick C. Crews:

> Let's see—I guess first off I should tell you that Al's book was for kids, I mean originally, before us longhairs got on to it. Now, of course, everybody's reading it, along with Kafka, Proust, Dostoevski, and the other really big people.[30]

In contrast, the following passage of Sir Thomas Browne's moves with a smoother, more regular pace:

> The particulars of future beings must needs be dark unto ancient theories, which Christian philosophy yet determines but in a cloud of opinions. A dialogue between two infants in the womb concerning the state of this world, might handsomely illustrate our ignorance of the text, whereof methinks we yet discourse in Plato's den, and are but embryo philosophers. . . .[31]

While a particular rhythm is often characteristic of the total work of an author and will help to distinguish one author from another, if the author has been careful, rhythm will also distinguish one character from another in the same work.

Style and Narrator Action

The pattern of movement created by the narrator's showing or telling in time and space is the primary level of action in the epic mode—its presentational form. Thus, action in the epic mode consists not only of interaction among characters, but also of the narrator's shifting of position in relation to the story being told. For you as a Chamber Theatre adapter, narrative movement becomes a major factor in scripting and staging, since both division of lines and the physical location of performers onstage are dependent on your analysis of the narrator's movement. Identifying the narrator's movement as a sequence of locus (or position) changes in time or space allows the adapter to ask, at each moment, "Where is the character (or narrator) in space? Where is she in time?" Changes in temporal locus are often signaled by verb tenses that bring into focus a complexity of time and action. Whether a narrator chooses to say "he walks," "he is walking," "he walked," "he will walk," "he would walk," or "he would have walked" gives the adapter information about the narrator's relationship in time to the walker and about the narrator's knowledge of the intentions of the walker.[32]

A first person narrator has a different frame of reference than a third person narrator, which results in a fundamental difference in movement. The first person narrator moves in **psychic time** between past and present; the third person narrator, although making use of time systems, moves in **psychic space** between the narrator's own consciousness and the consciousnesses of the characters. General language style (diction, syntax, rhythm, verb tense, and person) provides clues to immediate position and pattern of movement for both first person and third person narrators.

First Person Narrators. A first person narrator usually moves back and forth in time between telling in the present and showing and telling in the past. Once the past memory is set into motion, past and present seem to exist simultaneously, creating a dual presence: "I in the present" and "I in the past." The tensiveness created by the interaction of these two presences and the relative degree of control exerted by the present narrator over the past self combine to form the primary action of the first person narrator. (A few first person narrators speak only in present tense—"I am walking down Main Street"—in which case the illusion is given (through both showing and telling) that the story is happening as it's being told. The dual presence created by this use of tense is composed of "I as teller" and "I as actor.")

First person narrators use the techniques of reporting, reevaluating, recalling, and reliving to link past with the present. As the narrator moves into the past, characters and events from an earlier time become more vivid and immediate; the narrator's perspective and control over the story is less apparent. Figure 4.2 indicates the movement of the first person narrator between present and past, and reflects the narrator's use of time systems as narrative action shifts among reporting, reevaluating, recalling, and reliving.

Generally, narrators who tell in the present use condensed time, summarizing in a few moments events that took much more time in the past. As first person narrators move closer to

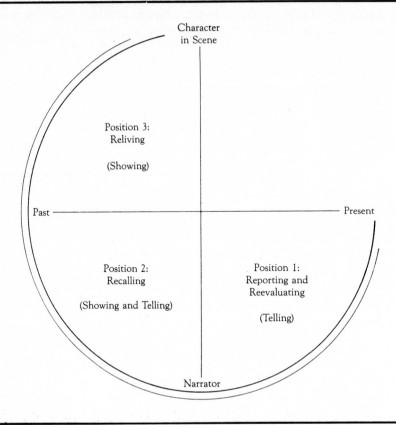

Figure 4.2: First person narrative movement in psychic time.

reliving the past, they begin to make greater use of suspended and equivalent time. During moments of recall, narrators often suspend time to give descriptions increasing in detail as events become more vivid in their memories. When reliving the past, first person narrators use equivalent time, letting the scene progress at its original pace. How do you, as an adapter, determine whether a narrator is speaking in present time or in past time? The checklist in figure 4.3 provides some guidelines to help you follow the first person narrator's movement in time.

Third Person Narrators. The general movement of the third person storyteller is located either (1) in the exterior—taking place in objective time and space or (2) in the interior—taking place in psychic space between the mind of the narrator and the mind of one or more of the characters. Although the third person narrator (objective or omniscient) who maintains an exterior position may constantly shift the reader's orientation in the external world of the story, the reader is always aware that it is the *narrator* who is speaking unless quotation marks are present. You can easily distinguish characters from the narrator because characters usually speak in dialogue.

Checklist for First Person Narrative Movement

I. Narrators are located in the present (position 1) when:
  A. They judge past experience in light of their present perspective
  B. They make references to their own present activity
    1. They address the reader directly
    2. They discuss the act of storytelling
    3. They refer to their present personal life or situation
  C. They exhibit a greater maturity than was evident in their earlier selves
    1. Their diction and syntax are more sophisticated
    2. Their attitudes reflect their development as persons.

II. Narrators are beginning to move into the past (position 2) when:
  A. Images of the past become more vivid and detailed
  B. They remember specific thoughts and feelings they experienced in the past
  C. They share indirect dialogue from the past in their present language style

III. Narrators are located in the past (position 3) when:
  A. They reproduce direct dialogue from the past
  B. They share indirect dialogue in the language style of past characters
  C. They relive immediate sensations, emotions, and thoughts of the past

Figure 4.3: Checklist for first person narrative movement.

Interior narrators (always omniscient to some degree) change position in relation to the internal worlds of characters, sometimes standing back and sometimes moving inside characters' minds. This movement causes the reader to ask, "Whose perceptions am I being given—the character's or the narrator's?" Generally, third person narrators with interior omniscience move from (1) external telling, in which the narrator's presence in the story is most visible, through (2) internal telling and (3) internal showing in which the consciousness of the narrator becomes intermingled with that of the characters in varying degrees, to (4) external showing, in which the narrator steps aside to let the characters speak aloud. These various positions represent hypothetical stations in the narrator's complex movement through psychic space. Language style and verbal actions help identify the narrator's locus at any given moment and tell you whose interior view is being revealed. Figure 4.4 gives a graphic representation of the third person narrator's movement, which affects the narrator's relationship to the characters and reflects the narrator's use of time and space. A narrator may be located at any point along this path of movement at any moment in the story; also the narrator may move in any direction among these four positions, without regard to the sequence implied by the chart.

Whenever an omniscient third person narrator is telling, the major focus is on the narrator and the quality of the telling. Whenever a third person narrator shows the words or actions of a character, the major focus is on the character. As the narrator moves from position 1, in which the narrator is most central, toward position 2 (internal telling), she seems to move closer to the character to report internal thoughts and feelings. The narrator in position 2 still retains a kind of objectivity, sometimes even an ironic perspective, that isn't found in the fully empathic stance of position 3.

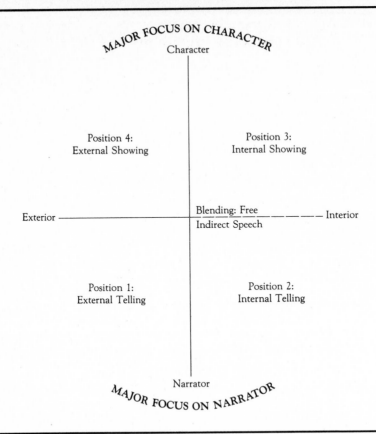

Figure 4.4: Third person omniscient narrative movement in psychic space.

Sometimes narrators blend their objectivity with the character's subjectivity, in a kind of intermediate stage between positions 2 and 3. You know this kind of blending is taking place when you see the syntactical structure termed *free indirect speech*.[33] In free indirect speech, the narrator refers to the character in the third person and uses past or conditional verb tenses to create the immediacy of the character's feelings. Free indirect speech differs from dialogue—" 'I hate that wreck of a house' "—and indirect dialogue—"He said he hated the house"—in that the statement comes with the emotional force of direct dialogue but the presence of the third person and past tense seems to hold it back—"He hated that wreck of a house."

Free indirect speech can take two major forms. On one hand, the narrator may sincerely feel with the character, in which case a kind of fusion occurs, a true empathy between narrator and character: "How time had ravaged the place; certainly he had been away too long." The reader feels no division in attitude here between the narrator and character. On the other hand, the narrator may only seem to feel with the character for ironic purposes. In this kind of merging, the narrator is seeking a true meeting with the mind of the reader at the character's expense: "To have come home to this! Why should he soil his hands cleaning it up?" Although the narrator

Checklist for Third Person Narrative Movement

I. Narrators are speaking from their own perspectives (position 1) when:
   A. They summarize external events
   B. They describe a character or scene
   C. They report observable action
      1. They comment upon the action
      2. They give a blow-by-blow account of the action
   D. They report indirect dialogue in their own words

II. Narrators are speaking from a position of contact with a character's consciousness (position 2) when:
   A. They reveal a character's thoughts and feelings in the narrator's own language
   B. They comment upon a character's internal actions

III. Narrators blend their objectivity with a character's subjectivity (free indirect speech) when:

   A. They create an immediacy of the character's feelings expressed in past tense and third person
   B. They remove the dialogue tags ("He said that," "She said") from indirect dialogue to give the statements the impact of direct dialogue without quotation marks.

IV. Narrators speak from a position inside the character's consciousness (position 3) when:
   A. They seem to be looking at the world through the eyes of the character
      1. The character's perspective totally dominates
      2. The character's language is used
   B. They show stream of consciousness thinking—both formed and unformed thoughts

V. Narrators show from an external location (position 4) when they present direct dialogue, with or without quotation marks

Figure 4.5: Checklist for third person narrative movement.

seems to help the character make this statement, as a reader, you feel that the narrator is really asking you to step back with him or her to take a criticial look at the character. Free indirect speech, therefore, blends position 2 and position 3.

The movement from the empathic identification between narrator and character (position 3) toward position 4 allows characters to speak for themselves in direct dialogue. In this position the narrator throws major focus on the characters by letting us see them in scene. The checklist in figure 4.5 provides guidelines for tracing the third person narrator's movement in space.

The plotting of the narrator's movement is a useful way to analyze point of view. Think of these positions as movement tendencies that occur in narration, rather than as fixed patterns. You'll discover you can look at a single narrative relationship in several ways, especially as you begin to work with these relationships more specifically in line division. Remember that what we've given you is a set of analytic tools that should reveal possibilities and help you to recognize false judgments; these are not rules.

CREATING A SAMPLE TEXT FOR CHAMBER THEATRE

We have chosen to adapt "The New Dress" by Virginia Woolf[34] for the Chamber Theatre stage, as a way of demonstrating how to transform a text from page to stage. We selected this short story because it's strongly epic—there's a strong sense of a story (or experience) and a storyteller, even though this narrator is often self-effacing—and because the deep interior view of this third person omniscient narrator presents problems for the adapter that can be shown best by example. The quality of the main character's consciousness is intriguing, as are the subtly shifting positions of the narrator as she probes that consciousness. (The gender of the narrator in "The New Dress" is not specified. We refer to this narrator as female, following our custom of endowing an unidentified narrator with the same sex as its author.) Furthermore, "The New Dress" has the environmental appeal of a polite social gathering that would be fun to stage, and it fits our practical considerations: it's short enough that we can reprint the entire story for you.

The New Dress

Virginia Woolf

Mabel had her first serious suspicion that something was wrong as she took her cloak off and Mrs. Barnet, while handing her the mirror and touching the brushes and thus drawing her attention, perhaps rather markedly, to all the appliances for tidying and improving hair, complexion, clothes, which existed on the dressing table, confirmed the suspicion—that it was not right, not quite right, which growing stronger as she went upstairs and springing at her with conviction as she greeted Clarissa Dalloway, she went straight to the far end of the room, to a shaded corner where a looking-glass hung and looked. No! It was not right. And at once the misery which she always tried to hide, the profound dissatisfaction—the sense she had had, ever since she was a child, of being inferior to other people—set upon her, relentlessly, remorselessly, with an intensity which she could not beat off, as she would when she woke at night at home, by reading Borrow or Scott; for, oh, these men, oh, these women, all were thinking— "What's Mabel wearing? What a fright she looks! What a hideous new dress!"—their eyelids flickering as they came up and then their lids shutting rather tight. It was her own appalling inadequacy; her cowardice; her mean, water-sprinkled blood that depressed her. And at once the whole of the room where, for ever so many hours, she had planned with the little dressmaker how it was to go, seemed sordid, repulsive; and her own drawing-room so shabby, and herself, going out, puffed up with vanity as she touched the letters on the hall table and said: "How dull!" to show off—all this now seemed unutterably silly, paltry, and provincial. All this had been absolutely destroyed, shown up, exploded, the moment she came into Mrs. Dalloway's drawing-room.

What she had thought that evening when, sitting over the teacups, Mrs. Dalloway's invitation came, was that, of course, she could not be fashionable. It was absurd to pretend to even—fashion meant cut, meant style, meant thirty guineas at least—but why not be original? Why not be herself, anyhow? And, getting up, she had taken that old fashion book of her mother's, a Paris fashion book of the time of the Empire, and had thought how much prettier, more dignified, and more womanly, they were then, and so set herself—oh, it was foolish—trying to be like them, pluming herself in fact upon being modest and old-fashioned and very charming, giving herself up, no doubt about it, to an orgy of self-love which deserved to be chastised, and so rigged herself out like this.

But she dared not look in the glass. She could not face the whole horror—the pale yellow, idiotically old-fashioned silk dress with its long skirt and its high sleeves and its waist and all the things that looked so charming in the fashion book, but not on her, not among all these ordinary people. She felt like a dressmaker's dummy standing there for young people to stick pins into.

"But, my dear, it's perfectly charming!" Rose Shaw said, looking her up and down with that little satirical pucker of the lips which she expected—Rose herself being dressed in the height of the fashion, precisely like everybody else, always.

"We are all like flies trying to crawl over the edge of the saucer," Mabel thought, and repeated the phrase as if she were crossing herself, as if she were trying to find some spell to annul this pain, to make this agony endurable. Tags of Shakespeare, lines from books she had read ages ago, suddenly came to her when she was in agony, and she repeated them over and over again. "Flies trying to crawl," she repeated. If she could say that over often enough and make herself see the flies, she would become numb, chill, frozen, dumb. Now she could see flies crawling slowly out of a saucer of milk with their wings stuck together; and she strained and strained (standing in front of the looking-glass, listening to Rose Shaw) to make herself see Rose Shaw and all the other people there as flies, trying to hoist themselves out of something, or into something, meager, insignificant toiling flies. But she could not see them like that, not other pepole. She saw herself like that—she was a fly, but the others were dragonflies, butterflies, beautiful insects, dancing, fluttering, skimming, while she alone dragged herself up out of the saucer. (Envy and spite, the most detestable of the vices, were her chief faults.)

"I feel like some dowdy, decrepit, horribly dingy old fly," she said, making Robert Haydon stop to hear her say that, just to reassure herself by furbishing up a poor weak-kneed phrase and so showing how detached she was, how witty, that she did not feel in the least out of anything. And, of course, Robert Haydon answered something quite polite, quite insincere, which she saw through instantly, and said to herself, directly he went (again from some book), "Lies, lies, lies!" For a party makes things either much more real or much less real, she thought; she saw in a flash to the bottom of Robert Haydon's heart; she saw through everything. She saw the truth. This was true, this drawing-room, this self, and the other false. Miss Milan's little work-room was really terribly hot, stuffy, sordid. It smelt of clothes and cabbage cooking; and yet, when Miss Milan put the glass in her hand, and she looked at herself with the dress on, finished, an extraordinary bliss shot through her heart. Suffused with light, she sprang into existence. Rid of cares and wrinkles, what she had dreamed of herself was there—a beautiful woman. Just for a second (she had not dared look longer, Miss Milan wanted to know about the length of the skirt), there looked at her, framed in the scrolloping mahogany, a grey-white, mysteriously smiling, charming girl, the core of herself, the soul of herself; and it was not vanity only, not only self-love that made her think it good, tender, and true. Miss Milan said that the skirt could not well be longer; if anything the skirt, said Miss Milan, puckering her forehead, considering with all her wits about her, must be shorter; and she felt, suddenly, honestly, full of love for Miss Milan, much, much fonder of Miss Milan than of anyone in the whole world, and could have cried for pity that she should be crawling on the floor with her mouth full of pins and her face red and her eyes bulging—that one human being should be doing this for another, and she saw them all as human beings merely, and herself going off to her party, and Miss Milan pulling the cover over the canary's cage, or letting him pick a hempseed from between her lips, and the thought of it, of this side of human nature and its patience and its endurance and its being content with such miserable, scanty, sordid, little pleasures filled her eyes with tears.

And now the whole thing had vanished. The dress, the room, the love, the pity, the scrolloping looking-glass, and the canary's cage—all had vanished, and here she was in a corner of Mrs. Dalloway's drawing-room suffering tortures, woken wide awake to reality.

But it was all so paltry, weak-blooded, and petty-minded to care so much at her age with two children, to be still so utterly dependent on people's opinions and not have principles or convictions, not to be able to say as other people did, "There's Shakespeare! There's death! We're all weevils in a captain's biscuit"—or whatever it was that people did say.

She faced herself straight in the glass; she pecked at her left shoulder; she issued out into the room, as if spears were thrown at her yellow dress from all sides. But instead of looking fierce or tragic, as Rose Shaw would have done—Rose would have looked like Boadicea—she looked foolish and self-conscious and simpered like a schoolgirl and slouched across the room, positively sinking, as if she were a beaten mongrel, and looked at a picture, an engraving. As if one went to a party to look at a picture! Everybody knew why she did it—it was from shame, from humiliation.

"Now the fly's in the saucer," she said to herself, "right in the middle, and can't get out, and the milk," she thought, rigidly staring at the picture, "is sticking its wings together."

"It's so old-fashioned," she said to Charles Burt, making him stop (which by itself he hated) on his way to talk to someone else.

She meant, or she tried to make herself think that she meant, that it was the picture and not her dress, that was old-fashioned. And one word of praise, one word of affection from Charles would have made all the difference to her at the moment. If he had only said, "Mabel, you're looking charming tonight!" it would have changed her life. But then she ought to have been truthful and direct. Charles said nothing of the kind, of course. He was malice itself. He always saw through one, especially if one were feeling particularly mean, paltry, or feeble-minded.

"Mabel's got a new dress!" he said, and the poor fly was absolutely shoved into the middle of the saucer. Really, he would like her to drown, she believed. He had no heart, no fundamental kindness, only a veneer of friendliness. Miss Milan was much more real, much kinder. If only one could feel that and stick to it, always. "Why," she asked herself—replying to Charles much too pertly, letting him see that she was out of temper, or "ruffled" as he called it ("Rather ruffled?" he said and went on to laugh at her with some woman over there)—"Why," she asked herself, "can't I feel one thing always, feel quite sure that Miss Milan is right, and Charles wrong and stick to it, feel sure about the canary and pity and love and not be whipped all round in a second by coming into a room full of people?" It was her odious, weak, vacillating character again, always giving at the critical moment and not being seriously interested in conchology, etymology, botany, archaeology, cutting up potatoes and watching them fructify like Mary Dennis, like Violet Searle.

Then Mrs. Holman, seeing her standing there, bore down upon her. Of course a thing like a dress was beneath Mrs. Holman's notice, with her family always tumbling downstairs or having the scarlet fever. Could Mabel tell her if Elmthorpe was ever let for August and September? Oh, it was a conversation that bored her unutterably!—it made her furious to be treated like a house agent or a messenger boy, to be made use of. Not to have value, that was it, she thought, trying to grasp something hard, something real, while she tried to answer sensibly about the bathroom and the south aspect and the hot water to the top of the house; and all the time she could see little bits of her yellow dress in the round looking-glass which made them all the size of boot-buttons or tadpoles; and it was amazing to think how much humiliation and agony and self-loathing and effort and passionate ups and downs of feeling were contained in a thing the size of a three-penny bit. And what was still odder, this thing, this Mabel Waring, was separate, quite disconnected; and though Mrs. Holman (the black button) was leaning forward and telling her how her eldest boy had strained his heart running, she could see her, too, quite detached in the looking-glass, and it was impossible that the black dot, leaning forward, gesticulating, should make the yellow dot, sitting solitary, self-centered, feel what the black dot was feeling, yet they pretended.

"So impossible to keep boys quiet"—that was the kind of thing one said.

And Mrs. Holman, who could never get enough sympathy and snatched what little there was greedily, as if it were her right (but she deserved much more for there was her little girl who had come down this morning with a swollen knee-joint), took this miserable offering and looked at it suspiciously, grudgingly, as if it were a halfpenny when it ought to have been a pound and put it away in her purse, must put up with it, mean and miserly though it was, times being hard, so very hard; and on she went, creaking, injured Mrs. Holman, about the girl with the swollen joints. Ah, it was tragic, this greed, this clamour of human beings, like a row of cormorants, barking and flapping their wings for sympathy—it was tragic, could one have felt it and not merely pretended to feel it!

But in her yellow dress tonight she could not wring out one drop more; she wanted it all, all for herself. She knew (she kept on looking into the glass, dipping into that dreadfully showing-up blue pool) that she was condemned, despised, left like this in a backwater, because of her being like this—a feeble, vacillating creature; and it seemed to her that the yellow dress was a penance which she had deserved, and if she had been dressed like Rose Shaw, in lovely, clinging green with a ruffle of swansdown, she would have deserved that; and she thought that there was no escape for her—none whatever. But it was not her fault altogether, after all. It was being one of a family of ten; never having money enough, always skimping and paring; and her mother carrying great cans, and the lineoleum worn on the stair edges, and one sordid little domestic tragedy after another—nothing catastrophic, the sheep farm failing, but not utterly; her eldest brother marrying beneath him but not very much—there was no romance, nothing extreme about them all. They petered out respectably in seaside resorts; every watering-place had one of her aunts even now asleep in some lodging with the front windows not quite facing the sea. That was so like them—they had to squint at things always. And she had done the same—she was just like her aunts. For all her dreams of living in India, married to some hero like Sir Henry Lawrence, some empire builder (still the sight of a native in a turban filled her with romance), she had failed utterly. She had married Hubert, with his safe, permanent underling's job in the Law Courts, and they managed tolerably in a smallish house, without proper maids, and hash when she was alone or just bread and butter, but now and then—Mrs. Holman was off, thinking her the most dried-up, unsympathetic twig she had ever met, absurdly dressed, too, and would tell everyone about Mabel's fantastic appearance—now and then, thought Mabel Waring, left alone on the blue sofa, punching the cushion in order to look occupied, for she would not join Charles Burt and Rose Shaw, chattering like magpies and perhaps laughing at her by the fireplace—now and then, there did come to her delicious moments, reading the other night in bed, for instance, or down by the sea on the sand in the sun, at Easter—let her recall it—a great tuft of pale sand-grass, standing all twisted like a shock of spears against the sky, which was blue like a smooth china egg, so firm, so hard, and then the melody of the waves— "Hush, hush," they said, and the children's shouts paddling—yes, it was a divine moment, and there she lay, she felt, in the hand of the Goddess who was the world; rather a hard-hearted, but very beautiful Goddess, a little lamb laid on the altar (one did think these silly things, and it didn't matter so long as one never said them). And also with Hubert sometimes she had quite unexpectedly—carving the mutton for Sunday lunch, for no reason, opening a letter, coming into a room—divine moments, when she said to herself (for she would never say this to anybody else). "This is it. This has happened. This is it!" And the other way about it was equally surprising—that is, when everything was arranged—music, weather, holidays, every reason for happiness was there—then nothing happened at all. One wasn't happy. It was flat, just flat, that was all.

Her wretched self again, no doubt! She had always been a fretful, weak, unsatisfactory mother, a wobbly wife, lolling about in a kind of twilight existence with nothing very clear or very bold, or more one thing than another, like all her brothers and sisters, except perhaps Herbert—they were all the same poor water-veined creatures who did nothing. Then in the midst of this creeping, crawling life suddenly she was on the crest of a wave. That wretched fly—where had she read the story that kept coming into her mind about the fly and the saucer?—struggled out. Yes, she had those moments. But now that she was forty, they might come more and more seldom. By degrees she would cease to struggle any more. But that was deplorable! That was not to be endured! That made her feel ashamed of herself!

She would go to the London Library tomorrow. She would find some wonderful, helpful, astonishing book, quite by chance, a book by a clergyman, by an American no one had ever heard of; or she would walk down the strand and drop, accidentally, into a hall where a miner was telling about the life in the pit, and suddenly she would become a new person. She would be absolutely transformed. She would wear a uniform; she would be called Sister Somebody; she would never give a thought to clothes again. And forever after she would be perfectly clear about Charles Burt and Miss Milan and this room and that room; and it would be always, day after day, as if she were lying in the sun or carving the mutton. It would be it!

So she got up from the blue sofa, and the yellow button in the looking-glass got up too, and she waved her hand to Charles and Rose to show them she did not depend on them one scrap, and the yellow button moved out of the looking-glass, and all the spears were gathered into her breast as she walked toward Mrs. Dalloway and said, "Good night."

"But it's too early to go," said Mrs. Dalloway, who was always so charming.

"I'm afraid I must," said Mabel Waring. "But," she added in her weak, wobbly voice which only sounded ridiculous when she tried to strengthen it, "I have enjoyed myself enormously."

"I have enjoyed myself," she said to Mr. Dalloway, whom she met on the stairs.

"Lies, lies, lies!" she said to herself, going downstairs, and "Right in the saucer!" she said to herself as she thanked Mrs. Barnet for helping her and wrapped herself, round and round and round, in the Chinese cloak she had worn these twenty years.

Analysis of "The New Dress"

At first glance the epic balance in "The New Dress" is not apparent; there seems to be so much more narration than dramatic scene. Yet scene, in this story, exists on two levels—on the literal level of the social gathering, and on the psychological level of Mabel's perceptions of herself in relation to the other guests. By probing Mabel's mind, the narrator often shows her consciousness in action rather than telling about it in a narrative voice. The storyteller of "The New Dress" creates a constantly shifting relationship between Mabel's perceptions and the progression of the party. Within Mabel's consciousness, the narrator reveals voices that speak different aspects of her tortured self-image.

Point of View

The narrator of "The New Dress" speaks from a third person, single omniscience point of view; she reveals both external and internal omniscient powers as she tells the story of the central character, Mabel, through whose eyes all action is reflected. As an indication of her external omniscience, the narrator can range in time—returning (in the recent past) to the evening when Mrs. Dalloway's invitation came and recapturing (in the far past) events in Mabel's life history. The narrator is even able to report Mabel's thoughts of future plans—"She would go to the London Library tomorrow." In addition to her ability to range in time, the narrator of "The New Dress" is also capable of moving freely in space with Mabel, following her physical progress as well as her mental journeys throughout the story.

What distinguishes this narrator, however, is not her external knowledge of Mabel, but the arresting quality of her interior probing of Mabel's consciousness. Few stories go as deeply or as quickly into a character's mind as this one; even the first line of the story is told from Mabel's viewpoint. The effect of such a full narrative commitment to sharing Mabel's thoughts and perceptions is that the reader gets a rather complete view of the paranoia that controls Mabel's life. The narrator seems to present Mabel's neurotic perceptions without undue commentary, and even with a certain sympathy. The reader senses the narrator's willingness to share this party experience with Mabel, no matter how painfully vivid or misdirected Mabel's emotions may be.

Plot

The progression of action in "The New Dress" is determined by Mabel's physical movement through Mrs. Dalloway's drawing room and her mental movement through the corridors of her mind. The time frame of the plot is the length of Mabel's stay at Mrs. Dalloway's party. Because the action of the story centers around a single experience (the party) as seen through the eyes of one character, rather than around a causal string of events, "The New Dress" may be considered a character sketch, rather than a piece with a defined story line. The plot comes through the structure of Mabel's mental images—the sequence of imaginative events that pass through her mind. In this story, external action is all in the service of internal action.

Ideas

One of the reasons we chose to work with "The New Dress" was that its ideas—its notions of social tension and feelings of personal inadequacy—are concepts and emotions shared by everyone. The irony in this story is exceedingly strong, because this narrator, without apology, reports and shows the thoughts of a paranoic character. We sense the narrator's gentle sympathy for Mabel's vulnerability, as the narrator reports that "she felt, suddenly, honestly, full of love for Miss Milan, much, much fonder of Miss Milan than of anyone in the whole world. . . . And now the whole thing had vanished." Yet the narrator's freewheeling exaggerated diction ("It was her own appaling inadequacy; her cowardice; her mean, water-sprinkled blood") and open commentary ("Envy and spite, the most detestable of the vices, were her chief faults") suggests a kind of ironic exposé of Mabel's overly dramatic self-centeredness. We'll discuss irony at greater length, under the power source of *character*, but we recognize that irony plays a major role in the appeal of the story.

Imagery

The physical setting of the story is very clear: this is an upper-middle-class drawing room in which a genteel party is taking place. Yet there is a strong sense of two worlds in "The New Dress": the polished social environment of the party and Mabel's private inadequate settings—"her own drawing room so shabby" and Miss Milan's workroom that was "really terribly hot, stuffy, sordid" and "smelt of clothes and cabbage cooking."

The recurrent metaphoric image of the fly in the saucer of milk becomes a **leitmotif** of Mabel's social desperation. Pervading the story, the image is also used to show Mabel's paranoia and poor self-image—"she was a fly, but the others were dragonflies, butterflies, beautiful insects, dancing, fluttering, skimming, while she alone dragged herself out of the saucer."

Two other images recur in the story as symbols of the action: mirror images and a haunting vision of a dressmaker's dummy. Four mirrors are mentioned in the story—Mrs. Barnet's hand mirror, the large looking glass in the corner of Mrs. Dalloway's drawing room, Miss Milan's "scrolloping looking-glass," and the "round looking-glass which made them all the size of boot-buttons"—and their presence reinforces Mabel's fixations about appearance and reality. On a more abstract level, the narrator acts as a kind of mirror for Mabel, reflecting her inner thoughts without distortion. The dressmaker's dummy is not physically present in the story; Mabel invokes the image by feeling "like a dressmaker's dummy standing there for young people to stick pins into." Furthermore, Mabel poses as a "human mannequin" in Miss Milan's workroom. The references to dressmaking may suggest a workable production concept to the stager of tales.

Character

As in all stories with single character omniscience, the personality of the major character commands the most interest. Mabel Waring's mental action is vivid, but she is apparently quite colorless externally. The tension between her lively thoughts and her rather plain appearance at the party, as she skillfully blends into the environment, constitutes much of the irony of the story. Similarly, there seems to be a considerable difference between the attention Mabel assumes other people are paying to her (especially her dress) and the attention they *really* pay. The narrator never shows other characters to be as judgmental as Mabel assumes they are; part of the charm of the story is in Mabel's dramatic interpretations of her social encounters.

Not only is Mabel's mind dramatic in its descriptions, it's dramatic in its personae as well. From the submerged voice that first tells her "it was not right, not quite right," to the dramatic scene of seeing herself as a fly, to her willingness to project dialogue and thoughts for others—"for, oh, these men, these women, all were thinking—'What's Mabel wearing? What a fright she looks! What a hideous new dress!'"—Mabel's mind operates dramatically.

As a character, Mabel is unreliable. The strength of her bold interior judgments often calls into question the quality of the judgment. Mabel's paranoia causes us to see an interior character very different from her own concept of what the exterior Mabel is like; to reinforce the singleness of paranoic vision, the narrator never shows us the exterior Mabel except through her eyes. Evidence of Mabel's unreliability comes through many sources, such as:

1. her excesses of diction, especially when she criticizes herself, as in, "It was her own appalling inadequacy; her cowardice, her mean, water-sprinkled blood that depressed her,"

2. the use of **hyperbole**, as in, "and all the spears were gathered into her breast as she walked towards Mrs. Dalloway,"

3. the assignment of hidden motives to relatively neutral comments, as in, "Mabel's got a new dress!' he said, and the poor fly was absolutely shoved into the middle of the saucer. Really, he would like her to drown, she believed,"

4. the exaggerating of the importance of a dress (or any material object) as a symbol of character: "But in her yellow dress tonight she . . . knew . . . that she was condemned, despised, left like this in a backwater, because of her being like this—a feeble, vacillating creature; and it seemed to her that the yellow dress was a penance which she had deserved."

Much of the interest in the story is in the unreliability itself and in the dry humor it engenders. Although stories based on unreliable characters are fascinating, there are inherent challenges and problems for those who wish to transform such stories from the page to the stage. What does Mabel really look like? Is her dress truly hideous? How should you view the interior Mabel—with humor, pity, sympathy, derision, understanding? Are the other characters considerably different from the vision Mabel paints of them?

Time

"The New Dress" has a very strong sense of present tense and equivalent time, but it weaves in the past with two major flashbacks: to the evening Mabel received the party invitation, and to the dressmaker's workroom. The final paragraphs of the story also weave in future time: "She would go to the London Library tomorrow."

Although "The New Dress" has a strong sense of continuing equivalent time—the ongoing party—the narrator relies on suspended time to record the stream of Mabel's consciousness, as in the moments when Mabel's thoughts return to the planning of her dress, or to her childhood and marriage, or to any lengthy elaboration of feelings and attitudes. The adapter of "The New Dress" would want to stage the *interacting* time frames and actions—the party scene in equivalent time and the summary of her past life and description of her feelings in suspended time. Finally, the transformer of this story would be sensitive to the simultaneity implied by that interaction: the party goes on while Mabel is thinking.

Style

Besides its word choice—the exaggerated diction and the hyperbolic images that reflect Mabel's paranoia and contribute to the humor of the story—the story is stylistically interesting for its syntax. Sentences are often very long (the opening sentence is 102 words and a sentence recalling Mabel's past life is 230 words) and complex, with rearranged word order.

The long syntactical structures themselves create a special rhythm, particularly when they are alternated with short sentences such as "One wasn't happy." Rhythm also comes through the parallelism and repetition of words and phrases, as in, "It was not right, not quite right," and, "Fashion meant cut, meant style, meant thirty guineas at least," and, "She would become numb, chill, frozen, dumb." An adapter of "The New Dress" may wish to feature the power source of rhythm in production because rhythm in this story is so strong.

The narrator of "The New Dress" features Mabel's thoughts and actions through most of the story. The narrator uses all four narrative positions, ranging from position 1 (external telling), as in, "She faced herself straight in the glass; she pecked at her left shoulder; she issued out into the room," to position 2 (internal telling), as in, "She meant, or she tried to make herself think that she meant, that it was the picture and not her dress, that was old-fashioned," to position 3 (internal showing), as indicated by, "No! it was not right," and to position 4 (external showing), as in, "I have enjoyed myself enormously." Positions 2 and 3, however, are used much more than the others.

Much of the story seems to be told in free indirect speech, in which Mabel's subjectivity is revealed in past tense, in a blending of the narrator's and character's language choices. We sense the narrator's ironic purposes as she shares Mabel's neurotic thoughts, as if the narrator were asking the reader (or audience member) to look critically at Mabel. Punctuation helps to differentiate the free indirect speech from the narrator's internal showing of Mabel's mind. Mabel's direct thoughts are often placed in quotation marks, as in " 'We are all like flies trying to crawl over the edge of the saucer,' Mabel thought," whereas lines of free indirect speech have no quotation marks: "But she dared not look in the glass."

The importance of analyzing narrator position, for the stager of tales, is that such information is essential for determining where the narrator stands in relation to Mabel, and *who* actually speaks the internal lines. This analysis also suggests possibilities for other interior voices that could be realized in a script.

STEPPING BACK

You've seen how to probe your story in many different ways. At this point you may be asking yourself, "Why must I do so much analyzing?" and "How am I going to put this machine back together, now that I have the nuts and bolts strewn all over the floor?" The answers to these questions lead to the heart of the Chamber Theatre form.

The epic mode is a particularly complex literary form, and Chamber Theatre stages that complexity. The epic mode's built-in tensiveness—created by the interaction of the lyric mode (the telling aspect of narration) and the dramatic mode (the showing aspect of narration)—is the essential presentational form actualized in Chamber Theatre. To begin to constitute a text for adaptation to Chamber Theatre, you must, at the very least, probe the double modality of narration and the probing is demanding because there's so much dramatic action to discover, even in a seemingly static passage of narration. The suggestion of different selves within one character, the presence of shifting time systems, and narrator movement in time and space suggest the division of lines for your script and stage movement for your production.

In the process of completing much of the analysis of your selection, you've constituted the text from which your script will be born. That text is your developed insight into the author's story. Now you're ready to decide which script you'll create from the many possibilities your text affords; that is, you're ready to verbalize your production concept. In Chapter 5, we'll explore how to transform a text from the moment you're able to verbalize a production concept to the completion of your script. We'll return to "The New Dress," sharing three production concepts and three short scripts.

NOTES

1. See Robert S. Breen, *Chamber Theatre* (Englewood Cliffs, N.J.: Prentice-Hall, 1978), for a discussion of the art form by its creator.
2. This begins the opening line of *A Tale of Two Cities* by Charles Dickens.
3. This is the first sentence of *Moby Dick* by Herman Melville.
4. Kurt Vonnegut, Jr., *Breakfast of Champions* (New York: Delacorte Press, 1973), p. 286.
5. Nathaniel Hawthorne, *Hawthorne's Short Stories* (New York: Dodd, Mead, 1962), pp. 63–71.
6. Percy Lubbock, *The Craft of Fiction* (New York: Viking Press, 1957), p. 251.
7. Cleanth Brooks and Robert Penn Warren, *Understanding Fiction*, 2nd ed. (New York: Appleton-Century-Crofts, 1959), p. 687.
8. Richard Eastman, *A Guide to the Novel* (San Francisco: Chandler, 1965), p. 31.
9. Ring Lardner, "Haircut," *The Love Nest and Other Stories* (New York: Charles Scribner's Sons, 1953).
10. Carson McCullers, *The Ballad of the Sad Cafe* (New York: Houghton Mifflin, 1941).
11. Bret Harte, *The Works of Bret Harte*, vol. 7 (New York: P. F. Collier and Sons, 1899).
12. James Joyce, *The Dubliners* (New York: Viking Press, 1962).
13. Saul Bellow, *Seize the Day* (New York: Viking Press, 1955).
14. We are using the generally accepted term, *style*, to refer to language structures in the epic mode; in chapter 2, we used the phrase, *sound structures*, for this power source because we were particularly interested in analyzing sound values for orchestration.

15. James Joyce, *A Portrait of the Artist as a Young Man* (New York: Viking Press, 1964), p. 50.

16. Ibid., p. 7.

17. Ibid., pp. 205–206.

17. Truman Capote, *A Tree of Night* (New York: Random House, 1945).

19. Jean Stafford "In the Zoo," in *Story: An Introduction to Prose Fiction*, ed. Arthur Foff and Daniel Knapp (Belmont, Calif.: Wadsworth, 1964), p. 303.

20. Ibid., p. 315.

21. John Fines and Raymond Verrier, "The Work of Dorothy Heathcote," *Young Drama* 4 (January 1976): 5.

22. Ibid., p. 5.

23. Stephen Crane, *Short Stories and Sketches of Stephen Crane*, ed. Thomas A. Gullason (Garden City, N.Y.: Doubleday, 1963), pp. 239–249.

24. Joyce, *Portrait*, p. 232.

25. Willa Cather, *Youth and the Bright Medusa* (New York: Alfred A. Knopf, 1932).

26. Vladimir Nabokov, *The Portable Nabokov*, ed. Page Stegner (New York: Viking Press, 1968), pp. 362–512.

27. See Susanne K. Langer, *Feeling and Form: A Theory of Art* (New York: Charles Scribner's Sons, 1953), especially chap. 17.

28. S. Alexander, *Space-Time and Deity*, vol. 2 (New York: Humanities Press, 1950), p. 218.

29. See Henri Bergson, *Time and Free Will: An Essay on the Immediate Data of Consciousness*, trans. F. L. Pogson (New York: Macmillan, 1959).

30. Frederick Crews, *The Pooh Perplex* (New York: E. P. Dutton, 1963), p. 66.

31. Sir Thomas Browne, "Hydriotophia, or Urn Burial" in *The Prose of Sir Thomas Browne*, ed. Norman Endicott (Garden City, N.Y.: Doubleday, 1967), pp. 241–286.

32. For a more detailed discussion of locus in all literary modes, see Wallace A. Bacon, *The Art of Interpretation*, 3rd ed.(New York: Holt, Reinhart & Winston, 1979), chap. 4.

33. For a more extensive discussion of free indirect speech in the epic mode, see Judith C. Espinola, "The Nature, Function, and Performance of Indirect Discourse in Prose Fiction," *Speech Monographs* 41 (August 1974): 193–204.

34. Virginia Woolf, "The New Dress," *A Haunted House and Other Stories* (New York: Harcourt Brace Jovanovich, 1972). Reprinted by permission of the publisher.

SUGGESTIONS FOR FURTHER READING

Booth, Wayne C. *The Rhetoric of Fiction*. Chicago: University of Chicago Press, 1961.

Eastman, Richard. *A Guide to the Novel*. San Francisco: Chandler, 1965.

Edel, Leon. *The Modern Psychological Novel*. New York: Grosset & Dunlap, 1961.

Espinola, Judith C. "The Nature, Function, and Performance of Indirect Discourse in Fiction." *Speech Monographs* 41 (August 1974): 193–204.

Humphrey, Robert. *Stream of Consciousness in the Modern Novel*. Berkeley: University of California Press, 1968.

Maclay, Joanna. "The Aesthetics of Time in Narrative Fiction." *The Speech Teacher* 18 (September 1969): 194–196.

———. "The Interpreter and Modern Fiction: Problems in Point of View and Structural Tensiveness." In *Studies in Interpretation*. Vol. 1. Ed. Esther M. Doyle and Virginia Hastings Floyd. Amsterdam: Rodopi N.V., 1972.

———. "Translating the Literary Form into a Performance Form." *Readers Theatre* (*News*), Spring 1976, pp. 3–4, 10.

O'Connor, Frank. *The Lonely Voice.* New York: World, 1963.

O'Connor, William Van, ed. *Forms of Modern Fiction.* Bloomington, Ind.: Indiana University Press, 1948.

Raban, Jonathan. *The Technique of Modern Fiction.* South Bend, Ind.: University of Notre Dame Press, 1969.

Scholes, Robert. *Approaches to the Novel.* San Francisco: Chandler, 1966.

Thompson, David W., and Fredericks, Virginia. *Oral Interpretation of Fiction.* Minneapolis: Burgess, 1964.

CHAPTER FIVE

Transforming for Chamber Theatre: From Text to Script

The function of Chamber Theatre is to use the art of the theatre and all its theatrical devices which encourage the illusion of direct apprehension in order to reflect 'the sort of world which mirrors itself,' the world which has already been distorted by the narrative point of view.

Robert S. Breen, *Chamber Theatre*

As you move into scripting for Chamber Theatre, your mind may be virtually bursting with action images. You feel the energy of the story inside you, as characters take on bodies and faces in your mind's eye, as they speak to your inner ear, as scenes seem to materialize in space, as the narrator takes moving form on the stage in your head. This is the beginning of emergence from linear space (the words on the page) to acoustic and pictorial space (the characters on a stage). Only when you can make the transformation from a perceptive silent reader to an imaginative auditor are you ready to become the *stager of tales*. As stager of tales, you'll need to transfer the performance in your head to a production onstage. The first step in that transfer is the formulation of your production concept.

VERBALIZING A PRODUCTION CONCEPT

The production concept is the master plan that tells you how to reassemble and shape the inner workings of your story, which you have laid bare through analysis. Now is the time to consult your earlier notes, the first impressions you recorded; compare them with your present feelings about the story. Give yourself time for creative maturation, a few days in which you free yourself from the intensity of analysis to let impressions flow together. Remember the dynamic quality of the epic mode: the richness of action that lies hidden in seemingly static blocks of narration and the constant movement of the narrator as she shifts position in relation to the characters.

Your production concept is both the result of the analytical choices you've made thus far and the foundation of your scripting and production choices to come. Your concept needs to be logical in relation to your literary text and practical in terms of the physical space and facilities you'll be using. As you visualize outlines of the finished product, consider possible stagings, audience relationships, and movement of performers. Play with the possibilities that the story now presents to you; soon you'll feel a master concept beginning to form that will be your vision of the story, a vision that will bind the action images together into a workable context.

To solidify your vision, write a statement of meaning that embodies your approach to the work. What is it you and the author, together, are going to say in this script? What themes are you choosing to emphasize? Will you need to eliminate any themes, scenes, or characters? What tonalities will predominate and from what sources are they coming—imagery, character, narration, style? Listen to the voices creating those tonalities. Your production concept shapes the way you listen by permitting some voices to dominate others.

In creating a Chamber Theatre script, recording your initial impressions of your story is the first checkpoint; enunciating your production concept after analysis is a second checkpoint, but not the finalized version of your approach. Only as you actually wrestle with the lines of your text, attempting to shape it into voices, will your production concept finally take on the dimensions of your analysis, and you'll see why you have spent so much time exploring your literary work.

FINDING AND RELEASING VOICES IN THE EPIC MODE

In Chamber Theatre, the division of lines into voices is closely tied to the physical movement of the narrator and characters. In the epic mode, the location of the narrator is central: what narrators are able to say depends upon what they're able to see. The movement of the narrator in psychic time or psychic space becomes a concrete physical reality on the stage. As you hear voices speak, you also begin to see bodies move in space.

We'll begin the process of identifying voices in the text by exploring some common scripting techniques for Chamber Theatre. As you examine each scripting technique in relation to your particular text, you'll begin to sense which ones are useful for your production concept.

Texts with First Person Narrators

The most important characteristic of first person narrators is that they have a double existence in psychic time: they live in the present and in the past. Their relationships with characters in both time frames helps determine the nature of their roles in the Chamber Theatre script. Two common ways of handling the voice(s) of the first person narrator are to use a single narrator who moves between past and present or two narrators—one in the present and one in the past.

Technique 1

The narrator is played by a single performer who exists in the present and moves in and out of the past. Using a single performer to play the narrator in both time frames tends to minimize the difference between past and present. Narrators who tell stories of the very recent past and who have changed very little between the event and its retelling are well portrayed by a single performer. And when a narrator is not really concerned with the interaction between past and present—when the major focus is on either the past story, or on the narrator's present condition—the use of a single narrator is appropriate. One narrative voice is also logical for a work in which the narrator's ego is so strong that we sense his or her desire to play all the parts. The narrators of *Catcher in the Rye* and *The Adventures of Huckleberry Finn* exemplify narrators who could be well represented by a single person playing both past and present selves, although other techniques could be used.

Finally, using a single narrator moving between past and present is appropriate for works in which the story is told by a minor character who doesn't exist as an important figure in the story being told. The barber in Ring Lardner's "Haircut" is a good example of this kind of narrator.

If you choose to cast a first person narrator as a single character, recognize that the narrator must be interesting enough to sustain the whole show. The role becomes a tour de force that will require a strong performer, as she must not only tell in the present, but move into scene and interact with other characters as the past self.

Technique 2

The narrator is played by two or more performers, one existing in the past and the others existing in the present. This technique can help clarify past and present; various kinds of temporal relationships can be shown by division of lines between the speakers and by skillful movement of the bodies onstage. One kind of temporal relationship that can be sharpened by casting two narrators is that between the present tense narrator and his or her past self, in a work in which the narrator undergoes a noticeable age progression or change in perspective. Giving the narrator two bodies features the character's complexity and development through time, and it emphasizes the condition of self-awareness; the present storyteller can react in a totally different way than did the self in the past.

When a narrator seems to be struggling to tell the story—when the telling is a process of coming to terms with the past or of gaining a focus upon past events—two performers playing the roles can help to show the struggle. Finally, when the narrator tells of events so traumatic that they cannot be recalled and relived at the same time, two bodies are needed—one to recall from the safe distance of the present, the other to relive the emotions that would be too powerful for telling. The narrator of *I'll Cry Tomorrow* by Lillian Roth, for example, would need her past self to help her re-create the horror of alcoholic delirium tremens.

Generally, lines are assigned to divided first person narrators in one of three ways:

1. The present tense storyteller takes all the narration; the past self functions entirely in scene with other characters. This division might be appropriate when reliving in scene tends to be the major narrative action:

NARRATOR 1 (*present*). I tried to tell him how I felt about it.
NARRATOR 2 (*past*). Joe . . . I just can't go through with it.
JOE. Why?
NARRATOR 2 (*past*). I—I—
NARRATOR 1 (*present*). The words stuck in my throat.

2. The present tense storyteller shares narration with the self in the past. As an adapter, you might divide the narration between present and past storytellers when there is a great deal of narration and when there are stylistic indications that two narrative voices are present. When the process of recalling dominates, a past narrator can jog the memory of the narrator in the present:

NARRATOR 1 (*present*). I remember that I had tried to tell him how I felt, but the hour was late and I
NARRATOR 2 (*past*). just couldn't get the darned words out. It was no good!
NARRATOR 1 (*present*). Not that he would have understood, but I didn't know that then.

3. Finally, more than one present tense storyteller can share narration, and both can share with the self in the past. Two present tense narrators emphasize contradictions in present tense interpretation of past events. For example, envision a submerged self, a conscience that pulls in a different direction from the narrator's conscious perspective, as when a narrator reevaluates past events with an ambivalent attitude.

NARRATOR 1 (*present*). I remember that I had really tried to tell him—
NARRATOR 2 (*present*). at least I told myself that I tried.
NARRATOR 1 (*present*). No—I really did try, but
NARRATOR 3 (*past*). nobody could tell that stupid oaf anything.

Texts with Third Person Narrators

Unlike the first person storyteller, who is always characterized by the author, third person narrators seem to have no bodies or distinguishing features. Although third person narrators may appear colorless, they're very colorful and powerful indeed; if they're relatively unobtrusive, it's because they choose to be. Chamber Theatre depends on the inherent vitality of the narrative voice; in a Chamber Theatre production, the narrator always has a central role.

Consider two observations about the kinds of roles you'll want to create for your third person narrators. First, since in production the narrator must be given a body, you'll want to give much thought to the kind of person evoked by the narrator's style of speaking; and you'll need to determine for yourself what the narrator's purpose seems to be. Second, some third person narrators stand apart from the characters they're showing and others stand so close as to be inside the minds of the characters. If the narrator seems to exist to show us the character's story, then she must be able to merge with the world view of the character. If, on the other hand, the narrator's main purpose is to comment on the characters, then the narrator assumes a more individualized presence.

Four major scripting techniques for third person narrators may be distinguished by the way in which lines of narration are divided among narrators and characters:

Technique 1

A single narrator is given all narrative lines; characters speak all direct and indirect dialogue. This division of lines is appropriate when objective narrators show much of the story in scene or when a dominating omniscient narrative perspective is divorced from, or stands at a distance from, the characters. Such narrators tell much of the story from position 1, in which they comment upon the scene or direct our attention to details. These narrators are often as interested in the audience and in the act of telling as in the characters. The narrator of Hawthorne's "Wakefield," for example, who is constantly reminding the reader of his task to keep the story together, would move close to the audience and speak directly to the listeners. In creating a role for this kind of narrator, it's often useful to establish a specific occupation or reason for the narrator's functioning in the story. Although this information is not given by the author, a creative adapter can find possibilities in the text of the story. The narrator of "The Jockey" by Carson McCullers, for example, might be the hostess of the restaurant in which the story takes place; the narrator of Jerzy Kosinski's *Being There* could be a television producer. These occupational roles are suggested by aspects of the physical scene. Other clues for narrator occupations are contained in language style. A narrator with a penchant for accurate historical detail might be cast as an archivist-librarian; a narrator who is concerned about the moral and ethical implications of the story could be a minister.

Technique 2

The narration is divided among two or more storytellers who are not characters in the story. When there seems to be more than one perspective in the narration, you may decide to feature that difference by creating two or more narrators. Philosophical differences, contrasts in imagery, embedded psychological forces, and parallel or multiple themes all suggest that the narration has more than one voice. By dividing the lines, an adapter calls attention to these differing qualities in the narration and gives them concrete bodies. In so doing, differences are emphasized to varying degrees; sometimes the relationships shown are subtle, sometimes they are deliberately made strikingly different. For example, if you sense a feminine strain in a male narrator that seems more obvious than the normal male-female impulses in all people you might give lines suggesting a kind of maternal instinct to a female narrator, making this submerged voice more apparent, while you use a male narrator for the major narration:

NARRATOR 1 (*male*). The boys came rolling down the hill, kicking and pummeling each other as they came.
   Greg was getting the worst of it—
NARRATOR 2 (*female*). his poor head was bruised and his lip was bleeding—
NARRATOR 1 (*male*). but he was manfully trying to give as good as he got.

Diffusing the narrative focus in this way has many creative advantages, but it sacrifices the complex centrality of the multileveled, single narrator.

Technique 3

The narration is shared by the narrator or narrators and the characters. In works with primarily exterior narration, characters may sometimes describe their own actions besides speaking in dialogue. When the lines are divided in one way, the narrator is allowed to retain objectivity while the character communicates the intensity of the action:

CHARACTER. He ran blindly against the door, throwing his entire weight against it. "Let me out,"
NARRATOR. he yelled. He was always getting himself into these kinds of messes.

By assigning the dialogue tag, "he yelled," to the narrator, we allow him to comment on the character's action. When the lines are assigned another way, alternating the narration rapidly back and forth between narrator and character, the effect may be a kind of shared intensity that isn't normally found in exterior narration.

NARRATOR. He ran blindly against the door,
CHARACTER. throwing his entire weight against it. "Let me out," he yelled.

NARRATOR. He was always getting himself into
CHARACTER AND NARRATOR. these kinds of messes.

In this line division, the narrator cannot remain objective, but enters into the action with the character. The narrator's omniscience is still maintained, but the shared narration gives a sense of self-awareness on the part of the character, and an impression of complicity between narrator and character. The dialogue tag "he yelled" is eliminated because the character action makes the narrative explanation superfluous. Although this kind of line division can produce a variety of tones, in this case the result would probably be comic.

Dividing interior narration between storyteller and character shows narrator position in relationship to the mind of the character, and features variations in style. In other words, when the language seems to belong to the perspective or to the cultural level of the character (even though it is part of the narration), the Chamber Theatre adapter may give those lines to the character, thereby creating a bond of intimacy between narrator and character. As in free indirect speech, this intimacy may be real, so that a fusion takes place, or it can be artificial, so that the narrator moves close to the character to comment ironically upon his or her intimate thoughts.

Line division can emphasize either the fusion or the ironic separation between narrator and character. Speaking in unison or sharing lines that show a single perspective emphasizes fusion; narrator and character are together, looking at a scene or looking at each other:

NARRATOR. Her gaze traveled out onto the terrace, drawn by the
NARRATOR AND CHARACTER. beauty
CHARACTER. of the garden by moonlight. There's no other place I would rather be, she thought to herself.

When there is an ironic separation between character and narrator, the adapter can emphasize the separation by giving the reliable aspects of the perception to the narrator and the individualized interpretation to the character. In this case the narrator might be speaking to the audience while the character is focused in scene, or the narrator might become an ironic mirror that reflects an altered image of the character:

NARRATOR. She moved out onto the terrace,
CHARACTER. to the absolutely divine little garden by moonlight,
NARRATOR. as she mentally saw herself glamorized by the glowing radiance, enshrined in gossamer.
CHARACTER. "Oh, there's just no other place on earth I'd rather be,"
NARRATOR. she exclaimed for the benefit of the young man standing at her side.

In a sense, although lines are divided in both cases, the assignment of lines in fusion results in a sharing of views, while the assignment of lines in ironic separation results in a division of views. Ultimately this difference is realized by narrator position and focus in production.

Technique 4

The central narrator is eliminated; narration is shared among major characters. As an adapter, you may choose this technique when the narration seems to be so much a part of individual character perspectives (as in some examples of multiple shifting omniscience) that there might reasonably be no central controlling mind. Each character then becomes his or her own narrator, playing two roles (narrator and character), and the story is seen from multiple perspectives. Be sure the lines of narration you retain are lines that would logically be spoken by the characters. Under some circumstances, you may wish to cut a few lines that suggest the presence of some kind of weak prevailing consciousness, but only if the content of the lines can be realized in staging.

JOHN. John said that he'd better be leaving. It was getting late.

BETTY. Betty asked if he couldn't please stay just a little while longer. After all, he didn't have to go to work in the morning.

Other Narrator Functions

In a third person narrative situation, when the narrator is not given a single occupational role, the adapter can use the narrator to fulfill many other functions. When characters appear for only brief scenes, for example, it's often useful for this kind of narrator to step into scene, chameleon-like, and play the character roles. Most third person stories allow the use of this technique. (First person narrators are so defined that they wouldn't usually be in a position to play other characters' roles unless they were overtly mimicking the character.) Besides the obvious casting economy, this use of the narrator creates a narrative dimension that isn't present in the original work: the narrator can be seen as both storyteller and role player. The dual function seems to increase the narrator's power and commitment to the story; he becomes the raconteur, the conjurer of tales, as he tells of the arrival of the "truant officer," for example, and then, donning a pair of glasses and adjusting his posture, becomes the official at the door. When the narrator plays more than one of these minor roles, he gives the small parts a unity, as if they were all aspects of the same force.

The narrator may also take on roles not directly created by the author, roles with no spoken lines in scene: he functions as doorman when the character enters a hotel and as bellhop when the character goes to his or her room. The narrator might be valet, salesperson, or conductor, or he might assume any functional role that relates to possible actions in the scene.

In a variation of this technique, the narrator can also play parts of the environment of the story. The narrator can, for example, become the tree in whose branches the Cheshire Cat reposes. Or the narrator could tick away the minutes as a teenage girl waits for the phone to ring.

The narrator might be a mirror, reflecting back to the character; the mirror image is so common in literature that this is often a useful role for the narrator to assume. This use of the narrator's body as living furniture enhances the narrator's power as a creator of images.

Similarly, the narrator's cane can become a turnstile, a sword, or any prop—belonging to any character—that the scene demands. Narrators are often keepers of the prop box, supplying props and costumes to the players as needed.

Occasionally an adapter may assign the narrator one or more assistants who take on cameo roles and who may engage in minor aspects of storytelling. This technique is especially valuable when there are many small character roles or when the action of the story is complex. This differs from actually sharing the narration in that the assistants take roles and bits of narration under the command of the narrator.

Character Roles

Finding the voices of other characters in your text and shaping their roles for Chamber Theatre has much in common with what you did in creating your Readers Theatre script, but you proceed in a slightly different manner. Since characters in the epic mode tend to be explicitly defined, you work primarily with characters who've been given some kind of physical description by the author. You need to decide which characters are major and which are minor, which minor characters might be played by the narrator or a narrator assistant and which need to be portrayed by a performer assigned exclusively to that character. Remember that many cameo roles, in which a character appears only once for a short scene, can be taken by the narrator. Sometimes very minor or incidental characters can be eliminated, or several incidental character functions can be combined in one character. The major problems in combining several voices in one character are the possible stylistic variations in the original characters' dialogue and the differences in their functions.

After you've made some of these basic decisions, you're ready to tackle one of the most interesting problems in prose fiction: how to give voice to characters who seem to contain several selves. You can make the existence of submerged selves, dramatized selves, and projected selves in literary characters explicit by **bifurcating** characters: giving a single character two selves. Thus a single character may be played by two performers, each of whom represents an aspect of the character.

When the narrator takes an exterior position in relation to the characters, divided characters probably will function autonomously from the narrator. A division of selves might feature an active self who wants to do things and go places and a reflective self who wants to think about them and is reluctant to make the effort to act. The active self might describe physical action and take dialogue in which the character exhibits the active trait. The passive self would then reflect on the consequences of action and take dialogue describing his or her reluctance to participate. The narrator might referee but would not take either of the roles.

NARRATOR. Joyce took off her coat and turned to her mother.
JOYCE 1. "I know I won't enjoy going. I never have anything to say to people I don't know."
JOYCE 2. But she held on to her gloves determinedly and she had not taken off her hat.
NARRATOR. She turned to the mirror.

JOYCE 2. The Parkers might be there,
JOYCE 1. but then she didn't know them very well either.
NARRATOR. She started to take off her hat,
JOYCE 2. but saw that she was messing up her hair. "I should at least put in an appearance—
JOYCE 1. "But why go to all of the trouble for appearances?"

This kind of situation is only one of many you may encounter and only one possibility for division of the lines.

A divided character is more likely to be found when the narrator moves into interior positions 2 and 3 and comes close enough to the character to reveal inner workings of the character's mind. In fact, one of the functions of interior views is often the examination of inner tensions and conflicts within a character. This narrator might actually take a part in the bifurcation or **trifurcation** (division into three selves). She might step into and out of one of the character selves to demonstrate either to the audience or to the character that the other self (or selves) exists:

JOYCE. Joyce knew she shouldn't go; in fact, she had taken off her coat and gloves.
NARRATOR. But in her head was a tiny hammering and her spine was rigid.
JOYCE. She was suddenly aware that she was still wearing her hat—
NARRATOR. her hair would look a fright if she took it off and then put it on again.
JOYCE. Should she go anyway?
NARRATOR. She really wanted to.

In this line division, one self has made a decision but the other self isn't willing to go along with it. By giving some lines to the narrator we see the division clearly and we also see a growing awareness on the part of one self of the existence of the other.

The possibilities for division of characters and narrators, and the resultant revealing of the hidden tensions in the story is one of the most exciting aspects of Chamber Theatre. The basic division of lines not only begins to carry out your production concept, it sets the pattern for all decisions about staging.

Influences on Line Division

When you confront the number of possibilities for line division offered by any story, some factors drawn from analysis can help you make your decisions. As you read your story, you gained certain impressions about the narrator's tone, the powers of the narrator, the reliability of characters and narrators, the self-consciousness of the narrator, and the degree of awareness or recognition of the others' existence between characters and narrators. Not all these elements will be present in a single story, nor would you wish to work with them all in a script, but at least one of these factors will influence line division in your script.

Narrative Tone

Fundamental to any decision about the dividing of lines of narration into voices is the tone of voice in which the narrator speaks; narrative tone is an especially important consideration in any script in which the narrator is separate from the characters. Even when the narration is divided among characters, each character will shift into a different tone when she is functioning as his or her own narrator.

To isolate the narrator's tonality, listen to the storyteller speak; hear the oral intonation that might be used in saying the lines. What are the dictional and syntactical choices that create the tone? Narrators will speak sympathetically, factually, with slight amusement, with sarcasm, or in any of the many attitudinal voices you hear in life. Sometimes the narrator's tone is complex and ambiguous, especially when a third person omniscient narrator probes deeply into the consciousness of a character. Often there is irony, but the irony may be so subtle and so mixed with human understanding of the character that a single tone may be difficult to isolate.

Besides determining the general feeling of the story, narrative tone, coupled with narrator position, is an important factor in determining the way lines should be divided. An ironic comment cannot be given to a character who is ignorant of the irony. A privileged view isn't usually taken by a character who couldn't have access to the information. A psychological insight is unlikely to be voiced by a character who isn't self-aware.

Degree of Narrator Control over Characters and Events

Some narrators stand back to observe the events they're relating, calling the reader's attention to particulars, interjecting comments, and assisting characters as they play out their stories. Other narrators exhibit a much stronger control over the showing and telling, even to the extent of standing centerstage and directing the symphony, with the characters appearing and disappearing at the narrator's command. Narrator power ranges between these two extremes. One of the farthest-reaching decisions in your script making will be your determination of the extent of power you'll allow your narrator to exhibit, because it sets a tone for the production and shapes the personalities of the narrator and characters.

The power of a first person narrator may be indicated by the extent of the telling as opposed to the showing she does or by the kind of character shaping that takes place. A dominant first person narrator will probably impose his or her viewpoint on everything you hear or see, and she may be so overbearing that a second narrator or alternate characters must be created to present the possibility of another view. Not all first person narrators are this strong, of course.

A third person narrator who dominates the act of storytelling will take the lines that move characters into action and initiate the movement of scenes. Characters will respond to the words and actions of the narrator and will act only at his or her bidding. This narrator will be a strong personality; she might physically propel characters about the stage, interrupt their actions, freeze them in space, make them sit down, or change their minds by showing them the submerged selves in their personalities.

A stylistic element you can check to determine the degree of dominance of a third person narrator is the use of adverbs in the syntax. A story filled with clarifying adverbs ("awkwardly," "innocently," "foolishly," for example) suggests a directing presence you may or may not feature. If the **dialogue tag**, "He admitted reluctantly," is spoken by the character, the narrator's control isn't featured. When the narrator speaks the entire dialogue tag, she has control. Focus and tone determine the degree of controlling power the narrator has. If the narrator were to look at the character and nudge him while saying, "He admitted reluctantly" as if to force the admission, we would have a strong sense of the narrator's domination. On the other hand, if the narrator were to deliver the same dialogue tag to the audience, it would become simply a way of explaining the character's action to the audience. Dividing the dialogue tag between character and narrator serves to emphasize the narrator's power and create interaction, as in the following examples:

CHARACTER. He admitted
NARRATOR. reluctantly

and:

NARRATOR. He admitted
CHARACTER. reluctantly.

In the first example, the character is willing to undertake the action, but the narrator controls its tone. In the second example, the narrator pushes the character to action, and the character either submits or bargains, depending on the intonation of the word *reluctantly.*

Such playing with language creates the magic of Chamber Theatre. If we can suggest so many ways to work with three words, imagine the many creative approaches you could take to a whole story. Don't be afraid to rely on intonation and visualized movement to help you make decisions about line division.

Reliability

Questions of reliability become most important when working either with first person narrators or with third person narrators who move deep into the consciousness of a character. Working with a first person narrator, your concern is the reliability of the narrator; working with a third person interior view, you question the character's reliability. In all matters of reliability, determine the value systems of the selection as best you can, and work out strategies in your script to probe the differences in perspective. First ask, "What clues give the unreliable narrator or character away?" "What are the values that seem violated by the character's unreliability?" Once you have answered these questions for your story, you're in a position to explore the reliability factor in scripting.

Many techniques are available to the creative adapter for featuring unreliability. For the first person narrator, using two contradictory narrative voices, shaping the narrator's occupational role to suggest possible instability, and using an alternate set of characters who repeat lines or actions in a contradictory manner are all effective techniques. The unreliable narrator of Truman Capote's "My Side of the Matter," for example, describes his wife's Aunt Eunice, "This big old fat thing with a behind that must weigh a tenth of a ton, she troops around the house, rain or shine, in this real old-fashioned nighty, calls it a kimono, but it isn't anything in this world but a dirty flannel nighty."[1] The Chamber Theatre adapter may wish to feature the narrator's unreliability by staging two Aunt Eunices simultaneously—one appearing as the boy describes her, and the other as a moderately heavyset woman in a respectable flannel kimono.

These two characters could share lines, speaking alternately or simultaneously (but with different attitudes), or one of the characters could mime the action while the other takes all the lines of dialogue.

The third person interior narrator is often given lines that correct the vision of the character being explored or comment on the human weakness of that character. In "Mother and Daughter" by D. H. Lawrence, for example, the narrator supplies information that the characters don't realize.

> It was tragic. Because Mrs. Bodoin wanted Virginia to fall in love and marry. She really wanted it, and she attributed Virginia's lack of forthcoming to the delinquent Henry. She never realized the hypnotic spell, which of course encompassed her as well as Virginia, and made men just an impossibility to both women, mother and daughter alike.[2]

The character could take the first part of the quotation, but the narrator has to speak the latter half. This division of lines ensures that the narrator's critical attitude is maintained in production, making the double perspective clear.

With characters in third person narratives, the presence of submerged, dramatic, or projected selves implies a multiplicity that might bring the character's reliability into question. By bifurcating these characters, an adapter can use one aspect of the self as a corrective to the other. Whatever the cause of unreliability, you need to take it into consideration in the shaping of your script.

Degree of Self-Consciousness

Narrators exhibit varying degrees of *awareness* that they're telling stories; when a special kind of self-conscious narrative awareness informs the story, you may wish to give it an individual voice. In *Breakfast of Champions* by Kurt Vonnegut, Jr., for example, the narrator who openly addresses his reader and who creates hand drawings to illustrate his story seems to live on a different plane of existence from the other narrator in the same novel who inhabits Kilgore Trout's private world. Similarly, in *The Princess Bride* by William Goldman, the implied author constantly interrupts the story to speak directly to the reader (or audience) about the original author, Morganstern, whose work he is abridging:

> This chapter is totally intact. My intrusion here is because of the way Morganstern uses parentheses. Either Morganstern meant them seriously or he didn't. Or maybe it was just the author's way of telling the reader stylistically that "this isn't real; it never happened." All I can suggest to you is, if the parentheses bug you, don't read them.[3]

One advantage of giving separate voice to the self-aware narrator is the possibility of neatly staging the relationship between the self-conscious narrator and his or her alter ego through line division, focus, movement on stage, and handling of the physical script.

The Recognition Factor

When a narrator or a character is divided into selves played by different performers, as when a bifurcated character's or a first person narrator's present self is different from the past self, the adapter must be aware of the relationship between the parts of the character.

In a story with a third person narrator, are characters aware of the storyteller? Are they conscious of any submerged part of themselves? Does the projected self recognize the original self, enabling the performers portraying the two selves to communicate with each other onstage? Or do these aspects of character influence each other without mutual awareness and direct communication?

In a story with a first person narrator, the whole structure of your script will depend upon whether the character in the past is aware of the character in the present and talks directly to him or her. Likewise, the present narrator may or may not move into the past and make communicative contact with the past self. These decisions help create a design for line division and help determine blocking and communicative conventions in production.

CONSTRUCTING THE SCRIPT

When you've decided on your strategy for assigning lines among voices, you're ready to shape your total script. One of the first considerations has to do with the arrangement of the original material. Where and when will your story begin? What parts of the story will you be able to use, and which must be discarded? Will your production follow the sequence of action in the original story, or will you rearrange plot to emphasize certain features of your story's presentational form? Your production concept has isolated the themes you'll emphasize and will act as a touchstone as you cut and arrange the text.

Cutting and Arrangement

Only after you've made some decisions about production concept and techniques are you ready to do the final shaping of your script. Some literary texts lend themselves to the deletion of whole sections. More likely, you'll have to do some internal cutting, lifting out themes and cutting individual lines. You've already considered the deletion and condensing of characters, which eliminates some individual speeches. Another possibility for cutting lies in blocks of description; often some aspects of description can be supplied in production by visual and auditory setting. However, the temptation to cut description should be resisted until you're certain what the description is accomplishing. Description can build suspense, create mood, give important factual information, and provide a means for the narrator to establish relationships with characters and with a reader (or audience).

Dialogue tags are another problem for the adapter. In Chamber Theatre, dialogue tags take on a particular significance because they may be important indicators of narrators' relationships with characters. As a general rule, eliminate dialogue tags when they're redundant—when they merely designate speakers or when performers can show what the dialogue tags tell. On the other hand, many seemingly superfluous tags (such as, "he admitted reluctantly") can be used to explore relationships or to provide a means by which a narrator asserts power. In many selections, dialogue tags are an important component of the prose rhythm. Look at dialogue tags carefully before you decide to cut them.[4]

When you're working with a long piece of literature, much that you'd like to include must be sacrificed. Be realistic both about the length of your production and about the basic information necessary for your script to make sense. Have you left out an important detail in favor of including a favorite but extraneous scene? (In the best literature, no scenes are extraneous; often, the more skillfully written the selection, the more difficult it is to cut. This is a problem we're always willing to face with good original works.) Be sure that the details you choose to include (incidents, descriptive passages, and so forth) are the most meaningful ones in terms of your production concept. Step back and ask, "How does my script hang together?" Your finished script should have an integrity that comes as much from the way you have cut the material as from the original work.

Usually an adapter trusts the original author's structure, but transforming a work to the stage sometimes calls for a reorganization of the order of events in the work. The particular dynamic structure found in most plays is often different from the dynamic structure found in novels and in most short stories. The novel may have a series of climaxes and may end in a very anticlimactic way. Often a novelist deliberately gives the reader information that would create suspense if withheld; emphasis is thereby placed on other aspects of the work. A short story may explore character rather than bring events to a climactic resolution. When you've discovered the pattern of tensions and releases in your work, consider how that pattern will operate in performance. Do you have a major organizing **climax** of events? If not, what other factors will sustain audience interest? Have you emphasized them sufficiently? How has your cutting affected the dynamic pattern of the work? Will you need to reorganize the plot sequence to make it more workable in performance? This is not to say that you should impose a play structure on your selection, but you need to be aware of some of the possibilities for restructuring to allow the work to reach its potential effectiveness in production.

Time structures in the work, for example, may be altered for purposes of performance. Whereas simultaneity of action must appear sequentially on paper, the Chamber Theatre practitioner can actually stage simultaneous sequences. Another kind of simultaneity occurs when characters act and narrators tell what the characters are thinking while they act or when characters later reinterpret their own thought processes. The Chamber Theatre adapter can construct a script to have thought and action occur at the same time. You may wish to create simultaneity where the author has only implied it. Bifurcating characters to show narrator unreliability (as in the example from "My Side of the Matter") creates a kind of simultaneous existence for the characters.

There are other reasons for rearranging the original plot. To realize your production concept, you may want a flashback to occur in a different place, or you may want to restore the flashback to a normal time sequence. On the other hand, you may want to create a temporal sequence that doesn't exist in the original story—by giving presence to a scene the author only suggests or by beginning the production at a late point in the story and presenting the earlier part in a flashback scene or reported summary. The latter technique is often used when very long works are adapted for the stage. Since adapters of texts have the advantage (over first-time readers) of knowing how the story ends, the adapter can begin the story at a decision point or in a physical locale that isn't suggested by the first line of the story.

To highlight differences in character perception, it's possible to stage the same scene more than once, even though the original author didn't write the repetition. By replaying the entrance of Star Drake into the household in "The Comforts of Home" by Flannery O'Connor, the audience can clearly see the difference between the mother's and the son's perceptions of the girl. The mother relates to Star Drake as a helpless waif who needs mothering; the son sees Star as a slut, an ominous threat to his way of life. In the first staging, Star may come into the house looking like an innocent young woman who simply needs a home. In the replaying of the scene, Star may move and talk as the worldly-wise seductress the son believes her to be.

In all rearrangements of plot sequence, take great care with climactic structure and exposition. You wouldn't want to destroy the climax in your selection or to leave out important details of information.

Finally, the way in which your text functions in relation to its reader and how that functioning can be transformed for the stage raises the subject of a particular kind of dialectic that is characteristic of Chamber Theatre.

The Dialectic of Identification and Alienation

Richard Eastman speaks of the **"distance"** between reader and story, stating that "all the narrative controls available to the author have as their proximate purpose the precise involvement or detachment of the reader so as to fix his response to the fiction."[5] According to Wayne Booth, the writer reaches out to the reader along certain lines of interest, or "axes of belief," through which he either draws the reader close or moves the reader away from certain elements of the story.[6] It is this tug between identification (or empathy) and alienation (or detachment) that the reader senses as a dialectic in the epic mode—a constant shifting between two or more positions. The reader may feel pulled simultaneously toward identification and alienation, and, in the resulting tension, he may become aware of the ironic nature of the epic experience.[7]

Because of the human qualities of the characters in a story, the readers are likely to be caught up in their experiences and to identify with characters more than with any other element in the story. The humanity of the characters reaches out to readers' humanity and draws them close. But the author may not want readers to become so involved with the lives and activities of characters that they're blind to other aspects of the literary work. For example, by keeping readers from identifying too closely with a character, the author enables readers to see the character in a broader context. Perhaps the character has brought on his or her own sufferings and the author wishes readers to think about the larger implications of any action that brings pain. When you step back to look critically at the character whose sufferings have so engaged you, you aren't less involved with the character, you're simply equally involved with another aspect of the story. You gain distance from character to achieve closeness with the story's ideas. In fact, readers become more deeply involved because of a double perspective. Not only have you experienced some of the the character's adversity, you've been lifted above those emotions and allowed to see the character in a new way, a way that gives insight into the causes of suffering; you feel that dialectic within you.

It's possible to isolate some of the elements in a script that may serve to draw an audience away from complete identification with characters in a story. First, the physical presence of the narrator is a signal to the audience that this is not a conventional theatrical situation. The fact that the narrator will initiate and interrupt action, will sometimes move characters around the stage as a demonstration, and will often suggest a critical or philosophical attitude to the audience by the nature of his or her commentary makes the narrator an alienating force. The narrator's very act of telling acknowledges the presence of the audience and recalls the existence of the physical world of the stage.

If the narration is divided between two narrators, both of whom approach the audience directly with their viewpoints, the audience may quickly become more engaged with the debate than with the seeming reality of the fictional world. Usually, the more the narrator uses the stage as a lecture platform, whether to view the characters from the inside or from the outside, and uses characters as a means of demonstration, the less the audience member tends to identify with the characters. Conversely, the more the narrator lets the characters play out their story without critical comment, or the more the narrator identifies with the characters, the more the audience will become empathically involved with the characters.

Time is another factor in controlling audience identification. The fact that characters often speak of themselves in third person and past tense forms a kind of barrier to our identification with them. The juxtaposition of the performers in the here and now and the past tense language creates an ironic tensiveness that constantly reminds the audience that a story, not real life, is happening before them. When a story is cast in past tense and has obviously already taken place, the verb tense may work against the suspense factor in special ways. We know that the first person narrator has survived the experience because she is here to tell us about it. Third person narrators will often tell us the outcome of the story and give most of their attention to exploring motivation.

The dynamically shifting attention the epic mode author requires of the reader becomes an important feature of Chamber Theatre. When we transform a story to the Chamber Theatre stage, the dialectic between identification and detachment forms the basis of much of the staging. As adapter, you should be able to visualize your script in production and make sure that your line division allows the dialectic to function.

As you work with the Checklist for Constructing a Chamber Theatre script, in figure 5.1, refer to your production concept. You may find that your answers to the checklist questions will reshape your production concept a bit. Don't resist that. Your notions of the story will continue to form, even during rehearsal and performance.

CREATING THREE SAMPLE SCRIPTS FOR CHAMBER THEATRE

To illustrate some of the concepts you've been learning, we'll continue our work with Virginia Woolf's short story "The New Dress"[8] and carry our text of that work into script form. From the

Checklist for Constructing a Chamber Theatre Script

I. Narrator
   A. In what person does the narrator speak?
   B. What is his or her degree of omniscience?
   C. Does there seem to be more than one narrator perspective? If so, identify each perspective.
   D. What is the narrator's general locus? Is she located close to the characters in the story or at a distance in time or space?
   E. What is the primary time structure used by the narrator—equivalent, condensed, or suspended?
   F. Does the narrator do more telling or showing?
   G. What are the narrator's attitudes toward self, toward reader or audience, and toward characters in the story? How will these attitudes affect scripting?
   H. In what general tone of voice does the narrator speak?
   I. What will be the amount and kind of power exhibited by the narrator over the characters in the script? What techniques will you use to allow narrative power to function in performance?
   J. Is the narrator reliable or unreliable? If unreliable, how do you plan to handle narrative unreliability in scripting?

II. Characters
   A. Describe each character individually (physically and psychologically).
   B. Are any characters unreliable? If so, how will you handle the unreliability in scripting?
   C. Do any of the characters seem to contain more than one self? If so:
      1. How many selves exist?
      2. Describe each self and explain how it functions.
      3. Check for consistency of this division throughout the story.
   D. Will you condense more than one character into a single voice? If so, which characters are to be combined, and what is the nature of the single voice?

III. Construction of Script
   A. What narrative technique seems to be the best choice for your selection?
      1. One narrator taking all narration?
      2. Dividing narration among two or more narrators? If so, describe each voice and explain how it functions.
      3. Dividing narration among narrator(s) and character(s)? If so, what narrative functions do the characters assume?
      4. Eliminating a separate narrator and dividing narration among characters (third person only)?
   B. What role(s) will your narrator assume?
      1. A single specific occupational role?
      2. A single undefined role?
      3. Any character roles?
      4. Any environmental functions?
   C. Recognition factor
      1. Do characters or aspects of characters communicate directly with their narrator?
      2. If the narrator or a character is divided into more than one self, do the selves recognize each other?
      3. When recognition takes place, describe the nature of the relationship.
   D. Cutting and arrangement
      1. Will you use the original plot sequence?
      2. If not, how will you rearrange events?
         a. When and where will the action begin?
         b. What events do you plan to reorder and how?
      3. Will you cut any scenes or characters? If so, will you need to compensate for their absence in some way?
      4. Does your script have a clear climactic structure?

IV. Dialectic
   A. As you view your plan for scripting, try to verbalize how the identification-alienation factors will work in production.
   B. With what aspects of the production will the audience be likely to identify?
   C. What features of your script will involve your audience to the extent that they'll become distanced from the normal involvement with the lives of the characters?

Figure 5.1: Checklist for constructing a Chamber Theatre script.

many possibilities for production that this story affords, we've chosen three to exemplify in scripts. The three scripts (created from the first portion of "The New Dress") illustrate how more than one production concept can emerge from a single text and show how the production concept affects line division and even the nature of characters in the script. In approaching the task of creating scripts for Chamber Theatre from the text of "The New Dress," some of the most important aspects to be taken into consideration come from our analysis of the character of Mabel and the narrator's revealing of her interior world.

"The New Dress": Production Concept 1

"The New Dress" is the record of a woman's paranoia. In our first script, we view Mabel as a socially inadequate individual with a vivid and paranoic inner life. She is fully aware of most of her inner feelings, but is powerless to stop their constant hammering. Likewise, her inner self is powerless to alter her exterior behavior, although this hidden force creates a colorful and chastising inner commentary. The narrator takes a position close enough to the character to facilitate and comment upon both the exterior and interior action, but control it only when necessary. The cast of characters, therefore, includes Exterior Mabel, who goes to the party, interacts with the other guests, and carries on a running dialolgue with her inner self; Interior Mabel, who goes to the party as an invisible guest and carries on the other half of the dialogue, constantly depreciating her exterior self, and a Narrator who sympathetically but ironically oversees the action. Interior Mabel is caustic, paranoic, and very vivid. Exterior Mabel is drab and socially timid, but sees herself very romantically at times. Since we wish to suggest the social context of the party, we will have a chorus of three performers, two female and one male, to take on the roles of the guests with whom Mabel interacts, and to pantomime generally the action and atmosphere of a cocktail party. Chorus 1 takes on the role of Mrs. Dalloway and acts as the hostess of the party; in a script of the complete story, she also would take the role of Miss Milan in the flashback sequence. Chorus 2 takes the role of Rose Shaw and Chorus 3 plays Robert Hayden and Charles Burt. The narrator plays Mrs. Barnet at the beginning and ending of the story.

Because Exterior and Interior Mabels are aware of each other and of the Narrator, there's a sense of dialogue among the three. Only the Narrator speaks to the audience, but, because there isn't a pervading sense on the part of the Narrator of her own act of storytelling, the moments of direct audience contact are carefully chosen. Most of the action resides within the closed arena of Mabel's world. Neither of the Mabels is reliable; therefore, our sense of the reality of the situation comes almost solely from the Narrator. The overall tone of the production is gently ironic with moments of humor.

"The New Dress": Script 1

Set is on two levels. Basic set pieces: hall tree, couch, standing oval mirror frame (without glass).

CHARACTERS:

INTERIOR MABEL
EXTERIOR MABEL

NARRATOR
CHORUS 1
CHORUS 2
CHORUS 3

[Chorus 1, Chorus 2, *and* Chorus 3 *are all in place on the stage, in party poses.* Narrator, Interior Mabel, *and* Exterior Mabel *enter from downstage right.*]

NARRATOR. Mabel had her first serious suspicion that something was wrong as she took her cloak off [*stepping into the role of* Mrs. Barnet] and Mrs. Barnet, while handing her the mirror and touching the brushes

INTERIOR MABEL. [*to* Exterior Mabel, *with an air of superiority*] and thus drawing her attention, perhaps rather markedly, to all the appliances for tidying and improving hair, complexion, clothes,

NARRATOR. which existed on the dressing table [*resuming* Narrator *role*] confirmed the suspicion—

EXTERIOR MABEL. [*embarrassed*] that it was not right, not quite right,

NARRATOR. [*directing* Exterior Mabel *upstairs to centerstage;* Interior Mabel *follows*] which growing stronger as she went upstairs and springing at her with conviction

EXTERIOR MABEL. as she greeted Clarissa Dalloway [Chorus 1 *responds as* Mrs. Dalloway],

NARRATOR. [*leading* Exterior Mabel *to the mirror frame upstage center,* Interior Mabel *moves behind open frame*] she went straight to the far end of the room, to a shaded corner where a looking-glass hung and looked.

EXTERIOR MABEL. No! It was not right.

NARRATOR. And at once the misery which she always tried to hide,

INTERIOR MABEL. [*needling*] the profound dissatisfaction—the sense she had had, ever since she was a child, of being inferior to other people—

NARRATOR. set upon her, relentlessly,

INTERIOR MABEL. remorselessly,

NARRATOR. with an intensity which she could not beat off,

INTERIOR MABEL. as she would when she woke at night, by reading Borrow or Scott;

EXTERIOR MABEL. For, oh, these men, oh, these women, all were thinking—

INTERIOR MABEL. [*mocking*] "What's Mabel wearing? What a fright she looks! What a hideous new dress!"—

EXTERIOR MABEL. their eyelids flickering as they came up and then their lids shutting rather tight.

INTERIOR MABEL. It was her own appalling inadequacy;

EXTERIOR MABEL. her cowardice;

INTERIOR MABEL. her mean, water-sprinkled blood that depressed her.

NARRATOR. [Narrator., Exterior Mabel, *and* Interior Mabel *move away from party to stage right*] What she had thought that evening when, sitting over the teacups, Mrs. Dalloway's invitation came, was that,

EXTERIOR MABEL. of course, she could not be fashionable. It was absurd to pretend to even—

INTERIOR MABEL. Fashion meant cut, meant style, meant thirty guineas at least—

EXTERIOR MABEL. but why not be original?

INTERIOR MABEL. Why not be herself, anyhow?

NARRATOR. And, getting up, she had taken that old fashion book of her mother's, a Paris fashion book of the time of the Empire, and had thought

EXTERIOR MABEL. how much prettier, more dignified, and more womanly, they were then,

NARRATOR.   and so set herself—

EXTERIOR MABEL.   Oh, it was foolish—

NARRATOR.   [to audience] trying to be like them,

INTERIOR MABEL.   pluming herself in fact upon being modest and old-fashioned and very charming, giving herself up, no doubt about it, to an orgy of self-love which deserved to be chastised, and so rigged herself out like this.

EXTERIOR MABEL.   But she dared not look in the glass,

NARRATOR.   She could not face the whole horror—

INTERIOR MABEL.   the pale yellow, idiotically old-fashioned silk dress with its long skirt and its high sleeves and its waist

NARRATOR.   and all the things that looked so charming in the fashion book,

EXTERIOR MABEL.   [Exterior Mabel and Narrator moving back to mirror; Exterior Mabel takes pose in front of glass] but not on her, not among all these ordinary people.

INTERIOR MABEL.   [moving to Exterior Mabel] She felt like a dressmaker's dummy standing there for young people to stick pins into.

CHORUS 2.   "But my dear, it's perfectly charming!"

NARRATOR.   Rose Shaw said,

INTERIOR MABEL.   looking her up and down with that little satirical pucker of the lips which she expected—

EXTERIOR MABEL.   [complimenting Rose] Rose herself being dressed in the height of fashion

CHORUS 2.   [throwing off the compliment] precisely like everybody else, always [Exterior Mabel and Chorus 2 pantomime conversation under following lines]

INTERIOR MABEL.   always. We are all like flies trying to crawl over the edge of the saucer.

"The New Dress": Production Concept 2

"The New Dress" is about the dramatic selves that lie beneath a person's social exterior. Mabel's world is so bound up within herself that other people exist for her only in relationship to her own ego. In fact, she doesn't see other people at all; she sees only herself as she thinks other people react to her. The people at the party, therefore, are represented only as cardboard cutouts which the Narrator moves around and represents in speech. Mabel's interior world, on the other hand, is teeming with real voices, some of which she brings with her to the party. There is Interior Mabel 1, who borders on paranoia and is constantly kicking her. Interior Mabel 2 is helplessly romantic and suffers from the biting remarks of her counterpart, Interior Mabel 1. The script will feature the conflict between these two aspects of Mabel's interior world. Exterior Mabel moves through the social charade, giving surface attention to the others at the party and speaking the direct dialogue. Sometimes she enters into the interior dialogue, but only in the flashback sequences can Exterior Mabel really be herself and freely voice her own thoughts. The presence of the two interior selves tends to balance Exterior Mabel, giving her a strange kind of reliability. We realize that Mabel has achieved a kind of unhappy stasis in her life, which will continue as long as she lives.

Mabel of the exterior world is conscious of the presence of the Narrator and is also fully aware of her two interior selves; she sometimes has difficulty keeping them concealed in social situations. Her two interior selves are also aware of each other, and of Mabel, but not of the Narrator. For them, the Narrator is a controlling but unrecognized force.

The Narrator, in this production concept, is a facilitator; he or she (because of this narrator's exterior position, the narrative voice might be either male or female) makes the party happen by describing and directing physical action, moving cardboard characters around, and speaking for them. He facilitates time shifts by either moving Mabel to another location on the stage, moving the party cutouts away from her, or calling for light and sound changes. The Narrator's attitude toward the scene is somewhat clinical, but he assumes professional responsibility for the "patient" and, therefore, looks out for Exterior Mabel, occasionally acting as a referee when the interior conflict becomes too heavy. Because of the artificiality of the cutout environment, the overall tone of the production becomes alternately comic and pathetic.

"The New Dress": Script 2

Set is on two levels. Basic set pieces: cardboard cutout guests, hall tree, large mirror frame, couch.

CHARACTERS:

INTERIOR MABEL 1
INTERIOR MABEL 2
EXTERIOR MABEL
NARRATOR

[*Cutouts are in place on the stage, as* Interior Mabel 1, Interior Mabel 2, Exterior Mabel *and* Narrator *enter from downstage right*]

INTERIOR MABEL 1. Mabel had her first serious suspicion that something was wrong

NARRATOR. as she took her cloak off

EXTERIOR MABEL. [*greeting her*] and Mrs. Barnet

NARRATOR. [*as Mrs. Barnet*] while handing her the mirror and touching the brushes and thus drawing her attention,

INTERIOR MABEL 1. perhaps rather markedly,

NARRATOR. [*as Mrs. Barnet*] to all the appliances for tidying and improving hair, complexion, clothes, which existed on the dressing table,

INTERIOR MABEL 1. confirmed the suspicion—

INTERIOR MABEL 2. that it was not right, not quite right,

NARRATOR. which growing stronger as she went upstairs and springing at her with conviction

EXTERIOR MABEL. [*greeting cardboard figure at top of stair*] as she greeted Clarissa Dalloway,

NARRATOR. She went straight to the far end of the room to a shaded corner where a looking glass hung and looked.

INTERIOR MABEL 1. No! It was not right.

INTERIOR MABEL 2. And at once the misery which she always tried to hide, the profound dissatisfaction—the sense she had had, ever since she was a child, of being inferior to other people,

INTERIOR MABEL 1. set upon her relentlessly, remorselessly, with an intensity which she could not beat off,

INTERIOR MABEL 2. as she would when she woke at night at home, by reading Borrow or Scott; [*looks around room, with a sweeping gesture toward all the cardboard figures*] for, oh, these men, oh, these women all were thinking—

INTERIOR MABEL 1.	"What's Mabel wearing? What a fright she looks! What a hideous new dress!"—
INTERIOR MABEL 2.	their eyelids flickering as they came up and then their lids shutting rather tight.
INTERIOR MABEL 1.	It was her own appalling inadequacy; her cowardice; her mean, water-sprinkled blood that depressed her.
NARRATOR.	[*as action moves to another location*] What she had thought that evening, when, sitting over the teacups, Mrs. Dalloway's invitation came,
INTERIOR MABEL 2.	[*to Exterior Mabel*] was that, of course, she could not be fashionable. It was absurd to pretend to even—
EXTERIOR MABEL.	[*to Interior Mabel 2*] fashion meant cut, meant style, meant thirty guineas at least—
INTERIOR MABEL 2.	but why not be original?
EXTERIOR MABEL.	Why not be herself, anyhow?
NARRATOR.	And, getting up, she had taken that old fashion book of her mother's,
EXTERIOR MABEL.	a Paris fashion book of the time of the Empire,
NARRATOR.	and had thought
INTERIOR MABEL 2.	how much prettier, more dignified, and more womanly they were then,
NARRATOR.	and so set herself—
EXTERIOR MABEL.	Oh, it was foolish—
NARRATOR.	trying to be like them,
INTERIOR MABEL 1.	pluming herself in fact upon being modest
INTERIOR MABEL 2.	and old-fashioned and very charming,
INTERIOR MABEL 1.	giving herself up,
EXTERIOR MABEL.	no doubt about it,
INTERIOR MABEL 1.	to an orgy of self-love which deserved to be chastened,
EXTERIOR MABEL.	and so rigged herself out like this.
NARRATOR.	[*moving the action back to the arena of the party*] But she dared not look into the glass,
INTERIOR MABEL 1.	she could not face the whole horror—[*satirically*] the pale yellow, idiotically old-fashioned silk dress with its long skirt and its high sleeves
INTERIOR MABEL 2.	[*gently defensive*] and its waist, and all the things that looked so charming in the fashion book,
INTERIOR MABEL 1.	but not on her, not among all these ordinary people.
EXTERIOR MABEL.	[*as if in dialogue with* Rose Shaw] She felt like a dressmaker's dummy standing there for young people to stick pins into.
NARRATOR.	[*as Rose Shaw*] "But, my dear, it's perfectly charming!" Rose Shaw said,
INTERIOR MABEL 1.	looking her up and down with that little satirical pucker of the lips which she expected—
NARRATOR.	[*as Rose*] Rose herself being dressed in the height of fashion, precisely like everybody else, always.
INTERIOR MABEL 2.	[*turning away from the scene, highly dramatic*] We are all like flies trying to crawl over the edge of the saucer.

An alternate concept, using a device similar to that of cutouts, presents a Mabel façade, a dressmaker's dummy on wheels wearing a rather hideous yellow dress. Interior Mabel, dressed in black, pushes the dummy around, speaks Mabel's dialogue, and comments caustically to the real Exterior Mabel, dressed in a nice Empire design yellow dress. The people at the party speak not to Exterior Mabel, but to the dummy façade; Exterior Mabel isn't noticed, although she occasionally tries to make herself seen; she carries on a dialogue with Interior Mabel and the

Narrator. The Narrator shares a partnership with Exterior Mabel as they watch Interior Mabel propel the dummy about the stage. In this approach, Mabel's somewhat shoddy world intrudes physically into the elegance of Mrs. Dalloway's world in the figure of the dummy; in the other approaches the two worlds remain separate spaces. Mabel is a little ashamed of her world, so she sometimes attempts to step in front of the dummy.

"The New Dress": Production Concept 3

"The New Dress" is about the nightmare of self-doubt. In this view, Mabel is less aware of the forces that move her and less able to keep them under the control of an exterior façade. The interior forces in this approach (in our script, two voices) are less personal, more a blending of the interior weakness of the character with the exterior, unfriendly world that Mabel has created for herself. The voices become a satiric, somewhat surrealistic chorus that exaggerates and reiterates the tragicomic nightmare of uncertainty and self-reproach in which Mabel lives.

Mabel voices many of her own self-doubts and uses the Narrator as a confidant and buffer against the sometimes flailing voices which she seldom confronts or sees, but to which she rather blindly reacts. The Narrator is closer to Mabel than in the other production concepts, more sympathetic and protective. She (for this narrator is female) sees Mabel's faults and sometimes voices them, but always speaks from a bond of sympathy. This Narrator doesn't control the action as completely as does the Narrator of production concept 2; rather she acts in response to Mabel's orgy of self-recrimination, sometimes protecting her, sometimes gently forcing her to face herself. There is a strong and direct interaction between Mabel and the Narrator.

The two voices that assail Mabel appear first wrapped in long black cloaks, as coats hanging in the cloakroom where we first meet Mabel. With their first lines, the mirror voices unwrap themselves and are revealed dressed in black leotards and tights, with long yellow scarves that echo the yellow in Mabel's dress with exaggerated deepness of color. They move throughout the production as Mabel's dancing, mocking, personal devils, always satiric, but never really sinister. We feature the rhythmic power source in this script by giving most of the parallel words and phrases in the text to these voices ("paltry, provincial," or "seemed sordid, repulsive"). We altered our cutting of the original story somewhat to feature the rhythmic parallelism.

In a longer script, the few lines of conversation would be taken by a chorus of three performers—two women and one man—who are always on stage, creating a party by pantomime and occasional ad lib party conversation. These characters function in much the same roles as in script 1.

Although the humor of the story is still apparent, it isn't emphasized as strongly as in the other scripts; rather, the pathetic nature of the character receives the primary focus.

"The New Dress": Script 3

Set is on three levels. Basic set pieces: a dressmaker's dummy wearing an awful yellow dress (placed upstage in the same position as the mirror frame in the previous two scripts), a prop table for the Voices, and a couch.

CHARACTERS:

MABEL
NARRATOR
MIRROR VOICE 1
MIRROR VOICE 2
CHORUS 1
CHORUS 2
CHORUS 3

[Chorus 1, Chorus 2, *and* Chorus 3 *are in place as party guests onstage.* Mirror Voice 1 *and* Mirror Voice 2 *are hanging as coats in the clockroom.* Narrator *and* Mabel *enter from downstage right*]

MABEL.	Mabel had her first serious suspicion that something was wrong
NARRATOR.	[*helping* Mabel] as she took her cloak off
CHORUS 2.	and Mrs. Barnet, while handing her the mirror and touching the brushes and thus drawing her attention,
MABEL.	perhaps rather markedly,
CHORUS 2.	to all the appliances for tidying and improving hair, complexion, clothes, which existed on the dressing table,
MABEL.	confirmed the suspicion—
MIRROR VOICE 1.	that it was not right,
	[*This is their first appearance; they have appeared to be coats hanging in the closet*],
MIRROR VOICE 2.	not quite right,
NARRATOR.	[*as herself*] which growing stronger as she went upstairs and [*moving with* Mabel *to the level of the dressmaker's dummy*]
MIRROR VOICE 1 *and*	
MIRROR VOICE 2.	springing at her with conviction [*jumping up on upper level; this is done always satirically, not threateningly*]
MABEL.	as she greeted Clarissa Dalloway,
	[Chorus 1 *responds*]
NARRATOR.	she went straight to the far end of the room,
MABEL.	to a shaded corner where a looking-glass hung and looked.
NARRATOR.	[*moving between* Mabel *and the imaginary mirror, as if to protect her*] No!
MABEL.	[*to* Narrator] It was not right.
MIRROR VOICE 1.	[*echoing*] Not right
MIRROR VOICE 2.	Not right
NARRATOR.	And at once the misery which she always tried to hide, the profound
MIRROR VOICE 1.	dissatisfaction—
MABEL.	[*perhaps leaning against* Narrator] the sense she had had, ever since she was a child, of being
MIRROR VOICE 2.	inferior to other people—
MIRROR VOICE 1 *and*	
MIRROR VOICE 2.	[*repeating, under next line*] inferior to other people—
MABEL.	set upon her, relentlessly, remorselessly, with an intensity which she could not beat off,

NARRATOR. [*stops* Mirror Voices] as she would when she woke at night at home, by reading Borrow or Scott;

MABEL. for, oh, these men, oh, these women all were thinking—

MIRROR VOICE 1. What's Mabel wearing?

MIRROR VOICE 2. What a fright she looks!

MIRROR VOICE 1. What a hideous new dress!—

MABEL. their eyelids flickering as they came up and then their lids shutting rather tight. It was her own appalling inadequacy;

MIRROR VOICE 2. her cowardice;

MIRROR VOICE 1. her mean, water-sprinkled blood

MABEL. that depressed her.

NARRATOR. And at once the whole of the room where, for ever so many hours, she had planned with the little dressmaker how it was to go,

MIRROR VOICE 1. seemed sordid,

MIRROR VOICE 2. repulsive;

NARRATOR. and her own drawing-room so shabby,

MABEL. and herself, going out, puffed up with vanity as she touched the letters on the hall table and said: "How dull!"

MIRROR VOICE 1

and

MIRROR VOICE 2. to show off—[*orchestrated repetition under next line*]

MABEL. all this now seemed unutterably silly,

MIRROR VOICE 1. paltry,

MIRROR VOICE 2. provincial.

NARRATOR. All this had been absolutely destroyed,

MIRROR VOICE 2. shown up,

MIRROR VOICE 1. exploded,

NARRATOR. the moment she came into Mrs. Dalloway's drawing-room.
[*Takes* Mabel *and moves her to another part of the stage, while* Mirror Voice 1 *and* Mirror Voice 2 *stay in the party area*] What she had thought that evening when, sitting over the teacups, Mrs. Dalloway's invitation came, was that,

MABEL. of course, she could not be fashionable. It was absurd to pretend to even—

NARRATOR. fashion meant cut, meant style, meant thirty guineas at least—

MABEL. but why not be original? Why not be herself, anyhow?

NARRATOR. And, getting up, she had taken that old fashion book of her mother's, a Paris fashion book of the time of the Empire, and had thought

MABEL. how much prettier, more dignified, and more—

NARRATOR. womanly

MABEL. womanly they were then,

NARRATOR. and so set herself—

MABEL. oh, it was foolish—

NARRATOR. [*consoling* Mabel] trying to be like them,

MABEL. pluming herself in fact upon being modest

NARRATOR. and old fashioned and very charming,

MABEL. giving herself up,

NARRATOR. no doubt about it,

MABEL. to an orgy of self-love which deserved to be chastised,

NARRATOR. [*with a sigh, gently*] and so rigged herself out like this.
[*takes* Mabel *back to the imaginary mirror*]

MABEL.   But she dared not look in the glass. She could not face the whole horror—

MIRROR VOICE 1. the pale yellow, idiotically old-fashioned silk dress with its long skirt and its high sleeves

MIRROR VOICE 2. and its waist

MABEL.   and all the things that looked so charming in the fashion book,

MIRROR VOICE 2. but not on her,

MIRROR VOICE 1. not among all these ordinary people.

MABEL.   She felt like a dressmaker's dummy standing there for young people to stick pins into.

At the end of the story, the two mirror characters would wrap Mabel in the cloak. Throughout the story, they would become the mirror images. They might also perform a dance that would suggest the "spears" image with their long yellow scarves, drawn from the line, "And all the spears were gathered into her breast as she walked towards Mrs. Dalloway and said, 'Good night.' "

The differences between these three scripts—in narrator-character relationships, in tone, and in characterization—would emerge even more clearly if you were actually to produce them. Much of the meaning of these scripts, as with any script, becomes apparent in production—when you can see the narrator-character relationships and hear the tonalities of the lines. Although we've tested these scripts in production, we think of them as works in progress. Different directors and casts would change some of the line divisions. The flexibility of the Chamber Theatre medium is that it allows—even encourages—the adapter to experiment continually with the script, shifting lines and adjusting movement patterns as new meanings emerge from the text.

DIRECTING CHAMBER THEATRE: SPECIAL CONSIDERATIONS

In describing Chamber Theatre, Robert Breen writes: "Chamber Theatre is dedicated to the proposition that the ideal literary experience is one in which the simultaneity of the drama . . . may be profitably combined with the novel's narrative privilege of examining human motivation at the moment of action."[9] The word *combine* is a key word for the director of Chamber Theatre. Chamber Theatre combines the lyric and dramatic modes, combines acoustic and pictorial space, combines past and present, and combines showing an action and telling a tale.

The richness of Chamber Theatre as a medium stems from these tensive combinations, which are the very heart of the form. The tensive complex both intrigues us and presents major directorial challenges.

Although many staging procedures are common to Chamber Theatre and Readers Theatre (see Part 3), some special staging considerations are so much a part of the total scripting process of Chamber Theatre that they're best discussed within the context of script creation. The success of your staging of prose fiction depends largely on your ability to use the narrator so that narrative point of view becomes a major action.

In Chamber Theatre, the blocking of the narrator becomes an **analogue** for point of view. Since the point of view is comprised of the physical and psychological positions the narrator takes toward the action of the story being told, the narrator's location onstage defines time as well as space and attitude as well as physical vantage point. Creating analogous movement depends on establishing narrator relationships and balancing the activities of showing and telling.

Establishing Narrative Relationships with the Audience

You first want to know how the narrator meets the audience. Since the narrator is the liaison between the audience and the story, every movement the narrator makes defines the nature of that relationship. Does the narrator recognize the existence of audience members by addressing them directly? Or is the verbal contact more indirect, as the narrator seems to be involved with the world of the story? Every story implicitly acknowledges a reader because telling is telling *to* someone; similarly, in every Chamber Theatre production, the narrator in some way contacts the audience directly, because presenting a story is presenting to someone. Some texts are more overt in their recognition of the reader or audience than others; whether the "Dear reader" of eighteenth-century novels or the "you" of twentieth-century fiction, direct address suggests that the narrator may move close to the audience members, sit among them, or perhaps even touch them. The narrator's entrance, whether from the audience area, from offstage, or from a discovered position onstage, should nonverbally as well as verbally establish the nature of the narrator-audience relationship.

The text, which suggests the narrator's tone of voice, will help determine the physical distance between narrator and audience. If a narrator speaks confidentially—"He didn't really have the money, but he thought the bluff would work"—or if the tone is primarily defensive—"I want you to know that it wasn't my fault"—the narrator might spend much time close to the audience to make a case, explain motives, or casually crack jokes for the benefit of the listeners. Even if such a narrator moves completely upstage, the audience feels closely included in the narrative process.

Some narrators are more stiff and formal; although they may physically approach the audience, they carry with them an attitude which keeps a psychological space between them and the listeners. An ironic narrative tone usually creates a communicative bond with the audience on a level different from that of the unfolding of the events of the story. At times, the ironic narrator will need to move out of the story's framework to communicate the ironic understanding; this action implies, for example, "Little does she know how serious a mistake this is." The cynical narrator may also use the audience as someone with whom to share an attitude, or she may be cynical toward the audience, in which case she might keep some physical distance. A compassionate storyteller, such as an intensely involved omniscient third person narrator, will spend a great deal of time in interaction with characters and will be mainly concerned with helping the audience to understand character feelings.

In our first script of "The New Dress," the narrator is gently ironic, establishing an immediate affinity with the members of the audience by delivering the opening line to them. This narrator guides the audience through the story, maintaining a dual attitude toward Mabel: the narrator understands her feelings but sees the humor in them. Lines such as, "And at once the misery which she always tried to hide," might be delivered to the audience to emphasize their ironic humor. The narrator of our second script, maintaining a rather clinical attitude, is much more interested in creating the environment of the party (chiefly by moving the cardboard figures around). This narrator might come onstage before the production, openly adjusting the placement of the cardboard cutouts. As a comic touch, this narrator may even try to propel Mabel around as a cardboard figure. The narrator of the second script is less emotionally involved with Mabel's predicament than the first narrator. The storyteller of the third script of

"The New Dress," however, is very sympathetic to Mabel and protective of her. This narrator is more interested in sharing Mabel's position than in siding with the audience; she never establishes contact with the audience at Mabel's expense.

Staging Narrative Action

Chamber Theatre is a process of discovery in space. What makes this medium so exciting is its specialized use of space—to depict psychological and temporal relationships, to reveal narrative attitude, and to expose unreliability—which is unlike its use in any other theatrical medium. Chamber Theatre uses pictorial space more than Readers Theatre, and differently than Conventional Theatre. Space in Chamber Theatre isn't principally a springboard into acoustic space, nor is it used primarily for visual or dramatic effect; stage space in Chamber Theatre is used analytically, as a critical reflection of implicit relationships in the text. The Chamber Theatre director uses the narrator as a kind of stylus, carving space to show character relationships and psychological states. The movement of that stylus also indicates the narrator's use of three time systems—condensed time, suspended time, and equivalent time.

The Narrator's Use of Time Systems

When a narrator condenses time, she is usually telling part of the story directly to an audience. The narrator's position in space, therefore, should be in direct relation to the audience—whether that means the narrator is close to the audience or physically removed with focus directed at them. In the activity of telling, in which time is condensed, the narrator's orientation is toward acoustic space, toward an imaginative connection with the audience. When the narrator is telling, she dominates the action of the story; stage position and movement should reflect that dominance.

A narrator suspends time to fill in descriptive details and to explore motivations. Two factors affect the staging of the narrator using a suspended time system: (1) what the narrator is focusing on, whether a visual scene, an impression, or an idea, and (2) how the scene or idea is perceived, whether from a close or distant position, through the narrator's eyes or through the eyes of a character. The narrator directs the audience's focus toward whatever is being explored either onstage or offstage. A motivation may be explained by using direct offstage focus to the audience (see Chapter 7), as in the narrator's delivery of the motivational line, "Trying to be like them," directly to the audience in script 1 of "The New Dress"; by using onstage focus to the character, as in the script 3 narrator's delivery of the same line to Mabel, as if consoling her; or by using a combination of both.

The narrator's location in stage space should correspond to the implied physical position of the storyteller in the text. When a third person omniscient narrator is seeing through a character's eyes, for example, she must literally be able to share that character's perspective. Obviously the director would want to block the narrator and character close together at such times. Script 3 of "The New Dress" is filled with "such times." The narrator moves physically close to Mabel, sharing her perceptions and sympathetically listening to her feelings.

In moments of equivalent time, the narrator either steps back to allow the characters to show their own scene, becomes a character in the scene, or employs vivid words to unfold an action which may or may not be staged. When the narrator steps back, relinquishing centrality, she should literally move to a more peripheral position onstage. The degree of the narrator's removal is determined in part by the number of verbal or nonverbal interjections the narrator must make during the course of the scene. In such moments of direct showing, the audience's orientation is toward pictorial space, while the storyteller's focus is on both the audience and the scene, creating a lively tensiveness between showing and telling.

When a narrator is in scene, either as a third person narrator who takes on a character or as a first person narrator who moves into the past, the narrator/character's orientation is onstage in pictorial space without acknowledgment of the audience. At one point in script 3 of "The New Dress," when Mabel and the narrator move (in what seems to be equivalent time) to the mirror, the narrator tries to prevent Mabel from looking in the mirror by saying No! as if to protect her from the vision she'll see. Notice that the narrator's line "No!" is taken from the longer expression, "No! It was not right," in the printed work. In its original context, the line revealed Mabel's feelings about her dress. By dividing the line differently, we've added another level to implied meaning: No! Do not look in the mirror. This is most fully realized when the narrator stands in front of the mirror and gestures toward Mabel. Finally, a narrator can use equivalent time to tell a scene directly to the audience, giving a blow-by-blow account. The scene may also be staged while the narrator describes it; in this case, the audience's orientation is simultaneously toward the onstage scene (in pictorial space) and the narrator's words (in acoustic space). Narrators can allow the scene to play while they describe it, freeze it from time to time while they go on with the action verbally, show the scene in slow motion, or accelerate it.

Staging Psychological States

To show psychological states of being—whether that of a character or of a first person narrator—space is usually used symbolically. The psychological state of memory, for example, is often staged so that one stage area refers to time present, while others represent times past. The action of the short story, "Sex Education," by Dorothy Canfield, is built around a series of three different memories of the same incident, which are relived a generation apart during the life of a single character. One production technique to differentiate both the time and substance of each memory is to assign a different stage area for each reliving. As another production idea, one section of the stage might be reserved as a place of memory, which the character enters three times; to distinguish between the memories, slide projections, lights, and costumes would be altered. In both techniques the state of memory is separated from the state of everyday experience spatially.

Another psychological state in which audiences are particularly interested is the degree of reliability with which the character or narrator tells the story. Each of our scripts of "The New Dress" shows a different degree of Mabel's reliability, from least reliable in script 1 (because the narrator seems to relate more to the audience than to Mabel) to somewhat reliable in script 2 (because Mabel is at least aware of the forces that drive her) and script 3 (because she receives some sympathy from the narrator who plays close to her).

A classic example of narrative ambiguity is Henry James's *Turn of the Screw*, in which the reader is uncertain of the reliability of the main character, the governess. A director has at least three choices in staging the James story: (1) the narrator can play close to the governess, obviously sharing her attitude and thereby reinforcing the validity of her impressions, (2) the narrator can become reasonably objective, keeping physical distance from the governess whenever possible, so that the audience is unsure as to whether they should believe the governess, and (3) the narrator can display an attitude contradicting the governess, even when he is looking over her shoulder. The resulting impression, of course, is that the governess is not to be trusted; this way the unreliability itself is staged. In the first and third versions, ambiguity is resolved, whereas in the second option, ambiguity is retained.

The appeal of many stories comes from their ability to probe psychological aberrations, such as hallucinations, wish fulfillment dreams, nightmares, or schizophrenia. Scripting will feature alternate states of consciousness verbally, usually through orchestration, but it's the director's responsibility to create visual analogues for these moments. Directors will often spatialize aberrant states of mind so that some stage areas are used to play the sane scenes while others are reserved for the realms of inner consciousness. On the other hand, in some scripts you may deliberately want to use the same space for normal and aberrant behavior to show a double existence in the guise of normality, as in "The Secret Life of Walter Mitty" by James Thurber. Producing "Walter Mitty," you might want to transform the stage space from the ordinary to the fantastic through media, although the narrator can suspend normal time through words alone while the daydream takes over.

Depending upon the text, the narrator signals transitions from one mental state to another in different ways. Strong narrators can cause characters to face their submerged selves either by materializing a second self or by playing the role themselves; can force characters to remember by leading them to the onstage place of memory; can initiate mental aberration by calling forth hallucinatory images, taking a role in the alternate world, or enticing the character toward the onstage place of insanity. Narrators who exert less control over characters can assist in the character's own depiction of psychological states by offering props, exemplified by the narrator's offer of a mirror to Mabel, by becoming a supporting rather than a dominating character, or by standing close to the audience, almost as a fellow observer.

Staging Narrator-Character Relationships

On a simplified level, you can assume that at any given time in a script a narrator either supports, or doesn't support, character action. By *support*, we mean that the narrator seems to sanction the character's action, to approve of it, and even to assist or share in it. When a narrator doesn't support the character's action, the narrator may be ironic, disapproving, or simply physically withdrawn from the character. The tensive shifts between the positions of support and nonsupport constitute a central action of Chamber Theatre. Many staging techniques have been used by directors to clarify these narrator-character relationships as they develop in the script. We can suggest several methods, but you'll discover your own techniques as you work with your script in rehearsal.

A narrator shows support for a character in many ways that real-life individuals encourage each other. The narrator and the character are physically close, they may touch, they send approving glances, and they seek to view life from similar perspectives. A narrator may hold a chair or a coat for a character, or, as in our script of "The New Dress," may step into the role of a servant who assists the action, thereby giving subtle support to the character. Very often support will come through tone of voice or lines of focus. Even though a narrator may be physically removed from the character in a scene—because the language of the text indicates a panoramic view of the action (as in position 1) or because the narrator decides to enter position 4 to show the scene—the storyteller can still indicate support by a warm tone, encouraging facial expression, and by simply looking at the character.

The most immediate way to show lack of support for a character's action is to withdraw from the character. Yet withdrawal can take many forms: physically the narrator can turn and walk away, glance knowingly at the audience, or dismiss the character with gestures and facial expressions. Vocally, narrators may indicate disapproval or disinterest through tone of voice. Many nonsupportive narrators are ironic. Irony can be shown by the narrator's focus and delivery being directed toward the audience at ironic moments, regardless of how physically close the narrator may be to the character. An ironic narrator can also indicate irony of statement or dramatic irony by materializing a scene or an alternate character for purposes of contradicting what has gone before. When a script indicates irony, contradiction is a key to staging. A director would be well-advised to establish contrasts between the character and narrator in such aspects as body position, eye focus, and tone of voice to highlight the irony.

A subtle way to indicate narrator support or nonsupport is based on the roles the narrator assumes in relation to the character. If the narrator of "The New Dress" were to take the role of Miss Milan, the dressmaker, for example, such a character assignment would automatically indicate narrative support of Mabel's feelings. To have the narrator take on the gossipy roles of the other characters at the party (who Mabel believes disapprove of her as in script 2) would reveal a nonsupportive narrator.

Of course, most narrative fiction—especially ironic works—continually shift nuances of narrative support and nonsupport. One way the shifts can be shown is by varying the kinds of roles the narrator takes. Another way is to direct the storyteller to mix support and nonsupport in a single piece of stage business. A narrator might hold a chair for a character but shove it under the table very abruptly, might light a cigarette with a disapproving look, or become a mirror for the character, as in script 1 of "The New Dress", seeming to support the character's actions by reflecting them, but actually forcing the character to see herself or himself. Since physical actions and vocal tones or words can contradict each other, the director has rich resources in human behavior for stating complexities of narrator-character relationships.

What can be achieved in Chamber Theatre staging is limited only by the relative complexity of the point of view of the text coupled with your imagination. A rich narrative text in the hands of an inventive director can produce an outstanding theatre experience.

NOTES

1. Truman Capote, "My Side of the Matter," *A Tree of Night and Other Stories* (New York: Random House, 1949), p. 121.
2. D. H. Lawrence, "Mother and Daughter," *The Complete Short Stories of D. H. Lawrence*, vol. 3 (New York: Viking Press, 1961), p. 812.

3. William Goldman, *The Princess Bride* (New York: Ballantine Books, 1973), p. 39.

4. For further discussion of dialogue tags in performance, see Lilla A. Heston, "A Note on Prose Fiction: The Performance of Dialogue Tags," *The Speech Teacher* 22 (January 1973): 69–72.

5. Richard Eastman, *A Guide to the Novel* (San Francisco: Chandler, 1956), p. 53.

6. Wayne C. Booth, *The Rhetoric of Fiction* (Chicago: University of Chicago Press, 1961), chap. 5.

7. For further discussion of alienation, see Robert S. Breen, *Chamber Theatre* (Englewood Cliffs, N.J.: Prentice-Hall, 1978), chap. 5.

8. Virginia Woolf, "The New Dress," *A Haunted House and Other Stories* (New York: Harcourt Brace Jovanovich, 1972).

9. Breen, *Chamber Theatre*, p. 5.

SUGGESTIONS FOR FURTHER READING

Breen, Robert S. *Chamber Theatre.* Englewood Cliffs, N.J.: Prentice-Hall, 1978.

———. "A Chamber Theatre Production of *Jealousy.*" *Interpretation Newsletter*, March 1966, pp. 4–6.

Heston, Lilla A. "A Note on Prose Fiction: The Performance of Dialogue Tags." *The Speech Teacher* 22 (January 1973): 69–72.

King, Judy Yordon. "Chamber Theatre by Any Other Name . . .?" *The Speech Teacher* 21 (September 1972): 193–196.

Maclay, Joanna H. *Readers Theatre: Toward a Grammar of Practice.* New York: Random House, 1971.

Parella, Gilda. "Through the 'I' of the Beholder: A Rationale for Physicalization in the Performance of Narratives." *Central States Speech Journal* 25 (Winter 1974): 296–302.

Park, Lea. "A Chamber Theatre Production of *The Centaur,*" *Interpretation Newsletter*, May 1967, pp. 4–5.

Sturges, Christine A. "The Effect of a Narrator's Presence on Audience Response to Character in the Staging of Narrative Literature." *The Speech Teacher* 24 (Januray 1975): 46–52.

CHAPTER SIX

From Assemblage to Collage: The Compiled Script

The whole difference between construction and creation is exactly this: that a thing constructed can only be loved after it is constructed; but a thing created is loved before it exists.

G. K. Chesterton, *Preface to Dickens' Pickwick Papers*

We are all collectors. It's human nature to surround ourselves with things we enjoy. Some people collect matchbooks or menus, others gather compliments. The truth is, we accumulate the things that fascinate us and we store or display them in our individual styles. As readers who are intrigued by literature, the more we read, the more we become collectors, not only of literary ideas and perspectives, but of phrases, speeches, and whole stanzas that stay in our heads. Listen to the following collection of voices speaking about women:

"She walks in beauty, like the night."

"My mistress' eyes are nothing like the sun."

"A woman, a dog and a walnut-tree,
The more you beat 'em the better they be."

"For the female of the species is more deadly than the male."

"I met a lady in the meads,
   Full beautiful—a faery's child."

"I expect that woman will be the last thing civilized by man."

"O woman! Lovely woman! Nature made thee
To temper man: we had been brutes without you."

"Frailty, thy name is woman."[1]

As any contemporary feminist would tell you, these quotations were definitely spoken by men! The "character" voices create a clamoring chorus of attitudes, opinions, witty barbs, and emotional tributes which make us smile or bristle as the case may be. We enjoy hearing each voice, but we also enjoy the chorus of collected ideas and perspectives they create.

By now, you've learned to open the pages of individual literary works and release their voices into transformed energy. In the process, you listen to the voices, become sensitive to the lines of force that create them, recognize their individuality. Through this intimate process, you become attuned to the literary worlds you penetrate, and value the uniqueness of each voice that speaks to you. As a seasoned reader, the more voices you encounter, the better you're able to perceive patterns of utterance and find new pleasure in seeking out the variety of voices that speak out on the same subject. You learn more about love by reading *A Midsummer Night's Dream* and *The Winter's Tale* than by reading *A Midsummer Night's Dream* alone. Your sensibility is expanded even more when you also read Murray Schisgal's *Luv*, within the context of all your previous reading (and experience with) love.

As you experience these contrasts in the tonalities of the voices, you may begin to be intrigued by the whole idea of love as reflected in a collection of voices from literature. The same is true of many other subjects. As the varieties of human experience in different literary works accumulate in your mind, an infinite number of patterns begins to emerge. And as a transformer of literary works, you'll experience a growing fascination with the scripting possibilities inherent in these literary perspectives you've collected. This chapter talks about collecting: kinds of literary collections and the creative vehicle for displaying them—the compiled script.

WHAT IS COMPILING?

Thus far our explorations into Interpreters Theatre have involved seeking presentational form in literature. From creating texts to designing scripts, the purpose has been to actualize the forms in a single literary work. Now, we're asking you to shift your focus from an individual work of literature to an idea from your own experience. When you shift from an overriding interest in a single literary work to a fascination with a concept, the entire relationship between transformer and text changes. Your love affair is now with your own idea or theme, primarily, rather than with a particular piece of literature. Your literary appreciation isn't diminished; you'll still respect the works that move you. But you'll have stepped onto another creative plane, where you're moved by a creative urge originating in you, which is larger than, or different from, any single piece of literature.

Such a creative urge can inspire an artist to create completely original works. The maker of the compiled script, however, is inspired to use the literary pieces he has collected to create a new form. Sometimes these pieces are whole works and sometimes they are as small as a single phrase from a work. As a creator of compiled scripts, you'll borrow segments of all sizes from literature. Rather than seek presentational form in literature, you'll now create presentational forms from literature. How you can make "new forms from old" is our present subject.

When you approach literature this way, you still have a responsibility to understand the original context so you know—at the very least—how you've altered the context of the lines you've borrowed. Regardless of the extent of alteration made to the original works, **juxtaposition** is the key to achieving new structural form.

To compile is to juxtapose literary or nonliterary materials or both to serve an idea or theme. Similar to the effect of montage in filmmaking, the effect of juxtaposition is the creation of new meaning in the juncture between selections, while retaining meaning within the component parts themselves. Juxtaposition affords the compiler an added source of power from which to tap energy, and tensiveness is created not only by the interaction of power sources within selections, but by the interaction between the selections themselves. The combination of the junctural meanings and the internal meanings becomes the real power of the new form.

In the world of objects, for example, crumpled pieces of paper often signify the act of discarding, while a typewriter may suggest the act of creating. If you juxtapose the two objects into a single image, with crumpled papers surrounding the typewriter, you create additional meaning—frustration, perhaps—which isn't inherent in either of the component parts, but arises from combining the images of discarding and creating. The power of that single image comes from three sources: the meaning of the paper, the significance of the typewriter, and the juncture between the two meanings.

Like the metaphoric writer, the compiler of scripts is interested in creating meaning through juxtaposition, which transcends, but includes, the internal meanings of two or more literary selections. If, for example, a section of a compiled script were to juxtapose the lines from John Donne's "Song," "No where / Lives a woman true and fair," with the lilting strains of the nursery rhyme, "Georgy Porgy, puddin' and pie, / Kissed the girls and made them cry," the resultant meaning would be greater than either single source. Combining them achieves a sense of the reciprocity of infidelity—that both men and women can be untrue. The power of the script is in that statement.

Types of Juxtaposition

To help us describe various approaches to juxtaposition, we've borrowed two terms from the related field of art: **assemblage** and **collage**. Each of these terms suggests a different way of bringing things together into a larger form.

In art, the assemblage is usually composed of found objects, already made materials not created by the artist; the artist assembles them. The assemblage is usually three-dimensional, the objects of which it's composed often being readily identifiable (see figure 6.1).

Assemblage, in relation to the compiled script, is a collection of identifiable units—literary selections—each of which relates to a central theme. Each part has its own identity and separate existence, but is linked to the other segments by transitions of various kinds. Popular kinds of literary assemblage bring together works by a single author, selections that represent a literary period or movement, or whole literary pieces relating to a single subject. (For an example of a literary assemblage, see "The Time of All Novembers," beginning on page 164 of this chapter.)

Collage in art is a composition made of fragmented materials cut and pasted together to form a new entity. The distinguishing feature of collage, in contrast to assemblage, is the use of pieces of original materials, put together so that, although the segments may be recognizable, they are more completely subservient to a new compositional arrangement. The created identity of a collage incorporates and overrides the identities of the components from which it is formed (see figure 6.2).

A literary collage is composed of phrases, stanzas, or paragraphs (small pieces) taken from many works. They're combined to create new contexts, new meanings, and a new form. The components of a collage do not necessarily retain their original meanings. Because of the fragmented nature of the segments of the collage, much of the cohesiveness of the script and the meaning created by the new arrangement is achieved and reinforced in performance. Therefore,

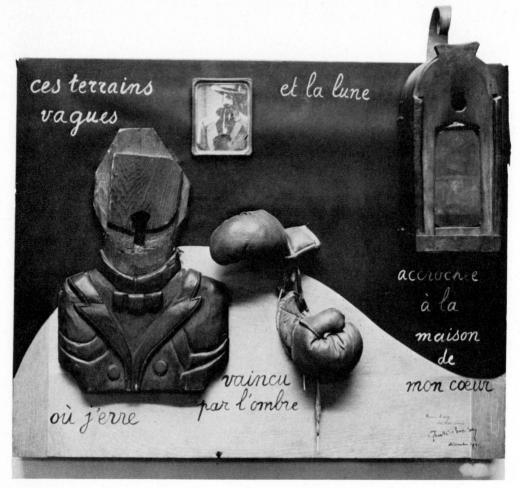

Figure 6.1: An assemblage: *Poem-Object*, 1941, by André Breton. Collection, The Museum of Modern Art, New York.

it's important for the compiler to write rather explicit production notes in the script. (For an example of a literary collage, see "November Hunt" on page 173 of this chapter.)

As techniques of juxtaposition, assemblage and collage represent a wide range of types of creative compiling; they may be considered to define the two extremes of a continuum. Assemblage and collage suggest different artistic attitudes that you, as the compiler, may take as you bring materials together. Figure 6.3 suggests the relationship between the type of compiled script you make, the methods of treating material you gather, and the structure of the finished script.

At one end of the continuum is the **collector** who, carefully preserving the integrity and beauty of each collected piece, arranges them together into a single program of the assemblage

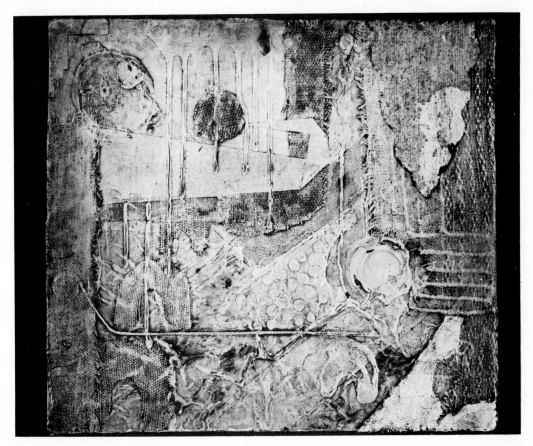

Figure 6.2: A collage: *Study II*, Author Unknown.

type. Although the theme or subject of the program provides a unity, the overall literary structure is actually a collection of individual works.

Excerpting occupies the midpoint of this progression from whole works to fragments of works; it is the process of lifting out segments from original works for use in a script. The compiler combines the excerpts into a single script, which usually has a more clearly defined overall form than does the assemblage. Because the parts of the script are excerpts rather than whole works, they cannot stand completely alone and must be woven more tightly together by transitional materials; yet, because an excerpt *may* be fairly lengthy, it may retain some of its own unity and be recognized as part of the original work.

The most radical treatment of literary materials is **fragmenting**, the process of breaking literature apart into separate voices made up of lines that can be combined with other literary fragments into a completely new structure: a collage. In collecting for an assemblage, the power source complex of a literary work is left intact: whatever is the dominant source of power in the

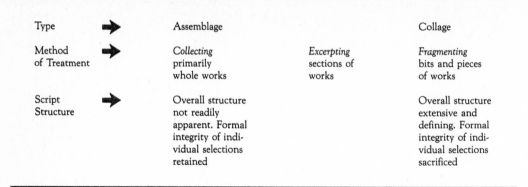

Figure 6.3: Techniques of juxtaposition.

original work remains a power source in the juxtaposition with other works. In fragmenting for the collage, the web of power of the original work is disregarded; individual fragments act as power sources, combining with each other to form the voices of the newly created script. Forming the other extreme of the continuum, the collage has a clearly defined comprehensive structure that constitutes a new form in which the individual parts are subsumed by the whole.

Combining Types of Juxtaposition

Although we've distinguished between types of juxtaposition, from assemblage to collage, and between methods of gathering and combining materials—collecting, excerpting, and fragmenting—in the practical creation of a script, the compiler often combines types and methods. Each subject tends to lead to its own formal realization; the final structure may be a pure assemblage or collage, or—more likely—it will be a mixture. It's useful, however, to recognize that differences in type and method exist.

SIX STEPS TO CREATING A COMPILED SCRIPT

Part of the fun of compiling a script is that no material is off limits—anything goes! The worlds of literature, documentary materials, news stories, cartoons, slides, songs—even graffiti—are all available to the compiler. The only restrictions are the limits of your imagination, audience analysis, and the parameters of good taste.

Because you are the author of your compilation, your purpose becomes the purpose of the script. As in any creative process, purposes range from the purely aesthetic to the utilitarian. A compiled script may be created solely for the beauty or dramatic power of the segments of which it is composed; it may carry an argument, communicate information, probe social issues, or merely entertain; or it may be based on any combination of the many reasons one person may wish to communicate with others.

Step 1: Finding the Core

How do you find the idea—the core or nucleus—around which you'll build your script? If you're interested in making an assemblage, many traditional ideas are available to you. The works of a single author often make a delightful evening. Imagine, for example, a program of selected works of Robert Frost interspersed with slides of the New England landscape; or of James Dickey's poems with transitions of bluegrass music. Literary movements or themes, such as Southern gothic fiction or the beat generation, provide excellent subjects for the collector. Famous assemblages you may have seen are *Thurber Carnival*, in which stories, dramatic sketches, and cartoons are combined with music; the television series *Anyone for Tennyson?* which features a variety of authors and literary themes in specific settings; and *The Belle of Amherst*, a one-woman show of the poetry and letters of Emily Dickinson.

If you're contemplating a collage, the core idea becomes more personal. Rather than assembling the already structured ideas of others, you're working from your private vision, which hasn't been stated in just this way by any one author. Start with yourself—your dreams, interests, far-out ideas, close-in concepts, ethical and moral beliefs, feelings about social justice—any idea that appeals to you and that seems to beg you to explore it. What are the themes of your life? What objects or ideas captivate you? Everyone has hidden interests, just as everyone has bits of musical scores and song lyrics that run through his or her head. You hum the tunes that haunt you; the compiled script is one way to play out the ideas that intrigue you.

Your working idea may be quite defined initially (for example, you're fascinated by the early romantic poems of W. B. Yeats and wish to show how he has used Irish folklore in his poems) or rather vague (you want to explore the emotional side of aging, but you aren't sure what you want to say yet). Let the idea solidify at its own speed; at this point in your creative process, there's much value in intentional vagueness. Leave your idea open enough that the discoveries you make in your search for materials can help shape it.

Once you think you've found a core idea for your script, ask yourself: Would others possibly be interested in this subject, too? Does the theme have potential audience interest, or is it too private to be made into an interesting presentational form for the stage? Think of the presentational value of the idea—its ability to engage an audience, to draw the audience members into the emotional, intellectual, physical, and sensory world of the idea. You might want to try out your ideas on some trusted friends who'll tell you honestly whether they'd be interested in being audience to explorations of such themes. Keep in mind good taste and general appeal for the kind of audience you intend.

Jot down your working ideas, with any supporting information you can think of—possible literary selections, sources of nonliterary materials, notions on staging. Refrain from the temptation to be prescriptive at this point; you're recording possibilities in full knowledge that the ideas will develop and change with time. Put your written statement aside for a while and relax.

Step 2: The Voyage of Discovery

After you have given yourself enough time to sleep on the idea, look at it again. Is it still as interesting to you? If you had more than one theme in mind, put all but one aside, keeping them, like the persona of "The Road Not Taken" by Robert Frost, "for another day." Commit yourself to one idea, and let it take you on a challenging voyage.

This is the time to gather literature and other materials to help actualize your theme. Begin with works you know, which seem to voice an aspect of your emerging concept, but don't limit yourself to what you already know. Read all you can find on your subject, copying selections or sections you sense may be useful for the script. Avail yourself of subject indices in the library, using them as guides, but also browse through the stacks. Subject indices list works that use the key word you are exploring, but often other works probe the ideas you have in mind as fully as works listed in the index. Let suggested bibliographies and footnotes from one source lead you to others; *The Reader's Guide* (or any other bibliography) is only a starting point, not the final word on what pieces are available. Also, brainstorm with your friends; many times a classmate will have read something just right for your script. We hope this period of creative detective work will be great fun for you, and a period of genuine discovery.

If your subject permits it, seek out various genres and modes; examine fiction and nonfiction, elite and popular literature, classic and contemporary pieces. Search for a mixture of tonalities—comic and tragic, dark and bright, smooth and rough, warm and cold—either in the same piece, or in the possible juxtaposition of pieces. Don't be afraid of contradictions in form, style, and context; a script that organizes selections with both similar and contradictory points of view may be very powerful indeed.

In addition to literary and nonliterary written sources, explore nonprint possibilities. Music, dance, art, cartoons—all can make central contributions to a script. Materials present themselves to you in unlikely places. You may discover graffiti you can use, or found art you can incorporate. One student's attention was caught by a crumpled Orange Crush can; the image of the crushed can (which is, of course, orange in color) became a working symbol for a compiled script on the use of double meanings and *trompe l'oeil* in literature. If you're sensitized to the environment, you may be surprised how many things are available to be used in your script!

As you gather sources, don't hesitate to write your own materials as well. Later on in the process of creating a script, you may sense the need to write transitional material. This is good, but don't limit yourself to writing only transitions. If you're a writer and sense the need for a selection your library search didn't yield, write it.

Survey all that you've gathered and make preliminary selections from your collection—selections that seem most valuable for your script. Keeping in mind variety and contrast, choose many more than you will probably use.

Step 3: The Gestation Period

It's important in any creative process to give yourself time for the creative juices to flow. Live with your idea for a while; read over your gathered selections and think about your subject at unusual times in unlikely places. Often when you are least anxiety-ridden about it, an angle of vision on the theme or a workable interpretation will occur to you.

During the gestation period, some selections will emerge as core materials, obviously quite usable for your theme, while others will need to be discarded. As you live with your potential selections, begin to probe them for their power sources. Your analysis will give you a solid understanding of the potential power generated by each of your sources, and may suggest ways to shape, excerpt, or fragment selections in accord with your purpose. (Review the methods of literary analysis in Chapters 2 and 4.)

Step 4: Crystallization

Crystallizing your theme and solidifying your perspective toward it is one of the most difficult steps. If you're exploring the works of a single author or historical period, what is the vision you'll take of it? If your subject is a state of being, such as loneliness, or a situation, such as racial inequality, how do you intend to tackle the issue? From whose (or what) perspective will you present material on the subject? How many perspectives do you intend to include? In other words, what is your production concept? It's better to develop a few well-chosen aspects of your subject than to try to explore all the possibilities your subject presents. The best script is often the simplest.

When you solidify your approach, you'll automatically see that certain selections will work with your concept and others won't. Begin to shape the material you've chosen. Try different sequences, combinations, and sizes of pieces to put together. These considerations lead you immediately to the next step.

Step 5: The Search for Form

In actual practice, steps 4 and 5 work together: what you choose to say determines and depends on how you plan to say it and how you plan to stage it. Furthermore, as your notion of a formal structure grows, your choices of material may alter.

Determine the voices or characters who'll speak your script and what lines of force they embody. Creating voices for the compiled script is much like finding and releasing voices in the adapted work. In compiling, you're again concerned with the voices (characters and other power sources) contained in the individual selections from which you've drawn your material. The script type and core idea largely determine the degree to which the voices in the individual segments will maintain their own identity. Each selection contained in an assemblage, for example, maintains its own voices; the assemblage is a series of adapted selections with the cast of character voices varying with each section of the script. In a collage, the voices are usually more consistent throughout the script. The compiler of the collage faces the problem of how to turn the voices contained in excerpts and fragments into the voices of the script—its special cast of characters. Individual voices for compiled scripts can be defined characters or ideological positions or attitudes.

The compiler has to be constantly aware of consistency and change in the role of the individual performer in the script. In the production of a compiled script each performer usually plays a series of parts, a task which can be bewildering if the script hasn't been carefully constructed. The problem is compounded in the collage by the original stylistic differences between the segments that compose the script. Although in a collage the segments are usually blended into a single formal unit, the form often contains shifting roles and scenes. When compiling a collage, you need to look carefully at the series of roles you've assigned each performer, making sure each is playable and consistent. In addition, a chorus of performers may take on a variety of roles in the compiled script; a chorus may be a necessity for a script that constantly shifts speakers and scenes.

As your script begins to come together, understanding how your script is to be organized for its dramatic, or emotional, effect is important. We use the phrase *dramatic form* to refer to the impelling movement of a script, not to suggest a mode or genre. Works in classical dramatic form move from an inciting action to a crisis or turning point, and then gather momentum once again to achieve a climax. At crisis points, the audience is moved, contacted on an emotional and sensory level. Many compiled scripts approximate classical dramatic form, gathering force and impact until a turning point or breaking point occurs, and then moving toward a climax. In a compiled script the climactic moment often embodies the impelling theme or idea of the script in such a way that the audience members think, "Aha!" Many compiled scripts aren't organized traditionally, moving instead toward a fullness of statement or a compelling emotional moment without going through a turning point. Such scripts gain power through accumulation of action.

Regardless of the kind of dramatic form your script takes, it must eventually build to some high point of intensity at which the audience is as moved by your script as they would be by a well-constructed play. You may feel as though you're part of a balancing act as you work with contradictions, contrasts in style and length, and individual structures, weaving them into a cohesive script with its own structural integrity. If you're making a collage, you'll find that the individual excerpts and fragments you're interweaving will create a logic of their own and tell you how they want to come together. As you work, check to see that your script is focused so the core idea is clear. Think in terms of the clarification of transitions. Imagine how the script will play. This is one of the most exciting and frustrating parts of making a script—shaping the materials into a new form that suggests something about the sources you have selected and something about you.

Step 6: Reevaluation

Put the script aside. After some time, reread it as if you were coming to it for the first time. Does the script do what you want it to do? Does it continue to evoke your imagination? Will an audience be able to follow your structure? Be sure that the main themes or ideas flow consistently through your script and that they're sufficiently reinforced to let the audience know they're main themes. Make sure you've worked out the reason for each shift of idea or attitude and that your audience will be able to follow the shifts. Check the attitude and perspective of the script for apparent inconsistencies. Reexamine emotional tension points and transitions and visualize how they will work in production. Be as objective as you can in your view of the script at this point; you may see some sections that need reworking.

Now you're ready to move into casting and rehearsal. You have a written script from which to work, but remember that the compiled script is particularly evolutionary; it grows and changes even through the rehearsal period.

These six steps are an overview of the procedures we follow when making a compiled script. Many of the decisions to be made during the script-making process are intuitive, but they are based on the compiler's knowledge of literature and ideas, analysis techniques, and formal construction. Since the overall structuring of the compiled script is an original process, the compiler needs to be familiar with some basic formal patterns in art.

SUGGESTED FORMS FOR COMPILED SCRIPTS

Think of yourself as an architect of scripts. No matter how you put your building blocks—the selections you have chosen—together, you'll have a form of some kind. As an architect's blueprints must pass the test of construction, your script has to stand the test of performance, and its formal properties determine much of its success or failure in production. Even with the assemblage, in which well-chosen literary works provide their own forms, the sequence of selections and the transitional devices between them can enhance or detract from the works themselves.

There are two major structural problems to solve in compiling a script: (1) How do you work with the structures of the individual selections you've chosen (whether literary or nonliterary) to form them into a script? (2) What will be the structure of the total script you're creating? Although we discuss these problems separately, the two questions have to be considered in relation to each other. It's difficult, for example, to excerpt and shape parts of works unless you have some concept of the total structure for which you're shaping them; also, you need to know the forms and textures of the pieces with which you're working to create the larger structure that can bring the pieces together. The compiler is constantly working back and forth between the smaller segments and the larger script concept.

Shaping the Segments

As you bring two or more pieces of material together, you have to deal in some manner with the individual forms of the pieces. Each literary genre or mode has characteristic formal shapes that help define it—the give and take of dramatic dialogue, the configuration of narrative movement, the rhythm of poetic meter—and each literary work molds these patterns into its own unique structure. Nonliterary materials have their own identifying forms, from the terse headlines of a newspaper article to the rambling flow of a conversational interview.

The problem of individual forms abates when you're working with assemblage, in which each segment brought together stands as an integral unit maintaining its own identity. In creating a collage, however, you work with a few lines from one poem, a paragraph from a story, a stanza from another poem, a passage of dialogue from a play, a line from a letter, and many other kinds of fragments. You face a variety of formal structures, each with a different rhythm, with different speakers, and with different language styles, tones, and attitudes. Although you may welcome these differences for contrast, the individuality of each piece with which you're working needs to be softened to some extent. To shape the larger structure of your collage, you often have to break down the formal structure of the original fragment or excerpt to enable it to become part of the larger work with a new structure and meaning.

As the creator of the script, you'll know how much you want each segment of your script to blend into the whole. In some sections of the script, you may wish complete submergence of the parts; in other places, you may want individual selections to be recognizable. Even a single line of a well-known selection may invoke the presence of the whole work for the listener. Such lines as, "Four score and seven years ago," or, "To be or not to be," cannot be included in a script without their bringing their context with them. This is useful for a compiler, because a whole situation can be invoked by the use of the first line of something as familiar as the Gettysburg Address, without having to include the whole text. It can also be a pitfall if you don't wish to invoke the context the line suggests.

The major processes by which individual selections are shaped toward inclusion in a larger form may be called, for convenience of discussion, **alteration, rearrangement**, and **conversion**. Which process you use and the degree to which you use it depend on the kind of script you're creating—from assemblage to collage. Obviously, the closer your script falls toward the collected assemblage, the less shaping you do with each individual selection. The collage requires the most work from the compiler.

Alteration

To alter means to adjust for a better fit. Unless you are creating a script that features a series of full-length, uncut original works, you'll need to alter your selections to make them fit together. The pieces in your finished script may differ in length, but it's important that no work overbalance the others; you may shorten some selections or delete passages from the middle of others to avoid this. With either a total work or an excerpted portion of a longer work, be certain that everything in the selection moves toward the point that you wish to make.

A dialogue sequence used in collage will blend into your script and into your cast of characters more smoothly if you delete names and other identifying specifics about the characters. Check the beginnings and endings of your selections: How do the ending of one piece and the beginning of the next fit together? What adjustments might you make to bring them into better harmony? As you alter the pieces of the script, you'll begin to get a sense of the kinds of transitions needed.

Rearrangement

To rearrange means to put in a different order. Many times, rearrangements of structural sequences are required in adapting a work to the stage. This is also true in creating the compiled script. The content of a selection may be just what you need, but the order of ideas or events may not match your structural concept. Don't hesitate to rearrange if you can do so without destroying the ideas you need. Rearrangement may be accomplished by changing the order of events within the selection, by scattering the events of a single selection throughout your script, or by inserting events from another selection into the original sequence. If you wish to repeat a whole selection several times in your script, you may want to vary its internal order. Rearrangement of the sequence will add variety to your script.

Conversion

Conversion, which means a change in the use, purpose, or function of something, is a fundamental process in creating a compiled script. The very nature of collage is the creation of a larger context different from any of the parts of which it's composed. To do this, the compiler makes use of various selections, many times reshaping the meaning to a different purpose or function. The juxtaposition of two pieces of literature adds dimension to both. When using fragmented materials, quite often a fragment will consist of a striking image or thought that, lifted out of the original work and placed in a new context, will carry a new meaning, perhaps even a reversed meaning. Because of the power of juxtaposition and the conversion of meaning or purpose it causes, take great care with the immediate context of each piece you use to make sure the sequence creates your intended meaning.

Creating the Overall Form

As you decide how to fit segments of your script together, you may become aware of an intuitive sense of overall form that suddenly guides your decision-making process. Every compiled script has (or ought to have) a central modality—either epic, dramatic, or lyric—that informs the entire structure of the program. Of course, your materials will likely be drawn from all three modes and, especially in the assemblage, such modal variety will be apparent in the final production. Yet, even with assemblages in which the collected parts maintain their own formal integrity and modality, it's useful to seek a central modality for the program that can be carried by the transitional framework of the program.

Epic Modality

Compiled scripts with a central epic modality rely on the presence of a story and a storyteller. The narrative voice becomes a liaison between the characters and the audience, directing the action in time and space. Epic scripts may combine all three modalities in the individual selections, but the pieces are juxtaposed in such a way that they unfold a story. Epic assemblages and collages often trace the chronological development of a period in history, an author's life, or an incident.

Scripts in the epic modality have a central narrative voice. The narrative lines may be spoken by one performer or several; the narrator usually introduces the script's subject, provides transitions, and concludes.

The script, *W. B. Yeats and the Little People of Ireland*[2], is an epic exploration of the work of William Butler Yeats. Selections from Yeats's early writings are interwoven with narrative Irish folktales into a modified collage form. Although many of the Yeats selections are either lyric or dramatic, they are part of the storytelling that permeates the script, parts of which follow.

W. B. Yeats and the Little People of Ireland

PEASANT 1.   It was one of the little people—a figure that kept changin' from a man to a woman and back again and walkin' round and round the bush in the forest.

PEASANT 2.   Ay—once I was standin' at the window, lookin' off toward Knocknarea, when the finest woman you ever saw came walkin' toward me—right across the mountain top. It was Queen Maeve herself, with a sword at her side. I covered my eyes, and when I looked again—she was gone.

NARRATOR.   William Butler Yeats, and the Little People of Ireland. Very early in life, Yeats decided that Ireland herself was to be an important part of his life work. He explored the legendary and supernatural heritage of the Irish people. Through his early poems and plays roam figures of the faery people, the Sidhe, who live in the wind; Maeve, their great queen who, according to legend, lies buried in a cairn of stones on top of Knocknarea in Sligo; Colite, Finn's friend; Niamh, who led Oisin on his merry chase; and many others. The symbols include the immortal white birds of fairyland and the wind itself, which whispers of man's vague desire and hope.

[*Sound interval*]

FEMALE VOICE.   The wind blows out of the gates of the day
The wind blows over the lonely of heart
And the lonely of heart is withered away
While the faeries dance in a place apart
Shaking their milk-white feet in a ring
Tossing their milk-white arms in the air;
For they heard the wind laugh and murmur and sing
Of a land where even the old are fair
And even the wise are merry of tongue.
But I heard a reed of Coolandy say
When the wind has murmured and laughed and sung,
The lonely of heart is withered away.

[*Sound interval*]

NARRATOR.   A little north of the town of Sligo, in Ireland, on the southern side of Ben Bulben, some hundreds of feet above the plain, there's a small white square in the limestone. No mortal has ever touched it with his hand. There is no more inaccessible place upon the earth and, to the Irish peasant, few more encircled by terror. It's the door of Faeryland. In the middle of the night it swings open, and the unearthly troop rushes out. All night the gay rabble sweep to and fro across the land, invisible to all, and the air is full of shrill voices—

[*Sound interval*]

PEASANT 3.   The host is riding from Knocknarea
               And over the grave of Clooth-na-Bare;
               Caolite tossing his burning hair,
               And Niamh calling

FEMALE VOICE.   Away, come away!
               Empty your heart of its mortal dream.
               The winds awaken, the leaves whirl round,
               Our breasts are heaving, our eyes are apart:
               And if any gaze on our rushing band,
               We come between him and the deed of his hand,
               We come between him and the hope of his heart.

PEASANT 3.   The host is rushing 'twixt night and day,
               And where is there hope or deed as fair?
               Caolite tossing his burning hair
               And Niamh calling

FEMALE VOICE.   Away, come away!

. . . .

NARRATOR.   There is magic in the sound of the Irish fiddle. In its music one seems to hear a voice of lamentation out of the Golden Age. It says that once the world was all perfect and kindly, and the kind world still exists, but buried under many spadefuls of earth. The faeries dwell within it, and lament over our fallen world in the lamentation of the wind-tossed reeds, in the song of the birds, and in the moan of the waves. With us the beautiful are not clever and the clever are not beautiful. The best of our moments are marred by a needle-prick of sad recollection. If only the faeries who live in the Golden Age could die, we might be happy, for the sad voices would be still; but they must sing and we must weep until the eternal gates swing open.

       [*Sound interval*]

PEASANT 1.   O sweet Everlasting Voices, be still;
               Go to the guards of the heavenly fold
               And bid them wander obeying your will,
               Flame under flame, till Time be no more;
               Have you not heard that our hearts are old,
               That you call in birds, in wind on the hill,
               O sweet Everlasting Voices, be still.

NARRATOR.   But they will not be still. And man will ever be reaching out toward them in desire. In the dim kingdom there is great abundance of all excellent things. There is more love there than upon the earth; there is more dancing there than upon the earth; and there is more treasure there than upon the earth. The Donegal peasants remember this when they sit beside the griddle at nightfall, and they tell stories and write songs about it that it may not be forgotten.

       [*Sound interval*]

PEASANT 2.   One time I was out cutting timber over in Inchy. I saw a girl picking nuts, with her hair hanging down over her shoulder, brown hair it was, and she was tall and comely. When she felt me coming she gathered herself up and was gone as if the earth had swallowed her up. And I followed her and looked for her, but I never could see her again from that day to this, never again.[3]

The entire atmosphere of *W. B. Yeats and the Little People of Ireland* is that of storytelling. Poems by Yeats are inserted into folktales and narrative explanations of Irish folklore; even though the poems aren't epic in themselves (consider, for example, "O sweet Everlasting Voices, be still"), they fit into the narrative framework of the script. The effect of the total script is a warm sharing of folklore, with the Narrator and Peasants 1, 2, and 3 acting as storytellers.

Dramatic Modality

Like literary selections that are dramatic in mode, compiled scripts with an overall dramatic structure tend to present individual voices speaking to each other, or to the audience, as characters in a setting. Although all literary power sources can function in every compiled script, the power sources of character and idea are central to scripts of dramatic modality. A dramatic assemblage collects works that present strong human perspectives or that seem to be spoken by individual voices or characters. In a collage, the dramatic modality is achieved by the juxtaposition of one point of view against another: who speaks the lines is as important as what is spoken. Dramatic speeches—whether long pieces or fragments of lines—are generally composed of all three modes, as is the dramatic dialogue in plays. However, the essential characteristic of the dramatic mode is its interest in the speaker of the speech, not—as in the lyric mode—in the beauty of the speech, or—as in the epic mode—in the narrative action of the speech.

In *I Dearly Love a Coal Mining Man*, a compiled documentary that depicts the role women have played in the development of better working conditions for coal miners, the action has a central dramatic modality.[4] The changes in the role of a coal miner's wife are seen by juxtaposing positions of early mining wives with those of their contemporary counterparts. Mine labor activist Mother Jones stands as a link between the past and the present, representing those who struggled to overcome the poor mine conditions of the past and symbolizing the continuance of the struggle. The script is composed of literature, documentary materials, and interviews—all organized principally in dramatic structure. To emphasize the life experiences of these characters in their setting, slide projections of coal miners' faces were used throughout the presentation. The opening section of *I Dearly Love a Coal Mining Man* reveals its dramatic nature.

I Dearly Love a Coal Mining Man

[*The stage is dark. From directly overhead a single light comes on a collection of mining articles arranged on a bench and a nail keg downstage left. The articles include a miner's hat, lunch pail, broom, picket sign, a wife's bonnet. Singer comes out and sings short selection from "I Love Coal Miners, I Do" in lighted area around bench. When she finishes, a light comes up silhouetting a group of miners' wives on centerstage platform. They are holding brooms, mops, and picket signs. Singer hears them as they begin to mumble and begins leading them in a strike song. General lighting comes up. After a short and heated singing session, the group freezes and* Coal Camp Wife 1 *steps slightly out of the group.*]

COAL CAMP WIFE 1. I'm twenty-six years a miner's wife.
        There's nothing harder than a miner's life,

> But there's no better man than a mining man,
> You couldn't find better in all this land.
> [*She freezes and* Coal Camp Wife 2 *speaks to the audience.*]

COAL CAMP WIFE 2. [*Said with sardonic humor*] Back when they used mules in the mines, the coal operators used to say they'd rather have a man killed than a mule, because they could always find another man.

[Modern Wife *steps from group to centerstage and* Miner *stands behind her on centerstage platform.*]

MODERN WIFE. My sole purpose in being here is to help the coal miner.

MINER. The women were the strongest ones on the picket lines.

MODERN WIFE. My father was a coal miner, I've got two brothers who are coal miners, and my husband is a coal miner; and I know what coal miners go through with.

MINER. The men weren't goin' to do nothing. The women just showed the way.

MODERN WIFE. I have lived through it and I was born and raised in it, but when a judge puts three men on a picket line—three pickets—and lets them scabs come in and spit in their faces and make obscene gestures at them and everything else, and those men have to sit there and take it, then it is time for the women to stop it.

MINER. You know men's always good about sneakin' around after dark where nobody can't see 'em. The women, they do it openly. I don't think it was just the thing of using their sex for protection either; they were just damned determined. That's all you can say about 'em.

MODERN WIFE. We knew there would be more violence. We knew if the women didn't come in there would be violence, because the men were getting fed up to the teeth with this. So the women came in. The women all went down there . . . and the women whipped them.

MINER. [*gesturing to the* Modern Wife] She was just a coal miner's wife until she got hungry and mad, like all the other women did.

[Mother Jones *leaves group and steps up on raised platform upstage center. Group of women turn to face her.*]

MOTHER JONES. Boys, this strike is called in order that you and your wives and children may get a bit of Heaven before you die.[5]

Although some of the characters' speeches tend to trace the history of labor struggles for the miner, and therefore seem to move into an epic modality, the narrative is nevertheless recounted by specific characters, not a central narrator. Characters represent specific positions that sometimes conflict, and many of the scenes are dramatic reenactments of events in coal mining history. Furthermore, the characters are likely to be fully or almost fully costumed, as one way of emphasizing the individual natures of the people who speak the script's lines.

Lyric Modality

The lyric mode speaker seems to stand in direct relation to the audience to share personal thoughts and feelings. Lyric mode personae often employ strong rhythms and musical language to move an audience; such speakers are relatively free from explicit time and space identifications, focusing instead on personal experience.

When the central modality of a compiled script is lyric, a chorus is often useful to help orchestrate the aesthetic qualities of the language. Musical forms—such as the sonata and

Figure 6.4: Mother Jones speaking to miners and miners' wives: "I Dearly Love a Coal Mining Man," compiled and directed by Ann S. Utterback.

rondo—can inform the whole script's structure, because music builds intensity through repetition and accumulation, hallmarks of the lyric approach to language. Even if some collected works in the script aren't lyric in individual mode, you can achieve a central lyric modality by having the speakers come forward and confront the audience with the emotional qualities of their selections, and by stressing the poetic dimension of the language.

An example of a script that is lyric in its central modality is *Lorca*, a program that features the poetry of Garcia Lorca.[6] Notice how repetition and emotional qualities of language inform the script. Much of the opening material and transitions are original. As in all scripts in the lyric mode, *Lorca* is essentially interested in the quality of a single voice—Lorca's voice. The script adds three additional voices, sometimes speaking separately and sometimes as a chorus, to support the single voice. The chorus is small enough to avoid overshadowing the Lorca figure, but it adds tonal variety to the script. The reprinted sections of the script are introductions and transitions that show the lyric qualities of its presentational form.

Lorca

VOICE 1. Federico Garcia Lorca—
       Voice of a people
       A gypsy voice.
       A voice that talked with death.

VOICE 2.   His poetry, a never-ending stream of life,
                   but life in which the veiled form of death
                   is ever present—demon-ridden poetry—
                   it baptizes with dark water those who take it in.

VOICE 1. Federico Garcia Lorca—
       Andalusian born;
       Close-rooted in her soil,
       Soil which held the seed of his death.

CHORUS. The voices of death are sounding
       Deep song of the human heart.
       The voices of death are sounding
       Torn out, the dark root of the cry.
       Liquid, multiplied voices—

LORCA.   My people, my work, my life.

VOICE 2.   The voices of death sounded for Federico Garcia Lorca in August 1936. Taken from
                   the house of a friend by the rebel forces of Francisco Franco—and for no reason—shot
                   at dawn.

VOICE 3.   The Spanish believe that it is possible for a man to so die that he kills his own death—
                   to find the "death of light" as they call it, and become greater than death itself.

VOICE 2.   Come with us to the room in which Garcia Lorca waits for the dawn and his own
                   death—as he listens to the night around him and remembers the words he has written
                   —as he listens to the last sounds of life, and seeks *his* "Death of Light."

CHORUS. The voices of death are sounding
       Deep song of the human heart.
       The voices of death are sounding

Torn out, the dark root of the cry,
Liquid, multiplied voices
LORCA.   My people, my work, my life.

* * *

LORCA.   I lose myself in light—
I lose myself in song,
I lose myself in the hearts of the people of Spain,
I have lost myself in the sea many times . . .
Ignorant of the water I go seeking
a death, full of light.
LORCA.   A death full of light . . .

CHORUS. The voices of death . . .

A dawn full of death . . .

The voices of death . . .

A death at the dawn . . .

The voices of death . . .

A dawn full of light . . .

The voices of death . . .

VOICE 1. Of death, of death
of terrible, terrible
death, of death
of death, of death

VOICE 2. voices of death
of voices of death
voices of death
of voices of death

LORCA.   The voices of death
that pound in my ear
like the shriek of the trumpets
that herald the Pasadobles.

VOICE 1 AND 2 [whispering]. Voices of death
Voices of death

And I am like the matador
Standing, waiting, pale
and with pounding heart
behind the portals of fear
that swing open to the
deafening roar of the crowd,
and the yellow sand of the
bull ring . . .
It is nearly dawn.
At dawn I must die.

Blood will run dark in the
dark of the dawn . . .

CHORUS. Green
how much I want you
Green . . .

My blood will run red in the
red of the dawn

Green wind, green boughs

Green
how much I want you
Green . . .

Voices of death will
sound in the dawn . . .

Green, oh green . . .

Portals of fear will
swing wide with the dawn . . .

> Green, how much I want you
> Green, how much I want you
> Green . . .[7]

This script features the poetry of a single writer, Federico Garcia Lorca, and focuses particularly on his early and tragic death. The script uses all three types of juxtaposition—collecting whole works, excerpting, and fragmenting—to achieve its effect. In the sections omitted, whole poems are often spoken, sometimes by a single voice and sometimes by a chorus combined with a single voice. A section of the poem "Somnambule Ballad"—"Green, how much I want you green"—is excerpted and later inserted as a haunting contrapuntal chorus voice underneath Lorca's poems of death, creating a montage of Lorca's multiple feelings toward life and death. Later in the script, single lines and phrases (such as "at dawn . . .") are fragmented and juxtaposed to create a musical form—an **antiphony** that uses materials from one poem and opposes them against another voice. The total effect of the script is a highly emotional presentation of Federico Garcia Lorca, as he seems to confront the audience lyrically with his personal poetry.

Musical Form

In addition to forms suggested by modal stance, some materials seem to urge the transformer toward musical structures. Musical form, like many of the forms around us, developed not as an arbitrary design, but as a result of human experience and impulse. The *a b a* of the **sonata** is a basic human pattern—to begin in one place, to venture forth to another, and to return home. To create a script around this pattern requires two themes or two distinctly different aspects of the same theme.

Suppose you're constructing a script on individual freedom and wish to say that personal freedom is ultimately a satisfying condition (*a* theme), but that there are some risks involved (*b* theme). The *a* theme begins the script, exploring various joys, satisfactions, and gently humorous aspects of being on one's own, using assembled materials of many kinds. Then the *b* theme is probed—stormy times, broken hopes, financial woes. Finally the *a* theme returns, but because you've lived through the *b* section, you're wiser. The joys of independence are reestablished (*a* theme), but they're deeper, with the recognition that personal freedom is not without its responsibilities. This approximates a traditional sonata form, which exists not only in music but in some poems, in which the last stanza repeats much of the first.

Another way of shaping a compiled script that uses two contrasting perspectives on a theme is the **antiphonal form**. Here the two perspectives alternate back and forth (*a b a b a b*), with an occasional surprise (*a b a a b*). Each *a b* interchange probes a different aspect of the theme, so the whole script has a forward ideational movement. A script on marriage, for example, might alternate a female comment on marriage with a male comment on marriage, with each unit centered on a different aspect of the subject—fidelity, children, in-laws, or finances. The antiphonal script works on the principle of meaning through accumulation.

When intermixing more than two themes or aspects of themes, the **rondo** form may be useful for the compiler. The rondo is similar to the antiphonal structure except that it keeps one theme relatively constant and alternates it with a progression of other themes or thematic aspects: *a b a c a d a e*. If there seems to be one dominant strain in your gathered materials, with a series of smaller contrasting pieces, you may wish to consider the rondo. The structure of the rondo, when used with literary materials, is like a "yes, but" argument. To continue our marriage theme, *a* may maintain consistently that marriage is the only truly satisfying relationship for men and women, but that argument is interrupted constantly by *b*, *c*, or *d*, which may object to this attitude (by citing the high rate of divorce, for example) or offer alternative plans ("What's wrong with the bachelor life?" or "Why not just live together?"). Each time, however, the *a* theme is reaffirmed by a new piece of literary or nonliterary evidence. In a script like this, you may end with the *a* theme triumphant, or the *a* theme may be gradually worn out by the constant attack from different directions and eventually give up.

Finally, **theme and variations** is a useful form for the compiler to consider. When you're making a single concise statement in which there is to be little evolution of meaning through the course of the script, you can gain variety and contrast by the different ways in which the single theme can be presented and elaborated. Of course, being able to use the theme and variations structure depends on the nature of your component materials. If you have a number of excerpts saying much the same thing ("Too much independence is a fool's paradise," for example), but they present the statement in different ways (humorously, tragically, or ironically, or, in dialogue, by lyric statement, in poetic meter, or with prose), you have ideal materials for a theme and variation structure. To gain greater variation, some of the excerpts can be orchestrated (see Chapter 3).

If you're doing a longer script and have amassed materials that seem to come together in several different groupings, you might try a **symphonic form**. A symphony is composed of several movements that contrast with each other in dynamics and tone. A standard four movement symphony has long movements at the beginning and the end with a slow movement and a short, fast movement between them. A symphony on marriage might begin with an exploration of the joys and good times of the married state. Movement two, the slow movement, might probe the sorrows—the loss of children, the near-loss of a mate, the reversals in fortune. The fast movement, number three, might be devoted to the marriage spat, the venting of anger that sometimes occurs. Movement four would weave these three strains together and make a statement about how joy, sorrow, and even fighting can ultimately bring two people closer together.

Other Forms

Two other forms useful for the compiler involve a small number of primary works: the **augmented form** and the **interpenetrated form**. Augmentation, a technique of orchestration (see Chapter 3), is used in a specialized way. You can create the augmented form by using one work, which reflects closely your own script idea, as the major framework of your script. A short story or a novelette can be augmented by nonprint materials that expand and add dimension to key scenes in the story; or inserted materials can play against certain aspects of the frame, either creating an ironic contrast in tone or a variation in point of view. An interesting compilation on the general subject of the negative things people do to each other and to their environment was created by using Louis MacNeice's poem, "Prayer Before Birth," as a frame. The stanzas of the poem were separated by inserted materials, each stanza signaling a different point of attack upon the subject—air and water pollution, war and violence, exploitation, and neglect. Literary works in which the original structure suggests a compiled script, such as *The Waste Land* by T. S. Eliot, may be augmented by inserting additional lines and scenes from the literary allusions. Such a production would be a creative explication of the literary sources and myths that inform the poem. Great care should be taken in selecting the excerpts and fragments to be inserted; otherwise, you can destroy the form of the frame without creating a new form.

The augmented form uses one major work as a frame. Interpenetration is the blending of two or more major works by interweaving their parts. To interpenetrate, each work is broken into parts that are alternated with segments from other works; the whole of each work need not be used. The difference between interpenetration and other compiled forms lies in the limitation of material to only a few (two to four) selections; most other compiled forms draw from many different sources. Further, not all works lend themselves to interpenetration; there must be commonalities among the works used, both in subject and in structure.

A compiler might choose to combine the fairy tale "Cinderella" by the Grimm brothers with "Cinderella" as rewritten in poetry by Anne Sexton and with "Passionella," the Cinderella story satirized in cartoon by Jules Feiffer. To interpenetrate these three works, the compiler would look carefully at their similarities and differences in content, tone, attitude, and structure. The Grimm piece is sympathetic in tone and simple in structure. Sexton's tone is heavily ironic and contains a prologue, which sets up the story, and several changes in content. Feiffer, in his cartoon version, exaggerates aspects of the story and adds his own satiric twists. A simple mixture of the three versions might begin with the Grimm story, which is interrupted by a narrator who, using all or parts of Sexton's prologue, poses an alternate approach to the tale and brings on a second cast of characters who begin the story again. A third group interrupts the second and interposes Feiffer's interpretation of the beginning of the story. The subsequent playing out of the story consists of the alternating versions interwoven together. As another way to begin, a group of performers is introduced, wanting to tell a story; they decide on Cinderella, but can't agree on the sequence of events or on tone and attitude. The group, then, answering to alternating storytelling narrators shows different versions of the same event, sometimes breaking for argument, sometimes agreeing on major incidents, but differing on other aspects of the scene.

As a compiler, you need an overall form for your script, but you also want to discover techniques for blending and enriching the script's individual parts.

Creating and Unifying Textures

The compiler has two major sources of life-giving tensiveness: the tensive nature of each piece within the script and the tension created by juxtaposition. The **texture** of a compiled script reflects both of these forms of tensiveness.

For the assemblage, identifying texture is provided primarily by the individual works included in the script. For the collage, the compiler has the task of creating and intensifying texture, blending the various parts of the script together into a cohesive whole that seems to be of one fabric. The method for doing this resembles that of orchestration (see Chapter 3), except that it involves synthesizing, rather than breaking apart. You're cementing together the scattered excerpts and fragments to achieve a feeling of unity rather than a feeling of isolated bits in a sequence.

Transition

The bringing together of different materials creates **juncture**, and juncture demands transition from one segment of material to another. Even silence becomes a kind of transition; although one excerpt may come immediately after another without words, music, or anything to create a bridge between them, there'll still be a feeling of change, unless the two pieces are very similar in idea or in tone and structure. A very important consideration in blending your script together, therefore, is the nature of the transitions to be used. In the collage, whether the script works depends on the way the excerpts and fragments are made to relate to each other. Visualize each transition carefully, whether verbal or nonverbal. Imagine it onstage. Hear it and see it. Know what you want to happen when two segments come together; then write those instructions into your script. Most compilers prefer not to provide the author's name and title before each selection as a means of transition; such information can be placed in a printed program.

A transition generally signals a change in mood and locus from one section of the script to another. Transitions vary with the type of script being compiled—assemblage or collage—and with the central modality employed—lyric, epic, or dramatic. Assemblage creates established tonalities because of the length of some of the units included; there's a need, therefore, to form bridges between the pieces. Since the collage is built from very small fragments, segments that serve as transitions often aren't distinguished from core segments.

Transitions may be accomplished vocally, by use of words, phrases, or vocal sounds; nonverbally through movement of the performers; or technically, through media of the stage—light, sound, movement of set pieces. Music is an excellent transitional tool, if not overused. Usually, transitions are composed of elements from several sources. For now, we're chiefly concerned with transitions created audibly by the performers.

If a chorus of performers is being used in the script, interesting transitions can be created through vocalized sounds that pick up the tone color of the last words of one selection and modulate it to match the tone coloring of the next selection:

> VOICE 1. A voice came o'er the waters far
> CHORUS. Ahhhhhhhh————————oo—oo—ooooooooooo
> VOICE 2. Two voices are there: one is of the sea

Quite often effective transitions are made by the imitation of imagistic aspects of the selections being bridged, such as the ticking of a clock, the sounds of the night, or the howling of the wind. A chorus can make sounds with their bodies, such as clapping, stamping, and beating, which will serve as percussive signals of change.

The use of verbal bridges, which can range from a single word to an elaborate sequence, depends upon the nature of the core idea and the kind of script being created. An assemblage on the works of a literary period, for example, might have rather long transitions which supply background information or might simply present the works with little between them. If the script is exploring dimensions of a complex idea—such as changing concepts of the nature of truth—the compiler may need to write transitional materials that mark the key contrasts or relationships in the progression of the idea. On the other hand, the simple repetition of words or phrases from the segments to be bridged can make an effective transition.

Seek variety in your transitions; occasionally surprise your audience. Musical transitions, for example, can depend on a single piece of music continuing through the whole script or on different musical works setting a changing mood for each transition. In either case, it's important to provide transitional devices other than the music for some transitions. The novelty provides that extra little twist that increases awareness in your listeners.

Two of the more common verbal techniques for creating both transitions and general texture are repetition and contrast.

Repetition

Among the texturing techniques available to the compiler, repetition is one of the most useful and versatile. Repeated materials can shape your script to a remarkable degree. Texturing is concerned with the repeated word, line, or very small section. Repetition as a transitional device can work in two basic ways: it can make the transition obvious, or it can help to mask it. In the following sequence, which moves from the tranquility of "The Lotos-Eaters" by Tennyson to the passion of Macbeth's speech (act 2, scene 2), there is a marked change of pace signaled by the dynamics of the repeated words "in sleep," which form the transition.

> Here are cool mosses deep,
> And thro' the moss the ivies creep,
> And in the stream the long-leaved flowers weep,
> And from the craggy ledge the poppy hangs in sleep.[8]
>
> Hangs in sleep . . .
> In sleep . . .
>
> In sleep
> Sleep!
>
> Methought I heard a voice cry, "Sleep no more!
> Macbeth does murder sleep!"

The transition acts as a turnstile, turning the mood and the substance of the script in another direction, and the shift is made obvious in rhythm and tone.

Repetition can also weld two sections together more closely; although there is a transition to a new direction, the shift is accomplished more subtly, so the listener is hardly aware of the change. The sequence below begins with the latter part of the same selection from "The Lotos-Eaters," and moves into the more thoughtful lines from "Mount Blanc" by Shelley.

> Here are cool mosses deep,
> And thro' the moss the ivies creep,
> And in the stream the long-leaved flowers weep,
> And from the craggy ledge the poppy hangs in sleep.
>
> In sleep,
> The poppy hangs in sleep

Some say that gleams of a remoter world
Visit the soul in sleep,—that death is slumber
And that its shape the busy thoughts outnumber
Of those who wake and live.[9]

The slide from one selection to another is accomplished by the shortness of the transition, by the rhythmic swing of the line, and by the tone color that pervades "sleep" and "gleams." It is particularly important, when making transitions between poetry excerpts, to give attention to sound and rhythm.

Repetition can also be used on a larger scale. For example, key lines or stanzas from a poem can be repeated in exact form at controlled intervals throughout a script. If the phrase or stanza is repeated often enough and at regular enough intervals, it becomes a theme, or leitmotif, for the script. To show this in a compiled form would require reprinting an entire script. Many poets, however, use this technique in single works of literature: "Do not go gentle into that good night" is a repeated motif in Dylan Thomas's villanelle of the same name, and "We are the greatest city, the greatest nation / Nothing like us ever was" from "Four Preludes on Playthings of the Wind" by Carl Sandburg is a counterpoint to the images of rats and lizards and crows. Repetition is a powerful force; the compiler, like the poet, can create effective rhythmic and thematic patterns by the careful use of repetition.

Contrast and Variety

The life-giving energy of a script is often created by the intersection of opposing forces, as in the rondo, for example, which is built by contrasting a series of different statements against a single core statement. Many power sources—idea, imagery, character, sound structures, or time—can be the subject of the contrast: the opposing of a strident character from one literary selection against a meek but forceful character from another, or the juxtaposition of a fast tempo against a slow one. A major source of power for your script resides in this kind of tensiveness. In addition, attention to smaller contrasts within the larger units of your structure becomes a way of increasing texture. As an example, within the third movement of the symphonic form exploration of a marriage, the spat, we might explore the fight from contrasting or varying angles of vision—the husband's, the wife's, the friend's, the lawyer's—or explore contrasting kinds of fights—the verbal duel, the smashed crockery fray, complete physical mayhem, the silent storm. In any script, little pockets of contrast or reversal add to the interest and ultimately to the strength of the major statement.

Besides these straightforward contrasts, a significant technique for elaborating contrast is counterpoint. Counterpoint, the playing of one element (idea, rhythm, image) against another element, is a contrasting technique explored in Chapter 3 in relation to orchestrating the individual work. Rather than lifting out an element from a work and playing it against parts of the same work, as the adapter might do, the compiler brings elements from several different works and juxtaposes them in contrapuntal arrangements. The following example uses some of the same sources as the illustration of repetition. Notice that the materials are reshaped through rearrangement so the thought lines and dynamics can be controlled.

Voice 1.

There is a music here that
    softer falls
Than petals from blown roses
    on the grass . . .
Music that gentlier on the
    spirit lies,

Than tired eyelids
Tired eyes
Music that brings sweet
Sle————ep

Here are cool mosses deep
And through the moss
The ivies cre——ep

Swe————et
Sle————ep

Sle————ep

Sle————ep

Voice 2.

Sle————ep

No————

Mo————re

Methought I heard a voice cry
Sle————ep

Sleep no more
Macbeth does murder sleep
The innocent sleep

The death of each day's life
Sleep that knits up the
ravell'd sleeve of care

No more
Sleep!

Macbeth does murder
Sleep!

Counterpoint usually involves an overlaying of one piece of material upon another, the simultaneous performance of two or more sequences. The sequences may contrast in idea or they may be alternate facets of the same idea. The example, intensifying the contrasting ideas of "sleep" and "no sleep," might be placed in a script immediately after the two literary units have been stated individually. Counterpoint needs to be used with care and discretion; if overused, it will lose effectiveness. Also be careful, especially when using more than two voices, that the performance is not just noise, that it's clearly paced so the audience hears the individual voices at least part of the time. Each voice may be highlighted alternately by having the other voices decrease in volume and intensity, or by spacing the opposing materials so individual voices sometimes speak alone, as in the example above.

THREE COMPILED SCRIPTS

We've created three short scripts to exemplify the script types: script 1, an assemblage, and script 3, a collage, fall at the two ends of the continuum. Script 2, using excerpts and short poems, combines aspects of both assemblage and collage. The genre has been limited to poetry for brevity.

The subject of all three scripts is hunting; the attitude taken is definitely against hunting for sport. We have deliberately adopted a polemic stance in the scripts to illustrate one of the uses of the compiled script: as a vehicle for persuasion.

Script 1: The Time of All Novembers—an Assemblage

Although all but two of the poems in the group contain a similar attitude toward the subject, there is considerable variety in methods of approach. "Deer Hunt," the first poem in the group, explores the tension between the persona's personal aversion to hunting, and the pressures from society to hunt. "Hunting Song" is a lyric invocation of the brotherhood felt by the Indian hunter toward the animal he must kill in order to live; the modern hunter follows the eternal ritual of the kill in "Trophy." Using a montage technique within the poem itself, "This Poem Is for Deer" projects kaleidoscopic glimpses of the deer, the disappointed hunter, the drunken triumphant hunter, and the hunter in touch with nature. The animal tragedy of the kill is explored in "Spring Hunt" and "Forgive My Guilt": the persona of the former is a sympathetic observer; the persona of the latter poem is the hunter who has killed uselessly. The final poem, "November," shows the reaction of wild animals themselves to the hunting season. The script moves from an emphasis on the hunter to a focus on the hunted in an overall lyric modality.

Each poem is given in its entirety, with a few choral repetitions inserted (in parentheses). Transitions are minimal, composed of music from guitar and flute and some lines repeated from the poems. The guitar begins and ends the program; lines from the last poem are used to introduce the subject, thus giving a *feeling* of *a b a* to the entire structure. No verbal transition is used between the first three poems—the choral refrain that begins and ends the "Hunting Song" serves a transitional function. The refrain is used again between "Trophy" and "This Poem is for Deer," but with a different tonality, as the guitar accompaniment changes to flute. The next three transitions are formed from repeated lines from the previous poem, which set a tone for the following poem. The program ends with a repeated line from the last poem spoken by a chorus.

There are no consistent voices throughout the script; each poem has its own set of characters. In the longest and most complex poem, "November," we heard five voices. Therefore, we decided to create a chorus of five voices to perform the whole script. Each selection is adapted for Readers Theatre, using the five performers in various ways—as narrator, as chorus, as personae, each performer taking a number of different roles. We attempted to keep the form of the poems intact, while adapting them for voices.

The Time of All Novembers

CAST:

VOICE 1: Male
VOICE 2: Either male or female
VOICE 3: Male
VOICE 4: Female
VOICE 5: Female

[*Guitar music*]

VOICE 2. Now when the brown and purple oaks defy the fall   "November"
        And the timid elms stand naked, blue and cold . . .
        And the night is still, beyond silence—

CHORUS. Now is the time of all Novembers

VOICE 2. Now is November
        And there is not room on earth for all creatures to survive:

[*Guitar up and out*]

VOICE 1. Because the warden is a cousin, my   "Deer Hunt"
        mountain friends hunt in a summer when the deer
        cherish each rattler-ridden spring, and I
        have waited hours by a pool in fear
        that manhood would require I shoot or that
        the steady drip of the hill would dull my ear
        to a snake whispering near the log I sat
        upon, and listened to the whelping cheer
        of dogs and men resounding ridge to ridge.
        I flinched at every lonely rifle crack,
        my knuckles whitening where I gripped the edge
        of age and clung, like retching, sinking back,
        then gripping once again the monstrous gun—
        since I, to be a man, had taken one.[10]

[*Guitar in and under the next poem*]

CHORUS.   Comes the deer to my singing,   "Hunting Song"
        Comes the deer to my song,
        Comes the deer to my singing.

VOICE 3. He, the blackbird, he am I,
        Bird beloved of the wild deer,
        Comes the deer to my singing.

VOICE 2. From the Mountain Black,
        From the summit,
        Down the trail, coming, coming now,
        Comes the deer to my singing.

VOICE 4. Through the blossoms,
        Through the flowers, coming, coming now,
        Comes the deer to my singing.

CHORUS. Through the flower dew-drops,
        Coming, coming now,
        Comes the deer to my singing.

VOICE 5. Through the pollen, flower pollen,
        Coming, coming now,
        Comes the deer to my singing.

VOICE 2. Starting with his left fore-foot,
        Stamping, turns the frightened deer.
        Comes the deer to my singing.

VOICE 3. Quarry mine, blessed am I
        In the luck of the chase.

CHORUS.   Comes the deer to my singing.
            Comes the deer to my singing,
            Comes the deer to my song,
            Comes the deer to my singing.[11]

     [*Guitar up and out*]

VOICE 3. Drew a fine bead   "Trophy"
            down at dusk in beaver meadow
            through the Nikon peep sight.
            Steady breath held half out.
            Squeeze the trigger.

            Dead shot
            centered behind the stiff
            right shoulder, where bristled hair
            points haunchward at the bend
            of muscle sheathed bone.

CHORUS. Wapiti at dusk, cud tucked into cheek,
            pranced head high of tines
            into the lodgepole,

VOICE 3. never looking back.[12]

     [*Flute under transition*]

CHORUS.   Comes the deer to my singing,
            Comes the deer to my song,   }   [*Transition*]
            Comes the deer to my singing.

VOICE 4. "I dance on all the mountains   "This Poem Is for Deer"
            On five mountains, I have a dancing place
            When they shoot at me I run
            To my five mountains"

VOICE 1. Missed a last shot
            At the Buck, in twilight
            So we came back sliding
            On dry needles through cold pines.
            Scared out a cottontail
             Whipped up the Winchester
            Shot off its head.
            The white body rolls and twitches
            In the dark ravine
            As we run down the hill to the car.

CHORUS.   deer foot down scree

VOICE 2. Picasso's fawn,

VOICE 5.   Issa's fawn,

CHORUS. Deer on the autumn mountain
            Howling like a wise man

VOICE 2. Stiff springy jumps down the snowfields
            Head held back, forefeet out,
            Balls tight in a tough hair sack
            Keeping the human soul from care on the autumn mountain.

CHORUS. Standing in late sun, ear-flick
        Tail-flick, gold mist of flies
        Whirling from nostril to eyes.

VOICE 3. Home by night
           drunken eye
        Still picks out Taurus
        Low, and growing high:
           four-point buck
        Dancing in the headlights
           on the lonely road
        A mile past the mill-pond,
        With the car stopped, shot
        That wild silly blinded creature down.

        Pulled out the hot guts
           with hard bare hands
        While night-frost chills the tongue
           and eye
        The cold horn-bones.
        The hunter's belt
           just below the sky
        Warm blood in the car trunk.
        Deer-smell,
           the limp tongue.

VOICE 2. Deer don't want to die for me.

CHORUS.   I'll drink sea-water
        Sleep on beach pebbles in the rain

VOICE 2. Until the deer come down to die
        in pity for my pain.[13]

        [*Guitar—more of a minor key—under transition*]

CHORUS. I dance on all the mountains

VOICE 2. In pity for my pain.   [*Transition*]

CHORUS. Until the deer come down to die
        in pity for my pain.

        [*Guitar under the beginning of the next poem and fade out*]

                                                                "Spring Hunt"

VOICE 5. A late snow drove the deer
        still lower to the greening meadows.

VOICE 4. She picked her way
        through the shivering aspen groves,
        slowly, head low, heavy with life.

VOICE 1. The practiced shot, well placed,
        clean and quick, staggered
        her pace,

        bringing her to bed beneath the browse.

        A whetted edge flashed along her
        taut undersides,

VOICE 5. her loins
      sprung wide
      by force of blade.
      The glistening gut slipped steaming
      onto the snow, spilling
      free a speckled fawn
      asleep in its caul-shroud.
CHORUS. It was cold that year in Colorado.[14]
      [Flute under transition]
VOICE 4. *[Flatly]* Cold
CHORUS. Cold that year——co——ld   }   *[Transition]*
VOICE 4. *[Flatly]* Cold
      [Flute fade out under next poem]
VOICE 3. Not always sure what things called sins may be,   "Forgive My Guilt"
      I am sure of one sin I have done.
      It was years ago, and I was a boy,
      I lay in the frost flowers with a gun,
      The air ran blue as the flowers, I held my breath,
VOICE 4. Two birds on golden legs slim as dream things
      Ran like quicksilver on the golden sand,
VOICE 3. My gun went off,
VOICE 4. They ran with broken wings
      Into the sea,
VOICE 3. I ran to fetch them in,
CHORUS. But they swam with their heads high out to sea,
VOICE 4. They cried like two sorrowful flutes,
CHORUS. *[Simultaneously]* $\overline{OO}$————————
VOICE 4. With jagged ivory bones where wings should be.
CHORUS. *[Simultaneously]* $\overline{OO}$————o————(continue "o" sound until "south")
VOICE 3. For days I heard them when I walked that headland
      Crying out to their kind in the blue,
      The other plovers were going over south
      On silver wings leaving these broken two.
      The cries went out one day; but I still hear them
      Over all the sounds of sorrow in war or peace
      I have ever heard, time cannot drown them,
      Those slender flutes of sorrow never cease.
      Two airy things forever denied the air!
      I never knew how their lives at last were spilt,
      But I have hoped for years all that is wild,
      Airy, and beautiful will forgive my guilt.[15]
      [Flute under transition]
CHORUS. Time cannot drown them
      They cried like two sorrowful high flutes   }
      Time cannot drown them   *[Transition]*
         Time cannot drown them
            Time cannot drown them
      All things wild and beautiful—

VOICE 2. Now when the brown and purple oaks defy the fall,
And the timid elms stand naked, blue, and cold,
And the woods-carpet yields lightly to the snuffling feetwall,
When the blasted rose droops withered by the garden,
The warty toad has found its cleft, the snake has holed,
And no birds sing
CHORUS.   (No birds sing)
VOICE 2. And the night is still, beyond silence—
CHORUS.   (still, beyond silence)
VOICE 2. Now is the time of all Novembers.

VOICE 4. In the sheltered clearing the star-eyed doe
Sniffs the frosty air, and remembers;
She smells the pungent thing
Whereby her yearling mate was stricken,
And she is afraid, her cud no longer sweet.
Wildly she starts to run, knowing not where to go,
CHORUS. But away with the wind she runs
To the spot where her fear will thicken
Into red on the trampled grass,
VOICE 4. And the hateful smells of man and guns
Torment her final breath.

VOICE 2.   Now is November—
Now when the wind tears at the cattails in the marsh—
VOICE 1. And the old mink and the three-footed muskrat remember
Their teeth sharp to tear the flesh or gnaw the root,
Their pelts growing prime and thick against the harsh
Cold to come.
VOICE 3.   Suddenly the rat forgets
His enemy the mink, and drops the tender shoot.
He feels on his slick body the man-made ripples and hears
The steel clank of chains
And sees a boat approaching by the shore.
VOICE 2.   Now is November—
CHORUS. [*low*] (and through the swamps and streams and sloughs)
VOICE 2. And through the swamps and streams and sloughs lie nets
To catch the slender feet, the trembling flesh, implanting fiery fears
In tiny brains.

VOICE 5. And the wild ducks remember—the teal,
The mallards, the pintails, the scaups, the canvasbacks—
CHORUS. And the geese they too remember.
Out of the clear-cold sky they wheel
And as of one mind drop down to rest and feed.
VOICE 5. With yaups and honks and gentle quacks
They bob up and down on the shining water. They dive
For the succulent root that makes them plump.

> See, over there, a tardy flock of redheads coming in,
> A lordly drake flying squarely in the lead—

VOICE 2. But now is November,
> And there is not room on earth for all creatures to survive:

CHORUS. (not room on earth for all)

VOICE 2. The fowler's eye this time has found its mark,
> And in a thousand avian breasts beats the pounding thump
> Of fright.

CHORUS.   With instant discipline
> The birds spring up and off in wild dismay . . .

VOICE 5. There is another lake a dozen miles away
> Where the wild rice still hangs ripe and sweet. There
> They will be safe—perhaps—after the kindly dark
> Has settled on the marshes and men are asleep . . . after
>   November.

CHORUS. But now they flee through the cold autumn air,
> Over the slough where the iron jaws lie concealed,
> Over the woods where the dead deer has lain,
> Over the brown earth in its fair fall dress—

VOICE 2. Now is the time of all Novembers,
> When the great thorn of fear pierces through the frail shield
> Of the world's loveliness;
> And the harvest is come, but bitter is the grain.[16]
>   [Guitar]

CHORUS. (Now is November—
> And there is not room on earth for all creatures to survive.)

Script 2: Comes the Deer to My Singing—a Rondo

Our second script falls in type between the extremes of assemblage and collage, using excerpts and shorter poems than those in script 1. "Comes the Deer to My Singing," which exhibits a definite attitudinal position against hunting, is structured in a rondo form: the *a* theme, created by the Navajo "Hunting Song," is carried throughout the script by Voice 1, alternating with different statements from Voices 2, 3, and 4. Because the Navajo poem carries the *a* theme throughout, the script structure is not only a rondo form, but an augmented form as well. In the *e* section, all the voices come together to create the segment, but each still maintains a consistent attitude carried over from the preceding statements: Voice 4 is the deer, Voice 2 is the hunter who kills the deer, and Voice 3, although becoming a kind of narrator, still shows his aversion to hunting. The overall lyric modality is maintained by the use of musical structure.

Comes the Deer to My Singing

CAST:

VOICE 1: Male or female; the singer, identified with the deer even though she may hunt the deer
VOICE 2: Male; the experienced hunter who hunts for pleasure

VOICE 3: Male; the reluctant hunter
VOICE 4: Female; the deer

Production note: Guitar music begins the script and runs under it, a simple tune in a minor key, to which the singer can sing the opening and closing of the "Hunting Song."

Form	Voice	Script	Source

a   VOICE 1. Comes the deer to my singing,
Comes the deer to my song,
Comes the deer to my singing.

"Hunting Song"

He, the blackbird, he am I,
Bird beloved of the wild deer
Comes the deer to my singing.

From the Mountain Black
From the summit,
Down the trail, coming, coming now,
Comes the deer to my singing.

Through the blossoms,
Through the flowers, coming, coming now,
Comes the deer to my singing.

b   VOICE 2. Missed a last shot
At the buck, in twilight
So we came back sliding
On dry needles through cold pines.
Scared out a cottontail
Whipped up the Winchester
Shot off its head.
The white body rolls and twitches
In the dark ravine
As we run down the hill to the car.

"This Poem Is for Deer"

a   VOICE 1. Through the flower dew-drops,
Coming, coming now,
Comes the deer to my singing.

"Hunting Song"

c   VOICE 3. Because the warden is a cousin, my
mountain friends hunt in summer when the deer
cherish each rattler-ridden spring, and I
have waited hours by a pool in fear
that manhood would require I shoot or that
the steady drip of the hill would dull my ear
to a snake whispering near the log I sat
upon, and listened to the yelping cheer
of dogs and men resounding ridge to ridge.
I flinched at every lonely rifle crack,
my knuckles whitening where I gripped the edge
of age and clung, like retching, sinking back
then gripping once again the monstrous gun—
since I, to be a man, had taken one.

"Deer Hunt"

a   VOICE 1. Starting with his left fore-foot,   "Hunting Song"
                  Stamping, turns the frightened deer,
                  Comes the deer to my singing.

d   VOICE 4. In the sheltered clearing, the star-eyed doe   "November"
                  Sniffs the frosty air, and remembers;
                  She smells the pungent thing
                  Whereby her yearling mate was stricken,
                  And she is afraid, her cud no longer sweet.
                  Wildly she starts to run, knowing not where to go,
                  But away with the wind she runs
                  To the spot where her fear will thicken
                  Into red on the trampled grass,
                  And the hateful smells of man and guns
                  Torment her final breath.

a   VOICE 1. Through the pollen, flower pollen,   "Hunting Song"
                  Coming, coming now
                  Comes the deer to my singing.

e   VOICE 3. A late snow drove the deer   "Spring Hunt"
                  still lower to the greening meadows.

       VOICE 4. She picked her way
                  through the shivering aspen groves,
                  slowly, head low, heavy with life.

       VOICE 2. The practiced shot, well placed,
                  clean and quick, staggered
                  her pace,

       VOICE 3. bringing her to bed beneath the browse.

       VOICE 2. A whetted edge flashed along her
                  taut undersides,
                  her loins
                  sprung wide
                  by force of blade:
                  The glistening gut slipped steaming
                  onto the snow,

       VOICE 4.   spilling
                  free a speckled fawn
                  asleep in its caul-shroud.

       VOICE 3. It was cold that year in Colorado.

a   VOICE 1. Comes the deer to my singing   "Hunting Song"
                  Comes the deer to my song.

Script 3: November Hunt—a Narrative Collage

"November Hunt" is also created from fragments taken from the poems in our assemblage, "The Time of All Novembers." The narrative sequence of "November Hunt" first sets the scene very briefly and then, with great economy, tells of the shooting and dismembering of a deer—the traditional hunting action. This action, however, is viewed from four different perspectives in this

Time Structure	Voice	Script	Source
	VOICE 3.	[*Watching* hunter] The limp tongue.	
	VOICE 1.	[*To audience*] And there is not room on earth for all creatures to survive.	"November"

NOTES

1. The quotations in order are from "She Walks in Beauty" by Lord Byron, Sonnet 130 by William Shakespeare, "Gnomologia" by Thomas Fuller, "The Female of the Species" by Rudyard Kipling, "La Belle Dame Sans Merci" by John Keats, *The Ordeal of Richard Feverel* by George Meredith, "Venice Preserved" by Thomas Otway, and *Hamlet* by William Shakespeare.

2. This script was compiled and directed by Marion Kleinau, for the WSIU-TV "Wordways" series of Readers Theatre productions.

3. Selections from Yeats's poetry in this script are taken from *The Collected Works of W. B. Yeats* (New York: Macmillan, 1956). Selections from Yeats's plays in this script are taken from *The Collected Plays of W. B. Yeats* (New York: Macmillan, 1953). Selections from Irish folktales are excerpted from W. B. Yeats, *Mythologies* (New York: Macmillan, 1959).

4. This script was compiled and directed by Ann S. Utterback at Southern Illinios University.

5. Materials in this script are taken from *Autobiography of Mother Jones* (Chicago: Charles H. Kerr, 1972); Guy and Candie Carawan, *Voices from the Mountains* (New York: Alfred A. Knopf, 1975); *Mountain Life and Work* (March 1975); and UMW Bicentennial Calendar (*United Mine Workers Journal*, 1976).

6. This script was compiled and directed by Marion Kleinau, Southern Illinois University.

7. Selections from Lorca's poetry in this script are taken from Arturo Barea, ed., *Lorca: The Poet and His People* (New York: Harcourt, Brace, 1949); Angel Flores, ed., *An Anthology of Spanish Poetry from Garcilaso to Garcia Lorca* (New York: Doubleday, 1961), and Francisco Garcia Lorca and Donald M. Allen, eds., *The Selected Poems of Federico Garcia Lorca* (New York: New Directions, 1955).

8. Alfred, Lord Tennyson, "Choric Song I" from "The Lotos-Eaters," *Poetry in English*, ed. Warren Taylor and Donald Hall (New York: Macmillan, 1963), p. 367.

9. Percy Bysshe Shelley, "Mont Blanc," *The Norton Anthology of English Literature*, vol. 2, rev. ed. (New York: W. W. Norton, 1968), p. 407.

10. Judson Jerome, "Deer Hunt," *Reflections on a Gift of Watermelon Pickle*, ed. Stephen Dunning, Edward Lenders, and Hugh Smith (Glenview, Ill.: Scott, Foresman, 1966).

11. Navajo Hunting Song, *The Indians' Book*, trans. Natalie Curtis (New York: Harper & Brothers, 1923).

12. Jerry Prater, "Trophy," *Blue Mushrooms*, ed. Jerry Prater (Greenville, Ill.: Scriblerus Club, 1972).

13. Gary Snyder, "This Poem Is for Deer," *Naked Poetry*, ed. Stephen Berg and Robert Mezey (New York: Bobbs-Merrill, 1969).

14. Jerry Prater, "Spring Hunt," *Blue Mushrooms*.

15. Robert P. Tristram Coffin, "Forgive My Guilt," *Apples by Ocean* (New York: Macmillan, 1950).

16. Paul Oehser, "November," *Fifty Poems* (Washington, D.C.,: Sherwood House, 1954).

17. Galway Kinnell, "To Christ Our Lord," *What a Kingdom It Was* (Boston: Houghton Mifflin, 1960). Two lines from this poem are used in our collage, but the poem does not appear in the assemblage.

SUGGESTIONS FOR FURTHER READING

Coger, Leslie Irene, and **White, Melvin R.** *Readers Theatre Handbook.* Rev. ed. Glenview, Ill.: Scott, Foresman, 1973. Pp. 60–64.

Haas, Richard, et al. *Theatres for Interpretation.* Ann Arbor, Mich.: Roberts Burton, 1976. Pp. 83–90.

Long, Beverly Whitaker, et al. *Group Performance of Literature.* Englewood Cliffs, N.J.: Prentice-Hall, 1977. Pp. 24–25.

PART THREE

Realizations: Moving into Production—From Script to Stage

In "Dance and the Poetic Image," Walter Sorrell observes that "somewhere in time, space and form, all the arts meet, cross, trespass, overlap, lean on, liberate, give, borrow and take from each other."[1] That "somewhere in time, space and form" for the Interpreters Theatre practitioner is the moment of production— that magic moment when the visual arts (stage design and technical media), the art of literature (the script), the art of dance (movement), and the musical arts (sound) fuse together to realize a literary text in space. If this description of production creates an image of theatricality, the image is intentional. Media of the theatre may be part of a production concept for Interpreters Theatre. George and Portia Kernodle observe, "The very center of the theatrical experience is the confrontation between two unstable, unpredictable elements: the living actor and the living audience."[2] This notion of the center of theatre indicates that the mere presence of theatrical accoutrements (stage settings, lights, costumes, and makeup) does not make theatre, nor does the lack of such media create theatre. What makes theatre is that living exchange of energies between performer and audience. Interpreters Theatre, as well as all other theatre forms, seeks that confrontation; what differentiates Interpreters Theatre as an art form—if indeed clear differentiation needs to exist today—is the nature of the confrontation and the methods of achieving it.

An Interpreters Theatre director needs to keep in mind the imaginative center of the medium. Production media, including a performer's movement and appearance, are used to guide the audience's imagination, but not to circumscribe it. Anything that tends to literalize will compete with free imagination. A director has to find the balance between imaginative freedom and tangible guidance that is right for the text and the production concept.

1. Walter Sorrell, "Dance and the Poetic Image," *Dance Observer* 27 (October 1960): 116.
2. George and Portia Kernodle, *Invitation to the Theatre*, rev. ed. (New York: Harcourt Brace Jovanovich, 1978), p. 4.

Interpreters Theatre production, as a search for imaginative balance, enables the power sources of the text, working through the script, to find living embodiment. It comprises both the ultimate releasing of the voices of the text and the screening out of some of those voices. Production is, therefore, a highly selective activity. Some critics argue that production is ultimately reductive—that a single staging can never capture the range of ambiguity in the literary work. A production is, by nature, a result of choices; although production may sacrifice the kind of appreciation for textual ambiguity that comes through silent reading, it creates a clearly focused in-depth experience with the text. As a work is richer in potential than the subsequent script (one work giving rise to many different scripts), a script is richer in potential than any single performance of it (one script giving rise to many different performances). The best production is one that gives an in-depth treatment to the greatest number of power sources in a text while retaining clarity. The value of production is that it truly features an informed vision of a work, presenting a literary experience with memorable vividness.

CHAPTER SEVEN

Presentational Action for Interpreters Theatre

I can take any empty space and call it a bare stage. A man walks across this empty space whilst someone else is watching him, and this is all that is needed for an act of theatre to be engaged.

Peter Brook, *The Empty Space*

The way of Interpreters Theatre is the way of nonillusion. Everything a director does, from creating the script to designing the production and blocking the performance, is designed to stimulate the audience's imaginative response rather than to provide a pictorial illusion of life onstage. The presentational, nonillusory nature of Interpreters Theatre allies it with those great presentational stages of history such as the Classical Greek and Elizabethan stages. The aesthetic of these theatres provides a model from which to develop an understanding of the informing aesthetic of the Interpreters Theatre art form. In *The Shakespeare Revolution*, J. L. Styan observes, "The flexible Elizabethan mode of performance, playing to the house, stepping in and out of character, generating a stage action allegorical and symbolic, making no pretence at the trappings of realism, encouraged a verbally acute, sensory and participatory, multilevelled and fully aware mode of experience for an audience."[1] This could be a description of the ideal audience experience for Interpreters Theatre. The staging techniques Styan describes for the Elizabethan theatre are also viable techniques for Interpreters Theatre.

As an initial step in establishing an informing aesthetic for Interpreters Theatre, we may observe that action in Interpreters Theatre has one major criterion: it is designed to establish primary focus in acoustic space rather than in pictorial space. When pictorial space is used, it is used symbolically. Whenever possible, the locus of action is pushed offstage rather than being carried out literally onstage. Although we may use the stage space fully and employ various media such as lights and costumes, the visual scene created onstage is usually serving an offstage or imaginative action. The greatest pitfall for the Interpreters Theatre director is a mode of production in which the illusion of real action is created onstage, replacing audience image-ination; we call this mode the "representational trap." A major way to avoid falling into the representational trap is to become aware of the techniques of presentational staging and how they function as alienation devices in Interpreters Theatre.

THE AESTHETIC OF ALIENATION IN INTERPRETERS THEATRE

At the heart of Interpreters Theatre production is the frank admission that there is no attempt to represent reality. Rather, Interpreters Theatre seeks to activate the imaginative, perceptual, and empathic abilities of an audience. Many of the techniques used are designed to prevent audience members from being caught up completely in the story being told, from being so submerged in an emotional experience that they lose sight of the structure and style of the text. Rather, this form attempts to place audience members at that ideal distance from which they can perceive both the literary experience and the way in which the experience is revealed. To accomplish this, Interpreters Theatre makes use of certain conventions, which may be termed **alienation devices**, or means to distance the audience from a natural inclination to escape into another created world.

Bertolt Brecht, a German playwright and critic who wrote in the 1930s and 1940s, is credited with introducing alienation to the modern theatre stage as a way of combating pictorial realism. Arguing that a kind of objective viewing of characters onstage is greatly preferable to identification with characters, Brecht called for the performers to confront the audience with their presence, so that "the spectator . . . says: 'I should never have thought so.—This is not the way to do it.—This is most surprising, hardly credible.—This will have to stop.—This human being's suffering moves me, because there would have been a way out for him.' "[2]

Since Brecht's theatre was termed Epic Theatre by its famous director, Erwin Piscator, and since it shares many attributes of narration (an interest in the past tense and in the act of storytelling, among others) with Chamber Theatre, the alienation principles of Brechtian Epic Theatre have been applied most fully to Chamber Theatre. In *Chamber Theatre*, Robert S. Breen explains, "Indeed it is the tensiveness created by the audience's disposition to respond emotionally and the Epic Theatre's insistence that they respond critically that gives the epic mode of Brecht's theatre its peculiar characteristic, its quality of 'alienation.' . . . Whereas Brecht used these alienation devices in rehearsal in the hope they would influence the performance, Chamber Theatre uses them in the performance itself."[3]

Yet all Interpreters Theatre—Readers Theatre as well as Chamber Theatre—employs alienation devices as part of its fundamental aesthetic, working against representationalism and illusion toward presentation and imagination. The most fundamental way in which alienation is achieved in Interpreters Theatre is through the use of presentational action.

THE NATURE OF PRESENTATIONAL ACTION

Action that is presentational symbolizes the experience of the text in acoustic space, whereas action that is representational re-creates the experience of the text in pictorial space. The key to understanding presentational action, then, is to recognize its essential symbolic nature. The ability of presentational action to symbolize—to stand for something else—is its distinguishing feature. Although all theatre forms are to some degree symbolic, presentational theatre features its symbolic nature, thereby providing a second level of communication. Representational theatre shows a created world; presentational theatre shows itself symbolizing a world, a world that exists in the audience's imagination. This is the heart of alienation in Interpreters Theatre. When interpreters gesture presentationally, either vocally or physically, the gesture is a stimulus for the audience's image response. Through presentational action, the Interpreters Theatre audience is invited directly to complete the symbolic process: to provide the "something else" that the presentational gesture suggests.

Presentational Vocal Action

The root of vocal action is presentational because words themselves are symbols. Words stand for certain agreed-upon meanings (denotations) but also suggest implied meanings (connotations) which are slightly different for each of us because we bring different experiences and contexts to our understanding of a word. In this way we help constitute a word's meaning by bringing our own meanings to its denotation. Literary language depends more on our ability to create its meaning than does scientific language, which attempts to resolve subtle differences of interpretation. In science, the language of numbers helps eliminate ambiguity of meaning, but in literature the language of images evokes deliberate ambiguity. As you've seen, your own image-ination helps you create a text and a script that is, at once, the original author's and significantly your own. Now your task is to tap the audience's image-ination through presentational vocal action.

Some critics have referred to the ability of literary language to engage its reader's imagination as a kind of gesture of language. Words move us. They reach out and grab us. "Words are made of motion, made of action or response," writes critic R. P. Blackmur. "When the language of words most succeeds it *becomes* gesture in its words. . . . Gesture, in language, is the outward and dramatic play of inward and imaged meaning. It is that play of meaningfulness which is moving, in every sense of that word: what moves the words and what moves us."[4] Words that are most presentational are the most playful. They gesture most broadly toward the audience, engaging their image-ination.

The voice, the communicator of words in performance, is naturally presentational because it lives in acoustic space. As the sounds of words swirl around them, audience members complete the symbolic transfer by imagining the action. The voice can create a setting by painting visual pictures with words. The voice can stimulate a sensory response or evoke emotions from the audience. These uses of the voice help feature such power sources as character, plot, idea, and imagery.

When voice is used to elaborate evocative qualities of language, it brings attention to language for its own sake and thereby serves as an alienation device. The orchestration of a text, for example, makes use of the human voice as an instrument to elaborate tone color, rhythm, and imagery. Often the voice is used in nonhuman or unusual ways, playing with duration, rhythmic patterns, and pitch to create atmospheric sounds. In these instances, the voice is most clearly presentational and symbolic.

Sometimes the voice can function more representationally, despite its natural life in acoustic space. When two characters exchange conversation onstage and their words refer to their own actions in pictorial space, vocal action is less presentational. The effect is similarly less presentational when the words of a character indicate something visual onstage. If a character speaks of "this barren tree," referring to an actual tree onstage, the words represent that tree. If, however, a character speaks of "this barren tree" when there is no actual tree onstage, the words present the image of tree to the audience, invoking their individual imaginative responses. Thus, the presentational qualities of the voice and words are greatly affected by the production's use of space. Typically, presentational theatre has depended on unlocalized space, relying instead on the power of the voice in acoustic space to evoke images that aren't realized literally onstage.

As a director of Interpreters Theatre, you are like the character who gives the Prologue in Shakespeare's *Henry V*. The Prologue addresses the audience prior to the beginning of the play, asking them to imagine that the small bare stage is a great battlefield, and that the movement of one or two characters symbolizes the marching of "a million":

> Can this cockpit hold
> The vasty fields of France? Or may we cram
> Within this wooden O the very casques
> That did affright the air at Agincourt?
> O, pardon!—since a crooked figure may
> Attest in little place a million;
> And let us, ciphers to this great accompt,
> On your imaginary forces work.

The stimulus to imaginative response in Shakespeare's day was, of course, the power of the play's language to evoke images of settings far beyond the confines of the "wooden O," the theatre of the King's Men for whom Shakespeare wrote his plays. Vocal action in Shakespeare's time, like vocal action in contemporary Interpreters Theatre, was—and is—presentational.

Presentational Physical Action

Unlike vocal action, which seems to penetrate all the air space in the theatre auditorium, physical action tends to be localized onstage. When a performer turns onstage to engage in some aspect of physical action—carefully untying a package, for example, or dueling—the audience looks in on the action, watching as though from the outside. If the performer is gingerly unwrapping a gift, it helps to have the actual package onstage, just as a sword fight staged believably onstage needs swords. This is the essence of representational action: that the action gives the illusion of a separate world of behavior onstage. Most physical action in the Conventional Theatre is of this type.

Interpreters Theatre will use some representational physical action, but the essence of presentational theatre is to break the illusion of real action happening onstage and to present the idea of action to an audience for imaginative completion. How is physical action, which seems naturally to inhabit pictorial space, transformed into presentational physical action? The key is to create physical action that functions much like vocal action in its ability to symbolize, to stand for an image of something that isn't literally provided onstage. When physical action becomes symbolic, the audience is imaginatively involved in the process of physical action. The physical movement of a mime artist is a good example of action that is symbolic. Everything the mimist does is accomplished through the suggestiveness of the human body. If the performer seems to be climbing stairs that aren't actually there, the audience provides the stairs through imagination and kinesthetic response. In this way, the audience is as involved in completing the symbolic action of the pantomime as it is in completing the image of a sunset that is conveyed in words. Action has been transformed from its natural representational state to a presentational gesture toward the audience.

TRANSFORMING LITERAL ACTION INTO PRESENTATIONAL ACTION

If a literary text seems to call for literal action, how does the Interpreters Theatre director transform it into presentational action? The answer to this question lies in the kind of relationship you want your performers to have with the audience. If you wish your audience to contribute to the action, then you must leave them something to contribute. In other words, literal action becomes presentational when parts of its "reality" are eliminated, so that the action stands for an image the audience can provide. In this way action in Interpreters Theatre becomes synecdochical; that is, a gesture is a part of a larger whole action. The audience imaginatively extends the part into the whole. Three major ways to transform literal stage action into synecdochical action are: (1) to take away physical properties, (2) to change spatial reality, and (3) to alter the usual continuity. In the process of directing your production you may discover others.

Pantomime is the most obvious example of action that has been stripped of physical properties. If a physical wall isn't present onstage, the audience will imaginatively provide it when the actions of performers suggest its presence. Among the advantages of pantomiming props and settings is not only that the audience is drawn into the experience by supplying the missing piece, but that stage space is fluid, unlocalized. When major set pieces are pantomimed, they can be changed at will without the clumsy necessity of blackouts and removal of stage decor. Furthermore, if the majority of props are pantomimed, then the presence of a crucial prop takes on added significance. Within the wide realm of pantomimic action, however, some pantomimed gestures are more presentational than others. When an object is meticulously pantomimed, the action tends to be more literal. (A prop that seems to require such detailed definition may need to be physically present.) The more presentational uses of pantomime involve symbolic gestures—raising a box by a single upward sweep of both arms, for example, rather than carefully grasping its imaginary corners, positioning the fingers, and then lifting. In the second instance, the box—even though it is pantomimed—seems to be located onstage; in the first instance, the box is more clearly part of acoustic space because the gesture symbolizes, rather than imitates, the lifting of a box.

In your Interpreters Theatre production, don't hesitate to pantomime articles you'd place onstage in a representational production. Explore the degrees of imitation in the pantomime itself. As a director, you can tap a wide range of pantomimic action, from specific and particular to general and symbolic. As a general rule, when props are not physically located in space, the physical action more clearly inhabits acoustic space.

Another technique for transforming ordinary physical action into presentational action is to change the spatial reality of the physical action. The clearest example of this technique is the use of offstage focus. [See pages 187–192.] If two lovers onstage turn toward each other while declaring their love, then the love scene is enacted in pictorial space and the audience observes the action. If the same two lovers stand side by side, playing their love scene out, as they address each other in the wide space of the auditorium, then the audience is thrust into the middle of the love scene, now in acoustic space rather than the pictorial space of the stage. When the spatial reality of a scene is altered, physical gestures become more symbolic than literal. If the two lovers were to kiss while enacting their scene onstage, they would perform the kiss as a natural part of their love scene. The two lovers who have turned toward the audience to declare their love would be ill-advised to kiss the air, unless a comic effect were desired. A better way would be to symbolize a kiss, to suggest the physical contact with graceful forward movement and appropriate emotional response. Very often the words in a text will carry enough explanation of the physical contact to make any actual physical touching unnecessary.

The technique of pantomiming the action and the technique of removing the action's spatial reality usually go hand in hand when a prop is involved in physical action. If you have decided to have the mailman hand a letter to the housewife by using offstage focus, with both characters reaching out to the audience (one in the gesture of giving, and one in the gesture of receiving), you will most likely choose not to use a physical letter. If the audience is capable of believing that the letter is actually being handed from the mailman to the woman, then they are also capable of believing that the pantomimed letter is actual. Keeping the props pantomimed, when using offstage focus, helps to smooth out the action considerably.

Offstage focus is not the only way to remove the spatial reality of physical action. When armies are moving across great miles of terrain but are actually traversing only a few steps on the stage, the physical action becomes presentational, with the few steps symbolizing great distances. Words usually play the major role in stimulating the audience to see the relatively small space of the theatre as a kind of magic space which can symbolize dimensions much beyond its own literal limitations.

A third technique for making physical action more presentational is to change its usual continuity. This technique, used most fully in Chamber Theatre, can exist without the other two techniques mentioned. In Chamber Theatre, a great deal of pictorial space is often employed. The narrator mediates between the sometimes representational scenes of the story as they unfold in pictorial space and the narrator's own presentational act of telling the story in acoustic space. As an art form, Chamber Theatre balances showing (representing action in pictorial space) with telling (presenting action to the audience in acoustic space). A great temptation in staging Chamber Theatre is to rely on the vivid picturization of showing in pictorial space, so that the narrative force is minimized. When this happens we see a production with a great deal of fully-staged representational action and a narrator weakly placed on the periphery of the action. Do not forget that in Chamber Theatre, as in all narrative forms, the narrator controls the action: the whole story is actually a presentation to the audience. Even though there may be extended moments of action believably staged in pictorial space, the narrator always has the capability to invoke and revoke the action at will. With a step forward, a gesture of dismissal, or a well-placed transitional word, the narrator can quickly remove the normal continuity of the action, holding the scene in abeyance or replacing it with another scene in a different time frame.

When the narrator exercises this scene-changing capability, we realize that all action in Chamber Theatre is really part of the presentation of a story—that even the most fully staged Chamber Theatre scene is an aspect of presentational action. Whenever the narrator adds a "he said" or "meanwhile," the audience is reminded that the action is not real in the sense that life is real, but that the snatches of action we see symbolize the ongoing lives of the characters the narrator is revealing.

As you transform ordinary physical action into presentational physical action, ask yourself: have I left a dimension for the audience to provide? Have I explored all the possibilities for symbolic action in this scene? Don't underestimate the power of an audience to participate imaginatively in the scene. If the performers place their energies well, indicating to the audience where props are to be imagined, or carrying out an offstage battle with the same tensive level of muscle involvement as an onstage battle, or controlling the narrative time shifts in scenes, then the audience will participate in the creation of the action.

Changing the expected direction of a movement, using only part of an ordinary gesture, or using pantomime are ways of transforming literal kinds of movement into symbols. Likewise, interrupting the continuity of action that's ordinarily representative attempts to shift the orientation of the audience from emotional identification with the characters to a more symbolic interaction with the narrator. Sometimes, though, the experience in the text isn't ordinary but is itself operating on a highly symbolic level. When performing such material, we make movement more symbolic by taking away its ordinary nature to call attention to other aspects of an action. The total pattern of the performer's movement becomes highly organized and formalized. In **formalized movement**, the design elements of the movement are exaggerated. Natural or ordinary motions are altered to allow other movement patterns to emerge.

Formalized movement signals that the performer is embodying something beyond usual experience. In some instances, the nature of the movement is suggested by the kind of role created by the author. It may be a very unusual kind of human being, as are the Red Queen and the White Queen in *Through the Looking Glass* by Lewis Carroll. Because these are playing cards come to life, the queens are human in form but they're merely exaggerated human types. Movement for these characters would be built from exaggerated human actions. When performers are not embodying human beings they may be animals, such as the pig and the rat in *Charlotte's Web* by E. B. White. Performers playing these roles might use movement abstracted from the ways in which the animals actually move, but the movement is reorganized. Symbolizing an animal or a playing card character may require that motion sometimes be created larger (or smaller) than life, that the rhythmic structure of the movement be altered to something other than ordinary human rhythms, or that the physical structure of the body be distorted in some manner.

Because the Interpreters Theatre script often assigns voices to power sources other than character, the Interpreters Theatre performer may be called upon to embody an abstract force, such as the sound or rhythm of a text. Or the experience being symbolized may be psychological, interior rather than exterior, so that the movement of the performer must create symbols for phenomena that cannot really be seen. When this happens, action in Interpreters Theatre becomes metaphorical; that is, one kind of action stands for another kind of action. Whenever a chorus is created to embody an internal state of a character, the external action of the chorus stands for the internal landscape of the character's mind. The audience perceives the analogy, and imaginatively makes the transfer from one kind of external action to an understanding of internal action. When creating movement patterns for metaphoric roles—forces, interior states of being, imagery—the movement approach may be very abstract, sometimes ritualistic in style.

When does the Interpreters Theatre director use literal movement presentationally, when are formalized movements most appropriate, and when is representational movement viable? This question can be answered specifically only in relation to a particular script, but a few generalizations apply. If your script depicts an ordinary situation with realistic characters, some of the movement of your performers will probably be representational. In such cases, always strive to involve the audience by transforming some aspect of the literal movement into a presentational form. In Chamber Theatre, you may be more likely to use larger segments of representational movement, but they're always in the context of an act of presentational telling. When you're working with exaggerated characters, with psychological forces, or with aspects of the text such as imagery and tone color, or when the experience of the text is supernatural, most of your movement may be formalized in some way.

Usually Interpreters Theatre directors combine all three kinds of movement—literal movement made presentational, formalized movement, and representative movement—to capture the experience of the text. Powerful effects can be achieved by changing movement style to make a point: by shifting into formalized movement to suggest a dream sequence in an otherwise realistically oriented production, by letting two lovers touch literally while others in the script remain on the symbolic level, or by contrasting characters who seem to move naturally with characters who move more formally and symbolically, to suggest that the latter stand for qualities or forces.

Since the informing aesthetic of Interpreters Theatre is that action is essentially presentational and inhabits acoustic space, you as director will always want to be conscious of the general spatial orientation of your production. Even though you've used moments of literal action in pictorial space for effect, is the overall impact of your production presentational? Have you trusted in the audience's ability to participate in the action of the text? So often, as directors, we're seduced into representing action onstage because we are familiar with recent developments in Western Realism in the Conventional Theatre. Resist the temptation to provide for the audience; otherwise, you'll surely fall into the *representational trap*. In approaching the construction of presentational movement for Interpreters Theatre, present—rather than represent—literal physical movement, and don't hesitate to explore the formalized movement possibilities in emotional and psychological states and in other power sources embodied by the script.

When the action carried by the words isn't essentially physical but is emotional, sensory, or psychological, the performer's action can be full and enriching. Organized rhythmic structure, whether in a poem, a story, or a play, suggests movement. Moments of intense feeling mobilize the entire body, urging a movement extension of the words. Even the most apparently static selection may have an inner dance of images, tones, rhythms, or presences which can be brought to life by overt movement. Just as performers give fullness to the noncharacter voices of a text through speech, they give them increased vitality through movement.

Movement, however, needs to serve the word and not itself. Many times the word is best served by little or no overt movement. Generally, when language is used to express conceptual relationships or to make intellectual distinctions, the verbal precision of the word will suffice. The power of such words may even be diluted by movement. Remember that moments of stillness can make moments of movement more meaningful. When interpreters choose not to employ movement, however, their decision should always be based on an understanding of the text and of the relationship between the language of the text and the kind of movement it calls into being, rather than on an arbitrary definition of the art form.

When planning a production, you'll need to come to an aesthetic understanding of the tensive relationship between word and movement in the script to be staged. Don't be afraid to trust in the power of the word. After all, Interpreters Theatre is interested primarily in acoustic space and in the way words evoke imaginative experience. On the other hand, don't be afraid to move freely when the text suggests it. Use movement to enhance or extend the literary experience, not to duplicate it. Only then can movement become a workable component of the language system of your script.

A CLOSER EXAMINATION OF TWO ALIENATION DEVICES: OFFSTAGE FOCUS AND THE USE OF A PHYSICAL SCRIPT

One aspect of movement that has become an identifying feature of many Interpreters Theatre productions is also a central alienating device for the art form. Offstage focus, which permits performers to confront the audience and to present themselves for inspection is one of the main tools of the Interpreters Theatre director.

The Use of Offstage Focus

Much of the communicative strength of the Interpreters Theatre performer resides in the power of the eyes to direct action and to evoke audience image-ination. The eyes are perhaps the most expressive agents actors possess; especially in an intimate theatre, the performers' eyes can communicate much of the inner tensiveness of the script.

Fundamentally, the eyes of the performer in Interpreters Theatre establish **focus**, thereby creating the very **location of scene** for the entire production. Since space in Interpreters Theatre tends to be used symbolically, with the vectors of energy emanating out from the stage space toward the audience, one essential technique informing the entire process is the technique of offstage focus.

The aesthetic principle of Interpreters Theatre is to use **offstage focus**, as if the action were happening in the boundlessness of acoustic space rather than in the pictorial space of the stage. A director has the freedom to pull scene onstage by shifting focus from offstage to onstage, but does so for a specific purpose with the conscious understanding that **onstage focus** is a break from the informing aesthetic of Interpreters Theatre. Such breaks are highly effective devices, which call attention to themselves, just as sudden moments of offstage focus (such as **asides** and **soliloquies**) in conventional, fully staged productions give extra theatrical weight to lines given out to the audience.

Most Interpreters Theatre productions employ a dynamic relationship between offstage focus and onstage focus, rather than a static insistence on a single kind of focus.[5] We encourage the dynamism of shifting focus in response to the demands of the text. Yet each decision about focus in Interpreters Theatre production proceeds from a base of offstage focus, just as each decision about focus in a Conventional Theatre production proceeds from an essential base of onstage focus. To use offstage focus skillfully and to know when (or if) it should be broken with onstage location of scene, the director should understand the nature of this central convention of Interpreters Theatre.

What is offstage focus? Literally, the performers address each other as though they were across the auditorium from each other, even though they may be standing side by side onstage. In this way, the audience is placed in the middle of the action. The offstage focus crosses over the audience's heads, locating the scene in acoustic space (figure 7.1). The effect on uninitiated audience members can be startling. At first, unused to such open encounters by performers who are seemingly addressing someone else, the audience may seem uneasy. Once they become more accustomed to the offstage focus technique, audience members begin to respond to the presentational advantages of such focus:

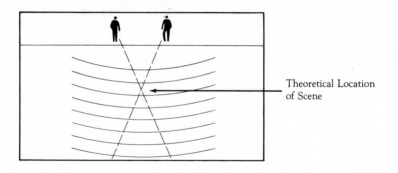

Figure 7.1: Offstage focus between two performers.

1. The audience seems to be in the middle of even the most highly charged emotional and intimate experience. On a practical level, offstage focus allows the audience to see more of the facial expressions of the performers, thereby intensifying many moments of the performance. In a Readers Theatre production of *Othello*, directed by Wallace A. Bacon, the strangulation scene (act 5) was played with offstage focus, so the audience saw simultaneously the anguish and anger on Othello's face and the mixed love and terror of Desdemona's response. (Usually, in a fully staged Conventional Theatre production of this play, at least one of the two faces is covered—most often Desdemona's, as Othello bends over her bed.)

2. The direct open stance of the readers and the offstage direction of the visual focus help to set in motion the imaginative orientation of the audience to the scene being presented. The active energies of the performers, thrusting out into the auditorium, engage the attentive energies of the audience members, turning them away from a literal identification with the action before them toward an imaginative constitution of experience. Literary images, along with the symbolic and presentational cues given by the performers (such as body movement, costume pieces, and vocal intonation), shape the imaginative completion of scene by the audience.

3. Offstage focus helps shift attention to the word, the acoustic dimension of the literary experience, rather than to the visual scene in space. Yet Interpreters Theatre performers can be highly interesting visually; the director's skillful blocking of movement helps achieve compelling stage pictures.

4. The audience is confronted by the performers' presence, a situation that heightens dialectical positions—as it did in the Broadway production of Peter Weiss's *Marat/Sade*, in which Jean Paul Marat and the Marquis de Sade turned full front to the audience, still arguing philosophically, as if to say, "Choose."

5. The face-to-face relationship between audience and performer can suggest a mirror image, a device used skillfully by Theatre of the Absurd playwrights such as Samuel Beckett. In *Endgame*, for example, the stage directions explicitly state that Hamm, in his chair, and Nagg and Nell, in their trash cans, are placed on stage facing full front toward the audience, as if to *confront*

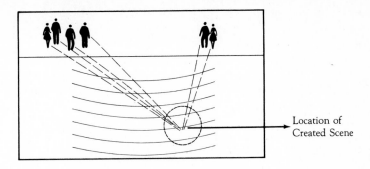

Location of
Created Scene

Figure 7.2: Group offstage focus on an object.

each audience member with an image of his or her own condition. Mirrored confrontations also occur in poems and stories between character and reader.

When more than two performers using offstage focus need to interact, the location of scene is established in the same manner as with two performers. If group members (either a chorus, or several more defined characters) are talking with each other, their lines of focus will cross. The crossing of focus lines looks more complicated on paper than it is in actual practice. The rule of thumb for each performer is: establish the central line of focus for the person you address first, then shift your line of vision slightly to the left or right for other persons, depending on their position in relation to you onstage.

Offstage focus is a powerful tool for creating imaginative objects and events in acoustic space. A group of performers (or a single performer) can act as a single focal unit; rather than crossing, the lines of focus run almost parallel and all performers turn eyes and body to face in the same direction, as illustrated in figure 7.2. Such convergence of energy toward a single point creates a happening in space. In a Readers Theatre production about the folk hero, Mike Fink, one episode involved Mike's famous jump across the Ohio River, during which he changes his mind halfway across, turns in midair, and comes back to the Illinois side. The group of performers virtually created Mike's incredible feat by following the non-existent figure with their eyes, their unified focus moving up and over the heads of the audience to the midpoint of the auditorium, then reversing the arc to follow him back down to the original jumping-off place. This use of focus, along with crowd reactions to the event, created a scene that could never have taken place literally onstage. The performers of *The Donner Party* by George Keithly (figure 7.3) are reacting to a sandstorm on the desert, created for the audience by a unified group focus.

Two more techniques of offstage focus are useful for the Interpreters Theatre director. First, when a character or a chorus is speaking introspectively, to themselves or to someone not literally present in a scene, the performers may confront space directly, without connecting in eye focus with any particular spot in space. In effect, the point of concentration is somewhere other than where the eyes seem to look, and the eyes are unfocused. Rather than seeing, the performer is

Figure 7.3: Unified focus: *The Donner Party* by George Keithly, directed by Jerry Mathis.

thinking or feeling, allowing the audience to participate in the projected interior state; the scene fills acoustic space.

Second, as an alternate way of visually contacting a character who is being addressed, the performer may place the character figuratively among the audience members, rather than contacting the character in space above the heads of the audience. Thus at brief moments during a performance an audience member may be addressed as "father," "members of the jury," or as whatever character is the recipient of the speech. It's important to distinguish between this kind of focal contact, which treats audience members as characters, and ordinary direct address to the audience as audience, as in figure 7.4. Both forms of direct address have considerable impact upon the viewers.

Often, during a production, a combination of kinds of focus is used—two or more types of offstage focus, or a blending of offstage and onstage focus. In figure 7.5, three persons are talking about the fourth. The fourth person, aware of the conversation, shares her feelings directly with the audience. Whenever focus types are combined, they should be crisply distinguished (but never simply mechanical), to enable the variation of focus to become a dramatic tool.

Although offstage focus is usually established by the eyes and reinforced by body position and posture, there are occasions when the body design will establish a strong focus even though

Figure 7.4: Direct address to audience: *The Scarlet Letter* by Nathaniel Hawthorne, directed by Margaret Dunn.

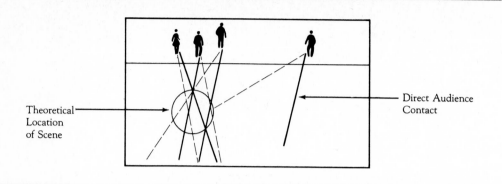

Figure 7.5: Combinations of offstage focus.

the eyes are looking in another direction [see Chapter 9, p. 247]. A performer who points away from the body, while the eyes are averted, establishes focus in the direction of the strong gesture. Although we've discussed focus almost exclusively in terms of the position of the eyes, a director shouldn't hesitate to use the effective power of a contrast in body design and eye focus. The sense of confrontation by no means depends upon a physical face-to-face relationship; confrontation is a state of mind. An audience can thus be confronted by a performer's back, if by that physical position the performer intends a statement aimed directly at the perceivers in the audience rather than at another performer onstage.

All kinds of offstage confrontation—between two characters, one character and a group, or a character and the audience—contribute to a sense of alienation, which ironically leads to audience participation in creating the action. When the audience and the performers mutually create an imagined world, there is a sense in which audience and performers look together at a literary text. This is the heart of presenting, that the literary world is offered for inspection. To heighten the central focus on the text, many directors utilize another important alienation device, the physical presence of the text (the script) onstage.

Use of the Physical Script

The script carried onstage isn't carried because the performer needs it for lines (Interpreters Theatre performers should be relatively free of dependence on a script); it's carried for aesthetic reasons. As the performer holds the text out toward the audience, it becomes a kind of offering—a genuine presentation—as if the performer were inviting the audience to share in the experience of the visible pages. (Some critics speak of the tripartite relationship between performer, text, and audience in theological terms, as if the performer and the audience were sharing a ritualistic communion with the text.[6]) We personally find the presence of a script on stage intriguing; its visibility becomes a very effective alienation device, helping to move the performance from the representational realm into the presentational.

Figure 7.6: Symbolic use of script: *Breakfast of Champions* by Kurt Vonnegut, Jr., directed by Janet Larsen McHughes.

We don't regard the presence of a physical script a defining feature of Interpreters Theatre, but when used symbolically the physical script can enrich the text. In a Chamber Theatre production of *Breakfast of Champions* by Kurt Vonnegut, Jr., the implied author figure came onstage dragging a huge copy of *Breakfast of Champions*, as shown in figure 7.6; this book became a drafting board for the drawing of illustrations that occurred during the performance. As a symbolic beginning of the story, the implied author constituted a narrator by handing a script to the performer onstage who was to play the narrator.

In a Readers Theatre production of Samuel Beckett's *Endgame*, the performer playing Clov was chained to a large durable script of *Endgame*, dragging it with him wherever he moved. The objective of such a symbolic use of the script was to show that Clov was entrapped by the words he had to utter as much as by the physical condition he had to endure. In a Readers Theatre production of E. E. Cummings' "Poem, or Beauty Hurts Mr. Vinal," the readers literally tore out paper from their scripts as they read them, littering the stage with remnants of the consumer society about which the poem was written.

Although such approaches to the physical presence of the script are striking, the held book can serve symbolic as well as aesthetic purposes. Often directors put script pages inside covers of other publications to make a statement—enclosing a clergyman's script in a Bible, for example, or placing a pretentious young woman's lines inside a *Glamour* or *Cosmopolitan* magazine cover. The script encasement serves as a character prop as well as an alienation device reminding the audience of the central interest in the text. Even without adornment, the plain black folder can become a prop—a shotgun, a tray, a fan, a mirror.

Many contemporary Interpreters Theatre productions don't use scripts at all. You may choose to perform without scripts present if the demands of physical movement are so great that scripts would literally be in the way, or if the nature of the literary experience seems to move away from an interest in the written text. Scripts wouldn't be appropriate in a production featuring the oral tradition, for example, during which a singer of tales seems to spin a story from his own imagination. In a staging of concrete poetry, scripts may be present as slide projections rather than as held manuscripts, as a way of sharing the poem's visual structure.

When shaping your production concept, think of the possibilities of retaining the physical presence of the script before you decide against it; it's altogether too easy to discard scripts because the performers and the director aren't skillful at using them. Scripts can sometimes serve an important artistic function because their presence contributes to the presentational form of the production. Whether to use scripts is a decision that should always be based on your understanding of the literary work. The presence or absence of scripts doesn't define the Interpreters Theatre form.

STEPPING BACK

Presentational action, including offstage focus and the presence of scripts, is an alienation device that helps to prevent an audience from being caught up in an illusion of real action onstage. Ironically, alienation devices also increase participation from the audience. By placing much of the scene in acoustic space, the performers invite the audience to share in the scene, even to the point of assisting in the scene's creation. Robert Breen notes, in writing of contemporary theatrical trends, "It is an irony of history that Brecht's Epic Theatre, based on the principle of alienation, should provide the nexus for a theatre of involvement."[7]

Alienation and participation may be strange bedfellows, yet the ability of Interpreters Theatre to alienate its audience from a primary illusion of action onstage allows the audience to help create action in acoustic space. The tensiveness between alienation and participation is a fundamental production tensiveness in Interpreters Theatre, and is therefore fundamental to production design. Although the use of offstage focus and the presence of the manuscript are not the only major means used by the director to illuminate the presentational form of a text, they are two conventions that have become identified with Interpreters Theatre. An understanding of their use and how they operate to promote both alienation and participation will help you understand better how to use other media of the theatre presentationally.

NOTES

1. J. L. Styan, *The Shakespeare Revolution* (Cambridge: Cambridge University Press, 1977), p. 5.
2. Bertold Brecht, "Vergneugungstheater oder Lehrtheater," *Schriften Zum Theater* (1936, p. 64; quoted in translation by Martin Esslin, *Brecht: The Man and His Work*, rev. ed., New York: W. W. Norton & Co., 1960, p. 136).
3. Robert S. Breen, *Chamber Theatre* (Englewood Cliffs, N.J.: Prentice-Hall, 1978), pp. 43–44.
4. R. P. Blackmur, *Language as Gesture: Essays in Poetry* (New York: Harcourt, Brace, 1952), p. 3.
5. For further discussion, see Marion L. Kleinau and Marvin D. Kleinau, "Scene Location in Readers Theatre: Static or Dynamic?" *The Speech Teacher* 14 (September 1965): 197–198.
6. See Wallace A. Bacon, *The Art of Interpretation*, 3rd ed. (New York: Holt, Rinehart & Winston, 1979), p. 527.
7. Breen, *Chamber Theatre*, p. 47.

SUGGESTIONS FOR FURTHER READING

Dalan, Nonna Childress. "Audience Response to Use of Offstage and Onstage Focus in Readers Theatre." *Speech Monographs* 38 (March 1971): 74–77.

Haas, Richard, et al. *Theatres of Interpretation.* Ann Arbor, Mich.: Roberts-Burton Publication, 1976.

Kleinau, Marion L., and Kleinau, Marvin D. "Scene Location in Readers Theatre: Static or Dynamic?" *The Speech Teacher* 14 (September 1965): 193–199.

Styan, J. L. *The Shakespeare Revolution.* Cambridge: Cambridge Univ. Press, 1977.

CHAPTER EIGHT

Designing the Interpreters Theatre Production

There are no bastard forms in art. There are only the living and the still-born.

George Beiswanger, *Theatre Arts*

Design in the theatre, like design in all other aspects of life, functions to impose order on chaos. Design in Interpreters Theatre functions either to embody and enliven the presentational patterns inherent in an original work, or to bring into being the composite design created by a compiler. The design of a production is the concrete fulfillment of a production concept.

In a highly structured production, everything the audience sees and hears is part of an integrated master plan: the design of the performers' movement and vocal action (see Chapter 9), the theatre space, the design of the stage environment, and the use of technical media all contribute to a total pattern that clarifies, intensifies, and unifies the power sources of the text. Often the complexity of a literary work poses a problem in clarity for an audience who hears and sees it only once. Simple identification of who is doing what, when and where, can be enhanced through the production design. When performers take more than one character role, for example, costume pieces that are changed with the role or consistent spatial locations for each role can make these character changes clear to an audience. Design enables a director-designer to give attention to individual elements while gathering all elements into a single perspective, creating a unity wherein everything in a production seems to move together.

Stage design for Interpreters Theatre production is as important—and should be as well conceived—as design in Conventional Theatre, although the stage setting may be no more elaborate than a few cubes placed in empty space. Anything placed on the stage becomes a design element; you're presenting a visual scene to an audience no matter how imaginative the action. If the formality of traditional stools and stands fits the total production concept and can be justified in terms of central values in the text, then certainly stools and stands should be the major element of the stage design. Arrange them skillfully in space, however, as part of the total production design. If the production concept calls for design approaches other than stools and stands, accept the challenge and create visual patterns that help actualize the presentational form with which you work. Sparsity rather than elaboration is the usual watchword, but the relatively few production elements to be used in realizing a script should be tellingly effective.

CREATING A PRODUCTION DESIGN

How does a production design idea arise? For every script you direct, the process will be different. Some texts seem to suggest their own production concepts quickly and the total design builds easily on that concept; from the very beginning of your work with those texts, you can see and hear the script in production. Others seem more obscure in their visual form, or they may present so many production design possibilities that it's difficult to choose. Much of the excitement of working with a variety of texts is that they each suggest their production form uniquely.

Generally, however, we can suggest three common ways a production design arises: through pervasive visual or auditory images, through focal characters, or through key actions. When auditory or visual images suggest staging ideas, the images usually begin to work on you early in the analysis and scripting process. Such images may arise in your mind as you read and analyze the work. Sometimes there'll be a series of images, sometimes a single informing image or guiding vision that sticks in your consciousness, subtly helping to shape stage arrangement and decor, order movement patterns, and define the use of all other production media. Such images often become the inciting spark that causes the script creator to attempt the arduous transformation process from literary work to production. In creating a script from *The Lord of the Rings*, for example, the beating of the orc drums in the Mines of Moria provided the initial impetus to production. The drums literally throbbed in the adapter's head throughout her reading of the work, and remained there until they sounded on the stage. Although the drumbeat, an underlying image that informed the rhythmic life of the production, was used overtly as a motif for evil forces in only four scenes, the implicit rhythm of the drums pervaded the whole production, setting a martial tone for much of the action. A visual image also guided the staging of this work; two towers—one good, the other evil—epitomized the major tension of the story and dominated both the stage setting and the use of focus in the production. Although the two towers were represented by abstract forms onstage, all focus was offstage, and the actual compelling force of the tug-of-war was created by setting up two widely separated focal points in the audience area. When Frodo felt the pull of the force of Mordor through the ring on his finger, he was physically drawn, through focus, in the direction of that tower. All the action of the production was shaped and unified by these two dominant images—the drum and the towers.

When such controlling images don't arise spontaneously, the director should seek some sort of unifying concept derived from the text. In almost every literary work, you can discern a fundamental pattern of action, which can usually be caught in a single phrase and which provides a workable design image. In dramatic terms, this pattern is called the spine of a play, the skeletal form that holds the dramatic body erect. In *Richard II* the fundamental pattern of action is vertical: Bolingbroke rises as Richard falls. In "*Richard II*: A Study in Movement," Lilla A. Heston explains the vertical spine of the play:

> The monarchial world of Shakespeare's *Richard II* might be described as a perpendicular one in which there are only two alternatives: to ascend or to descend, to rise or to fall, to go up or to go down. This movement of ascent and descent is revealed in a variety of literal and metaphorical ways. Primarily, of course, there is the fact that Richard falls from the throne as Bolingbroke rises. As Richard descends

from the heights of power, prestige, and divine authority, Bolingbroke ascends to these powers and ultimately *steps up*, in a literal sense, to seat himself upon the throne. Bolingbroke also steps up to mount himself upon Barbary, Richard's horse, so that Richard, by the end of the play, is not only unthroned, but unhorsed. Richard's fall and Bolingbroke's corresponding rise chart the dominant movement of the play.[1]

There are a number of ways that this image could control the design of a production of *Richard II*. First, the stage might be designed as a series of levels allowing for predominantly vertical movement patterns. The throne, Bolingbroke's ultimate goal, might be featured as a single dominant visual motif, elevated to require physical ascent. The characters of Richard and Bolingbroke themselves might ascend and descend as the balance of power shifts, or a chorus could symbolize the vertical movement patterns while the characters remain relatively stationary. A chorus might echo key lines that capture both Richard's fall and Bolingbroke's rise to power.

Pervasive visual and auditory images are especially important in the staging of compiled scripts as the "glue" that helps to hold the diverse pieces of the script together. Always try to be receptive to images as they arise from the text, even though you aren't fully ready to plan your staging design. Jot down the ideas that come to you; later they may form the nexus of a striking production design.

Often production ideas come through your fascination with a focal character whose nature and presence affects all the aspects of production. One adapter-director was drawn to stage *Breakfast of Champions* by Kurt Vonnegut, Jr., because of her fascination with the implied presence of the author. Indeed, the author becomes a character in the novel, recognizing the fictional characters as his own creations and, eventually, setting them free. The pervasive presence of Kurt Vonnegut, Jr., seemed so strong that this director conceived of a design image in which the author-figure could oversee all the action, entering the scene at appropriate moments. The image that evolved was a high narrow platform upstage, over the heads of the actors, on which the author-figure could perch. To reach the platform, the Vonnegut character climbed up a stepladder, at the top of which was built a large seat and drafting table (made out of a copy of the physical script, suspended from the ceiling), from which the author drew illustrations for the book, ate his lunch, and overtly controlled the action below.

Another instance in which the production idea came as a result of a focal character was a Readers Theatre production of *Hamlet*. There is a sense in which we see all the characters in *Hamlet* through the title character's eyes. To feature that psychological emphasis, the director staged a production in which all the characters except Hamlet wore masks given to them by Hamlet. Occasionally, Hamlet would offer a character a change of masks, as when he forced Ophelia to exchange her innocent face for the visage of a whore while he angrily shouted at her, "Get thee to a nunnery"; eventually, Ophelia herself donned the mask of madness. The production focused primarily on Hamlet himself, with the other characters serving as extensions of his troubled soul.

A practical solution to finding a production design is to examine key actions in your script for their design cues. Like the veteran puzzle solver who clusters the pieces around central images before filling in background, you as director may begin the design of your production by isolating key scenes. Key scenes are those that are central to the action of the script or that present special problems in staging. Almost every production has some scenes that pose a greater challenge to

Figure 8.1: The author-figure, left, gives advice to his narrator: *Breakfast of Champions* by Kurt
Vonnegut, Jr., directed by Janet Larsen McHughes.

the director than others. How you solve the problem of these scenes often determines the general
style of your production because, once you've discovered how to make difficult scenes work
onstage, the rest of the production will form itself around them.

Alice's fall down the rabbit hole and her rapid changes in size as she prepares to enter the
fantasy world of Wonderland, for example, are action problems that have to be solved early in
the planning stages for a production of *Alice in Wonderland* by Lewis Carroll. Solutions to these
problems have included, among others, a jungle gym through which Alice "falls" by a series of
acrobatic movements, a ladder on which she "grows" and "diminishes," defocused slide projections that create her fall and size changes, and, perhaps most satisfactory of all, reliance on the
power of words and focus alone to suggest an imaginative "fall." With problems that involve extraordinary happenings, usually the less specific the movement cues, the more the audience is
allowed to explore in imagination.

The solving of these kinds of problems is really an initial step in production design; until you know how Alice is to fall down the rabbit hole, you won't be able to solidify the style of your production or to put all of its pieces together into a total design. Perhaps some specific solutions to key scenes will clarify this concept.

A pivotal action in the C. S. Lewis story, *The Lion, the Witch, and the Wardrobe*, is the entry of the children into the land of Narnia. The entryway into this fantasy world is through an ordinary-looking wardrobe full of old coats, which opens out into a frozen world of snow inhabited by fauns, talking animals, and an evil witch. In a production of *The Lion, the Witch, and the Wardrobe* entitled "Narnia," the director isolated two basic problems: (1) how to present the contrast between the imaginary world of Narnia and the everyday world in which the children lived, and (2) how to deal with the somewhat preposterous idea that an ordinary wardrobe would be the gateway between the two worlds. The use of an actual wardrobe on stage was never seriously considered; rather, in this production, the four members of the narrating chorus stood in a block to become, in effect, the wardrobe. The chorus wore black capes with silver linings and carried scripts that were black on the outside and silver on the inside. As the children entered the chorus wardrobe, the chorus members moved slightly to encircle them. At the moment of the discovery of Narnia, the chorus dissolved the wardrobe formation, reversed their scripts, and with wide circling movements threw back their capes, transforming themselves into the icy landscape of Narnia. At the same time, the color of the whole stage changed from amber to blue. There was no spatial division between the ordinary world of the children's home and the fantasy world of Narnia. Because the wardrobe was created by performers, it was materialized and dematerialized as needed. In essence, the coloring of the visual scene changed, but there was no other changing of set pieces.

In a Readers Theatre production of *Rhinoceros* by Eugene Ionesco, the key scene was the famous transformation scene, in which one character gradually turns into a rhinoceros while engaged in conversation with a second character, who remains human. To solve the obvious problem of how to transform a man into a rhinoceros onstage, the playwright has provided several opportunities (in the lines and in the stage directions) for the metamorphosing man to step offstage into a conveniently located bathroom where deft makeup experts can daub his face with green makeup and crepe hair. With skillful cosmetic and costume changes, the man seems to become a rhinoceros before the audience's eyes.

The director of the Readers Theatre production of *Rhinoceros* was interested in adapting the play more to appeal to the audience's imaginations than to shock their sensibilities by the deliberately absurd presence of realistic rhinoceroses onstage. The key transformation scene, then, presented several problems. The solution was to center the process of transformation in the skills of the performer alone, rather than in the skills of the makeup and costume consultants. The interpreter playing the man-becoming-rhinoceros took one side step to place himself in the bathroom, and stared out toward the audience as though looking into the bathroom mirror. The effect of seeing a rhinoceros vision when looking at the audience added to the confrontation effect of this absurdist play. The transformation was accomplished entirely by the actor's gradual hoarseness, which evolved into the snorts and calls of a wild beast, and physical changes in bodily carriage and movement, from an erect human position to a stooped, hunched animallike crouch with pawing hoofs. Provided the performer is skilled enough in suggesting the metamorphosis to a rhinoceros, the advantage of such an appeal is that the audience is likely to imagine a more horrific rhinoceros than could ever be achieved by special technical effects. In this case, the inherent comedy of the scene seemed to be increased because there was a wildly absurd contradiction between what the man in his pajamas actually looked like and how he was behaving. Since the solution to the transformation scene was to rely on the skills of the performer, that decision affected all other aspects of the production: the set was minimal, as were costumes and makeup, and all focus was offstage to locate more fully the visual aspects of performance in imaginative acoustic space.

In all of these examples, the solving of the problem scenes led to a series of other decisions about the productions. Once slide projections are introduced to establish setting and action in *Alice in Wonderland*, for example, they can be used to create mood and character as well. Once it is decided that a four-person chorus will serve as the wardrobe in "Narnia," the chorus can become a means to create other tangible elements throughout the production. Once the skill of the performer alone is relied upon for the transformation in *Rhinoceros*, the director knows to avoid other more subtle reliances on pictorial space and representational staging in favor of a performer-centered presentation.

Responding to visual or auditory images, exploring the nature of a focal character, or solving key actions are three of the most common ways a director comes to an understanding of a production design. In your own work with your script, you may discover other avenues to design. Perhaps a particular communication strategy is at the heart of your text; for example, solving the problem of an unreliable narrator by replaying certain scenes may affect the design of your entire production. Perhaps another power source, such as time, will become the stimulus to a production design. In a staging of Laurence Sterne's *Tristram Shandy* or Robert Coover's contemporary short story, "The Babysitter," time is so convoluted that you may be led to work with a very unspecified set so that the characters can quickly move from one time frame to another.

However you arrive at your production idea, it's extremely important for you to find a pervasive design image that informs your entire production. Only with a controlling production design firmly in your mind can you ensure a consistency in production style and, at the same time, create a production that bears the unique stamp of you as its director.

Metaphoric Approaches to Design

When a controlling design image arises in your mind, it can present itself as a straight image or as a metaphoric image. Metaphoric thinking is one of the fundamental capabilities of all artists; whether your production design is a direct image or a metaphoric image, the idea of metaphor is at the heart of Interpreters Theatre. The very act of production is an exercise in metaphor because as directors we implicitly say, "This text is [like] this action in space." Performance becomes a metaphoric analogue for the action captured in the written text.

When your production design idea is also a metaphor, then you've completely engaged your power of metaphoric thinking. Not all design images will be metaphors, nor should they be; some texts give rise to metaphoric staging and others don't. When you sense a metaphoric image emerging, it's useful to understand more fully how metaphoric thinking can inform your production.

What Is Metaphoric Thinking?

To be able to "see something as something else" is a basic aspect of human perception.[2] To see faces in a cloud or to see familiar objects in the shapes of rocks is an experience most of us have shared. It seems that some visual forms trigger a double vision that allows us to juxtapose two images into one and, when such tricks of the eye happen, we feel the excitement of discovery. The same opening of our vision happens in larger ways when, in ordinary life occurrences, we suddenly catch a glimpse of what seems to be the larger design of the universe. These experiences are so common that we make use of such structures of language as metaphors or symbols, whereby one object or idea calls another into being, in our attempt to communicate with one another. In short, the metaphoric process, to see one thing in terms of another thing, seems to be part of the fundamental human experience. Friedrich Nietzsche went so far as to define *truth* as "a mobile army of metaphors."[3]

Norman Friedman once wrote that "metaphors have their source in the more primitive, undifferentiated levels of our consciousness."[4] It is no wonder then, that literature, which is "captured" human experience, is often filled with metaphoric and symbolic images. As you began to analyze your selection early in the process of transformation you may have discovered a strong underlying metaphor operating in the work itself; if this happened, you probably shaped your script to account for or expose the metaphoric life of the text (see Chapter 2). If your script is built on a metaphor, your staging of the script needs to reflect that metaphor.

Pilgrim's Progress by John Bunyan, for example, is structured by the metaphor of a journey: achieving spiritual salvation is like a literal journey through perilous places. To illuminate the metaphor of the journey in the script, the adapter employed a chorus and wrote orchestrated segments to emphasize the threatening forces encountered by the traveler. Stage space had to be fluid, without locales fixed by the stage setting, to allow the long journey to take place. Moving film projections suggested changes in terrain, and slide projections of splashes of color revealed changing aspects of the internal spiritual state of the pilgrim. The total flexibility of this production, with its nonspecific use of space and projected scenery, allowed the metaphoric form of *Pilgrim's Progress* to function in production.

Metaphor usually isn't as obvious in the original written form of a literary work as it is in the allegory, *Pilgrim's Progress*. Most texts are so richly ambiguous that they inspire directors to many kinds of treatment, including both straight staging (with a variety of production designs) and metaphoric approaches. In actual practice, most metaphors arise in the staging process (rather than the scripting process), with the original words of the work cast in a metaphoric frame onstage.

Metaphoric Stage Design

In the staging itself, metaphoric statements are usually made through either or both of two channels—metaphoric design of the setting or metaphoric qualities in the performers' actions. In the Readers Theatre production of *Hamlet*, described above, all the characters except Hamlet are wearing masks that reveal their roles in relation to the prince. A more metaphoric extension of that design idea would be to stage *Hamlet* in a funhouse, in which Hamlet perceives characters through distorted mirror images: the image of his mother looming large and frightening, or the visions of Rosencrantz and Guildenstern shrinking to almost laughable smallness, as Hamlet proceeds through the Hall of Mirrors. This particular metaphor would also illuminate the self-reflective aspects of the play. In actual production, a director may not choose to use literal distorted mirrors, because lights and audience faces might be reflected by them, but she could work with suspended odd shapes of shimmering mylar and then accomplish the distortions of image by slide projections.

Another metaphoric staging of *Hamlet* would be to place Hamlet in a maze built onstage. Whenever he is stopped by a wall, that moment corresponds to a scene or soliloquy in the play that further delays his action of revenge. Once he reaches the middle of the maze—where the play-within-a-play catches "the conscience of the king" or where Hamlet confronts his mother in her closet (depending on what you see as the central crisis of the play)—then Hamlet can see his way out of the maze more clearly, even though he still faces a number of detours (an aborted trip to England, a scene in the graveyard, the funeral of the woman he loved). Both the Hall of Mirrors metaphor and the maze metaphor are created essentially by set design. The performer, of course, must move in accordance with the arrangement of the set (wending his way through the maze, or proceeding cautiously through the Hall of Mirrors) but the set design is the controlling factor in establishing the metaphor.

Sometimes a staging metaphor comes not through set design, but through performer action primarily. "The Horse Dealer's Daughter" by D. H. Lawrence opens with the central character, Mabel Purvin, in a state of deep depression, so low that she attempts suicide by drowning. Dr. Fergusson sees Mabel walk into the pond, rescues her, and in the process of the rescue, restores her to new hope of happiness through his awakening love for her. The structure of the story suggested a ritualistic metaphor to one director, who staged it as the last rites for the dying. Most of the narration was carried by a chorus, three ritual figures and a celebrant who sometimes intoned the words as a Gregorian chant. The metaphoric level of the production was communicated primarily by the actions of this chorus depicting traditional events associated with the ritual.

The ritualist aspect was integrated with the more literal events of the story in various ways. Early in the story, for example, Mabel visits her mother's grave; one of the chorus members, seated with back to the audience, suggested both the mother and the grave site. The rest of the chorus, arranged as a choir, chanted the text, which describes Mabel's ordinary tending of the plot of ground above the grave. Rather than carrying out the literal actions described in the narration, however, "the performer playing Mabel ritually greeted the seated figure of her mother, arranging her hair and her dress. The mother figure remained motionless until Mabel's departure, when her hand reached out but did not quite touch her daughter's receding figure."[5]

A production of *The Bell Jar* by Sylvia Plath used both stage setting and performer action to create a circus metaphor that probed the major character's distorted vision of reality. The stage was composed of a series of levels at the rear with playing areas on stage right (defined by cubes) and stage left (defined by a swing).

Although not literally designed as such, the three major playing areas corresponded to a three-ring circus; the three-quarter round stage further approximated a circus arrangement. Three swaths of translucent cream-colored fabric were angled from floor to ceiling at the back of the stage, suggesting circus spotlights. Although the stage setting supported the metaphor, it was costume pieces and the actions of the performers that really carried the metaphor of the circus.

Figure 8.2: Stage setting suggesting a metaphor: *The Bell Jar* by Sylvia Plath, directed by Cindy Miller.

The major character, Esther, was trifurcated into an outward self and two narrators representing different psychological aspects of her character (one gentle, sensitive, naive, poetic; the other angry, witty, strong, and cynical). Esther's alter egos, donning uniform jackets and whistles, assumed the roles of twin ringmasters who signaled the actions of the other characters in the story and guided Esther through the events leading to her suicide attempt. The other characters wore costume pieces that corresponded to their different roles as circus performers. As the characters came into scene, their actions matched their circus role: Esther's boss, the lion tamer, for example, cracked her whip as she gave Esther her office duties for the day. At the point of Esther's suicide attempt, the dreamlike circus setting faded; circus performers moved off and the alter egos took off their jackets. Esther awoke from her suicide attempt to a stark black world, in which she was forced to struggle alone back to sanity.

Some Considerations When Using Metaphors in Production

Step back occasionally and ask yourself: does this production idea illuminate the text? In metaphoric design, in particular, the temptation is often to place the director's cleverness and in-

Figure 8.3 Character trifurcation: *The Bell Jar* by Sylvia Plath, directed by Cindy Miller.

genuity above the text. One of the values of metaphoric design is that it explores in depth a particular aspect of a literary work and it highlights that aspect by viewing it in a different way. In achieving this value, you ultimately sacrifice some of the multiple ambiguities of the text. Any production is a kind of reduction of the text (featuring a single director's informed vision of the work), and metaphoric production tends to be even more reductive. The artistic decision to make is whether the depth you achieve through metaphoric staging is valuable enough to offset the loss of breadth you could achieve through nonmetaphoric staging.

In the example from *Hamlet*, the metaphor of the maze focuses on the question of Hamlet's inaction, crystallizing and clarifying it for the audience. The production cannot equally emphasize other aspects of the text, such as the play's obsession with death or the pervasive contrast between disease and health. If the director wished to prove the play's fascination with death, this could be achieved metaphorically by casting the play's action in a ritual that prepares Hamlet for his own death, but the question of Hamlet's inaction is then left relatively unexplored. A nonmetaphorized production may attempt to maintain a balance among all aspects of the play, but such a production risks the criticism that it is unfocused. As a director, you must consciously arrive at an understanding of what you're gaining and what you might be losing in any production design. Only then are you ready to proceed in rehearsal with confidence that your production idea illuminates the text.

To show by example how a production design idea was conceived, expanded into all aspects of production, and eventually realized onstage, we shall describe in detail one Readers Theatre production of *Something Wicked This Way Comes* by Ray Bradbury, from production concept to production realization.

Something Wicked This Way Comes is set in a small town in which a carnival has just arrived. Although the carnival appears to be ordinary, mysterious happenings begin to occur and some inhabitants of the town disappear. Two young boys, Will Halloway and Jim Nightshade, are first excited by the prospect of the carnival, but then discover its strange and evil nature. They are aided in their explorations by Mr. Halloway, Will's father, who is the janitor in the town library.

The power sources of plot, character, and idea interact in the text to set up a dramatic conflict between good and evil, which is the major action of the novel. Evil, in the story, is the supernatural carnival that through the centuries has traveled the earth, capturing the souls (and bodies) of weak human beings, distorting them into a collection of freaks. The over-curious and the afraid are trapped by means of a strange carousel that whirls forward into age and backward into youth, thus luring the unwary person into the clutches of the carnival by promises of gaining immediate maturity or eternal youth. Good is primarily represented by the sensible maturity of the young boy, Will, and his father, Mr. Halloway.

Rather than being given to a single controlling narrator, the narration was divided along dramatic lines between a "good" narrator and an "evil" narrator. The characters in this script, therefore, are Will, his friend Jim Nightshade, Mr. Halloway, and their good narrator, posed against Mr. Cooger and Mr. Dark, the two owners of the carnival, the Dust Witch, a freak of the carnival, and the evil narrator. Miss Foley, the schoolteacher who falls prey to the carousel, is also included as a character.

The novel is about the inevitable process of aging and the human desire either for immediate maturity or eternal youth. Based on this production concept and its resulting script, the director determined that the carousel was central to the action of the script and that a centrifugal

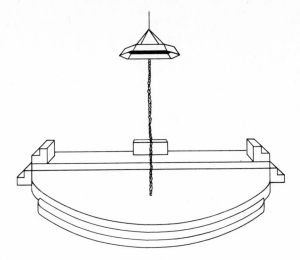

Figure 8.4a: Floor Plan: *Something Wicked This Way Comes* by Ray Bradbury, directed by Marion Kleinau.

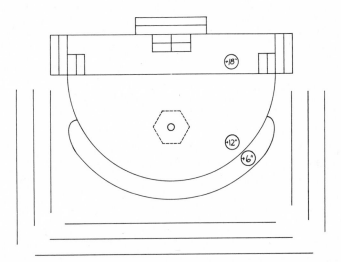

Figure 8.4b: Elevation: *Something Wicked This Way Comes* by Ray Bradbury, directed by Marion Kleinau.

experience of whirling on a carousel was the organizing image to control design decisions. The stage space, therefore, had to be organized so that circular movement patterns could be achieved. The audience was seated on three sides of the stage (the fourth side being needed for other practical aspects of the design). The set was built of a series of levels and organized around a pivotal point center stage, so that movement patterns could be naturally circular. The major set pieces were four L-shaped modular set pieces that were moved to different positions on the upper level for each of the three acts of the production. The stage space was not divided into defined locations; rather, the same space became various locations throughout the production.

Although the director wished to feature the circular movement of the carousel, the literal presence of a carousel onstage could never capture the fantasy image created by Bradbury. Also, rather than looking at something going around, the director wanted the audience members themselves to experience the sensation of motion. The solution to the problem was to create a revolving, multi-colored light source mounted in the ceiling over the center point onstage. When the light was in motion, it filled the whole theatre space. Music accompanied the motion of the "carousel" and helped to create a mood of eeriness. In a minor key, the tonality seemed to suggest a melancholy music box rather than the boisterous calliope normally associated with a carousel. The production technique seemed to work well, as many audience members reported being swept up in the circular movement of the light as if riding a merry-go-round.

The only physical representation of the carousel located onstage was a single heavy rope, hanging straight down below the light. Whenever the carousel was to be activated, the performers used the rope as if it were a pole on a merry-go-round, while the entire space of the theatre seemed to whirl with light. When the scene shifted away from the carnival, the rope was lifted out of the playing area.

Because of the fantasy nature of the story, much of the focus was offstage: the evil balloon, the midnight train, and the carnival freaks were created in acoustic space. Whenever human beings interacted, however, or whenever evil appeared in human form (Mr. Dark, Mr. Cooger, the Dust Witch), focus was onstage. The director chose to use carefully shaped symbolic movement to help create such fantasy action as the trip through the mirror maze. Stop action techniques were used to suggest the boys' running trips between the carnival and home. The explosion of the carousel was created through slow motion movement. Because of the extensive physical movement in the production, only the narrators carried scripts.

Because the whole concept of *Something Wicked* is metaphoric—the carnival being a metaphor for all evil that preys on mankind—the director chose to rely on the inherent metaphor in the text without further metaphorizing the script. The production sought audience identification through empathy with some of the characters and a participation in the imaginative creation of the supernatural elements of the story. Alienation was created through frankly symbolic techniques of staging and direct contact between both narrators and the audience, and between Mr. Halloway and the audience. A larger framework for the story, which suggested that the carnival waits for all of us, was created by a pre-show in which Mr. Dark, moving slowly and dispassionately through the half-lighted theatre, fastened up posters and studied the faces of the audience. To some he handed a ticket entitling them to "one free ride on the carousel."

As you read the above description of *Something Wicked This Way Comes*, you no doubt recognized areas of concern that you face as you are preparing to stage your script. You may find yourself asking: how does my text use stage space? What technical effects should I use? How should my cast members relate to the audience? and a host of other questions. There isn't a director alive who hasn't felt overwhelmed at times by these decisions. Have confidence in your production concept and carefully tackle each problem of the total production design as it arises. Rather soon, you will see a complete production design take shape, affecting all the components of the show.

THE COMPONENTS OF DESIGN

The creation of a complete production design never happens by accident, although many aspects of that design may arise intuitively. A good director makes artistic decisions about all the major aspects of the production—the nature of the theatre space and its effect on performer-audience relationships, stage setting, use of technical media, and the performance itself. The design of the human performers is so central to a production that we have devoted Chapter 9 exclusively to that aspect of production design; the other three aspects are discussed in this chapter.

Designing Performer-Audience Relationships in the Theatre Space

What is a stage for Interpreters Theatre? As the barest essentials, there need to be space for people and performers and enough freedom from distraction to allow the imaginative act to take place. What places meet these criteria varies with the nature of the imaginative act. It wouldn't be wise to perform the cerebral machinations of Henry James in the halls of a busy shopping center. On the other hand, the open confrontation and fragmentary nature of a polemic collage—a script challenging the exploitation of laborers, for example—might be enhanced by the presence of a more casual and transient audience.

Usually, Interpreters Theatre performances take place within some sort of defined room, which may or may not contain production equipment. Let your space challenge your ingenuity. No performance space is so poor that imaginative work cannot take place within it, provided the production is designed for the space or the space for the production. Whatever the nature of the script, the production should be built with space possibilities in mind, but don't let your space limitations shackle your imagination.

The question of performance space leads to further consideration of the audience who'll occupy the space and the role of the performer in relation to the audience. From the storyteller in the ancient marketplace, in close proximity to the audience both physically and socially, to the performer distanced by the proscenium stage, revealed only when the curtains part, the ways in which audiences and performers meet are many and varied. Ideally, the Interpreters Theatre audience is an active imaginative participant in the experience of the literature, but the nature of that participation depends on whether the performance is a formalized event or an informal sharing of literature among close acquaintances. The kind of audience participation expected is an important part of the production design.

The size and shape of the theatre space and how the space controls audience-performer relationships are primary considerations. Intimacy in a theatre space isn't necessarily related to size of the total auditorium. Even in a large theatre house, a sense of intimacy between performers and audience can be achieved through skillful arrangement of audience seating in relation to the stage area. Both New York City's Circle in the Square and the Arena Stage in Washington, D.C., have intimate atmospheres despite their size. Audience members can be seated on all four sides of the stage areas, and the seats are banked so that no audience member seems physically far away from the performers.

Theatre Shapes

In Interpreters Theatre, you usually work in one of the several traditional shapes diagramed in figure 8.5. If your performance space is a room without fixed seating, you may be able to use any of these arrangements. If, however, you have access to relatively inflexible theatre spaces, they'll probably be arranged in one of these five basic shapes. Each arrangement entails a different approach to designing a production that captures the intimacy of contact and primary identification with acoustic space. Each arrangement also requires different approaches to the placement of performers in the stage space.

The Proscenium

On the **proscenium stage**, extensive use of offstage focus techniques is necessary because the defined box shape of the proscenium stage can too easily become a separate, representational world for the audience to view. If there's no curtain, the danger of falling into the representational trap isn't as great. The curtain divides pictorial performance space from audience space, a division that can be detrimental to the creation of scene in acoustic space.

The size of the audience space presents another problem with the proscenium theatre. If it's too large, the performers may not be able to include those in the back of the auditorium to the same degree as those sitting in front. A director faced with a large proscenium space must make sure that the performers intensify their offstage thrust to reach the farthest extremes of the audience space. One way to achieve this is to open body angles more—almost to full front position. The success of the musical, *A Chorus Line*, on Broadway and on national tour attests to performers' abilities to reach every audience member, despite huge auditoriums and formidable proscenium stages. Essentially using offstage focus and other presentational effects, *A Chorus Line* was designed so that the dancers faced the audience in a full front position and proceeded, each in turn, to tell a story or share feelings with a casting director who was seated at the back of the auditorium. In this way, the audience was placed in the middle of the action, and was fully engaged in constituting the scenes of personal experiences that the dancers painted with verbal images in acoustic space.

Anything the Interpreters Theatre director can do to make the performance space reach into the audience space is desirable. In a production entitled "34 Witnesses," director Raymond J. Schneider, desiring to give the audience an experience of standing above a scene of action along with performers who were also viewing the scene, installed large speakers throughout the auditorium. The watching performers whispered to their fellow audience watchers through microphones. The effect for audience members was as if the performers were standing beside them.

The Arena Stage

As the stage area thrusts further out toward the audience and the performers move away from an enclosing space, the problem of the representational box diminishes and new difficulties

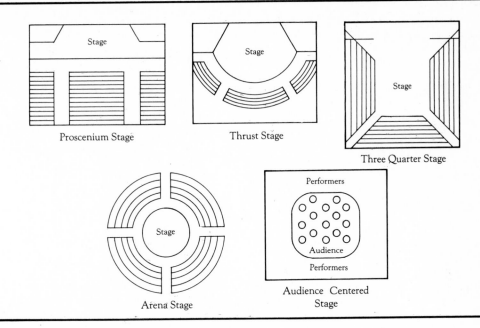

Figure 8.5: Common stage shapes.

arise. The shift from traditional proscenium staging, with audience on only one side of the per-formance space, toward **theatre-in-the-round**, or **arena stage**, with audience on all four sides of the performers, would seem to serve intimacy because of the proximity; but instead of softening the definition of the stage, the arena stage tends to intensify attention toward the defined stage area at the center of the arena. Because there's no longer a one-directional contact with the audience, the use of offstage focus to create scene in acoustic space becomes increasingly more complex. How does an Interpreters Theatre director working in theatre-in-the-round establish action in acoustic space? How can the vectors of force be made to go out when they seem to be pushed in so strongly by the audience on all sides? This is particularly critical if the director wishes to make contrastive use of offstage and onstage focus.

Despite the fact that the arena shape drives audience attention onstage, the design of the stage space is seldom realistic, and unless space is used very literally, all action will be symbolic to some extent. The director merely needs to be careful that all stage props and movement main-tain a symbolic identification. The director can still rely to some extent on the use of offstage focus, but the techniques vary; the use of body facing and focus to make contact with the audi-ence becomes a selective process, thrusting out first in one direction and then in another. A nar-rator may move in a circle or cross and recross the arena during the course of a production. Performers may shift position more frequently than in a proscenium production to vary body facing.

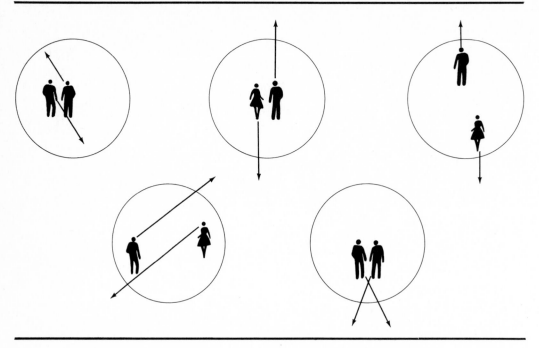

Figure 8.6: Offstage focus for arena staging—shared scenes.

The usual blocking of a shared scene between two people for arena production places them facing together, but in slightly different planes so that all of the audience members see at least one of the two faces (see figure 8.6a).

Because it appears artificial in such an arrangement for the performers not to look at each other, the Interpreters Theatre director using this physical relationship employs onstage focus. As an alternative (not to be overused), the performers can stand almost shoulder to shoulder, facing different directions (figure 8.6b), or they can stand back to back at different sides of the arena (figure 8.6c). This is an interesting way to stage an argument; the audience sees the arguing performers (and their positions) individually. As another alternative, performers may be spaced farther apart, allowing the direction of focus to encompass both the character addressed and the audience (figure 8.6d). Finally, if of short duration and if factors of audibility permit, a shared scene may be staged with offstage focus using one side of the audience as if it were a proscenium arrangement (figure 8.6e). Take care to shift this position frequently.

When more than two performers are sharing a scene, several stage arrangements permit the thrust of offstage focus to work, at least in varying degrees, as illustrated in figure 8.7. An important consideration in arena staging for Interpreters Theatre is not to hold to the offstage convention to the extent that you sacrifice believable performer relationships. The natural non-reality and the interactive nature of theatre-in-the-round make it relatively easy for the performers to sustain a presentational contact with the audience.

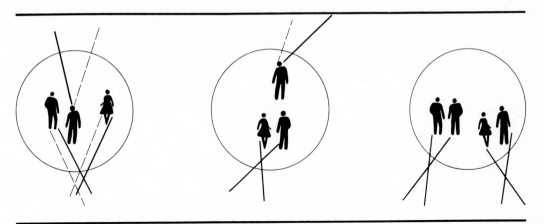

Figure 8.7: Offstage focus for arena staging—groups.

The Audience-Centered Stage

Offstage focus is a natural technique in audience-centered environments where the audience (which may be in swivel chairs or on pillows) is surrounded by the performance space. When performers look at each other, they look across the audience (figure 8.8a), shifting their body positions in space to facilitate the cross-audience focus; or they can stand side by side using traditional offstage focus (figure 8.8b). In this kind of theatre, because the focal energies of the performers are constantly crossing and recrossing the audience space, the action seems to be happening in the center of the room, where the audience is seated. The audience, very much a part of the action, becomes a strong participator in the imaginative experience.

Different kinds of theatre spaces suggest differing degrees of formality in performer-audience relationships. The arena stage, for example, suggests a greater informality than the proscenium, because the arena seems conducive to some openness and social interaction. Audience members have been known to become so engrossed in an arena production that they inadvertently participate by ad-libbing. Because Interpreters Theatre is the actualizing of presentational form in literature, the formality or informality of a performance should stem from the text itself and not from the shape of the theatre. Ideally, you might wish for a different kind of theatre space for each script you produce, a space that would reflect the uniqueness of the text; sometimes, this ideal can be partially achieved by using found spaces. More likely, however, you'll adapt the space in which you usually work, attempting to reshape the theatre space to coordinate with the cues in each text.

Directors and designers have solved the problem of inflexible theatre spaces in a number of ways. Thrust stages are added to the fronts of traditional proscenium arrangements. Sometimes the whole theatre, including the lobby, is redesigned as part of the set design, so that the atmosphere of the production begins as the audience enters the theatre. A large stage area can be turned into an arena theatre, the audience seated onstage. Theatre aisles are used as performance spaces and sometimes performers speak from audience seats. Preshows can be devised in

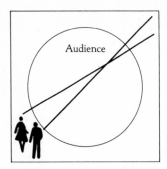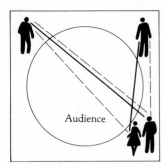

Figure 8.8: Focus for audience-centered staging.

which the performers contact the audience outside the framework of the text itself. To begin the production of a compiled script on whaling, individual cast members conducted audience members on a guided tour through the lobby, which had been turned into a small whaling museum.

If you normally work in a space that seems inflexible, attempt to see it from different perspectives to discover its potential for change. Think always in terms of the literary work to be produced, the nature of its experience, and the way it communicates with its reader or audience. Innovation for the sake of innovation makes little contribution to the literary experience, but innovation that comes from the nature of the text is a creative extension of that text.

Alternate Performance Environments[6]

Since oral interpreters often assume automatically they'll perform in one of the theatre spaces previously described, other kinds of performance environments are sometimes not explored fully. Upon encountering new and perhaps unique environments, we may habitually ask ourselves: "Where is the stage going to be?" and "Where is the front row?" Directors become so accustomed to using something approximating a traditional theatre environment that, although they may carefully consider all other aspects of production, they often fail to consider that important relationship between the place of performance and the experience of the text.

Although a more traditional theatre space may be well suited to some kinds of Interpreters Theatre productions, many texts suggest a less formal design in a less structured environment or different kinds of audience-performer arrangements than those we have examined.

The use of found space (any existing location that is used in its natural condition) is one way to seek a different kind of compatibility between literature and the environment. Reading the poetry of nature in a natural setting, performing literature that seems to connote a tavern setting in a bar, and using a church for a work such as *Murder in the Cathedral* by T. S. Eliot are

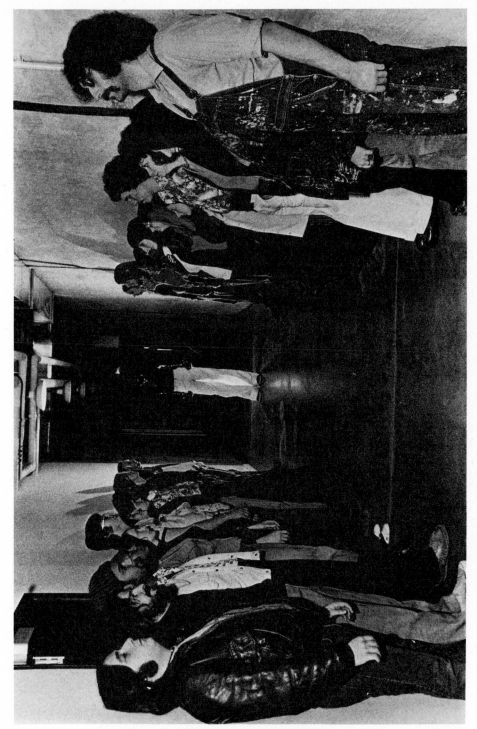

Figure 8.9: Use of found space: *Ashes and Asphalt*, a compiled script directed by Robert Fish.

production approaches that have been explored by many directors in various ways. The performance space in figure 8.9 was a basement hallway close to the throbbing sound of machinery. The script was built of poems that depicted voices of the city, people who might be riding a subway in any large metropolitan area. The audience stood or was seated in the long narrow hallway while the performers, sitting or standing among the audience, talked to their fellow subway riders.

The use of found spaces is a way to feature the more conversational style of some modern literature. In discussing twelve first novels by contemporary writers, Alfred Kazin refers to their "dominating quality of personal give-and-take—a story related among friends, who are probably in the book anyway." He notes their undisguised, relaxed, conversational tone; their "raw," "lived" look and plain, harsh, straight storytelling; their narrative openness and unselfconsciousness, their looseness of structure reflecting the increased commotion of late twentieth-century life through their antic rhythms, and their seeming indifference to form. According to Kazin, the writers' intentions seem to be simply to tell any story they can tell by any means, "so long as there is someone to listen."[7] Although Interpreters Theatre certainly doesn't focus exclusively on contemporary literature, many performance scripts are exploring a wider variety of casual literary forms, such as folklore, street poetry, protest literature, song lyrics from popular and rock music, contemporary social and political satire, and factual material from the world of advertising or from the new journalism. These works suggest an informal, rustic, perhaps even harsh environment. They often deal with immediate issues arising from a specific situation. Read by performers in the more formal atmosphere of the theatre, out of touch with the conditions that prompted their creation, this kind of material can sometimes lose the immediacy and sense of authenticity that gives it life.

You shouldn't think in terms of simply transplanting a traditional performance into a new environment; rather, you need to redesign the performance for these settings. In public places a good way to begin is to allow the event to form its own nucleus by having some performers act as audience members initially. Give attention to how an audience will be drawn to the event; performers should be prepared for spontaneous interaction with audience members during the performance.

It's also helpful to consider an alternate space-time orientation for some productions. We usually think of theatre as an event in which an audience occupies the same space for a period of approximately two hours. A more active use of space is to structure an event so that performers and audience members move to different locales or settings for various segments of the performance. An entire building may thus become the performance environment. In the production of "Ashes and Asphalt," the audience moved among four different performance locations—a subway, a city park, a nightclub, and a bookstore—all located within one building.

Interpreters Theatre has always recognized that the audience participates actively in the experience of the literature; the Interpreters Theatre experience may be seen as arising from a direct transaction between the audience member and the performed text. For some texts, therefore, you may want to emphasize the intimacy and informality of those performance situations in which we share the literature among a group of friends. You may also want to emphasize a strong sense of community among all participants, performers and audience alike. In this sense, the Interpreters Theatre performance may be viewed as a social occasion that brings people together to share a text. When the text permits, therefore, you may wish to emphasize the social

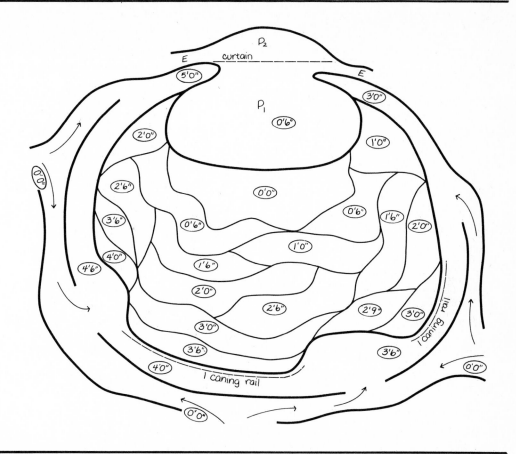

Figure 8.10: A proposed performance space for Interpreters Theatre, designed by Robert B. Loxley.

nature of the gathering by heightened interaction among performers and audience, with an emphasis on informality and active participation by the audience in the performance.

This kind of social emphasis may provide impetus not only for using found spaces, but for changing the entire performance environment that we traditionally use. How might we design a performance space flexible enough to facilitate more informality between performers and audience while at the same time accommodating those texts that require a more formal approach? You may never participate in the design of a new theatre space for Interpreters Theatre, but you might have occasion to suggest ways to remodel existing spaces. When such opportunities arise, it is well to think experimentally as well as traditionally, to think in terms of increased flexibility and fluidity of space.

Remember that the audience members and performers don't need to be segregated from each other. Designs such as the one in figure 8.10 offer alternative approaches to traditional theatre arrangements. This theatre consists of a multilevel, free-form audience area wrapping around a central performance space. The levels rise progressively higher as they sweep up and away from the performance area. The highest level encircles the audience, allowing audience members to move around the outer edge of the space and enter the space at any point. The environment would facilitate a varied, spontaneous, and informal use of space yet provide sufficient body support for the participants. Audience members could either sit on the forward position of a level with their feet on the next lower level or sit leaning back against the front of the next higher level. They might also assume a wide variety of body positions, orientations, and groupings. The structure would be carpeted, with large cushions or pillows placed randomly throughout the environment for additional comfort and body support. Certain areas of the structure might include built-in seats that would serve the more traditional function of chairs for audience members who required greater body support or who might feel uncomfortable using the freer parts of the structure. The levels might build gradually to a height of as much as five feet at one side of the main performance area, allowing a few audience members to perch on them overlooking the entire event. Leaning rails on the inner edge of the highest level provide places for those wishing to stand, or lean, on the periphery of the space.

If the performers need a larger amount of space or more depth, the performance area can be enlarged by drawing aside a curtain, behind which is an extension of the performance area. Performers can also use the areas immediately adjacent to the main performance area or any other part of the structure for performing; they can surround the audience, perform in their midst, or use various locations throughout the space. The structure has a single lighting system for the entire space, allowing possibilities for lighting audience areas as well as performance areas.

Although this design is only one of many possible approaches to the creation of a theatre, it may stimulate you to design your own ideal space for Interpreters Theatre. An interpretation space should be more than a neutral container for the performance, providing only for the necessary practical requirements for an audience watching a performance. It should also be a place to which people enjoy coming.

Stage Space and the Text

Because the confrontation between audience and performer in Interpreters Theatre is presentational, all techniques of production, including stage setting, should serve that essential act of presentation. Whether your production is to take place in a theatre space or a found space, you need to incorporate the visual scene into your total design. In found spaces, the design is usually minimal, consisting perhaps of a seemingly casual rearrangement of chairs. In a more traditional theatre space, stage settings may become an intrinsic aspect of the visual impact of the production.

The general atmosphere of the performance space when the audience member arrives will engender an emotional frame of mind. Audience members should feel that they have walked into a place where they can help to create worlds. To be a participating creator, the audience member needs an opportunity to absorb the "feeling tone" of the theatre space—happy, somber, folksy, regal—and to become accustomed to the shapes and coloring of the surroundings. Although a completely empty stage invites the imagination to fill it, carefully selected shapes,

Figure 8.11: Symbolic use of space: *The Donner Party* by George Keithly, directed by Jerry Mathis.

colors, and sounds can subtly persuade the audience to be ready to create with the performers when that moment arrives.

As the spatial images of the script build in your mind and you begin to create a visual setting, hold on to a concept of acoustic space. You'll be constantly tempted to literalize, simply because we live in a literal world where a hallway is a hallway and occupies a different space from the kitchen or the bedroom. This is one of the first pitfalls in the representational trap: the desire to carve the space of the stage in a literal manner. Once these specific divisions have been made, a whole set of obligations to representationalism arises: "Where does the sofa belong?" "I need a bed; it says she sits on the bed." "There's a scene at the dinner table so I have to have a dining room with a table and chairs." Particularly with more realistic novels, a director may soon discover that he has attempted to re-create the total materialistic world of the story literally onstage. In the first stages of design, therefore, it's well to think more abstractly and symbolically than literally. In figure 8.11 the set becomes a covered wagon, a desert, a mountainside, a cabin, and many other locales. The abstract design suggests a feeling of motion and entrapment that informs the entire production.

Begin with general questions about the space suggested by the text. These impressions may relate to actual space or to the space of the mind. How much space is involved and what is its general nature? Is the emphasis on specified physical space, or is the space orientation psychological? Does your script suggest wide open spaces or confined spaces? Does the action take place outdoors or indoors? Will the stage contain large groups of performers or only a few? Is the psychological condition free and open or smothered and bound? Is there physical isolation? Psychological isolation? Is the action epic in scope, covering many locations and much distance in time and space, or is it localized to one space and time?

When the action ranges in time and space, it becomes immediately apparent that the stage can't encompass the literal aspects of the space used. Many novels in particular will cover multiple space locations and time spans. *Gone with the Wind* by Margaret Mitchell encompasses the full time span of the Civil War and moves in space from Tara to Atlanta. The best solution for such a script seems to be the undefined setting, through which the same stage space can become any locale at any time. The stage may be designed with symbolic shapes and functional levels, but there's no division of parts of the stage to correspond consistently to specific locales. An undefined setting is also beneficial for scripts that are primarily psychological; certainly the mythic experience of the persona in Edna St. Vincent Millay's poem "Renascence" needs nonliteral, undefined stage space.

If the action in a script is localized, then you may use a generally specified setting, which designates areas of the physical stage space to help clarify aspects of the action such as time changes, symbolic locations, and areas of character dominance. In a production of *Breakfast of Champions*, the two sides of the stage were used to indicate the locations and sphere of influence of the two major characters in the work: Kilgore Trout's apartment on stage right, and Dwayne Hoover's Pontiac showroom on stage left. It's important to the concept of the text that the two characters not meet until almost the end of the story; the midpoint of the stage was reserved for that meeting.

The relation between the amount of the original stage space and the amount of space used for the action of the production can help both to clarify and to intensify the impact of a performance. An Interpreters Theatre production of *A Doll's House* by Henrik Ibsen might occupy only a mid portion of the stage space and use a literal barrier of some sort surrounding Nora's small world, so that when she finally walks out of it, she is moving from a secure and confined space to the undefined space of her future. In a work such as "How I Contemplated the World from the Detroit House of Corrections" by Joyce Carol Oates, in which the present tense narrator is incarcerated, the emotional impact of her confinement is reinforced if she appears physically isolated, limited to a very small and specific area of the stage, while the flashbacks of her life play before her and the audience as if on a movie screen. Conversely, the asylum hall that becomes a stage space in *Marat/Sade* by Peter Weiss doesn't seem to be able to hold the energies and the communicative thrust of the piece. Part of the power of the play is that its dialectical philosophy is greater than its specified locale, the 18th-century insane asylum. In Peter Brook's staging of the play, the characters literally spilled out of the playing area into the general audience space.

Creating a Stage Setting

The greatest stage setting in the world is, of course, the setting in your head. Throughout all your speculations about shape and texture, your script has undoubtedly been playing on the stage in your head, and definite images and forms have begun to emerge. Don't resist this kind of fantasy; indulge yourself as a director by permitting the performance in your imagination to become as rich as possible in its presentational form. You'll be able to visualize some moments fully. At other times you'll hear the characters speak. Listen. Watch.

When you have as much of your production in mind as you can—and have made notes on it—walk into the actual performance space you'll use. Unless you're using a specialized or found space, this is probably a familiar place to you. It may take some effort to look at it with a fresh eye; nevertheless, try to approach the space as if you've never worked in it before. Mentally place your imaginative production in that space. What do you have to do as a designer to come as close as possible to the ideal production space in your mind? What changes in your imaginative setting must you make so that your script can come alive in your actual stage space?

Each stage and text presents unique challenges for the director; much of your creativity as a director is exhibited by the ways you meet the individual challenges. There are, however, some basic deliberations each director should make when creating the physical setting in a conventional theatre or similar space:

1. Let your controlling image, rather than the nature of your theatre space, be the dominant shaper of your design. You may find that the actual performance space and the theatre in your head are very similar; in fact, your knowledge of the playing area may have helped you shape the script. But if your stage is square and your production is round or angular, find ways to modify the stage shape—through curtaining, construction, lighting, or rearrangement of audience position. If your stage is small and your image is of vistas of space, you may choose to use part of the auditorium or to extend the visual horizon through film projections.

2. Think in terms of playing areas and **levels**. See your setting vertically as well as horizontally. See it in motion. Would your production concept be best realized in an empty space, or do you need the variety of levels that platforms can provide? For many Interpreters Theatre directors, levels are useful nonrepresentational solutions for a variety of problems. Platform levels maximize the number of playing surfaces, adding flexibility to the set. This kind of versatility is valuable for the director with a small stage, because it makes use of vertical space, and for the director in a large theatre, because it breaks up the vastness of the space. The ways platforms are put together can accentuate the kind of balance or imbalance that exists in the text. Centered and regularly spaced platforms immediately connote an ordered world, whereas an asymmetrical level construction suggests an unpredictability of action. Platforms become symbolic structures as well as practical playing areas.

3. Consider the nature of your space. Will it be undefined or specified? If specified, where are your areas? What are their functions and their shapes? Will your space concept work for all scenes in the show?

4. Consider the nature of the action in your script. How much flexibility do you need? Go through the script and decide how each important action can happen presentationally in your setting. Begin with key scenes. If your stage shape works for these, it'll probably work for the rest of the performance.

5. Imagine the general movement patterns that will emerge from your stage setting. How will your performers move in relation to the locations of exits and entrances and in relation to playing areas and set pieces? In arena staging, for example, the general movement pattern tends to be circular. If you wish to change this predominant pattern, you might locate the set pieces in such a way as to elicit more angular movement.

6. Visualize your completed setting. What set pieces will you need to allow the action to be realized and to complete the visual form? If your production concept suggests the use of reading stands and stools or chairs, be as careful in designing their placement as you would be with any other set pieces. Experiment with interesting arrangements that may become analogues for the shape of action in the text. Remember that reading stands, like other set pieces, can be placed on levels as a way of achieving variety and interest in the setting. If your stands and stools are lightweight, consider them as portable stage pieces which the performers can readjust for scene changes.

Some of the finest Readers Theatre productions use only stools and reading stands, relying almost entirely upon the power of words to create setting. In such productions, stools and stands are often used symbolically as well as practically. Music stands can be held in various ways by the performers or can be placed together to suggest a prison cell, a forest, a cave, a city, and many other imaginative constructions. Experiment with decorating reading stands by painting them, draping them with fabric, or hanging banners from them. You may even want to create specialized reading stands that serve to hold a script and to designate a reader's station, but reflect a more specific element of the text's environment—pulpits for T. S. Eliot's *Murder in the Cathedral*, tree stumps for J. R. R. Tolkien's *Hobbit*, or giant chess pieces for Jean Anouilh's *Becket*, for example.

When your production concept involves more elaborate set pieces than reading stands, the following steps can help you avoid the representational trap:

a. Make a list of all the set pieces that are absolutely necessary to the performance.
b. When your list is complete, reduce it by at least 50 percent. This may sound facetious, but it's our experience that directors rarely need more than half the set pieces they expect to need.
c. See how many of the remaining objects can be combined into multifunctioning pieces. For example, a table may become a ticket counter or a bed, as well as a place to eat.
d. When you've reduced your list to the absolute minimum number of set pieces, decide whether your production concept calls for abstract forms or representational forms. Can the table actually be a box, or a series of boxes, or must it be a realistic table? As a general rule, avoid using very much realistic furniture and other decor onstage. Its presence tends to carve space literally and specify setting. Sometimes, however, a well-chosen realistic piece used flexibly can be extraordinarily effective. In a Chamber Theatre production of *Tristram Shandy* by Laurence Sterne, directed by Robert S. Breen, the central set piece was a large ornate mahogany table littered with piles of books, miscellaneous papers, food, items of clothing, and other objects. While the table was used functionally as a prop stand, a writing desk, and a dining table, it also symbolically reflected the teeming clutter of Tristram's mind.

    A basic consideration for any set piece is: How much information concerning time and place, meaning and mood, must your stage setting communicate? A simple column could denote the ancient Greek period, for example. In figure 8.13, a small group of symbols created a waterfront setting.

e. Whereas most set pieces are constructed for the show, almost any structure can be adapted for stage use, size permitting. Many directors have made creative use of playground

Figure 8.12: Decorative reading stands: *James and the Giant Peach* by Roald Dahl, directed by Raymond J. Schneider.

Figure 8.13: Use of key symbols to suggest place: *River Out of Eden*, written and directed by Joseph Robinette.

Figure 8.14: Found object as set piece: *I Never Promised You a Rose Garden* by Hannah Green, directed by Vance Fulkerson.

equipment—slides, swings, teeter-totters, sandboxes—to symbolize other structures or to enhance tensive shifts in the action. Peter Brook used large swings in his adaptation of Shakespeare's *A Midsummer Night's Dream*; Edward Albee wrote an entire one-act play featuring a sandbox; a production of Anton Chekhov's "The Bear" used a teeter-totter as the only set piece. Other found objects can also become intriguing set pieces. Ladders, for example, are commonly used; a ladder defined the fantasy world of Yr in a production of *I Never Promised You a Rose Garden*. In a Readers Theatre performance of the musical *Stop the World, I Want to Get Off*, a grocery shopping cart was used as a baby buggy, satirizing the commercialism of childrearing. One of the values of incorporating found objects into the stage picture is that they successfully work against representationalism and rather quickly establish a symbolic orientation to dramatic action.

As a director, don't overlook your performers as found objects. The human body can effectively become a set piece; witness Snout's portrayal of the Wall in *A Midsummer Night's Dream*. Performers have been used for chairs, beds, curtains, wardrobes, walls, and many other functional pieces. If you use human bodies in this manner, consider the possible personalities of the set pieces: a human chair might literally hold its occupant fast, and another chair might eject its overweight intruder. Could a bed with a twinkle in its eye tickle its occupants? Would a wall slyly provide a chink for some viewers and not for others?

7. Finally, stand back and look objectively at your design. Will it clarify your production to the extent necessary for audience understanding? Now is the time to work out any remaining problems. Does it have the intensity, the emotional impact that you desire? Sometimes the extending of a line, the adjusting of an angle or a slight change of color can work a miracle. Is your setting unified? Does it seem to be of a single piece? Be careful of too many isolated objects stuck in space. There should be a feeling of continuity to the stage picture.

Incorporating Media Effects

Early in the development of Interpreters Theatre in this century, many directors felt the necessity to break down the separation between audience space and performing space by leaving lights on in the auditorium and by using no theatrical effects whatever. This is still an exciting concept.

Today, however, the trend is growing toward full use of theatrical media, and with the integration of more of the effects of the theatre in Interpreters Theatre production, practitioners often find themselves in a dilemma: they want to use lighting effects and other media, which sometimes tend to locate scenes onstage, yet they want to maintain intimacy with the audience. Too often, in an enthusiasm for what the media of the theatre can achieve, the Interpreters Theatre director inadvertently cuts off the lifeline of direct contact that is the heart of our performance aesthetic. When this happens, media take precedence over the text. We believe a balance can be achieved wherein media of the theatre can work for, rather than against, intimacy of the performer-audience relationship.

The first thing you need to understand about media effects (lights, slide projections, sound, hand props, costumes, and makeup) is that usually the more of them you use, the more you'll tend to pull the action of the performance into pictorial space. All other things being equal, the more visual stimuli given to an audience and the more explicit the sound images, the less the audience will create in imaginative space. On the other hand, some media stimuli may facilitate audience participation. If you wish to use media and still keep the major thrust of your action in acoustic space, your media design will need careful planning.

Lighting

Light, by its mobility, can endow empty space with life, making it articulate. Changing the intensity of light on the stage can produce the feeling of movement. Changing angles or shifting from one angle to another through the use of differently placed light sources gives the impression of constant motion. Lee Simonson points out that Adolph Appia's supreme intuition was his "recognition that light can play as directly on our emotions as music does."[8] By its color, and by the rhythm of its mobility, light can enhance and augment the rhythm and intensity of a production. Light in Interpreters Theatre can help to stimulate a major mood in the audience and provide an impetus to imaginative participation. Changes in lighting, when nonliteral, can reinforce image changes in the words of the script.

For the most part, in Interpreters Theatre, faces should receive primary lighting and be visible to the audience. The light on a performer's face reveals the lines of offstage and onstage focus. Visibility in Interpreters Theatre is particularly important because of the synecdochical dimension of the art form; the audience simply must be able to see the performers' symbolic facial gestures.

If you have a sequence in which symbolic movement, rather than words, is the primary communicative medium, you might want to shift lighting emphasis to highlight the sculptural qualities of the body. To light the body rather than the face requires different angles, and sidelighting becomes important because it results in a separation between background and figure.

A director in cooperation with a lighting technician can use light to help clarify action. A cross fade from one stage area to another, with the light dimming on the performer and brightening another area of the stage into which the performer then moves, gives the effect of the light leading the performer; the audience moves with the performer through whatever space or time change is taking place. When the performer walks out of the lighted area and crosses to the new stage position before it's lighted, even though it takes only a brief moment for the new area to brighten, a break seems to occur.

In effect, light can function as an additional performer in a production. Assume, for example, that memory plays an important part in the literary work being performed. If the past is located in a specific stage area that remains lighted and active even when unoccupied, all other action by the performers will seem to relate to the lighted area. The light becomes a metaphor for the past and the past becomes a tangible force in the action. The angle of light projection can also function metaphorically; if a strong beam of light is angled diagonally across the stage, the light source and its angular pathway will affect all the movement of the performance. The light will seem a goal if movement follows its beam toward the source. If performers cut across the beam of light, the light will seem to be a barrier to movement.

These and other special effects make light one of the most exciting of the stage media. Although many effective Interpreters Theatre productions make no use of light beyond simple illumination, the use of lighting effects can help the director solve special problems, such as the whirling carousel in the production of *Something Wicked This Way Comes*.

Projections[9]

Slide and film projections can be an exciting presentational aspect of a production, or they can utterly destroy it. The measure of success is related to the level of abstraction with which projections are employed in relation to the text and the way in which they're integrated into the performance. Before you decide to use slides or moving projections, consider the following questions:

1. Why use a projection? How does a visual effect of this nature help you create your production? What is its particular function in relation to the text? Perhaps your production is a documentary and you wish to re-create some of the scenes and the people of the area or place on which you're focusing. Or perhaps you need an abstract atmospheric background—a forest, a city—and are unable to achieve the effect you want in regular stage setting. Maybe you wish to augment or extend some particular image—a memory sequence or hallucination. Or you want to contradict something that's happening onstage by suggesting that it didn't really happen this way. (This may be an interesting approach to staging an unreliable narrator.) You may feel that the addition of projected words could underscore some aspect of the text; a presentational approach to *The Rivals* by Richard Brinsley Sheridan might use projected words comically to emphasize the many malapropisms used throughout the script. The text you're staging may even call for visions, such as the ghostly presences the witches create in *Macbeth*, that could be realized best through projections. Usually slides and other kinds of projections are used to achieve what cannot be accomplished with performers or set pieces to the same effect. Sometimes a McLuhanesque montage of slide projections, moving projections, sound and spoken words is desirable.[10] These conglomerates which seemingly make use of chance juxtapositions and ask the viewer to provide personal connections can be effective, but effectiveness requires more care in selection of stimuli and in arrangement of sequences than appears to the viewer.

2. What kind of projections will you use? Will they be still or moving? How defined will they be as opposed to defocused images? How realistic will they be? Realistic photographs of the suburbs of Detroit were used in a production of Joyce Carol Oates's "How I Contemplated the World from the Detroit House of Corrections." The slides were used during the early scenes of the script, in which the central character is describing her home, to reinforce the juxtaposition between her well-to-do background and her present condition.

In fantasy, projections can be used to great advantage for entities such as Humpty Dumpty in Lewis Carroll's *Through the Looking Glass*, the Oompa Loompas in Roald Dahl's *Charlie and the Chocolate Factory*, and other elusive but important inhabitants of the land of imagination. It would be foolhardy to make these projections specific, however. The wonder and value of projections is that they can be created abstractly with just enough hint of specificity to tickle the imagination.

If the slides are meant merely to give a background to what's going on, they may work best in a soft focus or on a screen that diffuses them and probably in large scale, so the audience doesn't perceive individual objects as much as an overall wash of pattern. Here the problem is one of balancing levels of light between what's needed for the performers and how bright the projections can be in proportion. But if the projections are meant to supply specific images at specific times, then you need a smaller screen that focuses attention in a particular place.

3. How will the projections be used in the performance? As background or atmosphere only? In partnership with words or movement? As transitional devices? If used with words, how will the two entities interact? What about rhythmic relationships? How will the visual projections relate to the visual presence of the performer?

If the projections comment on the production or provide some sort of additional text, you need to consider how your script works, where its rhythm allows additional material, and how, visually, you can make the audience understand the relationship between the projections, the performers, and the text.

The interface between performer and projection is a crucial element in the use of any projected images, and it's an area of artistic exploration that needs much more attention than it has been given. In a documentary, the real scenes and real faces can make the performers seem almost superficial if the same level of emotional reality isn't reached in the performance as in the pictures. This is one of the greatest dangers in using realistic projections. With abstract projections, the problem is alleviated to a large degree, but the relationship of abstraction levels still remains.

Symbolic and abstract projections in general seem to be an excellent solution for some of the problems encountered by the Interpreters Theatre director. In a production of Ken Kesey's *One Flew Over the Cuckoo's Nest*, abstract moving projections were used to signal shifts from external action in the asylum to the Chief's internal thought processes. Although the Chief never spoke his thoughts aloud, the colored projections illuminated his emotion-ridden face as his recorded thoughts were heard by the audience.

When using projections, beware of allowing them to take over the performance: they're seductive to the eye, they have a life of their own, and they're notorious scene stealers. Think of projections as performers. You can have them do monologues: the performers freeze, projections come up, pause, black out, performers continue. This could be a viable method, but there are the same problems associated with it as for a theatrical script written as a series of monologues. Continuity is largely destroyed, the performance assumes a predictable rhythm rather than building in a climactic direction, and, because the projections are inevitably stronger visually than the human performers (human faces are only reflectors of light; the projections are light), the projections tend to take over the strongest role in the performance.

A much better method is to write the projections into the performance as characters so both projections and human performers can be active simultaneously. The size of the projections should be reduced to a more human scale than usual, except for projections that need the emphasis of larger proportions. They should be blocked in relation to the other performers so their position either balances that of the human performers or, when necessary takes the focus just as a lead character might. They may be given lines in a dialogue so the screen reflects answers to the other performers' statements or augments them. Like another character, the slides may interrupt other performers by being timed to appear at the right moment and in the right place with a contradictory or supportive statement, either in graphic form or in print. Human performers may interrupt the projections, also, by stepping into the beam of the projector and using it as a spotlight, forcing their shadows onto the screen as projection element. All your directing and design variables come into play now; you should direct the projections just as you do the performers. Don't let either of the two upstage or become subordinate to the other, unless that's your deliberate intent. Lastly, don't forget that there's a human part of your projection performer, too. The projector operator must understand the part the projections have been given. If the projectionist is well rehearsed and sensitive, the projections can respond to the rhythm onstage and to the mood of the audience, just as any good performer can.

Sound

Sound naturally inhabits acoustic space and can greatly enhance an Interpreters Theatre production. Don't hesitate to use performers as sound sources, especially for sound effects. The nightmare of shock treatments in *The Bell Jar* was created by abstract moaning sounds made by the performers who were onstage but not in the scene. A rainstorm that flooded a river town was created vocally by cast members of *River Out of Eden*, a compiled documentary. As you've learned (see Chapter 3), vocal orchestration of the text, elaborating the rhythm and tone color, may be used to accent selected moments in a production, or it may be used as a total production approach.

Performers can also manipulate sound-making equipment such as drums and woodblocks. In creating live sound, it's good to be frankly presentational. Place the sound-making instruments onstage if the performers are to use them. If live sound comes from a single instrument—piano, guitar, oboe, violin—or small orchestra, don't try to mask it; make it a visible part of the performance. In a compiled script, live music can be as much a component as the literary fragments used. You might also wish to experiment with choral music as part of a performance.

By far, the most commonly used sound source is recorded music. Most productions use opening music to set a mood for the ensuing performance. Choose this music as carefully as you would any other part of the production media, making certain that the tonality of the music creates the effect you desire in relation to the tonality of the script. Avoid clichés. Although the popular *Malagueña* is beautiful Spanish music, it wouldn't be the best choice for a production of Garcia Lorca's *Blood Wedding* because it suggests a mood very different from the mood of the play.

When using music as an interwoven part of the production, for transitions, to underscore certain scenes, or for emphasis, avoid well-known music unless you deliberately want to use the audience's recognition of the melody for an aesthetic purpose. The same principle applies to the use of music as to selection of literary materials for the compiled script—a well-known musical phrase brings its own context with it. The music from *Star Wars* would evoke the memory of the whole motion picture.

Recorded sound effects can often be used creatively in an Interpreters Theatre production, but generally don't try to establish verisimilitude with them. A sudden toilet flush, although literal in one dimension, was an explicit comment on Kilgore Trout's stated philosophy of life in

Breakfast of Champions and also served as a comic transition, thrusting Trout from the men's room of a rundown massage parlor into the next scene.

Begin very early to select your music. Find a good record collection, in either a library or a radio station, and listen to as many different selections as you can. Don't overlook electronic music or any of the other standard musical categories. Often the librarian can help you find relatively unknown works if you explain the effect you're seeking. Let the music for your show grow with your production concept.

There's no standard set of rules for using music with a production; common sense should prevail. When music underscores speech, it's almost always the speech that should be the primary focus. For the most part, music in a production works on the emotions, intensifying the impact of the action. Music can also be used thematically, so that specified music is identified with certain characters, or events.

Special effects can be achieved by such deliberate variations as playing a recording at the wrong speed. In a production of *Jack and Jill*, a compiled script about man-woman relationships, the nursery rhyme was set to music and played periodically throughout the production. At the point in the performance when the love relationship began to turn sour, the music also turned sour through manipulation of turntable speed. Using live music, the same selection may be played at different tempos to make varied statements as in *The Music Man*, where "76 Trombones" and "Goodnight My Someone" are essentially the same melody played at different speeds.

Music's rhythmic beat may interact interestingly with the rhythm of poetry. When the poetry isn't metered, then the rhythmic pulse of music might counterpoint the lines and suggest underlying emotional tonalities. Poetry with a strong rhythmic beat is usually best accompanied by music that isn't strongly accented. Sometimes interesting rhythmic relationships can be achieved using live music, if both interpreters and musicians are treated as equal rhythmic partners. A Spanish guitar and a group of readers, for example, orchestrated the rhythmic structure of Garcia Lorca's "Romance of the Civil Guard," establishing a creative partnership between the sounds of words and music.

Hand Properties

One of the most creative production aspects of an Interpreters Theatre performance can reside in its use of hand properties. As with set pieces, the sometimes long list of things seemingly called for by the text should first be reduced to barest essentials. Very often, directors will use abstract props instead of realistic ones. Many productions use no hand properties at all; in Interpreters Theatre, words are the ultimate props. Don't hesitate to trust in language to create an object. In a production of Evan Hunter's *Last Summer*, the wounded seagull was found, treated, released into the air, and killed without ever appearing in actuality.

One or two central hand properties may function nonrealistically or symbolically throughout the production. Certain kinds of otherwise neutral objects are extremely flexible and can be very effective. An exciting production of a script compiled of selections about rivers was built around the manipulation of two long pieces of cloth. The cloth, held by a chorus, slowly moved into different shapes and would sometimes reinforce a climax by sudden movement. In

Figure 8.15: Use of pantomimed properties: *Last Summer* by Evan Hunter, directed by Janet Larsen McHughes.

Figure 8.16: Use of symbolic properties: *The Lion, the Witch and the Wardrobe* by C. S. Lewis, directed by Wayne Worley.

another production, a simple piece of white cloth, held taut by the performers, became a table; later it formed a shroud for the sacrificed leader. A piece of rope has possibly been used more frequently than any other object in the history of symbolic staging because it functions so flexibly. A metaphorical approach to a production of John Millington Synge's *Riders to the Sea* used a rope, coiled in the mother's arms, as a symbol of manhood. When the last living son asks the mother for the rope so that he may also go to sea, she refuses to give it to him. They struggle briefly, the rope suggesting an umbilical cord. Later, during the lamentation, the three dead sons appear holding the rope, which symbolically becomes the boat being dashed to pieces in the sea. Ropes have also been put to such uses as whips, as the cord of fate, as a web of entanglement, and as a symbol of death by hanging. On the lighter side there are jumping ropes which can be used literally or symbolically. A simple stick or pole can serve some of these same functions, as well as those of an abstract umbrella, a pointer, a maypole, a flag, a divining rod, a ballet bar, something to hide behind, and many other presentational roles. You can probably think of other objects just as versatile.

Sometimes, a single object that seems to dominate a text can be created more literally, but still on an abstract level. The prop may be recognizable as the intended object, but its form can suggest mood or symbol. Knives often have a central function in a script: the knife with which Clytemnestra kills Agamemnon, the knife that moves through the text of Garci Lorca's *Blood Wedding*, the daggers with which Macbeth kills Duncan, or the dagger the Witch uses to kill the Lion in *The Lion, The Witch, and the Wardrobe*. In a production of the latter, the Witch's dagger was made of quilted white satin with iciclelike properties.

If you use tangible properties, stretch your imagination in their creation and use. Don't forget the possibilities for using the script as a prop (see Chapter 7). Always be sure that properties are organic to the text, that the manipulation of the prop arises from and is integrated with the words of the script.

Costumes

As with other production media, costumes should be a part of the general style and abstraction level of the production. Sometimes full costuming may be used, provided the other production elements, particularly offstage focus, work to maintain presentational identification. However, there's danger of inconsistency and overrepresentationalism if costumes are too realistic. Costume fragments, or symbolic costumes, are well-suited to Interpreters Theatre production.

Generally, costumes perform two communicative functions: they can suggest time and place, and help identify and define character. Time and place can be established by simplifying or exaggerating one part of the dress such as a sleeve or belt. A suggestion of Elizabethan dress, for example, might concentrate on sleeves, collars, and simple full skirts using stiff and full-bodied materials, but wouldn't use the elaborate pleating, lace, and other details of the costume. A simplified wimple alone can create a medieval feeling, as a neck piece and hat can suggest the male costume of the colonial period in America. If the period in which the script is set is an important aspect of its experience, then costumes with period suggestions can help the text establish a feeling of time and place. If there is no defined period or if the period shifts frequently, other costume approaches should be considered.

Costume color is often neglected in Interpreters Theatre production. So often directors dress performers in black, because they think it's a neutral color; in fact, black costumes set a tone of heaviness or formality. Uniform black is useful if this is the mood you want, or if you add enough color through costume fragments. Any color can create a uniform base for adding costume pieces, and another color may work more effectively than black for the specific tonality of the script. A dark green or brown might be used for a script set outdoors. Bright yellows or blues might serve as a basic color for a script about a carnival.

Uniformity of costume implies anonymity of character; thus choruses are often dressed similarly in design and color. Conversely, individuality of costume aids characterization. Often costume fragments—a skirt, a cape, a scarf—can serve as a whole costume change or delineate one character from another. Different kinds of hats have been used many times to change character. Costume pieces can also be used imaginatively as both garments and props. Long capes, for example, are extremely versatile. A simple square of cloth may become a shawl, an apron, a scarf, a piece of sewing, a bandage, or almost anything needed in a scene, so long as the changing identities of the cloth grow subtly from the action.

Modern dancers have long been adept at the presentational and symbolic use of both costumes and properties. As a notable example, Martha Graham used a costume in her section of *Episodes* that also became a set piece and a symbol in the dance. As Mary Stuart first appears, she is Queen of Scotland, costumed in a very stiff grey-black Elizabethan gown. She begins to march up a large scaffold as if to her death. As she reaches a landing halfway to the top, Bothwell enters; Mary slips out of her extra stiff court gown, leaving it standing erect on the landing as a symbol of the Queen, and comes down to meet him, all woman in a soft slim beige sheath. Later in the dance Mary's attendants enter and robe her in heavy red velvet, symbol of her conflict with Elizabeth and impending death. All the while, the first dress remains standing upon the landing, held up by its own stiffness. Mary passes it in her final ascension to the execution block, and as she kneels for the blow, the light on her fades and a red light spots the dress, the blood-drenched symbol of her ambition and misfortune. This kind of symbolic approach to costuming can also be a useful presentational aspect of an Interpreters Theatre production.

Makeup and Masks

Because performers and audience members are physically close to each other in many Interpreters Theatre productions, makeup isn't usually needed for simple accent of facial lines to the same degree as in productions played farther away from viewers. Often simple street makeup for the women, and a light pancake base for the men will suffice. If the production uses stage lights, which can wash out the face even at close distances, then a medium base and subtle reinforcement of facial structure may be desirable. Character makeup is difficult to use when performers shift from one character to another, as they often do in Interpreters Theatre. To maintain consistency in style, the same degree of character makeup should appear on all performers and, unless every performer retains a single character throughout the show, it's best not to use character makeup at all.

Even when each performer plays only one character, a director should hesitate before employing character makeup; once the decision is made to use it, the temptation to go to extremes of realism grows. If a young person needs to appear old, where does the makeup artist

Figure 8.17: A rehearsal break in *I Never Promised You a Rose Garden* by Hannah Green, directed by Vance Fulkerson.

stop in the transformation? And if the audience is close, it will take a skillful artist indeed to prevent the attempt to achieve age from calling undue attention to itself. As a general approach, make up only one or two features (such as the eyes or the mouth), or find other ways to suggest age—through movement, costuming, hairstyle, or hand props.

In more symbolic and abstract approaches to performance, where there's no question of realism, stylized makeup may be used if it blends with the total production style. The fantasy gods of Yr (as in figure 8.17) were suggested by stylized makeup in *I Never Promised You a Rose Garden*, but then the whole kingdom of Yr was a surrealistic place, contrasting with the exterior world. Characters such as the Dust Witch in *Something Wicked This Way Comes* need in some way to be distinguished from the ordinary humans, but attempting to realize literally the incredible picture of this character that Bradbury paints with words would take emphasis from the words themselves. Abstract makeup and a costume fragment are workable solutions.

The use of whiteface, which creates a mask in effect, is a nonreal approach that is most effective when emphasis falls on words and physical movement rather than words and facial expression. The body's movement in relation to the words is substituted for facial expression. Created masks that can be worn or held provide another experimental approach useful for some productions. Remember that the abstraction created by the mask should be carried out in the other production media and will clash with natural movement and vocal patterns. Among other possibilities, masks can suggest the presence of a dual personality, distinguish the interior person from the exterior person, or help create fantasy characters. A chorus can make interesting use of masks to symbolize its nature and its function. If a chorus is being used to accentuate tone color, to elaborate visual images, or to create abstract forces, masks can help achieve these nonhuman identities and can, by the way they're designed, suggest the tonal nature of the identities.

STEPPING BACK

Although the media of theatre in general is available to the Interpreters Theatre director, you shouldn't feel you must fill your production with technical effects to have a good show. If your production concept calls for the use of media, we hope our discussion will help you to use it freely and artistically; if, on the other hand, your production concept calls for an empty stage, we hope you'll have the good sense and artistic courage to leave your stage unadorned. The purpose of staging in Interpreters Theatre is to bring the text alive presentationally. All media of the theatre are subservient to that purpose.

NOTES

1. Lilla A. Heston, "Richard II: A Study in Movement," *Illinois Speech and Theatre Journal* 23 (Fall 1969): 3.
2. Virgil Aldrich, "Art and the Human Form," in *Essays on Metaphor*, ed. Warren Shibles (Whitewater, Wis.: Language Press, 1972), p. 108.
3. Friedrich Nietzsche, "On Truth and Falsity in Their Extramoral Sense," in Shibles, *Essays on Metaphor*, p. 5.

4. Norman Friedman, "Imagery: From Sensation to Symbol," in Shibles, *Essays on Metaphor*, p. 45.
5. Raymond J. Schneider, "Symbolic Transformation: The Visible Metaphor," unpublished manuscript, p. 17.
6. We are grateful to Robert B. Loxley, assistant professor at University of Maine at Orono, for contributing "Alternate Performance Environments."
7. Alfred Kazin, "Fiction as a Social Gathering," *Saturday Review*, 3 July 1971, pp. 19–22.
8. Lee Simonson, "Appia's Contribution to the Modern Stage," *Theatre Arts Monthly* 16 (August 1932): 631–639.
9. We are grateful to James W. Utterback, theatre manager at Shelby State College in Memphis, for contributing much of the information in this section.
10. See Marshall McLuhan and Quentin Fiore, *The Medium Is the Massage* (New York: Random House, 1967).

SUGGESTIONS FOR FURTHER READING

Bachelard, Gaston. *The Poetics of Space*. Trans. Maria Jolas. Boston: Beacon Press, 1969.

Berleant, Arnold. *The Aesthetic Field: A Phenomenology of Aesthetic Experience*. Springfield, Ill.: Charles C. Thomas, 1970.

Brook, Peter. *The Empty Space*. New York: Avon Books, 1968.

Burdick, Elizabeth; Hansen, Peggy C.; and Zanger, Brenda. *Contemporary Stage Design U.S.A.* Middletown, Conn.: Wesleyan University Press, 1974.

Cassirer, Ernst. "The Power of Metaphor." *Mythology*. Middlesex, England: Penguin Books, 1972.

Coger, Leslie Irene. "Staging Literature with Minimal Props for Maximal Meaning." *Scholastic Teacher* 11 (October 1971): 25.

Hudson, Lee. "An Application of the Operations of Metaphorical Expression to the Process of Oral Interpretation." Thesis, University of Illinois, 1969.

———. "Oral Interpretation as Metaphorical Expression." *Speech Teacher* 22 (January 1973): 27–31.

Hoff, Frank Paul. "A Theatre of Metaphor: A Study of the Japanese NO Form." Dissertation, Harvard University, 1966.

Izenour, George C. "The Origins, Evolution and Development of Theatre Design since World War II in the United States." *Theatre Design and Technology* 14 (Summer 1978): 5–14.

Mackintosh, Iain. "Old and New: The Rejection of the Fan-Shaped Auditorium and the Reinstatement of the Courtyard Form." *Theatre Design and Technology* 14 (Summer 1978): 15–26.

New Literary History. Issue on metaphor in literature. Vol. 6 (1974).

Payne, Darwin Reid. *Design for the Stage*. Carbondale, Ill.: Southern Illinois University Press, 1974.

Pilbrow, Richard. *Stage Lighting*. New York: D. Von Nostrand, 1970.

Schevill, James. *Break Out! In Search of New Theatrical Environments*. Chicago: Swallow Press, 1973.

Schneider, Raymond J. "The Visible Metaphor." *Communication Education* 25 (March 1976): 121–126.

Wilfred, Thomas. *Projected Scenery*. New York: Drama Book Specialists, 1965.

Wolfe, Welby B. *Materials of the Scene*. New York: Harper & Row, 1977.

CHAPTER NINE

The Performer Onstage

*Human movement, with all its physical, emotional, and mental impli-
cations, is the common denominator of the dynamic art of the theatre.*

Rudolph Van Laban, *The Mastery of
Movement on the Stage*

As you enter the arena of production, you stand at a crossroads—between a private vision and a public vision, between a design in your head and its realization onstage. As you step fully into the role of director, you're faced with the awesome task of transferring your private production to the public stage. For many, this is where the creative process falters a little. None of the performers who audition for the show may sound or look remotely like the agile, resonant-voiced, sensitive figures on your mind's stage, and no technical genius could match your mental stage decor. Be prepared for the shock and, when you've recovered, begin to look for the special creative energies your performers have to offer the script.

Your first responsibility as a director is to shift your focus from a private interaction to a communal effort, working to balance the world of the script with the worlds of the performers who enact it and the technicians who support it. You will soon come to understand that realization means more than the staging of an envisioned script: realization also implies the incorporation of a special kind of reality, the reality of the available resources, into your creative vision. The director who is able to work with the productive energies of all involved—making room for individual creative efforts while firmly guiding the growth of the performance—is the director who is most likely to achieve a dynamic realization of the script.

One of the exciting aspects of presentational theatre is that so much of the theatrical experience depends on the creative energies of the performers themselves. In an interview on the future of Readers Theatre, performer/director Frank Galati observed, "RT [Readers Theatre] tends to feature the performer's work; the performer is more in evidence, less disguised, less concealed, than in a full-scale theatrical performance. His vocal and physical skill is, perhaps, in higher definition for the audience."[1] When the performers step onstage, they set into motion the living exchange of energies—between the text, the performer, and the audience—that is the heart of Interpreters Theatre. No matter what other production media you choose to employ, the primary medium is the performer.

Throughout its history, Interpreters Theatre has placed major emphasis on the performer, but that emphasis has been primarily on the performer's vocal skills. Little attention has been given to developing the interpreter's physical skills. For much of the twentieth century, in fact, Interpreters Theatre performers have hesitated to move onstage, seeming to feel that lack of physical movement helped define their art. Regrettably, we still find this feeling reflected in some speech contest rules. Because movement is observable, it's easy to understand why some inter-preters, anxious to sort out artistic definitions, used the amount of movement as a major criterion for distinguishing acting from interpretation. We would like to put this false distinction to rest.

The theorists in the early twentieth century weren't misguided in defining the art of inter-pretation in terms of its commitment to verbal action. What is misguided is the impression that featuring verbal action requires elimination or severe reduction of physical action. As Joanna Maclay remarked in a symposium on Readers Theatre, "You don't go to Readers Theatre and close your eyes, because there are people on stage, and somehow a director has to deal with the fact that you have to give the audience something visual."[2] That something visual may involve any media of the theatre, but its primary element is the physical presence of the performer. Inter-preters, like actors, move in space. The design and skill of their movement is a major aspect of their art. In discussing the Interpreters Theatre performer onstage, therefore, attention needs to be given to both voice and body and to the kind of physical and vocal approaches to be used.

WORKING WITH THE INSTRUMENTS OF THE PERFORMER: VOICE AND BODY

The performer's voice and body are the most powerful media of the stage. One nuance of the voice, one shift of the eyes, one tension-filled gesture can capture the emotional power of a text and communicate it to an audience. The potential capability of the performer's body to express living experience is so great that serious performers are always striving to improve their vocal and physical instruments. Like athletes who stay in shape through constant training, theatre performers must tune their voices and bodies so that they can communicate even the most com-plicated literary experience.

The performers' voices and bodies are also the primary means by which the director builds a performance, creating characters, embodying power sources and shaping the style and design of the production. Considering the voices and bodies of your performers as instruments for creating the performance, you as director need to understand how those instruments function. What physical capabilities do performers have and how do you work with those capabilities to mold your production?

The Performer's Voice

Naturally, you hope you've cast performers with highly flexible voices capable of meeting the vocal demands of your script. In Interpreters Theatre, especially, performers are often asked to use their voices to enact power sources other than character; by taking on special nonhuman roles, interpreters vocally create imagery (such as the sound of wind whistling), explore tone color and rhythm (by sounding out contrapuntal patterns in an orchestrated script), become an indicator of time (by producing the chiming of a clock in the background, for example), em-phasize the power of an idea (through repeated words or phrases in an underlying chant), or any combination of power sources. The vocal demands on a performer, therefore, are perhaps greatest in Interpreters Theatre.

During auditions, you probably explored some of the ways the performers' voices needed to be extended for your particular script (See Appendix 1, "Hints on Casting and Rehearsing"). Your ear will learn, through experience, to be more and more sensitive to the tones and qualities it hears, alerting you to grating or inflexible voices as well as distinguishing the most pleasant voices from the rest. Beware of being too impressed with the deeply resonant "beautiful voice" that calls too much attention to itself to blend with the other voices in production. Very often such voices, like the radio newscaster's resonant tones, are trained to be predictable and steady and are not often capable of wide variations. On the other hand, you may encounter an actor with a "golden voice" that is also highly flexible and can blend or stand out; such a performer is a director's dream.

If you're working with amateurs, most of your performers' voices will tend to be more "leaden" than "golden." It is wise to recognize early that, in six weeks rehearsal time, you are unlikely to appreciably change the overall quality of each cast member's voice; such adjustments usually take a concentrated effort on voice quality alone for an extended period of time. Your attention is on more than the performer's personal vocal development. Yet, with an understanding of some of the special capabilities of the human voice, you can achieve fascinating effects with relatively untrained voices.

There are four dimensions of sound that we perceive with our ear and that can be manipulated to achieve dramatic vocal effects in acoustic space: **pitch**, **force**, **quality**, and **time**. When you alter any one of the four dimensions generally the others are unconsciously affected as well.

Pitch

Pitch is the primary vocal tool for creating logical meaning from a literary line; through variations in pitch level, a reading becomes expressive and intelligible. Subtle differentiations in meaning, such as contrasts and comparisons, are conveyed through pitch. Pitch also helps determine whether a question is being asked or a statement being made. Although a monotone is sometimes desired for special effect (such as a chant), generally the performers will deliberately vary their pitch levels to clarify the meaning of a passage. Very often a change in pitch level can cause a passage to have entirely opposite meanings. If the simple sentence, "I'll get you," is uttered with relatively stable pitch (either high or low) and appropriate intensity, it carries a definitely menacing meaning; if, on the other hand, pitch is varied widely with musical playfulness on the rising pitch on "get," the sentence can be coy, delightful, and anything but frightening.

Pitch is the most important component of sarcasm and some examples of verbal irony. Sliding pitch on a single syllable such as "Oh" can endow the interjection with a wide range of expressive feeling, from dripping sarcasm to joy to agony.

As a director, your ear should be sensitive to the pitches you hear emanating from the stage. Are the pitches pleasant to listen to? Do they work well together? Are the performers able to modulate their vocal tones appropriately to project nuances of meaning? Explore pitch level as an indicator of character as well as an expressor of meaning. The White Rabbit of *Alice in*

Wonderland by Lewis Carroll is likely to speak in a rather continual high pitch, like the fever pitch of his life, while the Walrus may tend to speak with a low pitch indicative of his size. For these characters, pitch changes will occur within a pitch framework or range similar to a performer's optimum pitch range, or range of pitches comfortable for that performer's voice.

The most flexible voice has a broad pitch range; such a voice can reach wide maximum pitch levels without sacrificing quality. So often, a tendency (with female voices, especially) is to raise pitch when volume and emotional intensity are increased. This increase can lead to a strident sound, which is very unpleasant to hear. Encourage your performers to practice increasing their volume without raising their pitch; the effect is powerful.

Force

Vocal force is the amount of energy expended by the performer in vocal production and is therefore a major component of the living exchange of energies that is theatre. As directors, we traditionally work with three aspects of vocal force—**volume**, **intensity**, and **projection**—to create the verbal life of our staged production. The first of these aspects, volume, is of enormous practical and aesthetic value because the fundamental rule of any production is that the performers must be heard. If the audience can't hear, even the most brilliant and subtle performance is wasted. As director, it's your responsibility to ensure that all the interpreters are clearly audible, speaking with enough volume to reach even the farthest corners of the theatre auditorium. Experiment with variations in volume—to help differentiate character, to indicate time shifts, and especially to build to emotional crises in the structure of the script. Remember that dramatic moments are featured by employing vocal contrasts—by sudden increases in volume, for example, or even by unexpected drops to a near-whisper.

Intensity, the amount of tension in the voice, is directly related to character and the emotional life of the script. A line delivered with deliberate intensity always gains dramatic focus, whether the high intensity is accompanied by an equally high volume or not. Encourage your performers to practice achieving intensity in a variety of ways, from an intense whisper to the almost hidden intensity of seemingly normal conversation to the intense shouting match. By the same token, be sure that all the intensity you hear in the performers' voices is workable tension and not just a function of stage fright. Intensity of the voice is often what commands us to listen; it's that compelling quality of the spoken word that reaches out to us and sweeps us up in its effect.

Projection, the third component of vocal force, isn't concerned with how much energy is expended, but with where the energy is directed in acoustic space. Projection is the placement of vocal energy. Fine performers can toss lines like they toss balls—deftly, swiftly, from one person to another. In Interpreters Theatre, especially, where lines of literature are often broken up into voices, the individual voices need to project their phrases with an appropriate continuity that indicates someone else will pick up the line. Similarly, interpreters are consistently responsible for projecting vocally out in the auditorium, toward a setting that is being described, toward the audience in an open act of presentation, or to another character in a conversation using offstage focus. It is projection that helps make the stage whisper audible because the whisper is tossed out, not left on the stage. It is projection that creates a sense of intimacy between performers and audience. Projection usually works hand in hand with volume, but it isn't the same thing. A performer who can speak loudly but doesn't know how to project the voice may seem to be speaking at the audience; a performer who can speak loudly and project well will seem to be speaking to the audience.

You can help your performers a great deal if you clearly understand the differences between volume, intensity, and projection, and can suggest how they work together. During rehearsals, try sitting in different parts of the audience area, listening for variations in volume and projection, especially. You can begin to use intensity as a structural component, building to moments of highest tensiveness in your script, then releasing.

Quality

Quality is the single most important vocal tool for establishing character, particularly for revealing the emotional state of a character. Although in real life we may know people whose voices do not seem to match their characters—a person with an outgoing, friendly personality and a fullness of spirit whose thin, nasal, pinched voice seems out of place, for example—in the theatre it is commonplace to assume that a character's voice is indicative of inner being. In scripts containing stereotyped characters, the correlation is strong and obvious; in more complex texts, the relationship between voice and personality is subtle and pervasive. Depending on its quality, the human voice can stroke, hit, tickle, rip open, tiptoe, or dance. The real artistry in vocal production is in the meaningful manipulation of quality. The human voice has a wider range of quality than any musical instrument.

Without introducing technical vocabulary, we can say generally that vocal quality tends to be full-bodied (with pleasant resonance) or thin, pinching, and difficult to listen to. A full voice depends on strong breath support and good reverberation of sound waves in the chest, nasal, and oral cavities. A harsh or thin voice has too little breath behind it, while a breathy voice is produced by too much air. Very often, unintentional tensiveness in the vocal mechanisms contribute to thinness or stridency. Performers should be able to introduce elements of harshness or stridency if such a voice seems appropriate for the character. By the same token, performers should be able to increase good nasality and resonance when you ask them to. You'll need to balance off the use of a thin or harsh voice for special characterization effects with the general need of the audience to listen to reasonably pleasant voices. From your perspective as director, it's most important to know what adjustment in quality is necessary, so you can help your cast members achieve good vocal characterization and, at the same time, appeal to the audience.

Time

The timing of speech, like the timing of all other aspects of production, is of central concern to any director. Theatre is a temporal art. It moves through time, building rhythmic patterns in acoustic space. Vocal timing usually includes concepts of **rate**, **duration**, and **rhythm**.

Rate is the speed with which words and sentences are put together. Most directors working with amateur performers face an immediate rate problem: performers often speak too fast, rushing through vocal lines without an appropriate rate of rhythmic action in the body. The result is often a garbled delivery that seems memorized and insincere. Remind your performers that the audience will be hearing the lines for the first time and may appreciate their speaking more slowly than normal. Generally, the more difficult or complicated the meaning of the line, the slower the rate should be. If the line is delivered too slowly, however, credibility and spontaneity are sacrificed. The action of your script should move right along, even though the performers are speaking slowly enough to be comprehended. One of the best ways to ensure meaningful pacing while maintaining intelligibility in your production is to give attention to how cues (responses to previous lines) are handled. If the initial response comes quickly, the rest of the line can come slowly if need be. Remember that a cue can be picked up by a physical response as well as by a vocal one.

One of the fine points of oral interpretation performance is to learn when not to speak as well as when to speak. Encourage the interpreters to use pauses for effect, but insist that the pauses be filled, not empty. A speaker fills a pause by retaining the energy level of the spoken line even through the pause; an empty pause is one in which the reader has simply stopped speaking and has dropped energy as well. Such pauses are usually not desirable in performance.

Duration refers to the extension of individual sounds and is often a component of good vocal accents. An elongation of Malvolio's vowels in Shakespeare's *Twelfth Night* can help achieve that character's pomposity and sense of self-importance. A clipping of the vowels and an emphasis on the consonants can suggest a businesslike, unemotional character. Although duration usually works hand in hand with rate, it's actually an independent factor of the timing of speech.

A major concern of the director is the overall rhythm of the performance. A production gathers momentum as it moves to a crisis, slackens, and then builds again to another high point, and so on. Although rhythm is clearly related to the timing of speech, it's also created by the patterning of other factors in directing. Therefore, we'll discuss rhythmic vitality in more detail.

Formalized Vocal Action

Pitch, force, quality, and time are all components of vocal production you'll need to adjust for the best vocal life of your staged script. These components are important in every kind of production, even with the most casual and conversational characters, but they become especially crucial when you're working with formalized vocal patterns.

Formalized vocal action is the most presentational speech and therefore the most removed from realistic, everyday action. Metaphorical characters who openly stand for qualities of life or thought, choruses who verbalize the orchestrated tone color of a script, or individual performers who take on vocal roles of atmosphere or setting (such as the ringing of a doorbell) are all using formalized vocal action. Anytime two performers speak in unison, you've moved to a more formalized approach. In formalized speech, all the components of the voice—pitch, force, quality, and time—are used more artfully and manipulated more deliberately. Pitch is carefully controlled, as in the orchestrated scripts of "Ozymandias" in Chapter 3. In formal vocal action, intensity is almost always increased; additional and sustained intensity is, in fact, one of the indicators that vocal action has become more formal than casual.

In choral work especially, duration is markedly extended so the individual tones and background sounds are featured. You can introduce more subtle formal elements into a script by having a character suddenly increase duration and volume while decreasing rate. A performer playing a public figure, for example, distinguishes in part the politician's life from public life by shifting into more formalized speech for public moments. With a knowledge of how to build formalized vocal action— by deliberately structured pitch patterns and volume, increased intensity and projection, and a reduced rate with a correspondingly increased duration and use of pause—you can build variety and lively energy into your production. The vocal energies of the performers, like the capabilities of their bodies, are the greatest ingredients of true Interpreters Theatre.

The Performer's Body

One of the Interpreters Theatre director's major tools for shaping a performance is the moving body of the performer. For bodies to become instruments of expression, however, performers need to become aware of their own movement potential. The body, an intricate lever system controlled by sets of antagonistic muscles, is capable of taking many different positions. The trunk, shoulder joint, hip joint, ankles, and wrists rotate in a complete circle; knees and elbows will flex, extend, and twist. All of this movement is controlled by the brain through the mechanism of the **kinesthetic sense**, the feedback system for body movement. The kinesthetic sense allows us to become aware of our bodies in space and to maintain an intricate control over the movement and position of every body part. A strong kinesthetic awareness helps performers integrate inner thinking and feeling with outer physical movement so that inner states can be externalized effectively and authentically.

The different positions made possible by moving body parts are many, yet each body tends to move in habitual patterns and to rest in habitual postures. Because the body is human and not an abstract form, we make judgments about human intention and feeling states by observing the general design of the body. When the trunk forms a curved line forward, we may judge that the individual is in pain, feeling grief, or looking at something on the ground, depending on focus and other aspects of facial expression and movement. The trunk of the body arched backward may connote pride, joy, sun worship, or any number of states, which are further clarified by arm and head position. There is infinite variety in the ways human bodies stand, sit, and relate to one another. It's important that performers break out of habitual body positions and learn to use their bodies in different ways. It's also important that the director learn how to use the design and movement potential of the performer's body to build characters, define performance style, symbolize forces, and create the many other aspects of a production that can be communicated by the physical body.

Because the body has four identifiable surfaces (front, back, and two sides), **body facing** (the position of the face in relation to the audience and to the direction of movement) is a meaningful element in design. An audience usually judges a performer's focus from the direction of body facing. Most of the action in Interpreters Theatre uses body facing to establish focus. In

(a) (b)

Figure 9.1: Bodily focus.

Figure 9.2: Body design to establish focus: *In Violence*, a compiled script directed by Raymond J. Schneider.

some cases, however, other aspects of movement design can negate the effect of body facing. For example, if a character is being drawn by some force against his or her will, the face may very well turn away from the source of the external power, although the body is being drawn in that direction. In figure 9.1a, the performer's whole body is focusing on the source of power, although the head is turned away. If the performer were to lift the head, however, and look strongly in the direction opposite from the source of power, extending the neck in one direction while being pulled in the other, a second focal point—away from the source of power—would immediately be created (figure 9.1b). By means of a performer's body design, a director can establish the ideological presence of outside forces in the environment, as shown in figure 9.2; the strength of the force relates directly to the amount of force seeming to be exerted upon the body.

When you place one body in juxtaposition with other bodies, the design possibilities become greater. As the sculptor works with line and mass in metal or stone, the director works with the lines of the performers' bodies and the mass of one or more bodies. Considering the body, for a moment, as a purely sculptural form, we can say generally that the closer the arms and legs are drawn into center, the more the body takes on properties of mass (figure 9.3a); as arms and legs are extended into space, the lines of the body become more apparent (figure 9.3b). Similarly, several bodies placed close together form mass (figure 9.3c), and bodies spread apart become more individualized and linear (figure 9.3d). When grouped with other bodies, the lines of the individual body merge and become somewhat effaced by the overall group design. In staging, therefore, when a group of performers are to represent a single unit—a presence or an attitude—they are better grouped as a mass and moved as a mass. When you wish to highlight the individual qualities of a character, that character is better removed from the group and given a body stance that calls attention to individual line.

Both line and mass can project varying illusions of strength and amount of force being exerted. Line appears in two forms: straight and curved. The straight line is forceful, dynamic, and direct, but the angle of the straight line greatly influences its meaning connotation. The vertical body line appears strongest, seeming to contain its forces because it indicates no directional tendency (figure 9.4a). Exhibiting the most direct manifestation of released energy is the diagonal line pointing in the direction of body facing (figure 9.4b). The diagonal line progressing backward (in relation to body facing) seems weak by comparison (figure 9.4c). The horizontal line seems to project complete resolution with very little energy expended (figure 9.4d). The curved line, quieter, more graceful, less forceful, seems generally to want to move in upon itself rather than to project out into space, but this is governed largely by the shape of the curve. An open, gentle curve connotes greater interaction with outer space (figure 9.4e) than a tight, closed curved line (figure 9.4f).

As the performer's body begins to move, it carves through space in a continuously changing configuration—a series of transactions with space that have strong communicative potentials. You can control these moving designs created by the performers' bodies when you understand that any movement requires three basic adjustments: a change of location in **space**, a consumption of **time**, and an expenditure of energy **(force)**. These obvious dimensions define all movement; an alteration in one of the dimensions may change the nature of a movement completely. A strong walk away from another performer, for example, may connote indignation; the same walk toward the other performer might suggest aggression. A combination of the context of the scene and changing the direction of the movement changes its meaning.

Figure 9.3: Line and mass.

Much of what we do in Interpreters Theatre is synecdochical—that is, part of a movement (whether it's realistic or formalized) may suggest a larger movement. The performer can aggressively thrust a shoulder and an arm forward, thereby suggesting a physical fight. Energetic walking in place can become climbing a ladder; a lifted fist can connote a howling mob; a run across the stage can suggest a chase scene. But these concepts won't be communicated to an audience without precision in shaping and timing. Like the actor, the interpreter aspires to skill and fullness in all movement, regardless of the kind of gesture. And, in fact, a suggested gesture *is* a gesture, no matter what its range.

Performers need to learn how to take stage, to give whatever movement they execute their full energy, and to direct that energy out toward the audience. Interpreters contact an audience not only through focus and vocal energy, but with all their physical power. Just as the voice must reach every member of the audience, the gestures must also. Make certain that your performers carry a gesture out to the full extent of its design. If the arm is to be extended, energy should flow from the interior of the body to the fingertips. If the arm is to be bent at the elbow, the angle should be sharp. Particularly in formalized movement all gestures and other kinds of movement need not only be fully energized, but should be controlled so the body design and movement quality can create the intended symbol.

Figure 9.4: Straight and curved lines.

To control movement patterns in *space*, you'll use the measurable conditions of **direction** (the movement pathway), **level** (the height at which the movement takes place), and **range** (the amount of space covered). The aspects of physical *time* you'll be concerned with are chiefly **tempo** (the rate at which a movement is performed) and **duration** (the relative length of time consumed by any one aspect of a movement pattern). *Force* in the performer's body can seem to be large or small in amount, can seem to flow freely or be inhibited. The movement of force can also seem to be in a single direction, suggested by the seeming ease of movement of a body part, or in more than one direction, such as when performers suggest the presence of two opposing forces within their bodies by initiating a counterdirectional movement in another part of the body (the left arm moving to the right while the right leg moves to the left).

As the time-space-force dimensions of movement operate together in various ways they create movement quality, which can play a major role in creating the atmosphere and style of your production. Quality of movement, like body design, is immediately communicative. When a body appears to move heavily through space, the body weight may suggest such feeling states as weariness or grief; when a performer moves with light buoyancy, the resulting judgment is commonly that the mover is happy. These kinds of judgments are modified by the context in which the movement occurs and by aspects of body design.

Although nuances of movement quality are as limitless as nuances of vocal quality, we can distinguish three major quality types that, when seen as interacting categories, describe most movement and provide you with a vocabulary to aid in communicating with performers. The *abrupt* quality is characterized by quick muscle contraction providing great accelerative force, with an equally quick antagonistic contraction to stop the movement. An abrupt movement thus starts and stops suddenly. The abrupt quality is useful, for example, when a performer is communicating anger or is creating a very high-strung character. *Sustained* quality exhibits a constant release of force permitting continually controlled movement. This results in a very smooth movement that continues at the same tension level, whether great or small. Sustained movement may be useful for communicating a state of lethargy, for depicting a character with great dignity, or for creating any action that requires steady control. *Swinging* quality involves the combination of acceleration and deceleration, the former occurring on the first phase of the movement, the latter on the final phase. The swing usually travels a curved directional pathway with first an increase and then a decrease in speed as the swing reaches the end of the arc. A swing is often a less controlled movement than movements using either sustained or abrupt qualities. Depending on tempo and apparent body weight, a swinging quality can suggest exuberance or complete body relaxation.

Performers and directors, working together, can use the infinite variety of body design and the interactive movement dimensions of time, space, and force as a kind of alphabet to build movement words and sentences, shaping them into characterizations and other stylistic aspects of performance. Some characters, for example, may suggest angles; others may suggest curves. Some productions may use vertical movements with strong force, and others may flow easily along predominantly horizontal pathways. You can manipulate movement and movement quality, increasing or decreasing the range of an arm movement, changing the body part involved in an abrupt movement from the arm to the head, increasing or decreasing the amount of force used in a sustained movement. You can combine qualities in the performer's body so that a swing halts abruptly or so that a sustained movement sequence contains abrupt accents. Quite often you can help a performer create a character by suggesting a simple change in some aspect of movement quality or body design.

Perhaps the greatest advantage in having some knowledge of how to manipulate movement is when you are working with more symbolic or metaphorically formalized movement, when performers must become atypical humans or animals, or when you must turn a group of performers into the embodiment of tone color and imagery. If you are aware of the design potentials of the body and have some knowledge of how to control the time, space, and force dimensions of movement, you are equipped to help performers make the transition to more unusual ways of moving.

Formalized movement is created by the **exaggeration** of recognizable movement patterns and the **abstraction** and manipulation of selected aspects of movement. Formalized movement subordinates the realistic elements of movement to some principle of design, making the design of the movement a major aspect of communication. The further the movement is removed from ordinary human qualities, the more the mover is changed from a human being into something else. Exaggeration can therefore call attention to certain ordinary human characteristics and make them larger than life, or it can remove a performer from the human realm.

Assume that there are two scripts dealing with pride. One script calls for the human quality of pride to be exaggerated. The performers in this production are used as human beings, but exaggerated synecdochical manifestations of pride dominate every movement—they may walk stiffly, look down noses, and curl lips in self-satisfaction. Such exaggeration tends to create characters who are stereotypes, who exist primarily to present a character attitude or trait. The second script calls for a chorus to suggest pride metaphorically as an abstract state of being. For this production the performers are not human beings who are proud, but are the embodiment of pride itself. The metaphoric embodiment of a state of being calls for much greater abstraction in body design and movement than does the depiction of a human in an exaggerated state of being. The script might use a chorus because the very fact of more than one performer moving together helps to remove the suggestion of an individualized character. The director of this script might want to use the chorus as part of a living sculpture symbolizing man's elevated self-esteem or might isolate certain elements of a proud bearing, such as the upward tilt of the chin and the arch of the back, and abstract them into full movement patterns using the performers' whole bodies. In the second script the performers' movement is used for thematic design rather than for individual character expression.

Performers' bodies can also capture the tensions of other power sources in a text, such as tone color and imagery. If the imagery is light and ethereal, you can suggest this atmosphere through movements with a slow, sustained quality using low tension that seem to float delicately. Hard rasping tone color can be reflected in tense, abrupt movements. The major design aspects of imagery can be captured through abstracted movement, making a chorus seem to become the vertical lines of city skyscrapers or the undulations of storm-tossed trees, for example. It's important that these movements not be carried out literally, though, because the attempt actually to become skyscrapers or storm-tossed trees would not only be ludicrous, but would destroy the metaphor that has been set up. A director would not be likely to have the chorus members waving their arms around during the line "The wind tossed the branches of the trees," unless she's seeking a comic effect. Arms are too much like branches and the movement is illustrative. Rather, if a serious stormy effect is desired, the movement pattern should build slowly through the scene, using a massed rather than a linear design, the group of bodies swaying together subtly, increasing their range until, at the height of the storm, they break apart, twisting across the stage in different directions. This is only one suggestion for the creation of a storm. In your work with a similar script, you will surely discover others.

If you explore movement with your performers, deliberately experimenting with atypical body positions and with all the time, space, and force possibilities for the movement you create, you'll discover that the design of movement can be another exciting aspect of an Interpreters Theatre production. Furthermore, as the design of the production begins to take shape, you'll find the vocal and physical dimensions of performance falling into certain functional patterns that intersect to create the total world of the script.

MODES IN PERFORMANCE

No matter what mode of literature you work with or in what mode you create your compiled script, every production employs some combination of lyric, narrative, and dramatic uses of the voice and body. Although all three modes of performance become an intricate gestalt in the finished production, in rehearsal you can use the vocabulary and concepts of performance modes to sharpen your critical perception of what's happening onstage.

The Lyric Mode in Movement and Voice

Since the lyric mode encompasses the individual expression of personal thoughts and feelings, lyric vocal and physical action reveals an individual's character and immediate state of being.[3] The tilt of the head, idiosyncratic gestures of the hands, characteristic vocal pitch and speech patterns, and tension in the walk are constant revelations of character. Whether we should or shouldn't, we often judge people by their lyric action.

The lyric mode of performance distinguishes one character from all other characters and is of immediate concern to the individual performer. The creation of lyric mannerisms in body and voice calls upon all the imaginative powers of the performer, assisted by the director. Impressionists, for example, spend many hours learning to imitate the lyric mannerisms of the characters they portray. The familiar and distinctive walk of Charlie Chaplin's Little Tramp became such an identifying lyric element that we can invoke the Little Tramp's presence simply by imitating the walk. Similarly, the characteristic vocal patterns of Humphrey Bogart or W. C. Fields are strong lyric identifiers of those actors. Any movement or vocal action that defines a character is in the lyric mode of performance.

The creation of lyric aspects of performance is usually the interpreter's first task. An initial problem facing the director and performer is dealing with the reality of each performer's body, the *body fact*, in relation to the role the body must play in performance, the *body act*.[4] In group performance, the interpreter, like the actor, correlates body fact and body act more fully than does the solo interpreter. When performing as a solo reader, a female may create a scene between Othello and Iago effectively, despite the obvious gender difference between body fact and body act. When staging *Othello* for Interpreters Theatre, however, the director almost always casts men in those roles because the act of casting roles individually and placing characters in space— even presentationally—demands a kind of matching of body fact and body act. The performer's first step toward achieving the body act of a character is the creating of the character's lyric movement and vocal patterns.

Occasionally, the character's lyric dimension is deliberately stereotyped, as in many children's fairy stories and folk tales. Part of the charm and comprehension of such stories results from their use of stereotyped characters; young children, in particular, delight in familiar behavior and predictable results. When performers approach the lyric dimensions of stereotyped characters, their task is to distinguish that particular stereotype—the evil force, for example, in the guise of the Big Bad Wolf—from other similar stereotypes—the evil force in the guise of the wicked stepmother. Usually performers of stereotyped characters exaggerate the vocal and bodily lyric elements in their performance, playing the character with colorful extravagance.

Usually a character's lyric movements and speech patterns are subtle and unique, and the performer strives to capture that uniqueness. To help your performers create the lyric mode of performance, show them how to look at the script first for character description, for the depiction of the character's subjective experience, and for the nature of other power sources that shape character. Once a performer has an understanding of the nature of the character, she can begin to explore vocal and physical patterns onstage. Encourage performers to let the character and the experience take over their bodies. Such experimenting, using the character's emotional state or sensory experiences, often helps uncover new ways of handling the performer's voice and body.

In another approach to the creation of lyric action, you and the performer may use a metaphorical image of a character to help create new ways of speaking and moving. A family patriarch may be seen as a teddy bear, or a seductress may have the qualities of a cat. This imagery may be used as a point of departure for characterization in more realistic approaches to staging or may be developed more fully for metaphorical designs.

To determine lyric qualities of a character:

1. Look for the character's vocal quality. This is suggested by the character's words, by descriptions of the character, and by metaphoric images of the person.
2. Determine the apparent vocal range and tempo (whether the character speaks in a measured monotone, or seems to range widely in pitch and tempo). Much evidence of this resides in the emotional qualities of the lines.
3. Look for the presence of a characteristic accent or dialect that must be captured if the character's full lyric dimension is created. (The performer may be able to achieve a sense of an accent by merely suggesting it—using clipped speech for a British accent or slowing the tempo and broadening the *a* for a Southern flavor.)
4. Estimate the amount of movement habitually used by the character.
5. Determine the range and direction of movement (whether wide and sweeping or close to the body, whether primarily curved or straight).
6. Check the rhythm of movement (whether fast or slow, regular or irregular).
7. Determine the force of movement (whether the character is tense or relaxed).
8. Look for body design (how the character sits, stands, and walks).

Almost all identifying lyric characteristics can be captured by careful attention to the quality of movement (determined by its space, time, and force dimensions), to body design, and to the elements of voice (pitch, force, quality, and time). Most scripts won't give the performer and director all this information; much of it must be deduced from general references to the character's appearance and actions. The creation of lyric mannerisms calls upon your imaginative powers as you work with your performers' creativity.

The Narrative Mode in Movement and Voice

Any vocal action or movement that indicates changes of events in time and/or space is narrative in nature. Entrances, exits, stage crosses, or any task-oriented action ("She lifted the suitcase") fall within the mode of narrative movement. The vocal element of narrative action usually comes in the actual words the character speaks. If the character says, "I'm dashing to the mailbox—be back in a moment," or, "She waited in silence," the words themselves carry narrative meaning. Vocal quality is affected by the lyric dimension of the character speaking and the dramatic tensions between characters, but it's primarily the words themselves that create the vocal dimension of the narrative mode in performance.

The character most responsible for carrying narrative action is, of course, the narrator. Vocal and physical flexibility are enormously important for the narrator. To indicate shifts in time and space the narrator can move physically to another part of the stage, can change vocal intonation, or (more commonly) can combine these techniques. Furthermore, the narrator uses narrative action to contact the audience, balancing the story's "showing" with the story's "telling" by moving fully onstage. Generally, it's wise to cast your finest performer as the narrator in a Chamber Theatre production; the narrator operates on more levels than the story's characters do, moving onstage as an analogue for narrative relationships (see Chapter 5) and using voice and body to signal shifts in the plot and setting.

Narrators are sometimes prone to wander in space unless the director helps them to know at every moment where they're to be located and to whom or what they're relating physically. One solution has been to give narrators stations (a reading stand or a chair) as home bases to which they return periodically. This mechanism works if the text permits it. In a production of *The Little Prince* by Antoine du Saint Exupéry, the narrator sat at a writing desk when he was talking to the audience from the present time. When he went back in memory and interacted with the Little Prince, he left the desk and moved to another part of the stage. This was possible, however, because of the way the book is written. There are long sections in which the narrator talks in general about the world of adults or goes into factual data about various planets. These sections allowed him to move out of the past and stay in the present for sustained intervals of time.

Changing Scene

That the same stage area may become different places without any change of tangible scenery is a major asset in presentational staging. To change physical environment through movement alone, the performer acts upon space, evoking objects that are part of the new environment. Structures and objects can be "placed" specifically onstage with the performer, or they can be created more generally in the audience space through focus and direction of gesture. Like the mime artist who creates a wall by extending an arm with the hand palm forward, seeming to brace against a solid barrier, the interpreter can create the physical environment through image making and movement. A doorway, a river, a teacup—any aspect of the environment— can be constituted imaginatively in space, in whatever detail necessary, and then revoked when the scene shifts. When such imaginative scenery is created onstage in detail, however, the performers must carefully observe the dimensions of the created space and not walk through walls or step on sleeping dogs. Also, the scene is changed only when the audience knows that performers are in a different locale. When you're working with imaginative scene changes, paying careful attention to the clarity of vocal and physical cues to the audience prevents possible confusion.

Sometimes a production design calls for shifting tangible set pieces to change scene, such as rearranging a set of cubes, revolving a structure, or bringing on or removing objects from the stage. While we believe these kinds of changes should be kept to a minimum, occasionally they may be central to the presentational form of a text.

Set changes can either facilitate or inhibit the flow of a production. Too often directors give scene changes little concern, assuming the standard techniques from Conventional Theatre will work for an Interpreters Theatre production.

One of the most common techniques for changing scenes in Conventional Theatre is the **blackout**. In effect, its purpose is to close the audience's eyes while changes in time and location take place, while actors exit and enter, or while the physical set is shifted. All these activities serve essentially representational functions. Presentational staging frankly admits the artificiality of the created world and has no particular need to mask the mechanics of changing scene. Rather, scene transitions can become a creative part of the ongoing action of the performance.

To maintain a presentational orientation, it's wise to avoid total blackouts for scene changes. A well-designed stage setting won't require cumbersome movement of set pieces. If some props or set pieces need to be shifted for scene changes, there are two major ways of handling them: (1) place a deliberate emphasis on movement of stage pieces, calling attention to the action of changing scene, or (2) arrange a subtle incorporation of set changes into the flow of the dramatic action. If you choose the first alternative, you may wish to cast a stage crew to do the moving. The crew could be characterized as undertakers, circus crewmen, waiters, or police officers, depending on the nature of the text. In a Readers Theatre production of *A Thurber Carnival*, set piece changes were choreographed in double time, with crew members spilling onto the stage as Keystone Kops.

Should you choose not to have a separate crew, the performers themselves may make the set changes, either emphasizing or deemphasizing the process. When attention is deliberately called to the scene change itself, the performers might need to drop out of character temporarily as a convention of the production. If the performers can unobtrusively move set pieces in character, then the scene change is incorporated into the action. A narrator in Chamber Theatre, for example, may pick up a chair and move it to a new location while narrating the scene change. A butler or a chorus can move many pieces around the stage without interrupting the flow of action. Depending upon the nature of the text, one performer (such as a Chamber Theatre narrator) can signal the scene changes by a snap of the fingers, by clapping hands, or by blowing a whistle. A more subtle transition is made with words and movement together or with light changes that, by cross fading, lead the performers from one stage area to another.

Entrances and Exits

A major narrative consideration is the nature of character entrances and exits. If space is used pictorially, there's something to exit from and to enter into, but the nonpictorial use of space eliminates the necessity to remove physically the exiting performer from the stage space. Conventional Theatre tends to remove the actor; Interpreters Theatre tends to remove the scene. One way to keep a presentational focus is to retain all performers onstage at all times.

The presence of all the performers onstage may seem awkward until you begin to understand the exciting presentational possibilities offered by this aesthetic. In productions using a chorus, there's little problem in finding continuous onstage functions for the group, since the decision to create a chorus usually denotes a pervasive presence of some kind. If there's no chorus, but cast members assume different roles, any one of a number of conventions may be used. When not performing in character, the cast member may sit in the audience and watch the show, provided the audience area is close to the stage. Performers may sit onstage and watch the show, becoming part of its general atmosphere. Quite often specific roles may be given to such spectators: they may become the audience at a circus, members of a courtroom or church congregation, or participants in whatever social occasion is created by the director's production concept. Performers who are temporarily out of character may also become set pieces and help with the stage decor.

The decision to retain all performers onstage or to use entrances and exits should be based on a consideration of the individual script. Entrances and exits can be used as selective aspects of the production for emphasis and for characterization. In Maxwell Anderson's *Elizabeth the Queen*, the director might want Elizabeth to make a sweeping entrance to emphasize her grandeur. Similarly, an Interpreters Theatre director would probably be ill-advised to eliminate Nora's dramatic exit in *A Doll's House* by Henrik Ibsen. Fantasy characters might be allowed to enter and exit to differentiate them from ordinary humans in nonrealistic works such as *Peter Pan* by J. M. Barrie, or perhaps the humans might make entrances and exits while fantasy characters remain present. Consider your script carefully. Seek ways to retain performers onstage when possible; don't rely on regular exits and entrances simply because you're familiar with them in Conventional Theatre.

Passage of Time

In addition to creating spatial scene and suggesting a different time frame, narrative vocal and movement techniques can be used for manipulating the passage of time. Some useful conventions available to the Interpreters Theatre director are the **freeze**, **slow motion**, **in-place movement**, and **accelerated movement**. The freeze is simply the cessation of all motion. Freezes are most artistically functional when they capture movement in progress, when the body design suggests that the vectors of force continue to move even though the body is frozen. An effective freeze is not easy to accomplish. The body position to be held must flow naturally from previous action and must be sufficiently balanced that the performer can maintain immobility in the face as well as the rest of the body. A vocal line immediately preceding the freeze should not anticipate the freeze. When it's well done, the freeze gives added emphasis to what is to come next, and helps to create, through cessation of movement and voice, a sense of "meanwhile." Very often, in a piece of literature, two events are literally occurring at the same time—interior thoughts and exterior action, for example, or two simultaneous physical actions in separate locations. If the director wishes to show simultaneity of action without sacrificing clarity of focus, the freeze is a useful technique.

Slow motion action draws attention to the process of the movement and its emotional and pantomimic significance. One of the most valuable functions of slow motion is the depiction of action that's necessary to the script but that shouldn't or can't be realized literally onstage. In a production of *Something Wicked This Way Comes*, physical violence (a fight between two characters and an electrical explosion that throws bodies through the air) was staged in slow motion, in recognition of the evocative power of slow motion to be greater than the spectacle of literal staging.

Producing a successful slow motion scene is a challenge for the director and the performers, requiring considerable rehearsal. The prolongation of the action requires strict attention to body design and facial expression. Slow motion is movement of sustained quality, usually using a great amount of force; the whole physical and emotional force is stretched out in time. If the body must be thrown off balance, a tremendous amount of physical control is required, as

Figure 9.5: Explosion staged in slow motion: *Something Wicked This Way Comes* by Ray Bradbury, directed by Marion Kleinau.

energy is transferred from one muscle to another—smoothly. A good rehearsal technique for preparing a slow motion scene is to have the performers locate the sets of muscles that must be activated in sequence to accomplish the movement and, at the same time, become aware of the alignment necessary to keep the body in balance. Once the performer is conscious of how energy transfers during the slow motion sequence, continual rehearsal will produce the necessary control.

Slow motion vocal action is often used to emphasize the unreality of a scene. Ghosts and imagined presences, for example, sometimes speak in a sustained slow motion. To prepare for successful slow motion vocal action, the performer should practice breath control and gradual sustaining of a vocal tone. In slow motion, vocal tempo should match body tempo—unless, of course, there's no speaking at all.

In-place movement is a technique for staging the passage of time and space, giving equal attention to action and word. Using a limited amount of stage space, the performer suggests traversing a larger distance. The timing of the in-place movement can be that of a normal action or can have elements of slow motion or acceleration. (When slow motion is used as in-place movement, the same principles apply as when slow motion movement displaces space.) It's important that the performers carry out in-place action with the same degree of reality that they would use if actually covering ground. Energy in place must be expended as fully as it would be in space, regardless of speed.

The sometimes frantic pace of accelerated action in movement or voice can be a highly effective comic device. The quality of accelerated action is often abrupt and the body design is exaggerated. Unlike slow motion, which calls attention to the developing stages of an emotional moment, accelerated action tends to depict immediately a single emotional level, often humorous. The fast-moving chase scenes in the Keystone Kops films are examples of comic acceleration through cinema. Accelerated vocal action, in which individual words may be lost, emphasizes the process of talking more than the word-products themselves.

The ability of accelerated movement to compact a great deal of action into a short time span can be used for tones other than comic. Gradually speeding up any action builds tension; set in a serious context, it can be terror-producing. Accelerating the daily routine of Mr. Zero in *The Adding Machine* by Elmer Rice accentuates the meaninglessness of his existence and builds an atmosphere of a mechanistic society. Such creation of atmosphere and event through accelerated movement serves an essentially narrative purpose because it is closely tied to the sequence of events.

Although freezing, slow motion, in-place movement, and accelerated action are most commonly used as narrative movement to create event-time-space orientations, all of these techniques can be used for lyric or dramatic purposes as well. A character who paces the floor in slow motion, for example, is indicating a lyric state of being. When characters freeze in body positions that reveal interrelationships, the technique is used for dramatic purposes.

The Dramatic Mode in Movement and Voice

Any movement or vocal tonality that depicts character relationships is dramatic in mode. Characters in literature respond to each other, exhibiting emotions and sharing ideas central to the action of the text. How they typically respond to other people in various situations is usually more a function of the lyric mode in performance, but the *interaction* of characters in a specific scene is part of the dramatic mode. Two characters can engage in a heated argument, as in the series of confrontations between George and Martha in *Who's Afraid of Virginia Woolf?* by Edward Albee or between Rhett Butler and Scarlett O'Hara in *Gone with the Wind* by Margaret Mitchell. *That* they are confronting each other intensely is an aspect of the dramatic mode in performance; *how* they, because of the nature of their characters, choose to reveal their emotions is an aspect of the lyric mode in performance. As you can see, the dramatic and lyric modes of action can be closely related.

We engage in the dramatic mode of behavior so often that it's almost unconscious. All social gestures serve a dramatic function by clarifying roles and relationships. Everyone uses social gestures every day—waving hello, saluting, shaking a finger—to interact with others. Ritual gestures are dramatic in mode because ritual is usually a communal activity, involving people in defined power structures. Fraternal organizations, for example, use ritual movement and the ritualized exchange of words to honor those in high office and to acknowledge a hierarchy. In these social examples, lyric differentiations hardly affect the dramatic responses; the gestures and greetings are standardized.

Conventional social gestures can become a basis for showing changing character relationships, however. The taking of tea, for example, is a kind of social ritual that is followed stringently in some social and ethnic circles. In a Readers Theatre production of *The Importance of Being Earnest* by Oscar Wilde, the ritual of tea taking was used by the director to depict the dramatic relationship between two young women, Cecily and Gwendolyn. The director arranged Cecily and Gwendolyn onstage as though they were having tea (as indicated by the text), but the director had the performers use offstage focus and pantomime the actions rather than use a real tea set. As the scene progressed, the director gradually exaggerated the force and range of the movements associated with tea taking. By this kind of exaggeration—which, incidentally, would have been impossible if real cups and saucers were used—the action of taking tea evolved into a presentation of the state of being of the two women. By a gradual distortion of the act of sharing tea, the director captured an essential presentational form of the scene: the disintegration of the relationship between Gwendolyn and Cecily, from polite friendship to antagonism.

In figure 9.6 character relationships are suggested by proximity, facial expression, and gesture. Although the woman is using a supportive gesture (hand on the shoulder), and is clearly the silent partner at this moment, her elevated position and the hint of disdain on her face suggest that she has power in reserve, which may be revealed in due course. In figure 9.7, showing a scene from a Readers Theatre adaptation of *The Lord of the Rings* by J. R. R. Tolkien, the antagonistic character relationships are shown by implied physical contact created through facial expression and body design; the body designs of the two combatants suggest a large magnitude of force channeled in defined directions.

As figures 9.6 and 9.7 indicate, at any given moment in a production the bodies of the performers onstage form a sculptural shape that in some way holds and communicates the tensive focus of that instant. As the production moves in time, those tensional forces interact and develop through the movement design. If a photographer were to take a series of still photographs of your production, each picture would capture a relationship between performers, frozen in time. One performer in the picture might reveal dominance, subordination, isolation,

Figure 9.6: Exploring character dominance: *Time and the Devil*, a compiled script directed by Frank Gonzales.

Figure 9.7: Implied physical contact: *The Lord of the Rings* by J. R. R. Tolkien, directed by Marion Kleinau.

Figure 9.8: Triangular blocking using offstage focus: *The Prince and the Pauper* by Mark Twain, directed by Lynn Bradley.

unity, rejection, affection, or any number of possible relationships with other bodies onstage. When you, as a director, are able to use body position effectively, the series of photos would capture much of the sequential meaning of the script. Alexander Dean terms the use of body arrangement to convey ideas **picturization**; he notes that picturization "contributes the meaning, or thought, or subject, in a stage group."[5] Although Dean uses picturization as an element of Conventional Theatre staging in pictorial space, the concept of picturization is a useful one for Interpreters Theatre. Coining a term, we may say the Interpreters Theatre director works for

Figure 9.9: Triangular blocking using offstage and onstage focus (one character behind scrim): *Light in August* by William Faulkner, directed by Tom Anderson.

presentational picturization. Rather than illustrating ideas in the stage space, Interpreters Theatre uses stage pictures to activate the mental imaging and sensory responsiveness of an audience. All of the performers' movements and physical positioning, including body facing and focus, seek to make presentational contact with the audience or to create symbolic suggestions for the audience.

Skillful arrangment of exciting stage pictures is an ability that usually comes with directing experience. However, there are some general principles directors follow to help them achieve aesthetic interest in presentational picturization:

1. A useful directing technique (if not overused) involves thinking in terms of triangles for stage pictures. Since an arrangement of three is generally pleasing to the eye, and since the apex of a triangle can give emphasis to one character over others, triangular arrangement is used as a basic stage form. Generally, when using triangular shapes, avoid equilateral triangles and identical body angles. With the triangle as a fundamental shape, other forms (circles and squares) may be built on it, adding complexity and tensiveness through the juxtaposition of shapes, as in figure 9.10.

2. Avoid placing two performers with the same body angle in the same plane. Vary either the body position or the **stage plane**. Also vary the distance between bodies onstage, grouping some and isolating others as action and psychological relationships dictate. Study artworks to learn interesting groupings.

3. Change nuances of lyric movement so that characters aren't always identified by the same gestures and body positions.

4. Unless your production concept requires stationary readers, shift the stage picture often enough to maintain visual interest. Besides basic changes of scene, which can be indicated effectively by changing the stage picture, find scenes of physical action, points of psychological movement, contrasts in idea, and other dynamic aspects of the script that allow picture changes to take place. A change of position or other movement patterns may be used to emphasize an important idea or to intensify an emotional moment. As you shift the stage picture, make sure it's always in the balance you desire—that you don't have holes in your shifting stage pattern. Check the flow of power, which is embodied in the changing stage pictures, to be sure that the right performers are always receiving emphasis and that your moments of greatest intensity are supported by the total stage picture, as in figure 9.11.

Staging Physical Contact

The staging of physical contact so that it occurs in acoustic space may pose a problem for the director in Interpreters Theatre. Even in productions using essentially offstage focus, a great deal of onstage physical contact can be achieved if the planes and levels of the performers are varied. As in figure 9.12, one interpreter standing upstage of another can place a hand on the shoulder, or fondle the hair of the downstage performer, for example. Directors tend to use such physical contact sparingly because it generally pulls scene onstage, yet direct physical contact can be a very effective means of emphasizing important moments in a script.

How is physical contact requiring face-to-face confrontation generally handled in Interpreters Theatre? If onstage focus is being used in the scene in which such confrontation occurs,

Figure 9.10: Variations on triangular blocking: *The Phantasmagorical Fantasy Book*, a compiled script directed by Larry Parrish.

Figure 9.11: Blocking to achieve character emphasis: *In Violence*, a compiled script directed by Raymond J. Schneider.

Figure 9.12: Literal physical contact: *The Bell Jar* by Sylvia Plath, directed by Cindy Miller.

as in many scenes in Chamber Theatre, the action is handled naturally just as it would be in Conventional Theatre staging. If offstage focus is the convention, however, the director need not suddenly switch to onstage focus to accomplish the action. Any object can be handed from one person to another by one performer offering—and another receiving—the imagined object out toward the audience.

Physical violence can also be staged using side-by-side full front positions and offstage focus. Consider the strangulation of Desdemona by Othello, in which he pantomimes the pressure on her neck while she reacts in terror and pain. Fights of any kind can also be blocked with offstage focus as in figures 9.7 and 9.13; the combatants need never look at each other literally so long as they connect with each other in space. Coordinating offstage action and reaction is a delicate challenge and takes considerable extra rehearsal.

Think of physical action in Interpreters Theatre as a creative challenge. Very often a great deal of the intrigue of directing in this medium results from the apparent problems of staging physical action nonliterally. Don't overlook the power of the voice to create many of the dramatic relationships you might be tempted to stage physically. Whereas in dramatic texts written for the realistic stage characters often become speechless at the height of their emotion, showing their feelings by action instead of voice, in texts written for the presentational stage

Figure 9.13: A fight using off-stage focus: *The Wind in the Willows* by Kenneth Graham, directed by Carol Gaede.

characters often find voice at their highest emotional peak. Shakespearean characters, for example, almost always find the right words in a crisis; language rarely fails them. When the moment of crisis is reflected in language, make use of the richness of those words. As a director, you may be intrigued by the power of words and the voice alone to create dramatic interactions in more presentational literature. When crises depend on physical action alone, however, don't be afraid to stage those moments in movement. Take those instances of literal movement and transform them into presentational action.

Whatever text you're staging, the guidelines of good acting apply in every way. A performer's bodily action should be appropriate and clear. Vocal intensity should always seem to hold something more in reserve; otherwise we in the audience become painfully aware of the interpreter's body fact straining, rather than the character's body act enacting.

All three modes in performance interact to serve the text in production. The lyric and dramatic modes help the performer capture the full scope of body act, while the narrative mode controls the sequence of events. The value of determining the primary mode of a given action is that it helps you as director know what to emphasize: whether to give major attention to an individual character's reaction, to the nature of interaction among characters, or to the narrative movement of the action. As director, your responsibility is to keep all three modes in a working balance that reflects your particular text.

SHAPING THE PERFORMANCE

As your production begins to take shape, careful attention to such elements as production style, the relation of words and movement, how offstage focus is managed, the handling of manuscripts, and the building of rhythmic structure will make a difference in the unity and vitality of the final performance.

Production Style

Reaffirm your image of the overall style of your production. Where in the spectrum of presentational action does your production lie? Is it highly symbolic (perhaps metaphoric) or will it make use of some representational action? What is its tonality? Is it comic, serious, straightforward, ironic? Try to picture the whole production as a person speaking and moving. Is your production primarily stately or slouched, smooth or erratic, fast or slow, square or round? To what extent have power sources other than character been developed into voices in the script? Does the script contain vocal orchestration? Usually, the more orchestration a script has, the more it will suggest some degree of formalization in movement and voice.

Style in Interpreters Theatre production evolves from a combination of the nature of the text and from the levels of abstraction in your production concept. Consistency in style is important. If your setting makes use of pictorial space, for example, then the design of the action usually will be shaped to some extent by pictorial space. In the play *Marat/Sade* by Peter Weiss, the stage directions place the character Jean-Paul Marat in a bathtub at center stage. As an Interpreters Theatre director of this play, your production concept may lead you to respect the stage directions and localize Marat literally onstage. Even though you use blocks instead of a bathtub, Marat's position will be defined in pictorial space and the paths of other characters' movements will probably be defined by his position. His attendant, Simonne, might use onstage focus and possibly physical contact as she serves him.

On the other hand, if your stage design is highly symbolic, organized around shapes that objectify interior worlds or create analogic forms, the performers' actions should reflect this emphasis. Another production concept for *Marat/Sade* may lead you to symbolize the struggle for power between the two main characters, Marat and the Marquis de Sade. Such a production might use scaffolding as a set piece, with Marat and de Sade on opposite sides, continually adjusting their positions as the balance of power shifts. In a performance this symbolic, the other action onstage would also be very formalized. You might, for example, wish to stage Charlotte Corday's killing of Jean-Paul Marat in dancelike movement.

Styles mixed for no apparent reason create a dissonance that can seriously interfere with the experience you're communicating. In some cases, the dissonance is so great that it elicits laughter from the audience, even at highly charged emotional moments. Just as a vaudeville-type tap dance wouldn't usually occur in a serious classical ballet, realistic movement and style of delivery wouldn't belong in a highly symbolic approach, unless the realism itself is used as a symbol. If a living evergreen Birnam wood, represented by fully costumed warriors with branches on their helmets, were to descend en masse upon a Dunsinane castle created of presentational stage levels, even the greatest actor playing Macbeth might have trouble preventing audience laughter. A better solution might be to break up the literal mass of actors who are playing Malcolm's armies (obviously eliminating the evergreens) and have them enter singly from different locations as though they were converging on the castle from all sides. A nonrealistic woods could be suggested by slide projections. In a televised production of Verdi's opera, *Macbeth*, the director solved the problem by bathing the actors in green light as they ran to the stage area that symbolized Dunsinane castle. Consistency is a matter of maintaining the shape and the tone of the controlling image of the production.

Bringing Words and Movement Together

One of the major problems in many attempts to combine movement and words in Interpreters Theatre is that the movement tends to become overliteral and lose its presentational identity. Movement often appears to be overly illustrative chiefly because of the timing between movement and words. Whether to say the line and then move, to move and then speak, or to do both together is a question that is basic to both the rhythm and the meaning of a performance.

As a general rule, if a clause such as "he picked it up" is spoken *simultaneously* with a movement that symbolizes picking up, the movement will seem to blend with the words, unless it's too pantomimic. The director in this case needs to be sure that the movement is generalized enough to provide the needed accent but not so literal that it usurps the communicative function of the word.

When the performer executes a movement *before* speaking the line, depending upon the specificity of the movement, this repetition may make the word seem redundant unless the tone of the words adds a dimension or clarifies something about the movement. When movement and words seem merely to duplicate each other, the director may wish to reexamine the relationship between movement and words to determine which to retain. There are some occasions, although relatively rare in Interpreters Theatre, when a more literal kind of movement can be substituted for words. This is usually in the narrative mode when the storyteller provides behavioral information that could just as easily be realized in physical action. When a character actually seems to pick up an object in place of the narrator's words, "He picked it up," the result is a transition from telling to showing. So long as the line doesn't represent an important interaction between narrator and character—such as the narrator directing him to pick it up or disapproving of his action—movement can be substituted for the word. Make such substitutions very cautiously, however; explanations of movements combined with the movements themselves often create an important narrative rhythm.

When the interpreter performs the action *after* speaking the line, the movement becomes redundant unless movement creates an additional statement of its own. Comic effects can be achieved by this kind of timing, because a comic style of action can carry a surprise effect not necessarily indicated by the line itself.

Regardless of how movement is timed with the words, movement in Interpreters Theatre should always extend or refine the emotional, sensory, or psychological aspects of language. Unless the performer's physical action adds an attitudinal dimension, it merely duplicates the words instead of enhancing them. In a line such as, "He handed her the flowers," it's the director's responsibility to make sure that the performer doesn't merely go through the motions of handing her the flowers. When an emotional quality is written into the language—"He handed her the flowers reluctantly"—the challenge to the performer is to use movement to refine the state of reluctance. Should he bring the flowers slowly from behind his back? Should he continue to hold the flowers close to his body when he ought to be extending them? Is his reluctance caused by shyness or by shame? These considerations, not specified in the words, can be vividly communicated through movement.

Similarly, in drama, when literal action itself isn't always carried by words, the performers may need to supply the missing movement in some way. Stage business in Interpreters Theatre is just as important as it is in Conventional Theatre. A major difference is that when Interpreters Theatre performers engage in stage business involving hand props, the props themselves are usually symbolic or pantomimed. Furthermore, the focus of the Interpreters Theatre performer is often offstage.

In producing drama for Interpreters Theatre, the director usually ignores many of the stage directions, because stage directions are often designed for a more realistic setting. It isn't usually important, for example, that one character be seated while another stands, unless that physical arrangement is central to the scene. When you've created presentational action by removing the spatial reality of the literal movement, you've eliminated the responsibility to create realistic stage pictures in pictorial space. Presentational picturization operates on the principle of symbolic rather than literal relationships between characters.

Overt physical action carried in stage directions (such as "They fight bitterly") is carried out in Interpreters Theatre as a presentational fight, unless you've deliberately chosen to break the convention of acoustic space to bring the focus of movement onstage in pictorial space. Most likely, even in onstage physical contact, your production will utilize symbolic movement. Although drama probably has more movement without accompanying words than other literary forms, it's important that the movement maintain a consistent presentational style.

Bringing words and movement together is an orchestration process much like the orchestration explored in Chapter 3. Movement and words can move to the same beat, which integrates them, or movement can move in double time, half time, or a syncopated relationship with the words, which creates a contrapuntal pattern between words and movement. Generally, integrative combinations will give a simple, uncluttered effect. If you, as a director, wish to feature the rhythmic pattern of a work through movement, while preserving the clarity of the words, it's usually best to integrate the timing of movement and words to some extent.

On the other hand, contrapuntal combinations between words and movement can add an interesting complexity to the literary experience. When the language seems to suggest another level of experience that the words themselves are unable to capure completely, a contrapuntal combination may be useful. In stream of consciousness or dream sequences, for example, words struggle to show the constantly shifting images that flash to the mind's surface and then disappear. By counterpointing movement to the verbal sequence, the director can materialize more fully some of the intangible forces suggested by the words.

A production may be shaped with some performers moving and others speaking, or the same performers may both move and speak. When speakers and movers are separate, integration of the two sets of performers becomes a major task of the director. If the speakers don't sense the movement in their own muscles and if the movers don't have a feeling for the words, blending is difficult. A good rehearsal technique is to have the movers also speak and the speakers move, to help all performers gain the same sense of timing and quality before breaking them into two groups. When performers both move and speak, the skillful integration of movement with words depends on the ability of the performers to feel the rhythms of the words in their bodies and to let the voice reflect the physical impulse of the movement.

Precise timing of voice and movement can make performances hang together. In a collage, for example, where the script is composed of small pieces from various works, the verbal dimension of the text is likely to be disjunctive. Images and events are placed in sequence without the logical progression and motivational aspects of action being apparent in the words alone. Although vocal tonalities and movement are unifying media for all kinds of scripts, movement itself is particularly useful as a unifying and clarifying force in a collage.

In the production of the collage, "November Hunt" (Chapter 6), a delicate chain of gestures, shifts of focus, and vocal tonalities between narrator and characters provided a continuity of action only suggested by the verbal text. A special communicative link was established between narrator and hunter by a glance and a carefully controlled gesture of permission that captured in one silent moment the production concept of the script: that death is a fact of life and helps to maintain the ecological balance of the earth.

These kinds of subtleties require control from both performer and director. In many cases, the director needs to consider the performer as a kind of dancer and the word-movement pattern as a form of choreography. The resulting movement usually isn't dance, but it is highly refined and rhythmically precise. Vocal subtleties need the same careful attention. Although it's useful in rehearsal to work improvisationally, letting the performers help discover their own vocal and movement patterns, when the final shaping of the performance occurs (unless the total production is improvisationally based) you'll need to make meticulous choices in relation to the style of the production. Generally, the more formalized the style, the more necessary that the timing of voice and movement be precise.

A word of caution: Some directors become so fascinated by movement that their productions fail to maintain a complementary balance between words and movement, and the literary work becomes lost. Whenever movement (whether literal or formalized) calls attention to itself for its own sake instead of serving the literary experience, the movement is too extensive or of the wrong kind. There are many times when you can use movement fully, but you need always to keep in mind the necessities of the words of the text. Since movement always takes focus onstage (the audience's eyes will follow a moving figure rather than a static figure), it's easy for movement to overpower a text. A few well-selected and integrated movements are usually stronger than a movement extravaganza. The Interpreters Theatre director should use movement as the chef uses spices; more isn't necessarily better.

Blocking Offstage Focus

Whenever offstage focus is used, whether established by body design or by position of the eyes, it's important that the lines of focus be sharp and clear. The performer must see the character she is addressing in acoustic space just as clearly as if the character were being addressed onstage. One way to achieve such clarity of focus is for the performer to locate an object in the theatre auditorium that corresponds to the imaginative location of the other character in space and to concentrate on transmitting energy toward that specific object. A common rehearsal technique to increase the believability of energy flow is to have the addressed character go to the offstage spot in space at which she is being addressed and carry on the conversation from that locale, so that the onstage performer can have the experience of seeing the other character offstage. Offstage focus will be successful and evocative only if it's believable, if the individual characters really contact each other or objects or events in space (as in figure 9.14), or if the audience feels genuinely addressed when audience contact is intended.

Figure 9.14: Intensity in off-stage focus: "A Late Encounter with the Enemy" by Flannery O'Connor, directed by Tom Isbell.

Offstage focus presents a special challenge to the director to vary body angles and to arrange interesting stage pictures while still maintaining the performers' openness to the audience. Since offstage focus generally limits the performer to three body angles—one quarter right, full front, and one quarter left—how is the director to achieve variety in creating stage pictures?

First, the director can vary body angles in interesting ways, playing with degrees of openness to the audience. In figure 9.15, the two performers are in the same stage plane (simulating a truck ride) but their body angles are somewhat altered to create visual variety. Figure 9.16 is a group picture using a different body angle for each performer, even though they're all in the same plane.

Second, the director may make use of more than one stage plane in the stage picture, a common technique, shown in figure 9.17.

Third, the vertical level of the performers (whether they are in the same plane or not) can be varied for visual interest, as in figure 9.18.

Even though performers are in different positions with different body angles, their focal points of connection need to be coordinated. The director can help greatly in this regard by stopping action periodically and viewing the pictures from a series of different positions in the audience, checking sight lines and offstage focal points. Make certain also that important characters in each picture are given primary emphasis. Because, in using offstage focus, other performers cannot help create emphasis by turning and looking at the speaker, the director has to make sure that the speaker takes emphasis by contrast in position or movement.

Take similar care with focal points during shifts to onstage focus, especially when the stage is essentially bare. If an interpreter is looking at another performer onstage, there is usually no difficulty with clarity of focus; but if one or more interpreters are creating an imaginary object (onstage or offstage) through focus alone, the director should make sure that all lines of focus converge on the same location, that each performer has a similar notion of the size of the imagined object, and that accompanying movement contributes to the imaginative presence. In figure 9.19, the two boys in a Chamber Theatre production of Evan Hunter's *Last Summer* are stoning a seagull to death. The director created the presence of the seagull through the boys' onstage focus and through a small pool of red light that grew deeper in color as the violent act progressed.

Once performers have imaginatively constituted an object onstage, the rules of good pantomimic action prevail: unless the object (or scene) has been clearly dematerialized, the performers must regard the imagined object as physically present and avoid walking through walls or stepping on sleeping dogs. A narrator, of course, can cancel an imagined setting with one wave of the hand or simply by changing the environment through words. The richness of an essentially empty stage is that it can be filled as well as empty; generally it is filled through the skillful use of focal connections. These problems with focal points are somewhat unique to Interpreters Theatre; generally a Conventional Theatre director doesn't face the problem because objects of focus tend to be provided onstage.

Handling Physical Scripts in Performance

If the director has decided to use physical scripts, there are practical problems to solve. First, in accordance with your production concept as director, you should decide whether the physical

Figure 9.15: Variation of body angle: *Breakfast of Champions* by Kurt Vonnegut, Jr., directed by Janet Larsen McHughes.

Figure 9.16: Variation of body angle: *The Bell Jar* by Sylvia Plath, directed by Cindy Miller.

script is to be a symbolic prop or a plain folder. When scripts are held, the performers should refer to their scripts from time to time (as if engaged in the act of reading), catching a glance at the text and the audience in one sweeping eye movement, so as to use the physical script. Probably, as an audience member, you've had the experience of gradually becoming aware of a performer's turning page after page without ever glancing down (or never even bothering to turn the pages at all); when that happens, viewers become so concerned that the performer might suddenly need to go for a line that they're in danger of losing sight of the action being performed. As long as the interpreter looks at the script periodically and seems to be in control of where the lines are on the page, the audience doesn't give the presence of the physical script any undue attention, yet the book still serves as a reminder of the medium's essential interest in the text.

As a director, check the angles at which your performers are holding scripts; encourage them to hold the books far enough in front of them that they needn't bob their heads down to glance at a line. If the script is to be plain, choose unobtrusive but sturdy binders that allow pages to lie flat and be turned easily and silently. You may want to use folders smaller than 8½ inches by 11 inches for ease of handling. Beware of the popular plastic casings for script pages; the plastic sheets can glare under bright performance lights.

Figure 9.17: Variation in plane: *Jacques Brel Is Alive and Well and Living in Paris* by Eric Blau and Mort Schuman, directed by Steve Webster.

Figure 9.18: Variation in level: *Trumpet of the New Moon*, written and directed by Joseph Robinette.

Figure 9.19: Creating objects through focus: *Last Summer* by Evan Hunter, directed by Janet Larsen McHughes.

Figure 9.20: Relating to imagined objects: *Winnie-the-Pooh* by A. A. Milne, directed by Laurie Bruce.

Handling a script skillfully isn't as easy as it looks. During rehearsal you may need to give attention to the turning of pages, to moving with the script, and to any other special uses of it. You may also wish to run a few rehearsals without book to avoid undue dependence on the script for lines. If the script is to be used occasionally as a prop, plan the transition from held script to prop carefully. Beware of falling into the representational trap with scripts as props; a book used as a rifle, for example, shouldn't be held up for literal aim any more than book covers should clash together as actual swords. The act of employing scripts for props is already an abstraction; try to maintain the same level of abstraction in the ways scripts are handled.

Achieving Rhythmic Vitality in Production

A well-conceived production design maintains a balance between satisfying the expectations of an audience and providing surprise; good productions rely on both suspense and release of suspense. Although dramatic interest is often achieved by the tensiveness between what the audience expects to happen next and what actually occurs, dramatic satisfaction results when the expected retribution or triumph is finally attained. Given the beginning of an action with which they are unfamiliar, audience members anticipate its completion, are excited by being outwitted in their expectations, but are left unsatisfied if the outcome doesn't seem to justify the beginning of the performance. The basis for final audience satisfaction lies in the creation of the script, but a good script may be poorly realized in production unless the director understands how to work with the underlying rhythmic patterns.

The rhythmic progression of suspense and release of suspense is ensured by making certain that key lines and actions are clear to the audience and shaped to make the intended point. Sometimes directors are so familiar with a script and become so preoccupied with other aspects of production that they fail to listen as if they were audience members who don't know the text. As the production grows, make sure that the audience will be able to hear and understand every key action.

Rhythmic movement can be controlled by carefully building climaxes and sharpening changes in tempo. One of the basic rhythmic problems you may encounter occurs in individual rhythmic variation. Most scripts contain what would be called in musical terms an **underlying beat**, a rhythmic pulse that permeates the entire piece. Some texts are essentially slow paced, others fast paced. *The Trojan Women* by Euripides moves more slowly than a Noel Coward comedy. The poetry of Edith Sitwell's *Façade* skips erratically, yet the poem "Still Falls the Rain" by the same author marches steadily. On top of the underlying pulse, the lyric movement of individual characters and the pacing of individual scenes happen at different tempos and in different rhythmic patterns. Puck, in Shakespeare's *A Midsummer Night's Dream*, moves with lively rhythm; Oberon, in the same scenes, moves at a stately pace. These rhythmic characteristics permeate both physical movement and vocal delivery. Likewise, a total scene may be whimsical, heavy, long, or short. Each character and each scene has a particular rhythmic identification, which should be maintained in its individuality but must ultimately blend into the whole. The individuality gives rhythmic variety; the underlying pulse contributes unity and consistency to the production. You need to discover both kinds of rhythm in the script and make them work together.

Ultimately, the art of performance is creating an air of seemingly spontaneous reality, which emerges from careful rehearsal. This is sometimes called the illusion of the first time, the sense of an action happening only now. A well-rehearsed and precisely timed production is always desirable, but beware of falling into the trap of creating an overslick or canned production. When the smooth timing of words and movement seems to leave little room for depth of emotion, the audience may get the impression that the performers are programmed to execute their actions on cue, with little or no spontaneity of feeling. Always strive for the well-rehearsed production that is nevertheless fresh and vital. When you feel a sequence becoming stale in rehearsal, deliberately contradict the established rhythm of the scene by a double-time or slow-motion rehearsal to break up the predictability of the performers' actions. The best freshness to be achieved in performance is the spontaneity of actors who know exactly what they are supposed to do and sincerely contact the sensory and emotional life of the script each time they do it. Only then can you achieve a true illusion of the first time.

Using a Chorus

The chorus—a group of performers who move and speak together in various relationships—may fulfill any number of functions in your production. If the text to be performed is a Greek play or a drama such as Peter Shaffer's *Equus*, the chorus is written into the script; in most other kinds of literature, however, the chorus is created by the adapter-director. Anytime a collective voice is suggested by the literature or anytime the collective strengths of more than one voice and body are desired, a chorus provides a flexible performing instrument.

Sometimes the major forces in a work may be embodied in a different form through the use of a chorus (or choruses). In *Antigone* by Jean Anouilh, the title character is caught between the force of her cultural heritage, which says to bury her brother's body, and the political force of the state, represented by her uncle Creon who says the body must not be buried. These two major forces of the play, one within Antigone (the power of conscience) and one outside her (the power of the state) may be embodied in movement by the Interpreters Theatre director in a number of ways. In one Readers Theatre production of the play, the director used two moving choruses to create these forces: Creon was no longer an individualized performer, but was part of a group that embodied the political state in all its various roles; Antigone's conscience spoke to her through several performers who echoed the cultural tradition of burial. Antigone herself stood as a lone character buffeted by those forces. Movement and voice helped to define the two groups: the state group used vertical linear design, abrupt movement quality, and loud vocal volume with limited pitch variation. The forces of Antigone's conscience were curved and massed, with a slow swinging quality of movement that receded and surged back again as Antigone was badgered by political authority. Movement was used sparingly through much of the production (sometimes occurring in slow motion) but moments of extensive physical motion accented points of highest tension in the play.

A chorus is an efficient way to solve the problem of fragmentary roles—characters who are in one small scene only and never appear again or characters who pop in and out throughout the script, such as maids or postmen. Members of a small chorus may step into these various roles by using different voices and movements, by picking up a prop, or by donning a costume piece and then moving back into the chorus again. It's necessary to differentiate between a chorus of performers who play a series of different individual roles in a production (or who have individual character roles within the chorus) and a chorus that acts as an ensemble. Usually, the more abstract the role of the chorus, the more the group moves and speaks in a unified pattern. When a chorus functions as rhythm or as tone color, for example, both the movement and the vocal techniques are unified and create a single entity rather than a group of individuals.

A chorus doesn't have to be one or the other of these two types. In many productions, the chorus members may change characteristics, acting as a single entity in one scene and as individuals in another. The same chorus may portray a group of people reacting to a fight in one scene and create a sound effect in another scene. The director needs to be aware, however, that different kinds of choruses require some differences in handling.

When the chorus is composed of individual characters, the lyric aspects of voice and movement for each chorus member are created individually and the chorus acts together in performance chiefly for narrative and dramatic purposes. In some scripts each chorus member is assigned a particular character, but in most cases the chorus is designated only by "townspeople" or given some other generalized identity, as in figure 9.21. You usually need to help your chorus members create their character roles, (discover who they are in the town and how they interact with other chorus townspeople, for example) or find characteristics for a series of multiple roles, if the script is of this nature. A director has to be aware of chorus continuity—the moment-by-moment existence of the chorus throughout the production—to make sure that the role of each chorus member is well defined at every instant. In blocking a chorus of individuals, the director strives for interesting individual positions for each performer that project character and attitude and will contrast with the physical positions of other chorus members.

In a unified chorus, all members are parts of a larger whole and together they create a single personality. Each performer's lyric movement and voice is like that of at least some of the other members of the chorus. This need for similarity may cause problems in casting. Be aware of how performers' voices blend together in tryouts and how well a series of bodies can work in unison. Any performer who cannot modulate tone or who isn't somewhat flexible in movement style probably shouldn't be cast as a member of a unified chorus.

A director needs to allow ample rehearsal time for working with a unified chorus, because the **ensemble** awareness that underlies vocal and physical unity often develops slowly and requires time for maturation. Generally the first step in molding a unified chorus is to work for individual kinesthetic awareness, general voice and body flexibility, and an awareness of the other members of the chorus. Any exercise that depends on one performer sensing the physical patterns of another (such as a mirror exercise) is a good beginning procedure. Chants or any vocal exercise in which the group attempts to create a single tone will help attain vocal unity. Seek first to help the group breathe, speak, and move as a single being to establish the base or core of your ensemble. As the performers begin to move and speak together as a total group, be aware of the ways individual movement patterns and speech rhythms, pitches, and qualities affect the blend of the chorus. You may have to work particularly hard with some bodies and voices to tone them into the group. No matter what contrasting vocal or movement patterns a chorus performs, all individualized speech and movement should seem to emerge from and melt back into a solidly unified body.

Chorus continuity is especially important when working with a unified chorus. Since the chorus often acts as a single being, the chorus role should be as consistent as any other role in a production. When the chorus is broken into subgroups working either antiphonally or in

Figure 9.21: Chorus as individual characters: *The Singer* by Calvin Miller, directed by Randy Taylor.

counterpoint, you need to give special attention to the continuity of the action for each subgroup, so at every moment it has an identity and a purpose.

The almost limitless contrapuntal patterns make the vocal and physical orchestration of choral sequences an exciting process. Once chorus members gain the awareness basic to unified performance, they should also have the control necessary for contrapuntal effects. You learned some vocal orchestration possibilities in Chapter 3; consider now a few methods for achieving movement orchestration.

A chorus can engage in a movement conversation as well as a vocal conversation. Dividing the ensemble into two or three subgroups and alternating movement among them can create the effect of carrying on a dramatic dialogue. Repetitive patterns—one group moving in the same pattern as the preceding group—gain the effect of, "Oh yes, that's the way." Contrastive patterns, either in body design or in movement quality, seem to say, "No, it's this way." Such antiphonal movement phrases can also vary in length and in timing of response. Some movement sequences may involve a long and complex conversation, and other phrases may be as short as a single gesture. Movement response may come quickly, almost overlapping the end of the preceding phrase, or may be delayed and deliberate in its pacing. In this way, a chorus can engage in an argument, convey affection, gossip, or create any number of communicative effects.

Overlapping these varying movement patterns so two or more groups are moving simultaneously, either using repetitive or contrasting patterns, creates movement counterpoint. A single performer may move in contrast to the whole group, or various segments of the ensemble may be in simultaneous motion. The rhythmic relationship among the moving groups becomes an important factor in the total stage picture; it can follow some of the contrapuntal patterns illustrated in Chapter 3 for vocal orchestration. Movement orchestration, like vocal orchestration, requires precision of execution and needs a choreographic approach.

A well-trained chorus using precise timing can create stunning moments of illumination and extension of the text. Overused or poorly executed, however, choral orchestration can work against the clarity of the action. Counterpoint entails the chorus being broken into at least two subgroups. If the two groups are both moving and speaking against one another, chaos might well result. Pay particular attention to the kind of movement used in contrapuntal sections. Good options are to use no movement at all when the vocal patterns are complex and to use movement selectively for accent. Work always from the experience of the text. Often contrapuntal patterns that look good on paper are unworkable when put into operation and have to be adjusted. In orchestrated sections, you need to experiment with your particular chorus, not hesitating to change the script when necessary and not letting yourself be carried away by the pyrotechnics of sound and movement. As with all other aspects of production, the chorus and its functions are there to serve the literature.

Incorporating Dance Movement

The use of dance or dancelike movement combined with a literary work has been a fascinating area of exploration for many Interpreters Theatre directors. The line between **stage movement** and **dance** is not always distinguishable, but, in general, dance calls attention to itself as movement and movement in performance functions to serve the word primarily. For the most part, dance has a tighter, more repetitious rhythmic base, a more abstract body design and often makes use of identifiable steps or movement combinations. The best distinction between the art of dance and dancelike stage movement, however, is that a dance has an artistic integrity of its own that doesn't depend on any other context. A dance, although it may incorporate spoken language, can stand alone as a work of art.

Sometimes a script calls specifically for a dance. In most cases, the dance called for will be a social dance form, as in *A Doll's House* by Henrik Ibsen, in which Nora dances the tarantella, and in works with scenes involving characters attending a dance, such as the party scene in Shakespeare's *Romeo and Juliet.* When you're working with such a script, you might have the performers actually dance or you might use other movement conventions, such as a frozen position, to suggest a dance taking place. Recognized dance forms can also be used as part of the background and transitional materials for a script; a production of *Spoon River Anthology* by Edgar Lee Masters used square dance formations to change the physical arrangement of the stage between some of the poems.

Experimenting with social dance and other kinds of choreographed dance is exciting, but it's much more likely that your production design will call for dancelike movement, which serves the word primarily, rather than dance as an art form by itself. Regardless of whether you're trained in the use of dance movement, don't hesitate to explore heightened movement possibilities suggested by your text. Many times the combination of your skills as a director, the ideas and feelings of your performers, and some improvisational movement exercises in relation to specific moments in a script will produce movement that's dancelike in its authentic expression of the text. Some kinds of textual experience that may profitably be explored through dance movement are moments of intense interior struggle (including dream sequences), expressions of universal feeling, the supernatural, and any writing that is highly symbolic.

Movement for highly emotional material, especially if the story is told from an interior point of view, may become dancelike because of the personal intensity of the feelings involved. A production of *I Never Promised You a Rose Garden* by Hannah Green, for example, used dancelike movement extensively to suggest a schizophrenic state. *Rose Garden* is the story of a mentally deranged girl, Deborah, and her fight for sanity. Deborah's self-punishing forces are objectified into the figures of gods who inhabit a kingdom called Yr, which exists in Deborah's mind. Yr is a place for self-punishment in which the destructive forces within her war with objective reality for possession of her mind. In this production, at the highest peak of her suffering, Deborah's movement was very dancelike. The intensity of her feelings caused Deborah to lose contact not only with her surroundings, but with her usual ways of speaking and moving. As she moved toward Yr, the movement took over her whole body with strong rhythmic contractions, spiraling her through space; the movement seemed to contain the character rather than the character embodying the movement. Although this movement approached dance, it had no artistic life outside the framework of the story. It was an exaggerated symbol of very personal human suffering, cued by and blended with the words of the script.

Dance movement may also evolve from a textual situation in which emotion seems to reach a universal level. The last scenes of both John M. Synge's *Riders to the Sea* and Federico Garcia Lorca's *Blood Wedding* contain such elevated feeling that they create universal expressions of grief. To capture the power of such scenes, the characters need to become larger than life in

Figure 9.22: Symbolic exploration of supernatural shapes through movement: *The Dunwich Horror* by H. P. Lovecraft, directed by Robert Fish.

the classic sense. Both vocal utterance and physical movement are formalized. If the director chooses, movement can become dancelike, but this is dance very different from that of Deborah's in *Rose Garden*. The vectors of movement might go out and up rather than in and around; the pace would probably be slow and measured rather than fast and convulsive. In *Rose Garden*, the character is consumed by a personal emotion; at the end of the Synge and Lorca plays, the characters are beyond personal grief.

Symbolic material also can sometimes best be communicated by highly formalized or dancelike movement. Whenever the script is operating in a metaphoric manner or whenever the text itself is ritualistic or mythic, the symbolic nature of dance may complement the symbolic experience being embodied by the performers. In a compiled script entitled *Sweet Medicine*, which portrayed American Indian myths concerning rites of passage, dancelike movement symbolized such actions as the flight of birds and the transformation of a mouse into an eagle. The ritualistic nature of Indian dance was created by movements that used elements abstracted from actual Indian dances. The initiate character traveled over rough terrain (both physical and spiritual) carried in the arms of dancers or rolled over their backs in a series of back flips. The symbols of myth became the symbols of dancelike movement.

Lyric poetry, which may be not only emotional and symbolic but highly rhythmic, often suggests dance movement. The persona's impulse to reveal self is ultimately an impulse to move; in performance, that impulse can sometimes find fulfillment in dance. The musical sweep of the poetic line and its emotional intensity may urge that an ordinary action be extended and heightened. The following passage from Federico Garcia Lorca's "Lament for Ignacio Sanchez Mejias," for example, seems to signal the simple action of turning away.

I will not see it!

Tell the moon to come
for I do not want to see the blood
of Ignacio on the sand.[6]

The action, when examined, isn't simple at all, but captures the total and overwhelming gesture of consuming grief. It is a cry that seems to override the ordinary range of the action of turning away. The rhythmic structure of the line coupled with the strength of the emotion can carry the body into an exaggerated movement based generally on the action of turning. In one production of the poem, both a speaking performer and a moving performer were used as two aspects of the same personality. This treatment created a simultaneous presence of both the mourner and the extension of the mourner's grief in dance movement.

When your script seems to suggest the use of dance movement, look carefully at the context in which the movement will occur. Dancelike movement usually needs to evolve from greater exaggeration and a more structured organization of the same movement patterns used immediately before and after the dance sequence. The unity of the production as well as its rhythm may be destroyed if the design and quality of the movement suddenly change. Even in those works that call for dance as a set piece within the performance (see figure 9.23), the movement should not stop the forward progression of the action. To keep production momentum requires that the movements chosen have an integral relation to the experience of the script and

Figure 9.23: A danced climax: *I, Diary*, a compiled script directed by Raymond J. Schneider.

be woven into the progressive action so completely that the performance flows both verbally and visually.

Sometimes it's useful to enlist the help of someone trained in movement if you don't have the training yourself and feel hesitant to attempt it. Be careful, however, about asking a professional choreographer to design movement for your production when you need dancelike movement rather than dance itself. It's important that the choreographer understand the relationship you wish to create between the words and the movement. The difficulty in using a choreographer, as in working with any collaborative artist, is that the choreographer may not have the same muscle feeling for the script that you have or see the same visual images, and she may rely on combinations of previously constructed movements rather than evolving new movement patterns from the text. In most cases, any dance forms that rely on combinations of movement—such as the ballet or tap dancing—are dangerous to use in an Interpreters Theatre production. Dancers are accustomed to working from a movement premise rather than from a textual one, and often previously constructed movements such as ballet combinations have no relation to what is going on in the script. The choreographer does, however, have a developed ability to shape movement. If a choreographer is willing to digest the text and begin fresh with the creative movement ideas coming from the text, and if the director will work closely with the choreographer in the creation of the movement, stunning movement sequences may be created that will enrich the production.

Trained dancers can add an exciting dimension to a production, if handled skillfully. If only the trained dancers are to move, then a problem may reside in the kind of movement used. Dancers tend to rely on learned movement patterns and, unless a director or choreographer is very meticulous in constructing the movement, the movement may be far removed from the words in the text. If trained dancers are to work in conjunction with untrained movers, even greater attention has to be paid to the nature of the movement given each kind of performer, or the difference in ability will call attention to itself to the detriment of the performance. Don't hesitate to make use of the trained dancers available to you, but don't be in awe of their art; their purpose is to serve the art of the script.

Since there are so many possibilities for the combination of words and movement—what kind, when, how much, and how timed—a beginning director needs to leave time in the rehearsal schedule for considerable experimentation with performers. The prospect of free use of movement in an Interpreters Theatre production may seem awesome to the director who has no previous experience with movement or training in its use. But, regardless of experience and training, no director should hesitate to explore movement possibilities in a script. Not the least among the rewards of such exploration is the discovery that you do have within you a wealth of movement ideas and that, with practice, you can make them work in a performance.

TO THE DIRECTOR: A FINAL WORD

Directing for any theatre medium requires creative dedication, which is the mark of the artist. Art is exciting, self-fulfilling, expanding, exhilarating—but it is also plain hard work. As you watch your show take shape, there may be times when you feel there are so many different production elements that you can never blend them into a whole, and there may also be times when the sensitive images you had in your head seem far away indeed. When these moments of artistic frustration hit you, remember: the process of creation often requires a disintegration, a breaking down of resources, before new forms can emerge. Performers in Interpreters Theatre productions must objectively probe their inner selves, even to the point of denying part of their personalities, to become new characters. A director sees the early precasting visions of the production disintegrate as performers struggle for lines and blocking, as lights won't work, and as the set color is all off. In times like those, trust your artistic instincts. Remember the excitement you felt when you chose your text (or your idea for a compiled script) to stage. As you see your production begin to take artistic shape—and it inevitably will—you'll know the immense satisfaction that a director feels when a production works. That feeling is worth all the hours of preparation you have spent, and more.

NOTES

1. Frank Galati, in "Informal Conversations with the Leaders of Readers Theatre," *Readers Theatre (News)* 5 (Spring 1978): 5.
2. Joanna Maclay, "Convocation of the Advisory Board for the Institute for Readers Theatre: Advisory Board Symposium Excerpts," *Readers Theatre (News)* 5 (Fall 1977): 3.
3. Many theatre directors use the term *lyric action* to suggest a flowing, almost ethereal quality of the actor's bodily and vocal action. Although our concept of the lyric mode in performance can include this kind of action, we are using the term *lyric action* in a much broader sense, to include the characteristic behavior of any literary persona or created presence.
4. Wallace A. Bacon, "The Dangerous Shores a Decade Later," *The Study of Oral Interpretation: Theory and Comment*, ed. Richard Haas and David Williams (Indianapolis, Ind.: Bobbs-Merrill, 1975), p. 221.
5. Alexander Dean, *Fundamentals of Play Directing*, rev. Lawrence Carra (New York: Holt, Rinehart & Winston, 1965), p. 173.
6. Federico Garcia Lorca, "Lament for Ignacio Sanchez Mejias," *The Selected Poems of Federico Garcia Lorca*, ed. Francisco Garcia Lorca and Donald M. Allen (New York: New Directions, 1955).

SUGGESTIONS FOR FURTHER READING

Benedetti, Robert. *The Actor at Work.* Englewood Cliffs, N.J.: Prentice-Hall, 1970.

Cohen, Robert, and **Harrop, John.** *Creative Play Direction.* Englewood Cliffs, N.J.: Prentice-Hall, 1974.

Davis, Martha. *Understanding Body Movement: An Annotated Bibliography.* New York: Arno Press, 1972.

Dell, Cecily. *A Primer for Movement Description: Using Effort, Shape, and Supplementary Concepts.* New York: Dance Notation Bureau, 1970.

King, Nancy. *Theatre Movement: The Actor and His Space.* New York: Drama Book Specialists, 1971.

Klein, Maxine. *Time, Space, and Designs for Actors.* Boston: Houghton Mifflin, 1967.

Lessac, Arthur. *The Use and Training of the Human Voice.* Drama Book Specialists, 1967.

Linklater, Kristin. *Freeing the Natural Voice.* New York: Drama Book Specialists, 1976.

Penrod, James. *Movement for the Performing Artist.* Palo Alto, Calif.: National Press Books, 1974.

Pickering, Jerry V. *Readers Theatre.* Belmont, Calif.: Dickenson, 1975.

Shepard, Richmond. *Mime: The Technique of Silence.* New York: Drama Book Specialists, 1971.

Sievers, W. David; Stiver, Harry E., Jr.; and **Kahan, Stanley.** *Directing for the Theatre.* Dubuque, Iowa: William C. Brown, 1974.

Von Laban, Rudolf. *The Mastery of Movement.* 3rd ed. Rev. Lisa Ullman. London: MacDonald and Evans, 1971.

CHAPTER TEN

Interpreters Theatre in Special Contexts

Not art for its own sake, but art as a heightened awareness of the world.

Alan Trachtenberg, *America & Lewis Hine*

Interpreters Theatre is moving beyond traditional theatre spaces and reaching out to new audiences. Although we're never likely to forsake our ties to the formal theatre space, the horizons of Interpreters Theatre have recently been reextended to the whole arena of social culture.[1] As we combine highly structured Interpreters Theatre productions in theatre auditoriums with more informal performances in such places as prisons, hospitals, children's homes, and shopping centers, we recapture the full spectrum of our tradition, where the informal storyteller in the ancient marketplace existed side by side with the rhapsode performing Homeric epics formally to an audience of twenty thousand.

Today Interpreters Theatre is both literature-centered and audience-centered. We recognize, as perhaps never before, the value of Interpreters Theatre as a way to come to terms with literature by using the full resources of presentational theatre. Once we're able to recognize the real power of Interpreters Theatre performance, especially its ability to engender image-ination, it's natural that we become interested in extending that power to all kinds of audiences in all kinds of theatres.

In the past decade, a strong trend in interpretation has emerged that parallels our interest in Interpreters Theatre as an art form and as an academic subject. More and more adapter-directors are interested in exploring Interpreters Theatre as a persuasive medium, as a tool for social understanding, as a therapeutic technique, and as a means for expanding the arts to audiences previously ignored.

THERAPEUTIC AND SOCIAL VALUES OF INTERPRETERS THEATRE

Many ongoing experiments are testing the value of Interpreters Theatre as a therapeutic tool. At Menard Psychiatric Center, a branch of the state penal system in Chester, Illinois, a special arts therapy program was started in 1973 by Leigh Steiner Craine, exploring the potential therapeutic values of Interpreters Theatre. Craine used poetry readings, adapting and compiling, improvisational performances, Interpreters Theatre productions of scripts, and original writing as methods of achieving rehabilitation and reintegration of the residents at Menard. Her program was so popular and successful that when she left Menard to apply the same techniques in a mental health center, the prison administration hired another Interpreters Theatre director, Kevin Purcell, to continue the program. Purcell established a regular coffeehouse event at which residents and visitors share informal poetry readings, directed productions of many selections—including *Hamlet, A Midsummer Night's Dream*, and "The Love Song of J. Alfred Prufrock"—using inmates as performers, and continued to encourage adapting, directing, and original writing. The program at Menard and many similar experiments are being conducted by interpreters throughout the country.[2]

It's important to note that successful interpreter-therapists either have received special training, and usually certification, as therapists or work closely with trained therapists in every phase of the program. The potential therapeutic values of literature and Interpreters Theatre hold a fascination for the imaginative director, but even the most well-meaning directors who lack training in rehabilitative therapy may create more problems than they solve. Interpreters Theatre should not be casually used for therapy. When your understanding of Interpreters Theatre is combined with sound training in therapy, you have a viable and powerful tool.

Although it may take years of special training for the Interpreters Theatre director to act as therapist, there are many other social contexts in which you, as a skilled adapter-director, can function now. Experiments that seek to engender greater understanding of special segments of our society, such as cultural minority groups and the aged, use Interpreters Theatre for raising social consciousness. A project funded by the Maine Council for the Humanities and Public Policy combined the talents of script compilers and directors and a group of elderly people to probe the "potential contribution of the elderly to daily life"[3] and to question public policy for the aging. The script, "Old Age: Tradition Shelved or Shared," was compiled primarily from oral histories derived through interviews with the ten elderly people who performed it. These people were, in effect, performing their own lives in an attempt to show that older people can be of worth to society but that they're often not allowed to contribute.

This project had a strong impact, not only on the audience members who witnessed it and on the performers themselves who gained increased self-respect, but on the interpreters who created the scripts and who have had their belief in the social value of Interpreters Theatre confirmed. JoAnn Fritsche writes that "the responses and evaluations we have received . . . have given us reason to believe that oral interpretation is indeed an effective medium for raising public awareness and influencing public policy."[4]

Another developing social application of Readers Theatre is the documentary. As more sophisticated communication techniques make our world shrink to a kind of global village, we find ourselves more aware of world problems, political concerns, and social causes. The documentary form, which uses essentially factual material, is becoming generally more popular, as documentary films, issue-oriented television programs, and nonfiction books gain widespread acceptance. Since the first production of *In White America* by Martin Duberman, the use of Readers Theatre as a documentary form has become more and more popular. Adapter-directors have discovered the inherent drama in real-life experiences of human beings and in the way people express the meaning of their own lives.

READERS THEATRE AS DOCUMENTARY[5]

What makes the creator of literary scripts, who has worked with the richness of shaped human experience in literature, turn to the real world for script materials? Why would a creative adapter want to use words spoken by the common man on city streets when the lines of Shelley and Shakespeare and Joyce are even more accessible resources? The language of real people caught in the tensions of real life carries a drama that has another kind of appeal—often equally as moving —as the language of great writers. Most of us have experienced the frustration of watching a news program on a topic such as the plight of migrant farmers or hearing about the crowded living conditions of the poor in Watts, Harlem, or any poverty area—not knowing what we can do to help the situation. Maybe you have been overcome with curiosity when looking at an old photograph album, reading epitaphs in a cemetery, or coming into contact with an ethnic group in your city or town. Such frustration and curiosity brings the talents of the artist together with the talents of the research scholar to create documentaries.

Lewis W. Hine, a documentary photographer, describes very succinctly the possible directions of the **documentary** when he says of his work, "There were two things I wanted to do. I wanted to show the things that had to be corrected. I wanted to show the things that had to be *appreciated*" (italics ours).[6] Documentary creations work within these parameters, from the fiery attacks on social injustice of *Bury My Heart At Wounded Knee* by Dee Brown to the more intimate attempts at consciousness raising of Alex Haley's *Roots* or Studs Turkel's *Working*. Or a documentary may have a combination of motives, as in the nonfiction novel *In Cold Blood* by Truman Capote. Whatever the impetus, a documentary Readers Theatre script, like any documentary, begins as an involvement with the world around us and introduces us to the whole range of research possibilities in nonfiction sources. And what rich sources these are:

No Crystal Stair: The Black Woman in History

Conflict and Cleavage in Northern Ireland

My name is Kate . . . I am a drug addict and an alcoholic . . . I was an intellectual flower child . . . I was looking for my mystical experience, I just wanted to get stoned.

I'm a dying breed. A laborer. Strictly muscle work . . . pick it up, put it down, pick it up, put it down.[7]

Each one of these quotations taken from these nonfiction sources could be the start of a documentary script dealing with real-life drama.

A Creative Treatment of Actuality

Borrowing John Grierson's much quoted definition of documentary film, Readers Theatre as a documentary becomes "a creative treatment of actuality," and as a creator of such scripts, you're a Readers Theatre documentarist.[8] Just as documentary filmmakers have all reality to capture on film, documentary Readers Theatre creators have a limitless supply of factual material to explore. Libraries, courthouses, and attics are filled with documents that may not in themselves speak eloquently but that have the potential to say a great deal when selected and arranged by a Readers Theatre documentarist.

Readers Theatre documentaries are created from primary source material. The result is a very different creation from most historical dramas where nonfiction material works only as a research source for the playwright who invents the final script. Historical playwrights go to the primary sources to research their subjects, and then they usually create dialogue for characters that captures the essence of history as the individual playwright interprets it. In documentary Readers Theatre, the primary source material is used as dialogue for the participants, and it can become as entertaining as any created dialogue with added persuasive potential that no invention can achieve. Erik Barnouw summarizes this when he says of the film documentarist that he "has a passion for what he *finds* in images and sounds—which always seem to him more meaningful than anything he can *invent*."[9]

Yet Readers Theatre documentarists cannot presume to be creators of factual scripts any more than documentary filmmakers can presume to show us reality. Filmmakers show us their reality or their creative treatment of actuality, because they make the choices of what to film and what we shall see. As script compilers, we select, arrange, and edit material to create our actuality; this is where our creative abilities are used. We create a presentational form by transforming through selection, alteration, rearrangement, and conversion a collection of nonfiction sources (see Chapter 6).

Selecting a Theme

As with any compiled script, you begin a Readers Theatre documentary by determining the theme you want to explore. Generally, documentary subjects are found in one of four categories: persons; historical or current events; cities, towns, and places; and cultures.

The lives of real persons have always been popular topics for nonfiction works. Perhaps our desire to learn from others' successes and failures keeps us interested in knowing about them. Autobiographies, biographies, and documentary films dating back to Robert Flaherty's famous *Nanook of the North* (1922) have allowed us to glimpse into others' lives. The array of persons—famous or not—who might be interesting characters to bring to life in a documentary Readers Theatre script is limitless.

Every area of the country has its own important historical or current events that can be brought to life in a documentary Readers Theatre script. Battles, expeditions, and natural phenomena are some types of events that are locally significant. You might also consider national events: the bicentennial, the revolt of the 1960s, or an important legal confrontation such as that in Phillis Rienstra Jeffrey's *No Sense of Decency*.[10] Any socially important issue may become the basis of a script. Newspapers, journals, history books, and other nonfiction sources can help you discover possible script topics based on historical or current events.

Similar to an historical event is the history of a city, town, or other place that might work as a theme for a Readers Theatre documentary. If you live in a metropolitan area, you can consider not only your city, but all the neighborhoods or smaller towns that exist within and around the city. Town celebrations and anniversaries such as centennials, diamond jubilees, or pilgrimages provide excellent opportunities for a Readers Theatre documentary using a town's history as its theme. On a pilgrimage of old homes within a town, for instance, different events from the town's history could be staged at different homes to augment the historical tour.

Community conflict often exists, and a documentary can be compiled dealing with such a conflict. The struggles between the Nazis and the predominantly Jewish community of Skokie, Illinois, for example, would provide a good topic for a script focusing on community conflict. In a script of this nature, you'd look at a situation that needs to be corrected rather than at a town's history that is to be appreciated.

A more general thematic category for a Readers Theatre documentary is that of cultural groups, structured by racial, ethnic, socioeconomic, religious, or experiential parameters. Any group that has the characteristics of a culture, meaning that its members have ways of living that are passed from one generation to another, might provide an interesting group to research and use as the theme for a documentary Readers Theatre script.

Researching Your Theme

Gathering material for a documentary Readers Theatre script is the same process as collecting for any compiled script, except that you turn to the nonfiction world primarily. Explore newspapers, books, and journals, and talk to people who know about your subject. After you've considered the usual written sources, turn to miscellaneous materials that are often overlooked, such as publications by local organizations and clubs. The chambers of commerce in many towns may be able to provide interesting material, and it's always a good idea to contact the local historical society. Even an industry in a town may have brochures or publications that would be applicable.

Depending upon your location, you may begin visiting the area of interest in your script as soon as you become interested in your theme or after you have done the preliminary reading. If you're interested in Shakers in America, for example, a trip to a Shaker settlement would be most helpful. Nothing you can read can be as valuable as actually seeing and experiencing something for yourself.

When you visit a location, some important considerations will make the trip more worthwhile for you and for those with whom you talk. First of all, don't visit a site for interviews until you have done some preliminary work on your subject. If you make a trip before you're prepared, you'll most likely be wasting your time because you won't know what you're looking for. During your visit, take plenty of photographs that relate to your theme. These will help you put yourself in the mood while compiling and might be used as slide projections in your production. Photographs also can be used for lobby displays and posters.

Your visits to the area of interest also give you an opportunity to do research in the local library. Many times the public library in a town or area of a city has material that isn't available anywhere else. For instance, it may have boxes of old letters or diaries, not even catalogued, that are just what you need to see. The local librarian can be a great help since she is usually aware of other sources for printed material that relate to that area. The more you can collect, the more you'll have to use for the compilation process.

Interviewing

Once you've done some preliminary research and visited areas of interest to your theme, you may want to talk to some people closely related to your subject. Talking with dock workers or garment workers, for instance, would tell you more about their jobs than you could learn from a book.

Interviewing can provide great rewards as well as great frustrations. It takes a certain skill to know how much to prod without offending an interviewee. Because interviewing is time-consuming, few things are more disappointing than arranging an interview and driving a long distance only to be rewarded by a series of "yep" and "nope" responses. The goal in interviewing is to elicit specific information without using a direct inquiry structure. Kenneth S. Goldstein's book, *A Guide for Field Workers in Folklore*, contains excellent suggestions for an interviewer and is a concise, readable guide. Goldstein goes into great detail about establishing rapport, recording and transcribing data, and other interview techniques.[11]

A useful piece of equipment for interviewing is a small cassette tape recorder with an omni-directional microphone that gives you and your subject freedom to talk without taking notes or handling the microphone. The recorder often causes interviewees to be reluctant to talk at first, but it's soon forgotten if you don't have to adjust it or change tapes. By using the longest tapes available and a recorder with an automatic level control, you'll be able to turn the recorder on and forget it.

It's usually better not to write out specific questions to ask interviewees; instead, plan general areas you're interested in exploring. A script about coal miners' wives, for instance, required information about their feelings concerning strikes, what problems they felt existed today in miners' lives, and their knowledge of folklore such as mining songs and tales. The interviewer established an informal, conversational situation by asking questions such as, "What do you think about all those women getting involved in the Brookside strike?" Few people respond positively to general, naive questions like "Wow, what's it like to be a coal miner's wife?" If you ask superficial questions, you're apt to get superficial answers. You'll profit from using your preliminary research to ask intelligent questions.

Don't waste others' time by having them tell you information you can read. Interviewees respond negatively if you don't know the basic information about your subject. They rightly feel you're wasting their time and should come back when you know what you're talking about. Learn all you can before you interview, then let your interviews provide additional data that may not be available in printed sources.

Completing Your Research

If you've gone through the research process with an eclectic approach, you should have voluminous material on your subject. Truman Capote's research for *In Cold Blood* is said to have consisted of six thousand pages of notes as well as boxed and filed documents bulky enough to fill a small room to the ceiling.[12] You may not accumulate quite that much data, but, as with a documentary filmmaker, the ratio of material collected to material used will be great.

As you begin to shape your materials into a completed script, let the artistic principles you learned in Chapter 6 guide you. Readers Theatre documentaries are created as a good compiled script is constructed, except that they are more likely to be persuasive. If you have taken a polemical approach to your subject, then you need to interface the artistic techniques with the techniques of persuasion. See, for example, *Persuasion: Understanding, Practice, and Analysis* by Herbert W. Simons.[13]

The possibilities for the development of Readers Theatre as a documentary medium are challenging and exciting. Whether you're compiling a thirty-minute script to illustrate conflicts that exist within your university or a two-hour documentary on slavery in America, you can become a documentarist with your "creative treatment of actuality." You may be concerned with things that need to be corrected or appreciated but your "noble intention," as Thomas W. Bohn and Richard L. Stromgren say of Grierson, will be "to focus upon real conditions in a real world faced by real people."[14]

INTERPRETERS THEATRE FOR SPECIAL AUDIENCES

Another result of our new understanding of the social value of Interpreters Theatre is that many directors are for the first time considering audiences other than those for whom they normally perform, especially when touring a production. There is growing awareness of the value of arts for the handicapped.

Interpreters Theatre is for *all* people. When we look at the handicapped, we're often too aware of how they differ from us, but the truth is that handicapped people are more like us than different from us. Their dreams, their feelings, their imaginations are just as vivid—perhaps even more so. What is different is their incapacity to realize some of their dreams—to run like others, or see, or hear, or sing. For these special audiences, Interpreters Theatre is a way to share literature they can relate to in a manner they can respond to.

The Physically Handicapped

Physically handicapped people find it easy and rewarding to be members of an Interpreters Theatre audience, because the emphasis on imagined action allows those who cannot physically move to be fully imaginatively involved from their seats. By stimulating sensory awareness, you are giving the handicapped a gift beyond compare: the ability to dream of other times and places.

If you're playing to a wheelchair audience, try to arrange for their chairs to come as close to the playing area as possible; if you can, opt for arena staging. Make every effort to involve the handicapped audience in as many ways as possible. When audience response is called for, be patient; since some muscle afflictions also affect speech, some audience members may be a bit slow in responding.

Interpreters Theatre is a medium that allows physically handicapped persons to become performers, because the demands of presentational staging and the emphasis on imaginative action are much easier for a person in a wheelchair to handle than fully representational staging. When you cast disabled persons, try to give them parts they can handle skillfully even with their disability. Kings and queens tend to remain seated (wheelchairs make marvelous gleaming thrones); in fact, any production using stools and stands can easily incorporate a wheelchair. By casting a handicapped child, for example, in a relatively stationary role (the Caterpillar in *Alice in Wonderland* or the Wizard in *The Wizard of Oz*), you're using the child's disability and built-in chair to augment the dignity of the character.

On the other hand, don't hesitate to cast disabled people as parts of normal crowds on-stage. It would be perfectly natural for some of the children watching the Emperor's parade in *The Emperor's New Clothes*, for example, to be on crutches or in wheelchairs; a handicapped child shouting, "But he has nothing on!" adds an important additional point to the story.

Mentally Retarded or Emotionally Disturbed Audiences

When you plan a production for the mentally retarded, use your understanding of the mental age of your audience to guide your selection of material. Many retarded people are like children who love repetition, especially when there are opportunities for their own responses. Fairy tales and poetry are excellent sources for Interpreters Theatre scripts for such people.

Emotionally disturbed audiences present one of the most difficult problems for interpreters because we often understand so little about their afflictions. If you're planning an Interpreters Theatre performance for an audience of emotionally troubled people, check your script with their therapist to be sure it's acceptable. Some general guidelines are:

1. Unless the therapist suggests otherwise, don't plan to use masks in the performance. Persons with emotional difficulties (and, we might add, very young normal children) are frightened by masks. Seeing a person's unadorned face is comforting, even if the rest of the body is fully costumed.

2. Avoid sudden movements, especially if they appear to be aggressive toward the audience.

3. Similarly, avoid unexpected loud noises such as gongs, screams, or bangs.

Seriously disturbed people often need to make sense of their environment before they can enter another. For this reason, realism is generally preferable to fantasy. (A very generalized rule is that the mentally retarded tend to be more responsive to fantasy, whereas the emotionally disturbed prefer realistic literature.) As with all handicapped persons, emotionally troubled people need love more than anything else. Sharing the magic of theatre with these audiences is one of the greatest expressions of love we can make.

Blind Audiences

There's a saying that a blind person would enjoy Readers Theatre more than Conventional Theatre, and a deaf person would enjoy Conventional Theatre more than Readers Theatre.[15] However oversimplified the maxim, it refers to the essentially acoustic dimension of Readers Theatre and the visual (pictorial) emphasis of Conventional Theatre. Blind audiences respond to the sounds of literature in performance. Their sensitivity to tone color is keen. In Interpreters Theatre, where words often create the setting, visually impaired audiences are very comfortable.

To appeal to the blind, you may wish to feature a chorus as part of the production. Your audience will love the rich vocal tones that a chorus of well-attuned voices can make. Partially sighted audiences can respond to large motor movements and strong primary colors; these will enhance the power of the spoken word. Choruses that move together in sweeping gestures can be seen to some degree by those with limited vision.

Blind children are especially responsive to participatory moments in which they're asked questions. Be sensitive to the type of question posed, checking that it doesn't require sight to be answered. Questions to the audience that ask where someone is are inappropriate, but the performer could ask *what* or *how* questions, such as, "What shall I do? How can I explain the mess I'm in?" Subtle "where" questions that don't depend on actual knowledge are fine, such as, "Where do you think he went?"

A blind audience is an excellent challenge for Interpreters Theatre performers because they must rely on the tonality of the word, on the infinite variety of the human voice; they cannot rely on visible externals—such as set design, costumes, or makeup—to establish character and setting for them.

Deaf Audiences

If a blind audience requires an Interpreters Theatre performance to heighten the essential resources of sound, then a deaf audience is surely the most challenging because the acoustic dimension—the hallmark of an Interpreters Theatre production—is removed. For hearing impaired people, the stage is more a place of light and movement than of sound. As Taras B. Denis explains in "Drama and the Deaf Child," "For them it [theatre] is where actions always speak louder than words, and direct participation loudest."[16] Performers for the deaf need to rely a great deal on presentational movement cues, including pantomiming directly toward the audience.

Mark Nutial, director of a professional Readers Theatre company, Peanut Butter Readers, explained how his ensemble of performers prepared for a Readers Theatre performance for hearing impaired children.[17] Some techniques they found useful were concentrating on adapting literature with simple vocabularies and much repetition; speaking slowly, without distorting facial muscles; arranging for stage lighting on the faces of the interpreters; shaving beards and mustaches to make the lips more easily seen; avoiding speaking and moving at the same time; and using presentational staging to have the performers face the audience directly. "What happens to stress, rhythm, intonation, melody, onomatopoeia?" asks Nutial. He answers his own question by declaring:

> Throw them out, fall back on the essence of reading: the reader's internal response to the printed word, magnify this important internal response and adopt new mechanics to allow the hearing impaired to perceive and follow this response. Bypass the ears? No, flood the ears with so many sensory stimulators that the speechreader will suffer the illusion of hearing.[18]

What is "this important internal response?" It's the chill up the spine when the cellar door creaks in a mystery story, the pounding of your heart when you—alongside the main character—finish the race no one said you could, the internal vision of what your Shangri-la looks like. This is image-ination at its best: the full bodily and mental response to literature, the response that comes before sound and gesture. This is the living exchange of energy between literature and reader that is transformed to the stage and becomes the heart of Interpreters Theatre: the inexplicable bond between performer and audience as they share in the creation of another world. Does it take an audience of deaf people to make us see what Interpreters Theatre really is—that it is a living connection between a human soul and literature that precedes audible speech? Perhaps so. But, then, that's one of the joys of special audiences. Working with real human beings in a performance situation is the only way to fully realize the nature of our art.

NOTES

1. The title of this chapter was suggested by a 1978 Speech Communication Association convention program, "Interpretation in Social Contexts."
2. The work of David Williams at University of Arizona, K. B. Valentine at Arizona State University, Martin Cobin at University of Colorado, and Margaret Dunn at Kean College in New Jersey are examples of some of the ongoing projects using interpretation in prisons.
3. Maryann Hartman, Beth Hartman, Burton Alho, and JoAnn Fritsche, "Using Oral Interpretation to Affect Public Policy," unpublished manuscript, p. 2.
4. *Ibid.*, p. 26.
5. We are grateful to Ann S. Utterback, instructor at Memphis State University, for contributing the material in the section, "Readers Theatre as Documentary."
6. Larry A. Viskochil, *Lewis W. Hine, 1874-1940: A Retrospective of the Photographer* (Chicago: Chicago Historical Society, 1978), n.p.
7. The quotations are, in order: L. Bennett, Jr., *Ebony*, August 1977, pp. 164–165; R. J. Terchek, Bibliographical Footnotes, *The Annals of the American Academy of Political and Social Sciences*, 433 (Summer 1977): 47–59; drug addict quoted from *The New York Times*, 2 Aug. 1976, p. 14, col. 1; Studs Terkel, *Working* (New York: Avon Books, 1974), p. 1.
8. John Grierson, *Grierson on Documentary*, ed. Forsyth Hardy (London: Faber & Faber, 1966), p. 13.
9. Erik Barnouw, *Documentary: A History of the Non-Fiction Film* (London: Oxford University Press, 1974), p. 288.
10. For more information about this script see: Phillis J. Rienstra Jeffrey, " 'No Sense of Decency': A Readers Theatre Production Based on the Army-McCarthy Hearings." Austin: University of Texas, 1970.
11. Kenneth S. Goldstein, *A Guide for Field Workers in Folklore* (Hatboro, Pa.: Folklore Associates, 1964).
12. George Plimpton, "The Story Behind a Nonfiction Novel," *New York Times Book Review*, 16 Jan. 1966, p. 43.
13. Herbert W. Simons, *Persuasion: Understanding, Practice, and Analysis* (Reading, Mass.: Addison-Wesley, 1976.)
14. Thomas W. Bohn and Richard L. Stromgren, *Light and Shadows: A History of Motion Pictures* (Port Washington: Alfred, 1975), p. 300.

15. See Wallace A. Bacon, *The Art of Interpretation*, 3rd ed. (New York: Holt, Rinehart & Winston, 1979), pp. 461–462.
16. Taras B. Denis, "Drama and the Deaf Child," *Drama with Children*, ed. Geraldine Brain Siks (New York: Harper & Row, 1977), p. 203.
17. See Mark Nutial, "Readers Theatre for the Deaf," *Readers Theatre* (News) 5 (Fall 1977): 10–11.
18. *Ibid.*

SUGESTIONS FOR FURTHER READING

Gillies, Emily. *Creative Dramatics for All Children.* New York: Association for Childhood Education International, 1973.
Goldstein, Kenneth S. *A Guide for Field Workers in Folklore.* Hatboro, Pa.: Folklore Associates, 1964.
Grierson, John. *Grierson on Documentary.* Ed. Forsyth Hardy. London: Faber & Faber, 1966.
Leedy, Jack J., ed. *Poetry Therapy.* New York: J. B. Lippincott, 1973.
Levin, G. Roy. *Documentary Explorations: 15 Interviews with Film-Makers.* New York: Doubleday, 1971.
McHughes, Janet Larsen. "Interpretation in the Prisons: A Further Note." *Interpretation Newsletter* 15 (Spring 1976): 3.
Nutial, Mark. "Readers Theatre for the Deaf." *Readers Theatre (News)* 5 (Fall 1977): 10–11.
Schattner, Regina. *Creative Dramatics for Handicapped Children.* New York: John Day, 1967.
Schloss, Gilbert A. *Psychopoetry: A New Approach to Self-Awareness Through Poetry Therapy.* New York: Grosset & Dunlap, 1976.
Ulman, Elinor, and **Dachinger, Penny, eds.** *Art Therapy in Theory and Practice.* New York: Schocken Books, 1975.
Williams, David. "Interpretation in a Prison," *Interpretation Newsletter* 14 (Fall 1975): 5.

Appendix 1: Hints on Casting and Rehearsing

Having spent so much care in adapting or compiling a script, you naturally want the best production possible. Yet even the most creative script adapters falter when they turn to direction unless they have a solid view of production organization. Appendix 1 suggests some ways to set up auditions and handle rehearsals. Although there are as many ways to organize the production process as there are directors, these procedures are some we have found useful. What's most important is that the whole production process be as pleasant an experience for all concerned—director, cast, technicians, audience, and especially the characters in the text—as the private script creation was for you.

PRIOR TO AUDITIONS

I. Before you can cast your show, the script must be in a form that can be read easily.
- A. Type your script, double-spaced. Remember that a forty-to-fifty-page eight-and-a-half–by–eleven–inch script runs about two hours. You may wish to type the script on smaller sheets—six by nine inches or five-and-a-half by eight-and-a-half inches (one eight-and-a-half–inch page folded in half)—so performers carrying scripts find them easy to handle. Leave a wide left-hand margin (at least three inches).
- B. As you type the script, indicate placement of intermissions by dividing the script into units of action that might correspond to acts of a play. Let the structure of the script guide you; there may be one or two comfortable places where the production could be halted for an intermission. Be conscious of the dramatic structure; a crisis point should precede an intermission break to entice the audience to come back into the theatre. Generally, if your production is longer than one hour, you need at least one intermission; if it is a two-hour show, think in terms of two intermissions. Try to keep each unit reasonably the same length; if you are unable to do so, arrange for the longer units to be earlier.
- C. Make enough copies for each of your cast members, your technical crew (lights, sound, props, costumes), your stage manager, and your assistant director, and make several for yourself.

II. Choose an assistant director as soon as possible so you can work together on the various stages of production.

III. If you're working with technicians (set designer, lighting designer, costume designer, sound technician), consult with them early enough that they have as much time to work on the production of the script as you have. If you aren't working with technicians, take time early to design your set (making notes of any building you need to do) and make other technical decisions.

IV. Check on all deadlines for audition poster design, publicity releases, poster design, program design and copy.

V. Do preliminary blocking for the entire show.

    A. It's helpful to have your script on sheets of paper with three outlines of the stage area on the backs. As you turn the pages of the script, the back of each previous page shows diagrams for blocking.

    B. Move chess pieces, Monopoly pieces, thimbles, or whatever is handy around on a board (a chess board is a good size) on which you have drawn the outline for your set.

    C. Transfer the blocking (always in pencil) to the stage outlines on your script. (See Appendix 2)

VI. Prepare for auditions

    A. Choose times for auditions. Try to schedule auditions for two different times—once in the afternoon and once in the evening, for example.

    B. Design your audition poster to include: name of production, original author (if adaptation), and director; production dates; audition dates, times, and locations; where to obtain advance copies of the script.

    C. Post audition posters at least one week before tryout date.

    D. Make several scripts available to prospective performers on a checkout basis.

    E. Make copies of tryout sheets for auditions.

    F. Prepare lists of scenes that feature various characters and scenes that call for a variety of combinations of characters.

    G. Ask the assistant director to aid in auditions.

    H. Prepare a very general introduction about the show to give to those who come to auditions.

AUDITIONS

I. Ask each prospective cast member to fill out an audition form, such as the one in figure A1.1.

II. Guidelines for casting

    A. Appearance: How will each performer's physical appearance work for the role she is to play? How will each performer's appearance work in relation to the other performers?

    B. Flexibility

        1. Voice: Can the performer read a line believably? Can the performer achieve different vocal qualities when directed to do so? Can you hear and understand the performer?

        2. Body: Does the performer seem to have a sense of movement and rhythm? Does the performer's body seem stiff or pliant? Can the body take on different shapes easily? Does the performer use facial expressions and gestures naturally and effectively?

        3. General performance ability: Does the performer seem interested and energetic? Does the performer seem able to respond to direction? How believable are the performer's emotional qualities? How does the performer seem to work with others? Does the performer possess a comic or tragic tonality that is either appropriate or inappropriate?

AUDITION SHEET

Name_____

Local address_____ Telephone_____

Year in school_____ Major_____Age_____ Sex_____

Hair color_____ Do you sing?_____Vocal range_____

In what capacity would you like to work with us on this production:

    _____ Performance
    _____ Technical work (e.g., lighting, costumes, set
             construction, etc.)
    _____ Poster design, photography
    _____ Publicity or box office
    _____ Stage manager

List previous performance experience:

Schedule: Cross out times you will be *unable* to rehearse

	Mon.	Tues.	Wed.	Thurs.	Fri.	Sat.	Sun.
12 PM							
1 PM							
2 PM							
3 PM							
4 PM							
5 PM							
6 PM							
7 PM							
8 PM							
9 PM							

Director's Comments:

Figure A1.1: Sample audition sheet.

C. Special considerations
  1. If a performer is to take more than one role, note her ability to make a genuine difference between characters.
  2. If a character is divided among two or more performers, similar height and appearance may be important, but the performers need not be mirror images of each other. Check to make sure that any contrast in appearance among performers playing a single character makes the statement you intend about the personality or attitude of the character.
  3. If you'll be working with a chorus, be conscious of voice types. You may want to cast light and dark voices for variety. Check each performer's ability to blend his or her voice with others. Dissonant voices should not be placed in a chorus.

REHEARSALS

The purpose of the rehearsal period is to allow you and your performers to mature in your understanding and mastery of the script. Try to think of the rehearsal period as a time of growth and creative change—even in your production concept and the design of the script—because in the Interpreters Theatre medium you function very much as playwright as well as director. Your script is untested; even if the work is a play, chances are you have adapted it for the Interpreters Theatre stage by opening up its lines of tension—finding new voices or orchestrating sound structures, for example. Because your script is still evolving, it's especially important that you treat rehearsals as a creative interchange of ideas among an ensemble of artists, not as a time when the performers simply carry out your preconceived ideas on staging. Even though you've done some preliminary blocking, moving characters in your mind without seeing actual bodies onstage is always tentative.

For the director, the most precious commodity is time. In our experience, a two-hour production requires a minimum of six weeks rehearsal time. Even if the performers will be carrying scripts, this amount of time is needed to bring all the elements of the show together successfully. If you are planning a shorter production, you may be able to mount it in less time than six weeks —but not proportionately less. Even with shorter scripts, performers and directors need time for maturation.

A Suggested Six-week Rehearsal Plan

  1. During the first rehearsal period, read through the script. Discuss the production concept, stage plan, and general line interpretation.
  2. Remember to open each rehearsal with vocal and physical warm-ups to get the performers' creative energies flowing and their bodies and voices limber.
  3. Devote the first two weeks of rehearsal to blocking the movement of the entire show. Include direction on focus as well.

4. If you're using a chorus, begin to work on blending immediately. Devote fifteen minutes of each blocking rehearsal to some kind of voice blending exercises. When the blocking is completed, increase the amount of time devoted to choral ensemble practice. It usually takes the full six weeks to achieve a unified chorus.

5. During the third week, while performers are still on script, concentrate on line interpretation and character motivations. This is the time to break the script into smaller units for intense rehearsal. You may need some extra coaching sessions outside of rehearsal time for the next few weeks. Performers should be entirely off script, whether they are carrying scripts or not, by the end of the third week. (It almost always happens that some performers aren't off script by this time, but you should aim for this date.)

6. During the fourth week, focus on movement, stage pictures, and eye focus.

7. Beginning with the fifth week, rehearse the show in complete run-throughs so the performers can gain a feeling of the continuity of the whole production. Check on consistency of characterization, transitions, pacing, and climactic builds. Begin to work with sound. If the costumes require special attention to movement, have performers work in rehearsal costumes that approximate what they'll be wearing in the performance.

8. During the sixth week, the following schedule may be of assistance:

    Previous weekend: Hang lights and rehearse technical crew

    Monday: Full technical rehearsal

    Tuesday: Complete run-through with technical cues

    Wednesday: First dress rehearsal

    Thursday: Final dress rehearsal with invited audience. (Some directors prefer to have no advance audience at all; others prefer to schedule the invited audience for Wednesday night, reserving Thursday night for a private rehearsal.)

    Friday: Opening night!

Appendix 2: Making a Promptbook for Interpreters Theatre

A promptbook is a complete record of your production. Each time you produce a show, you should construct a promptbook of some kind—using a large ring binder—so that all the cues, blocking, and script materials are together. Promptbooks for Interpreters Theatre are similar to those for Conventional Theatre productions, except for differences in script form (division into voices and the use of orchestration, for example) that influence blocking, technical matters, and the question of focus. Figure A2.1 shows sample pages from a promptbook. It may also help you to consider a list of contents for a typical Interpreters Theatre promptbook:

1. cast and crew list with addresses and telephone numbers
2. rehearsal schedule
3. list of warm-up exercises
4. written production concept
    a. metaphor for the production, if used
    b. discussion of rationale for division of voices, including descriptions of characters
    c. staging concepts: notes on audience contact and handling of scripts, if used
5. scale diagram of stage setting
6. description of sound, including sources of recordings, if used
7. list of costumes, including any special costume designs
8. list of props
9. script with complete blocking, focus, light, and sound cues; include permission citation if applicable
10. extra paper for taking notes

Blocking   Focus   Lights

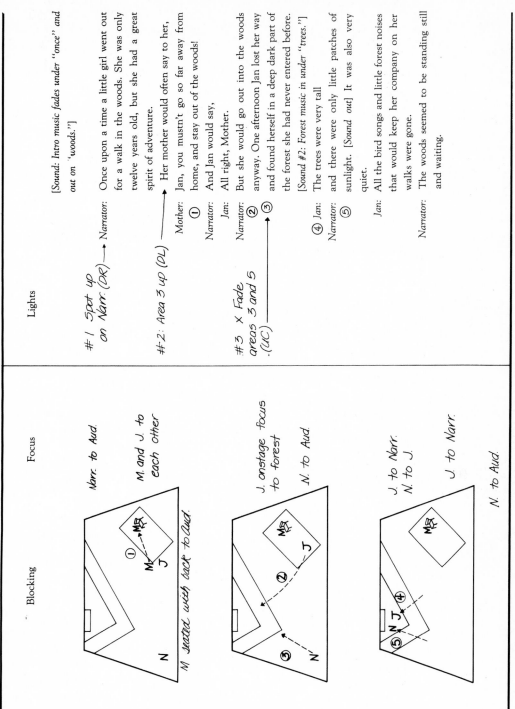

Focus

Narr. to Aud.

M. and J. to each other

J. onstage focus to forest

N. to Aud.

J. to Narr.
N. to J.

J. to Narr.

N. to Aud.

Lights

#1 Spot up on Narr. (DR)

#2: Area 3 up (DL)

#3 x Fade areas 3 and 5 (UC)

[Sound: Intro music fades under "once" and out on "woods."]

Narrator: Once upon a time a little girl went out for a walk in the woods. She was only twelve years old, but she had a great spirit of adventure.
Her mother would often say to her,

Mother: ① Jan, you mustn't go so far away from home, and stay out of the woods!

Narrator: And Jan would say,

Jan: All right, Mother.

Narrator: ② ③ But she would go out into the woods anyway. One afternoon Jan lost her way and found herself in a deep dark part of the forest she had never entered before.
[Sound #2: Forest music in under "trees."]

④ Jan: The trees were very tall and there were only little patches of sunlight. [Sound out] It was also very quiet.

Narrator: ⑤

Jan: All the bird songs and little forest noises that would keep her company on her walks were gone.

Narrator: The woods seemed to be standing still and waiting.

Figure A2.1: Sample prompt book page: Chamber Theatre.

INDEX